Best Practices in Mentoring for Teacher and Leader Development

A Volume in
Perspectives in Mentoring

Series Editor
Frances K. Kochan, *Auburn University*

Praise for *Best Practices in Mentoring for Teacher and Leader Development*

This volume, *Best Practices in Mentoring for Teacher and Leader Development*, forwards principles of effective mentoring, including the role and importance of talk in mentoring, using tools that make mentoring talk more purposeful, analyzing teaching practice, involving mentors in opportunities to share their practice, providing space for mentees to have a voice in mentoring conversations, and promoting teacher learning at all levels as part of instructional leadership in schools. This edited book highlights trends that we need to consider for future research, including the need for mentor development, the importance of carefully building school-university partnerships that support teacher learning, and providing networks for mentors to talk to other mentors about their practice. Especially important in this volume is the focus on benefits of mentoring for mentors to improve their own teaching practice. Much research is still needed to build a sense of urgency that mentoring can matter in new teacher learning, and ideas promoted within this book can contribute to this important conversation.

> **—Randi Nevins Stanulis,** Professor, Department of Teacher Eduction, *Michigan State University,* and Director of *Launch Into Teaching.*

How do you respond to the changing nature of schools today and the continuing pressure to improve teaching and leadership? Searby and Brondyk believe that good mentoring practice is one answer. In *Best Practices in Mentoring for Teacher and Leader Development* the authors present 13 unique and diverse examples of new teacher and principal mentoring program best practices. Individually and collectively, these case studies illustrate the value, utility and pragmatics of applying empirical research methods to evaluate the effectiveness of mentoring practices in P–12 mentoring programs. Read the book. Digest its summary of best practices. Mull over the list of emerging mentoring trends. And then meet with your leadership team to evaluate your best practices and next steps. There is plenty of grist for the mill in this book for sure!

> **—Lois Zachary,** Author, *The Mentor's Guide, The Mentee's Guide, Creating a Mentoring Culture,* and *Starting Strong: A Mentoring Fable*

Perspectives on Mentoring
Frances K. Kochan, Series Editor

Best Practices in Mentoring for Teacher and Leader Development (2016)
edited by Linda J. Searby and Susan K. Brondyk

Uncovering the Cultural Dynamics in Mentoring Programs and Relationships:
Enhancing Practice and Research (2014)
edited by Frances K. Kochan, Andrea M. Kent, and André M. Green

Mentoring for the Professions: Orienting Toward the Future (2014)
edited by Aimee Howley and Mary Barbara Trube

Global Perspectives on Mentoring:
Transforming Contexts, Communities and Cultures (2006)
edited by Frances K. Kochan

Creating Successful Telementoring Programs (2005)
edited by Frances K. Kochan

The Organizational and Human Dimensions of
Successful Mentoring Programs and Relationships (2002)
edited by Frances K. Kochan

Best Practices in Mentoring for Teacher and Leader Development

Edited by

Linda J. Searby
Auburn University

and

Susan K. Brondyk
Hope College

INFORMATION AGE PUBLISHING, INC.
Charlotte, NC • www.infoagepub.com

Library of Congress Cataloging-in-Publication Data

CIP record for this book is available from the Library of Congress
http://www.loc.gov

ISBN: 978-1-68123-298-0 (Paperback)
      978-1-68123-299-7 (Hardcover)
      978-1-68123-300-0 (ebook)

Printed in the United States of America

CONTENTS

Foreword
Frances Kochan .... *ix*

Book Introduction
Linda J. Searby and Susan K. Brondyk .... *xi*

1. Introduction: The Complexities of Identifying Mentoring
   Best Practices
   Linda J. Searby and Susan K. Brondyk *1*

2. Developing Mentors Across Contexts: The Reciprocity of
   Mentorship in School/University Partnerships
   Danielle V. Dennis and Audra K. Parker *19*

3. Impactful Mentoring Within a Statewide, Comprehensive
   Induction Program
   Amanda R. Bozack and Amy Nicole Salvaggio *31*

4. Reflection Rounds in the Context of Virtual Mentoring
   Carmen Gloria Núñez, Verónica López, Bryan González,
   Carola Rojas, Evelyn Mujica, Evelyn Palma, and Cristina Julio *57*

5. Face-To-Face, Online, and Hybrid Mentoring in
   a Professional Development Program
   Ya-Wen Cheng, Deborah L. Hanuscin, and Mark J. Volkmann *73*

6. Empowering Teachers Through Mentoring
   Elizabeth Doone, Karen Colucci, Laura Von Staden, and
   Dominique Thompson *93*

7. Crossing Borders on the Border: Implementation of a
    Mentoring Network
    Etta Kralovec and Laura Gail Lunsford *109*

8. Building Induction Capacity: Collaboration, Formative
    Assessment, and Systems Thinking
    Lara H. Hebert and Elizabeth A. Wilkins *125*

9. Promising Practices for Developing Teacher Leaders in
    High Schools: The Principal's Role
    Tricia Browne-Ferrigno, Amanda Perry Ellis,
    and Matthew Douglas Thompson *151*

10. How an Assistant Principals' Academy Evolved Into
    Dynamic Group and Peer Mentoring Experiences
    D. K. Gurley and L. Anast-May *173*

11. Mentoring for New Principals in Urban School Districts:
    One Size Does Not Fit All
    Constance Magee and Charles L. Slater *197*

12. Leaders Helping Leaders: Mentoring After Mentoring Ends
    John Daresh *219*

13. Best Practices for Supporting Beginning Principals as
    Instructional Leaders: The Consultant Coaching Model
    Mary Bearden Martin and Linda J. Searby *241*

14. Mentoring Midcareer Principals to Build Capacity for
    Change in Schools
    Kenyae L. Reese, Jane Clark Lindle, Matthew R. Della Sala,
    Robert C. Knoeppel, and Hans W. Klar *279*

15. A Summary of Best Practices in Mentoring for Teacher and
    Leader Development
    Linda J. Searby and Susan K. Brondyk *313*

About the Editors/Authors *325*

FOREWORD

Frances Kochan
Series Editor

Searby and Brondyk have written a groundbreaking book that features a firsthand examination of mentoring processes and practices in the modern world through the lens of best practices. Identifying and implementing best practices in mentoring programs and relationships are elusive goals. The authors have moved us closer to achieving these goals through their creative and dynamic approach to this issue.

In their first chapter, they establish a foundation for research and action by sharing the complexities of identifying best practices and then providing a framework for judging the degree to which an activity can be considered a best practice. The book includes examples of programs from a wide-range of perspectives within education. The authors then demonstrate how the framework can be applied by providing an analysis of the programs described within the book chapters. Although the book concentrates on programs within education, the focus on best practices should have relevance to mentoring in all areas as should the drive toward categorizing and sharing those practices that foster mentoring success.

Best Practices in Mentoring for Teacher and Leader Development, pp. ix–ix
Copyright © 2016 by Information Age Publishing
ix

BOOK INTRODUCTION

Linda J. Searby and Susan K. Brondyk

Mentoring has been identified as a critical factor in retaining new teachers (Menter, Hume, Dely, & Lewin, 2010) as well as new principals (Crow, 2012). The benefits of mentoring for these two groups of educators is widely understood. However, the ways that mentoring for P–12 educators is enacted in schools and districts can be quite different, and can range from feeble attempts to models of excellence (Crow, 2012; Savickas, 2007). Mentoring for new teachers and leaders is delivered through a variety of programs, with a myriad of purposes, structures, and practices. Because contexts can differ so greatly, it is difficult to identify mentoring practices that work in every situation (Clutterbuck, 2013). Though this challenge exists, we believe that it is still important to conduct empirical research in an attempt to find those mentoring practices that have been effective and can meet rigorous criteria for being labeled as "best practices."

With the growing interest in best practices, the time is ripe in education for a marriage of theory and practice in the area of mentoring. Therefore, when we put out the call for chapters for this book, we specified that the authors report original empirical research in mentoring, with the aim of highlighting and recommending those programs and practices that would meet our identified criteria for being "best practices": attainable, accessible and affordable in practice and based on theoretical research found in peer-reviewed literature.

Best Practices in Mentoring for Teacher and Leader Development, pp. xi–xiii
Copyright © 2016 by Information Age Publishing

This book is unique in that it highlights empirical mentoring research conducted with the two primary forces in P–12 education: teachers and principals. The chapters report on mentoring programs in diverse contexts (rural, suburban, urban, international), different types of mentoring (one-on-one, small group, network), and mentoring through different modes (face-to-face, virtual, blended).

In Chapter 1 of this book, we outline the specific challenges in identifying best practices in mentoring in education and suggest a process by which we can begin the work of identifying and cataloguing them. We chose 13 submissions for inclusion in the book, based on the criteria stated above. The book is divided into two parts: Research on new teacher mentoring (Chapters 2–8) and new principal mentoring (Chapters 9–14). Chapter 15 is our summary of the best practices identified through these research studies, as well as our identification of new emerging trends in mentoring.

This book serves multiple purposes:

- To show the value of using empirical research methods to evaluate the effectiveness of P–12 mentoring practices;
- To identify mentoring practices and programs for P-12 teachers and administrators that meet one or more of the criteria of a best practice, so that we may replicate them in future mentoring endeavors;
- To highlight any emerging new trends in P-12 mentoring that may be important to consider.

We draw attention to the ways in which these purposes have been fulfilled in the book's concluding chapter. Mentoring will always be complex, contextual, and full of possibility for those who engage in it. In this volume, we endeavored to move beyond narrative anecdotal reports of P–12 mentoring, and show the importance of using empirical methods to study mentoring for new teachers and leaders. We hope that you, the reader, will recognize the impact these 13 studies will have on the changing landscape of mentoring for teacher and leader development.

Whether you are a P–12 teacher or leader, or a mentoring researcher in higher education, our hope is that you will find this book helpful to you in your work.

REFERENCES

Clutterbuck, D. (2013). Where next with research in mentoring? *International Journal of Mentoring and Coaching in Education, 2*(3).

Crow, G. M. (2012). A critical-constructivist perspective on mentoring and coaching for leadership. In S. J. Fletcher & C. A. Mullen (Eds.), *The Sage handbook of mentoring and coaching in education* (pp. 228–242). Los Angeles, CA: Sage.

Menter, I., Hulme, M., Dely, E., & Lewin, J. (2010). *Literature review on teacher education in the 21st century*. Edinburgh, Scotland: Education Analytical Services.

Savickas, M. L. (2007). Forward: The maturation of mentoring research. In T. Allen & L. Eby (Eds.), *The Blackwell handbook of mentoring* (pp. xviii–xix). Malden, MA: Blackwell.

CHAPTER 1

INTRODUCTION

The Complexities of Identifying Mentoring Best Practices

Linda J. Searby and Susan K. Brondyk

In 2010, the authors of this book joined a group of other mentoring scholars at the American Educational Research Association Conference in Vancouver, British Columbia, in a newly-formed consortium named The Global Mentoring Research Network. Organizers of the group, Dr. Frances Kochan and Dr. Philip Feldman, stated that the initial purpose of this network was to create a repository for research articles on mentoring, because "there did not appear to be a high quality, cohesive, easily accessible body of research available focused on the primary issues of mentoring theory and practice in education" (Kochan, 2013, p. 1). Members of the network identified five broad topic areas under which mentoring research could be organized: foundations of mentoring, best practices in mentoring, culture and mentoring, policies/politics in mentoring, and technology and mentoring. Although the creation of the central repository for mentoring research articles is still an ongoing challenge, Dr. Kochan has extended the work of the Global Mentoring Research Network by creating this book series, *Perspectives in Mentoring*, to highlight research around important issues in mentoring in education. In addition, she edited a special issue of the *International Journal of Mentoring and Coaching in Education* (2013, Volume 2, Issue 3), in which leaders of the network topic groups published overviews of their mentoring topics and outlined potential research agendas in those topics. We published our article, "Best Practices in Mentoring: Challenges and Possibilities," in that special issue, to outline the breadth of the field of mentoring in education and the complexity of defining the term "best practices." We also suggested how researchers might begin to engage in identifying mentoring best practices across educational contexts.

What follows is our rationale for why it is so difficult to identify best practices in mentoring and our specific advice for how researchers could begin to catalog those practices. We conclude the chapter with a description of what we discovered as we attempted to "take our own advice" and began the work of identifying best practices in mentoring for new teachers and leaders.

WHY MENTORING IS IMPORTANT

Mentoring in educational contexts has become a rapidly growing field of study, both in the United States and internationally (Fletcher & Mullen, 2012). The prevalence of mentoring has resulted in the mindset that "everyone thinks they know what mentoring is, and there is an intuitive belief that mentoring works" (Eby, Rhodes, & Allen, 2007, p. 7). While mentoring may not have a positive effect on individuals in all circumstances, there is much documentation of the benefits of mentoring, both in the areas of career development and psychosocial enhancement (Johnson, 2007; Mullen, 2011). For example, in an analysis of over 300 research–based mentoring articles in the fields of education, business, and medicine, Ehrich, Hansford, and Tennent (2004) found that mentoring yields positive outcomes of learning, personal growth, and development of professionals. In another meta-analysis of 426 journal articles on mentoring, Dominguez (2012) identified 34 different positive mentor outcomes, 49 mentee benefits, and 13 organizational enhancements from mentoring endeavors. In education, mentoring for new teachers has been identified as a strong factor in retention (Menter, Hulme, Dely, & Lewin, 2010), as well as in the development of these teachers' self-confidence, ability to make changes to practice, understanding of subject matter, and use of a wider repertoire of strategies to match pupil needs (Cordingley & Buckler, 2012). Thus, there *is* empirical research undergirding the premise that mentoring is a construct that enhances growth in individuals (educators and noneducators) and in organizations of all types.

Although research is slowly emerging that identifies specific knowledge, skills and dispositions that contribute to mentor effectiveness (Allen & Eby, 2011; Campbell, 2007; O'Dell & Huling, 2004), the educational field has yet to begin distinguishing universally agreed upon "best practices" in mentoring. We propose that this is due to the complexity of both the practice of mentoring and the term "best practices."

THE COMPLEXITY OF MENTORING

Best practices in mentoring are difficult to identify due partly to the complexity of the mentoring process. This complexity is related to the context of mentoring, which in turn impacts its definition, and the way in which it is conceptualized. The variety of mentoring program purposes and settings in education is also extremely diverse. These complexities are described in detail in the sections that follow. Although we attempt to focus our sources on mentoring literature in education, at times we incorporate literature from other fields as they provide background and context.

Mentoring Context, Roles, and Conceptualizations

Mentoring can be found in almost every professional context. Each context has its own unique characteristics that influence the mentoring that occurs (Blake-Beard, Murrell, & Thomas, 2007; Giscombe, 2007; Kochan, 2002; Mullen, 2012). Mentoring programs are offered to individuals of all ages, to meet a wide variety of purposes in and across many professions. For example, many community and governmental agencies use it to foster personal and professional growth. Mentoring in business and industry has become a common practice as a strategy for recruiting, retaining, and promoting high potential talent (Eddy, Tannenbaum, Alliger, D'Abate, & Givens, 2001). Schools of medicine and nursing are implementing mentoring programs to enhance individuals' socialization into the profession (Grossman, 2013).

Within education, mentoring occurs in multiple contexts and levels. For example, in higher education contexts, new faculty members receive support, undergraduates and graduate students participate in mentoring programs, and more experienced faculty members are mentored into administrative roles. In P–12 schools, mentoring is often used to induct, develop and retain teachers and administrators. The contexts of these programs differ not only in terms of location and structure, but also in relation to the roles mentor and mentee play and when and why the mentoring occurs. For example, preservice teachers are mentored in field placements, newly employed teachers are inducted into the profession with assigned mentors, and veteran teachers receive ongoing support (Achinstein & Athanases, 2006; Feiman-Nemser, 2001a). Likewise, new assistant principals, new senior principals, and new superintendents receive mentoring for different needs and purposes, although the research on administrative mentoring is much less developed than that for teacher mentoring. Even in these subcontexts within education, organizational cultural differences exist related to the purposes of mentoring, some intentional, and some unintentional, as documented by Kochan and Pascarelli (2003).

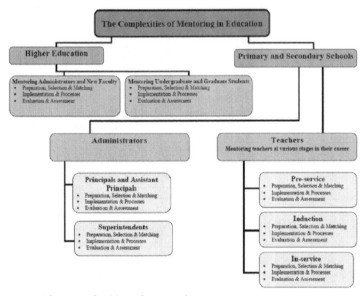

Figure 1.1.   The complexities of mentoring.

The complexity of mentoring in education is also reflected by the many terms used for "mentor," as well as those used to describe the person being mentored. For example, several terms are used in the present-day literature to characterize mentors of beginning teachers and each indicates different underlying assumptions and expectations. The most common term is "supervisor" or "university supervisor" (Slick, 1998), which is derived from the Medieval Latin word *supervidue* "meaning to 'look over and oversee'" (Slick, 1998, p. 821). Some researchers have proposed alternative terms that characterize the supportive nature of the role, like "advisor" or "helper" (Stone, 1987, p. 71). Others have used the language of coaching, evoking images of athletic coaches or, more recently, life coaches—individuals who often work one-on-one and who are in charge of training or teaching.

Terms like "field instructor" (Denyer, 1997) and "university–based teacher educator" (Millwater & Yarrow, 1997) imply responsibilities and actions that are more educative in nature (Feiman-Nemser, 2001b). Denyer (1997) views the word "instructor" as key, since it encompasses the heart of the role—"a person who will engage in instruction in the field, a person who will teach … teacher candidates about teaching, a person who will learn from teaching" (p. 39). It is particularly interesting to note that each term carries its own connotation and reflects how mentoring relationships might be conceptualized and enacted.

The multiple mentoring terms used are just semantics as they reflect understandings of what a mentor is and what he/she is expected to do. Put another way, not everyone in education shares the same paradigms regarding mentoring. For example, some scholars view teaching as a practice to be learned over time and a term like "novice," which means learner or beginner, best fits their developmental conceptualization of the mentee. In this conceptualization, the mentor is someone who helps teachers develop their practice (Feiman-Nemser, 2001a). Mentoring, in this case, "moves beyond emotional support and brief technical advice to become truly educative, focused on learning opportunities that move novices' practice forward and challenge their thinking and practice" (Achinstein & Athanases, 2006, p. 9). However, when a mentee is labeled as a protégé, the relationship carries very different connotations. Blackwell (1989) describes this mentoring as "a process by which persons of superior rank, special achievements, and prestige instruct, counsel, guide, and facilitate the intellectual and/ or career development of persons identified as protégés" (p. 9). Here the mentor would appear to be someone who is more directive with the mentee. There is a hierarchical nature to their relationship, for it is the mentor who holds the knowledge and power, while the mentee is expected to emulate the mentor. The purpose of this type of mentoring is to transmit knowledge and skills to someone with less experience and expertise, in order to help the individual assimilate into a new role.

Alternate Forms of Mentoring and Diverse Cultures

In addition to roles and conceptualizations of the mentoring relationships, the way in which mentoring relationships are structured and the cultural understandings about their purposes differ, creating another issue when attempting to identify which practices are best. The traditional form of mentoring described by Kram (1985) was based on a mentoring dyad, in which one mentor was paired with one protégé. The traditional form of mentoring involves the transfer of skills within authoritative and apprenticeship contexts and is male-based in its origins. In more recent mentoring literature, the concept of a developmental network of mentors has been explored (Higgins & Kram, 2001), which is referred to as a mentoring "constellation," (Higgins & Thomas, 2001), or a mentoring "mosaic" (Mullen, 2005). Other structures and hybrid forms of mentoring are also emerging, such as mentoring as a developmental learning partnership (Mullen & Lick, 1999; Zachary, 2012), peer-mentoring, e-mentoring, mentoring circles (Kram & Ragins, 2007), cascade mentoring (Davis, Ginorio, Hollenshead, Lazarus, & Rayman, 1996), reverse mentoring (Scandura & Viator, 1994), and synergistic comentoring (Mullen & Lick, 1999).

Further complicating the issue of complexity in mentoring is that these forms and types of mentoring vary culturally (O'Neill & Blake-Beard, 2002; Pellegrini & Scandura, 2006; Ragins, 2007). This cultural diversity demands that organizations identify ways to support mentoring relationships among people from different cultures, backgrounds, and perspectives. Blake-Beard, Murrell, and Thomas (2007) acknowledge that "the impact of race on mentoring relationships is an important question to raise, first and foremost because the changing composition of the workforce means that individuals will experience more cross-race (and cross-cultural) interactions within organizations of today and tomorrow" (p. 225). Ragins (2007) concurs, stating that diversity characterizes most aspects of organizational life, but goes beyond race to include diversity in age, sexual orientation, religion, gender, disability, and economic class.

Challenges Associated With Defining Mentoring

Variations in forms and contexts make defining mentoring a challenge. There is also a lack of a universal definition of the term mentoring (Crow, 2012; Eby et al., 2007). While Dominguez's (2012) review of a large database of mentoring articles found that most used either Kram's 1985 definition or that proposed by Levinson and colleagues in 1978, Crisp and Cruz (2009) found more than 50 definitions of mentoring when examining just the social science literature. Definitions of mentoring denote a variety of components. Some definitions describe the people (mentors or mentees), some describe behaviors, and others describe mentoring processes. Traditionally, mentoring has been defined as a relationship between an older, more experienced mentor and a younger, less experienced protégé for the purpose of helping and developing the protégé's career (Kram, 1985). This definition describes the people involved and the purpose, and a definite hierarchical relationship. In sharp contrast, Zachary (2005) defined mentoring as reciprocal and collaborative learning between two or more individuals who share mutual responsibility and accountability for helping a mentee work toward achievement of clear and mutually defined learning goals. This definition describes the people involved and the purpose, but a very different nature of the relationship (mutual, reciprocal).

Crow (2012) noted that defining mentoring is problematic in the following ways: (1) historically, the definitions have described mentoring attributes rather than the meaning of the concept; (2) the expanding types of mentoring have moved the field away from the traditional mentoring dyad concept; (3) the boundaries of the concept have become blurred with other supportive roles, and (4) assumptions about the goals of a mentoring relationship have been largely unexamined. Crow also pointed out that the lack of a solid mentoring definition limits the ability to develop theories of mentoring, as well as making it difficult to build a research base in the field.

In addition to the ambiguity of mentoring definitions, the terms "coaching" and "mentoring" are often used interchangeably in educational contexts (Fletcher & Mullen, 2012). Some scholars contend that these terms are different in several respects, and should be researched separately (Clutterbuck, 2007; Ensher & Murphy, 2005; Feldman & Lankau, 2005). Clutterbuck (2007) clarified this by stating that coaching can be either directive or nondirective, but is focused on performance goals, specific tasks, or competencies, while mentoring is "concerned with helping people achieve longer-term career or other personal goals" (p. 265). Fletcher and Mullen (2012) sought to bring the terms "mentoring" and "coaching" together with the following perspective: "We recognise that mentoring and coaching theory are not simple or uniform concepts but complex educational ideas that inevitably change because of their contextual dependency, philosophical rootedness and political idiosyncrasies" (p. 2).

Clearly, the wide range of mentoring contexts, concepts and definitions has made synthesis difficult and the mentoring literature has been "disparate and fragmented, having been the product of several disciplines, each with a unique orientation" (Savickas, 2007, p. xvii).

THE COMPLEXITY OF "BEST PRACTICES"

Another complexity in defining best practice in mentoring is trying to determine what the term "best practices" means. The term "best practices" has been used in management (Francis & Holloway, 2007), computer software development (Ambler & Lines, 2012), and health care (Frampton & Charmel, 2008) to describe practices that "work" and have consistently shown to be superior. Across the disciplines, best practices are described as an amalgamation of practice and research, meaning they are both useful and tested in practice yet firmly rooted in current, rigorous research In other words, they are practices that are "solid, reputable, state-of-the-art work in a field" (Zemelman, Daniels, Hyde, & Varner, 1998, p. viii). Despite this commonality, there are different conceptualizations of best practices (see Figure 1.2).

Figure 1.2.   Best practices.

Some disciplines use the term, best practices, to standardize the field, offering prescribed methods or premade templates for people to follow or a framework outlining an array of appropriate practices (Francis & Holloway, 2007). This standardization becomes problematic when best practices are reduced to a list from which practitioners can pick and choose, because a fixed list ignores the fact that best practices are by nature fluid and ever–changing, as new research emerges. Lists of best practices also often fail to account for the contextual nature of practice as not every practice is appropriate for every context, nor are they implemented the same way every time.

Some disciplines take a more rigorous stance in determining what makes a best practice and suggesting that people use it. The U.S. Department of Health and Human Services, for example, stipulates that there must be evidence of effectiveness and generalizability in order for something to be considered a best practice (U.S. Department of Health and Human Services, 2003). We believe this to be a more viable definition of best practices than creating a list of things to do, because by their very nature, best practices imply a measure of quality, meaning that they make work more effective by utilizing "the latest knowledge, technology, and procedures" (Zemelman et al., 1998, p. viii).

In education, the notion of best practices gained widespread appeal in the late 1990s with the advent of the standards movement (Dufour & Eaker, 1998; Zemelman et al., 1998). A growing body of practitioner-friendly literature now provides teachers with empirically based instructional frameworks and strategies to improve their teaching (Danielson, 2007; Marzano, 2007; Zemelman et al., 1998).

While there is a set of empirically based *International Standards for Mentoring Programs in Employment* (ISMPE), and an assessment process to identify the degree to which these standards have been applied in a particular situation, the mentoring literature in education has been slow to develop in terms of creating standards and best practices in mentoring. Despite the many how-to manuals available for mentors, most of the information within them is anecdotal in nature (Barnett & O'Mahony, 2008; Crow, 2012). In fact, one of the major criticisms leveled against "best practices" in education is that many of the examples found in practitioner-oriented literature are unsubstantiated by research, and in many cases, merely describe the latest fads or fashions (Francis & Holloway, 2007).

There are several factors that might explain this lack of empirically substantiated mentoring best practices in education. As a relatively new practice in education, mentoring is in the theory-building phase, where researchers are beginning to describe what is happening in the field, such as the roles that mentors play and the knowledge, practices, and skills that they use in their work with novices.

Another factor has to do with the nature of mentoring research itself. Most studies that examine mentoring in education are small-scale, qualitative studies (Cochran-Smith & Zeichner, 2005; Levine, 2006). While these cases help to identify promising practices, they do not allow generalization across mentoring contexts. Yet another challenge is that the research in various mentoring contexts is uneven. For instance, the preponderance of research on mentoring in education is in the area of P–12 teacher mentoring, with much less on school administrator mentoring and mentoring in higher education (Dominguez, 2012). The time is ripe for the field to begin looking across these studies to analyze and identify what we know about what is working well in mentoring.

As a field, we are beginning to build a body of evidence that supports the effectiveness of mentoring, but in this age of accountability, we need to begin substantiating how mentoring works—what mentors do that lead to more effective and successful students, teachers, administrators, or faculty within varied educational contexts. It is time to begin to develop an organized, focused approach to identify the structures that people are creating to prepare mentors or ensure that they are paired with mentees in their content area; the practices that mentors are employing that lead to instructional improvement; and the evaluation measures that lead to improved practice in education.

IDENTIFYING MENTORING BEST PRACTICES IN EDUCATION

The complexity of both the practice of mentoring and the term "best practices" make it difficult to draw broad conclusions on what is working well in mentoring in education based on research. However, we are optimistic that as a field, we can begin to engage in a process that will help us empirically identify those practices that are consistently—across contexts—having an impact and also suggest areas for future research. We propose the following:

Define Best Practices

The first step involves developing an operational definition of best practices that will enable the field to describe effective practices in education mentoring that can also be empirically substantiated. In order for a practice to qualify as a best practice, we propose that it must meet all of the following criteria:

- be effective in practice
- be empirically proven
- achieve the stated purpose

The challenge becomes knowing how to identify each of these characteristics. The following descriptions offer concrete ways to think about each of them (see Figure 1.3).

Effectiveness in practice. Consideration should only be given to those practices that are regularly and effectively being used by practitioners in the field. To qualify, these practices must be attainable, accessible and affordable. Attainable means that the practice is feasible and not so complicated that it is impractical. For example, suggesting that mentors observe their mentees daily might be productive, but is not a viable option for most people and would therefore be considered unattainable. Accessible means that it is virtually universally possible and not so extreme as to exclude certain groups. For example, online resources that require a subscription may not be available to all districts or universities and therefore would be ineligible for consideration as a best practice. Finally, best practice must

Figure 1.3. Determining best practices.

be affordable. Suggesting that schools hire full-release mentors to support administrators or teachers, for example, is unrealistic for most districts and therefore could not be considered a best practice.

Empirically based. As previously stated, much of the mentoring literature is based on anecdotal observations by an individual, or promoting a "how to mentor" practice that may not be tested in multiple educational settings. To be considered exemplary, a practice must be empirically substantiated in research-based literature—reputable, international peer–reviewed journals, scholarly books containing reports of sound research that have been conducted according to widely accepted methodologies, or dissertation research conducted under scrutiny of an institutional review board. It will be important to look for and develop both quantitative and qualitative studies that are broader in scope than isolated case studies or individual observations. Grounding practices in research will also help to ensure that they are conceptually founded and not based solely on practitioner experiences.

Achieve their stated purpose. To be considered, a practice must demonstrate that it realizes its goals. One of the primary purposes of mentoring in education is to increase effectiveness by creating highly effectual faculty members, administrators and teachers (Casavant & Cherkowski, 2001; Fairbanks, Freedman, & Kahn, 2000). Therefore, mentoring practices that achieve this goal should be eligible for consideration as best practices.

Campbell, Kyriakides, Muijs, and Robinson (2003) offer a definition of effectiveness—"that which produces, or is certain to produce, the intended effect" (p. 354). Therefore, a practice would need to demonstrate that it produced its intended effect. In other words, for each best practice, there would need to be some stated objective and corresponding evidence that the objective was met. For example, if a mentoring practice claimed that it increased retention among new faculty members, then there would need to be corollary data that substantiates this claim.

PUTTING THIS FRAMEWORK INTO PRACTICE

The next step in this process would involve cross-case analyses, wherein researchers determine if there ARE practices that seem to be effective across contexts. We suspect that some practices will be common across contexts, while others will be more uniquely suited to their specific group. Identifying common practices found in multiple contexts will allow us, as a field, to specify standards that can be used broadly by practitioners. Looking across contexts will also provide opportunities for researchers and practitioners, alike, to learn from one another. Perhaps most importantly, we believe that this exercise can provide another way for those of us who work in mentoring to evaluate what we do, in order to determine whether our practices are empirically grounded. This cross-contextual lens may help us consider questions such as: Are the mentoring practices used in our area substantiated by research? Are any common practices counter–productive or in need of alteration? Are there practices that still need to be empirically investigated? By engaging in this process, we can begin to build a common body of knowledge about effective mentoring that will allow us to respond concretely to critics and to substantiate our belief that mentoring works. This exercise also has the potential to contribute significantly by identifying gaps in the literature on mentoring, thereby indicating where future research needs to be conducted.

This book is a first attempt at gathering current empirical examples of practices in mentoring in P–12 education. With this initial work as a back-drop, we determined to begin following our own advice by conceptualizing a book for the *Perspectives in Mentoring* series that would hopefully identify some best practices in mentoring in two areas: new teacher mentoring and new principal mentoring.

Certainly, with the growing interest in best practices, the time is ripe in education for a melding of theory and practice, for us to think not only about the "how–to" but also the empirical support for specific strategies and behaviors that make mentoring effective, for there is a definite need to "figure out 'what counts' amidst the glorious complexity of practice, and how to characterize it in careful ways" (Schoenfeld, 1999, p. 12). Therefore, when we put out the call for chapters for this book, we specified that the authors report original empirical research in mentoring, with the aim of highlighting and recommending those programs and practices that would meet our identified criteria for being "best practices": attainable, accessible and affordable in practice and based on theoretical research found in peer-reviewed literature.

After accepting chapter submission proposals of empirical studies from around the world, we chose the ones that we felt would offer a diversity of perspectives in both new teacher and new principal mentoring. We were optimistic that this group of empirical reports would add to our knowledge of "what works" for these two populations (teachers and principals). After a careful review of the submissions chosen for this volume, we feel that we can state that we are *beginning* the work of identifying best practices in mentoring, following the criteria set forth in this article. Every practice reported in these chapters met one or more of the characteristics of the definition of best practice, and in the concluding chapter, we summarize those. However, we were also struck with the realization that the authors of these studies were also presenting practices and programs that demonstrated new and innovative formats for mentoring, representing a changing landscape in P–12 education. While they were indeed bringing forth effective mentoring practices, it became readily apparent the researchers in the field are currently focused on responding to many of the realities and challenges facing those who create mentoring programs: time, distance, budget constraints, and demands for results tied to student achievement.

As a result, we became "bifocal" as editors of this book: describing both enduring constructs of mentoring that can be labeled as best practice, and also highlighting some of the emerging trends in mentoring that result from the current realities of P–12 education. What we present here is a sampling of the many ways that mentoring programs are being conceived in P–12 education in response to changing standards, demographics, and fiscal challenges. Indeed, the creativity and resourcefulness of educators who are being asked to do more with less in this accountability-driven era are highlighted in this book. The landscape of mentoring teachers and school leaders includes vistas of enduring and effective mentoring constructs as well as new horizons, and we present the evidence of both in this volume. Whether you are a P–12 teacher or leader, or a mentoring researcher in higher education, our hope is that you will find this book helpful to you in your work.

ACKNOWLEDGMENT

This chapter is adapted from an article published by the authors in *The International Journal of Mentoring and Coaching in Education*, 2013, 2(3), pp. 189–203, titled "Best Practices in Mentoring: Complexities and Possibilities," and used with permission from Emerald Publishing Company.

REFERENCES

Achinstein, B., & Athanases, S. (Eds.). (2006). *Mentors in the making: Developing new leaders for new teachers.* Columbia University, NY: Teachers College Press.

Allen, T. D., & Eby, L. T. (Eds.). (2011). *The Blackwell handbook of mentoring: A multiple perspectives approach.* New York, NY: Wiley.

Ambler, S. W., & Lines, M. (2012). *Disciplined agile delivery: A practitioner's guide to agile software delivery in the enterprise.* Indianapolis, IN: IBM Press.

Barnett, B. G., & O'Mahoney, G. R. (2008). Mentoring and coaching programs for the professional development of school leaders. In J. Lumby, G. Crow, & P. Pashiardis (Eds.), *International handbook on the preparation and development of school leaders* (pp. 232–262). New York, NY: Routledge.

Blackwell, J. E. (1989). Mentoring: An action strategy for increasing minority faculty. *Academe, 75,* 8–14.

Blake–Beard, S. D., Murrell, A., & Thomas, D. (2007). Unfinished business: The impact of race on understanding mentoring relationships. In B. R Ragins & K. E. Kram (Eds.), *The handbook of mentoring at work: Theory, research, and practice.* Thousand Oaks, CA: Sage.

Campbell, C. D. (2007). Best practices for student-faculty mentoring programs. *The Blackwell Handbook of Mentoring: A Multiple Perspectives Approach, 325–343.*

Campbell, R. J., Kyriakides, L., Muijs, R. D., & Robinson, W. (2003). Differential teacher effectiveness: Towards a model for research and teacher appraisal. *Oxford Review of Education, 29*(3), 347–362.

Casavant, M. D., & Cherkowski, S. (2001). Effective leadership: Bringing mentoring and creativity to the principalship. *NASSP Bulletin, 85*(624), 71–81.

Clutterbuck, D. (2007). An international perspective on mentoring. In B. R. Ragins & K. E. Kram (Eds.), *The handbook of mentoring at work: Theory, research, and practice* (pp. 633–655). Los Angeles, CA: Sage.

Crisp, G., & Cruz, I. (2009). Mentoring college students: A review of the literature between 1990 and 2007. *Research in Higher Education, 50*(5), 525–545.

Crow, G. M. (2012). A critical-constructivist perspective on mentoring and coaching for leadership. In S. J. Fletcher, & C. A. Mullen (Eds.), *The Sage handbook of mentoring and coaching in education* (pp. 228–242). Los Angeles, CA: Sage.

Cochran-Smith, M., & Zeichner, K. (2005). *Studying teacher education: The report of the AERA panel on research and teacher education,* Mahwah, NJ: American Educational Research Association and Lawrence Earlbaum Associates.

Cordingley, P., & Buckler, N. (2012). Mentoring and coaching for teachers' continuing professional development. In S. J. Fletcher & C. A. Mullen (Eds.), *The Sage handbook of mentoring and coaching in education* (pp. 215–227). Los Angeles, CA: Sage.

Danielson, C. (2007). *Enhancing professional practice: A framework for teaching* (2nd ed.). Alexandria, VA: ASCD.

Davis, C. S., Ginorio, A. B., Hollenshead, C. S., Lazarus, B. B., & Rayman, P. M. (1996). *The equity equation: Fostering the advancement of women in the sciences, mathematics, and engineering.* San Francisco, CA: Jossey-Bass.

Denyer, J. (1997). Constructing a practice: How an educational vision shapes the work of a field instructor and her teacher candidates. In S. Feiman-Nemser

& C. Rosaen (Eds.), *Guiding teacher learning: Insider studies of classroom work with prospective and practicing teachers* (pp. 37–52). Washington, DC: American Association of Colleges for Teacher Education.

Dominguez, N. (2012). *Mentoring unfolded: The evolution of an emerging discipline* (Unpublished doctoral dissertation). University of New Mexico, Albuquerque, NM.

DuFour, R., & Eaker, R. (1998). *Professional learning communities at work: Best practices for enhancing student achievement.* Bloomington, IN: National Educational Service.

Eby, L., Rhodes, J., & Allen, T. (2007). Definition and evolution of mentoring. In T. Allen and L. Eby (Eds.), *The Blackwell Handbook of Mentoring* (pp. 7–20). Malden, MA: Blackwell.

Eddy, E., Tannenbaum, S., Alliger, G., D'Abate, C., & Givens, S. (2001). *Mentoring in industry: The top 10 issues when building and supporting a mentoring program.* Technical report prepared for the Naval Air Warfare Training Systems Division (Contract No. N61339-99-D-0012).

Ehrich, L. C., Hansford, B., & Tennent, L. (2004). Formal mentoring programs in education and other professions: A review of the literature. *Educational Administration Quarterly, 40*(4), 518–540.

Ensher, E., & Murphy, S. (2005). *Power mentoring: How successful mentors and protégé get the most out of their relationships.* San Francisco, CA: Jossey-Bass.

Fairbanks, C., Freedman, D., & Kahn, C. (2000). The Role of Effective Mentors in Learning to Teach. *Journal of Teacher Education, 51*(2), 102–112.

Feiman-Nemser, S. (2001a). From preparation to practice: Designing a continuum to strengthen and sustain teaching. *Teachers College Record, 103*(6), 1013–1055.

Feiman-Nemser, S. (2001b).Helping novices learn to teacher: Lessons from an exemplary support teacher. *Journal of Teacher Education, 52*(1), 17–30.

Feldman, D. C., & Lankau, M. J. (2005). Executive coaching: A review and agenda for future research. *Journal of Management, 31*, 829–848.

Fletcher, S., & Mullen, C. (2012). *The Sage handbook of mentoring and coaching in education.* Thousand Oaks, CA: Sage.

Frampton, S., & Charmel, P. (Eds.). (2008). *Putting patients first: Best practices in patient–centered care* (Vol. 33). San Francisco, CA: Jossey-Bass.

Francis, G., & Holloway, J. (2007). What have we learned? Themes from the literature on best–practice benchmarking. *International Journal of Management Reviews, 9*(3), 171–189.

Giscombe, K. (2007). Advancing women through the glass ceiling with formal mentoring. In B. R. Ragins & K. E. Kram (Eds.), *The handbook of mentoring at work: Theory, research, and practice* (pp. 549–571). Los Angeles, CA: Sage.

Grossman, S. (2013). *Mentoring in nursing: A dynamic and collaborative process* (2nd Ed.). New York, NY: Springer.

Higgins, M. C., & Kram, K. E. (2001). Reconceptualizing mentoring at work: A developmental network perspective. *Academy of Management Review, 26*(2), 264–288.

Higgins, M. C., & Thomas, D. A. (2001). Constellations and careers: Toward understanding the effects of multiple developmental relationships. *Journal of Organizational Behavior, 22*(3), 223–247.

International Standards for Mentoring Programmes in Employment. (2003). Retrieved from http://www.ismpe.com

Johnson, W. (2007). *On being a mentor: A guide for higher education faculty.* New York, NY: Lawrence Erlbaum Associates.

Kochan, F. K. (2002). *The organizational and human dimensions of successful mentoring programs and relationships.* Greenwich, CT: Information Age Publishing.

Kochan, F. (2013). Extending the research agenda on mentoring in education. *International Journal of Mentoring and Coaching in Education, 2*(3), 1–4.

Kochan, F., & Pascarelli, J. T. (2003). Culture, context, and issues of change related to mentoring programs and relationships. In F. K. Kochan & J. T. Pascarelli (Eds.), *Global perspectives on mentoring: Transforming contexts, communities, and cultures* (pp. 417–428). Greenwich, CT: Information Age Publishing.

Kram, K. E. (1985). *Mentoring at work: Developmental relationships in organizational life.* Lanham, MD: University Press of America.

Kram, K., & Ragins, B. (2007). The landscape of mentoring in the 21st century. In B. R. Ragins & K. E. Kram (Eds.), *The handbook of mentoring at work: Theory, research, and practice* (pp. 659–692). Los Angeles, CA: Sage.

Levine, A. (2006). *Educating school teachers.* Washington, DC: The Education Schools Project.

Levinson, D., Darrow, D., Levinson, M., Klein, E., & McKee, B. (1978). *The seasons of a man's life.* New York, NY: Knopf.

Marzano, R. (2007). *The art and science of teaching: A comprehensive framework for effective instruction.* Alexandria, VA: ASCD.

Menter, I., Hulme, M., Dely, E., & Lewin, J. (2010). *Literature review on teacher education in the 21st century.* Edinburgh, Scotland: Education Analytical Services.

Millwater, J., & Yarrow, A. (1997). Practernship: A theoretical construct for developing professionalism in preservice teachers. *Teacher Education Quarterly, 24*(1), 23–35.

Mullen, C. A. (2005). *The mentorship primer.* New York, NY: Peter Lang.

Mullen, C. A. (2011). Facilitating self–regulated learning using mentoring approaches with doctoral students. In B. Zimmerman & D. H. Schunk (Eds.), *Handbook of self-regulation of learning and performance.* New York, NY: Routledge.

Mullen, C. A. (2012). Mentoring: An overview. In S. J. Fletcher & C. A. Mullen (Eds.), *The Sage Handbook of Mentoring and Coaching in Education* (pp. 7–23). Los Angeles, CA: Sage.

Mullen, C. A., & Lick, D. W. (1999). *New directions in mentoring: Creating a culture of synergy.* London, England: Falmer.

Odell, S. J., & Huling, L. (Eds.). (2004). *Quality mentoring for novice teachers.* Lanham, MD: Rowman & Littlefield.

O'Neill, R. M., & Blake–Beard, S. D. (2002). Gender barriers to the female mentor–male protégé relationship. *Journal of Business Ethics, 37,* 51–63.

Pellegrini, S. C., & Scandura, T. A. (2006). Leader-Member Exchange (LMX), paternalism and delegation in the Turkish business culture: An empirical investigation. *Journal of International Business Studies, 2,* 264–279.

Ragins, B. R. (2007). Diversity and workplace mentoring relationships. In T. D. Allen & L. T. Eby (Eds.), *The Blackwell handbook of mentoring* (pp. 281–300). Malden, MA: Blackwell.

Savickas, M. L. (2007). Forward: The maturation of mentoring research. In T. Allen & L. Eby (Eds.), *The Blackwell handbook of mentoring* (pp. xviii–xix). Malden, MA: Blackwell.

Scandura, T., & Viator, R. (1994). Mentoring in public accounting firms: An analysis of mentor–protégé relationships, mentorship functions, and protégé turnover intentions. *Accounting, Organizations and Society, 19*(1994), 717.

Schoenfeld, A. (1999). Looking toward the 21st century: Challenges of educational theory and practice. *Educational Researcher,* 4–14.

Slick, S. (1998). The university supervisor: A disenfranchised outsider. *Teaching and Teacher Education, 14(8),* 821–834.

Stone, E. (1987). Teaching practice supervision: Bridging between theory and practice. *European Journal of Teacher Education, 10*(1), 67–79.

U.S. Department of Health and Human Services, Administration for Children and Families Program Announcement. (2003). *Federal Register, 68*(131).

Zachary, L. (2005). *Creating a mentoring culture: The organization's guide.* San Francisco, CA: Jossey-Bass.

Zachary, L. (2012). *The mentor's guide* (2nd ed.). San Francisco, CA: Jossey-Bass.

Zemelman, S., Daniels, H., Hyde, A. A., & Varner, W. (1998). *Best practice: New standards for teaching and learning in America's schools.* Portsmouth, NH: Heinemann.

CHAPTER 2

DEVELOPING MENTORS ACROSS CONTEXTS

The Reciprocity of Mentorship in School/University Partnerships

Danielle V. Dennis and Audra K. Parker

INTRODUCTION

The preparation of preservice teachers is an endeavor best shared between university supervisors and collaborating teachers. However, studies indicate that this relationship is often fraught with miscommunication, and conflict, regarding the roles and responsibilities of each partner (Hamel & Jaasko-Fisher, 2011; Rikard & Veal, 1998; Stanulis, 1995; Waring, 2013). Despite knowing the power of field experiences and collaborating teachers on preservice teachers' development (Bullough & Draper, 2004; Valencia, Martin, Place, & Grossman, 2009), little attention has been paid to developing and studying a shared understanding of the roles and responsibilities of each member of the triad: preservice teacher, collaborating teacher, and university supervisor. Collaborating teachers feel they lack

Best Practices in Mentoring for Teacher and Leader Development, pp. 19–29
Copyright © 2016 by Information Age Publishing
All rights of reproduction in any form reserved.

voice and power in regards to how preservice teachers are trained, and often rely on their own personal experiences to mentor university students (Rikard & Veal, 1998; Stanulis, 1995). University supervisors lament lack of time to develop triad relationships (Koehler, 1988; Slick, 1998). Preservice teachers report a tension between university supervisors and collaborating teachers and subsequently, the theories learned at the university and the expected practices of the classroom (Derrick, 1971; Feiman-Nemser & Buchanan, 1985; Labaree, 2004; Rikard & Veal, 1996; Shipman, 1967; Vick, 2006). Many studies indicate that it is the perceived responsibility of the university supervisor to set and communicate student teaching expectations, rather than a shared effort with the collaborating teachers (Rikard & Veal, 1998; Slick, 1998; Stanulis, 1995). Further aggravating these issues is the fact that most university supervisors are graduate students or adjunct faculty who themselves are separated from program development (Slick, 1998). Combining all of these factors, the mentoring of preservice teachers is generally narrow in focus and built upon emotional support and advice, rather than on the skills needed to develop as a highly effective educator (Norman & Feiman-Nemser, 2005).

To this point, we shifted our thinking about the roles of the triad toward Norman and Feiman-Nemser's (2005) concept of "educative mentoring" (p. 680), which views the learning of novice, and in our case, preservice teachers as developmental, and mentoring as essential to this development. Norman and Feiman Nemser view mentoring as a form of professional development, and offer that all novice teachers "need situated and sustained guidance and support as they tackle the challenge of learning to teach in a particular school context" (p. 694). Such a notion suggests that the university supervisor has much to learn from the collaborating teacher (Rikard & Veal, 1995). This supports Stanulis's (1995) claim that collaborating teachers have a "valuable voice in creating university- and field-based portions of teacher preparation" (p. 331). School/university partnerships, often referred to as Professional Development Schools, are uniquely positioned to heed the call for more robust triads. Goodlad (1994) coined the term "simultaneous renewal" to illustrate the iterative process of K–12 schools and Colleges of Education developing together, both to become stronger partners, and to create stronger teachers.

We believe that simultaneous renewal requires educative mentoring amongst all stakeholders, and that learning from one another will allow for greater growth across contexts. The purpose of this chapter is to profile how two school/university partnerships engaged in educative mentoring within and across settings. The chapter will explore ways in which school administrators, classroom teachers, university faculty, and graduate assistants develop as mentors that support preservice and in-service teacher development, with a focus on simultaneous renewal. We begin by providing contextual descriptions of two University Partnership Schools, and the ways in which each engaged in this work. We then discuss our methods for data collection and analysis, as well as our shared findings. Finally, we offer the lessons learned from our work, and how this work may inform both practice and future research.

CREATING SPACE FOR RECIPROCAL MENTORSHIP

This research took place at two University Partnership Schools in the Southeastern United States. One school, Watkins Elementary, is situated on the university campus, but under the authority of the local school district. The other, Thomas Elementary, is a Bank Street model K–8 charter school situated in the local school district. In each, a university supervisor used unique approaches and structures to foster opportunities for robust, reciprocal mentoring relationships.

Watkins Elementary

Built on the campus of a university in the Southeastern United States, Watkins Elementary School serves 650 pre-K–5 students. Although a partnership school with the local university, Watkins is operated by the local school district. The school has a diverse student population with 82% qualifying for free or reduced lunch, 21% identified as students with disabilities, and 25% identified as English Language Learners (ELL), with 27 different languages represented at the school. Forty-one percent (41%) of the student population is Black, 28% Hispanic, 18% White, and 9% identifies as multiracial. The faculty at Watkins varies in experience, though most have five, or fewer, years. Historically, the school endured high faculty turnover, though with a strong administration and an increased partnership with the local university, this has decreased in recent years.

Using Watkins's School Improvement Plan (SIP), university faculty and school administrators determined teachers' professional development needs. With this knowledge, university faculty and school administrators developed Professional Learning Communities (PLCs) as job-embedded professional development. Professional Learning Communities are largely used as a tool for analyzing student data and making instructional decisions to support students' needs (DuFour & Mattos, 2013). Grade level teams met weekly to review data, discern patterns, and discuss themes identified. Grade level teams then determined their specific professional development needs, and university faculty offered opportunities for classroom teachers to engage in professional development. After two years of grade level PLCs—focused on K–5 student data—two collaborating teachers, Jennifer and Emily, met with the university supervisor to suggest PLCs as a way to receive information beyond the logistics shared at weekly mentor meetings. Jennifer and Emily wanted to learn more about being strong mentors broadly, and they believed there were several teachers on the faculty who would support the PLC. We sent an invitation to all teachers who were currently serving as mentors to preservice teachers. Of the 14, nine shared an interest in participating in the PLC, though only six were able to participate once the dates were determined. The teacher leadership PLC was developed to support the professional needs of those teachers who were (a) engaged in the mentoring of preservice teachers, and (b) interested in developing their expertise as mentors.

Establishing community among the PLC members was a priority. At the first meeting, each teacher was given time to share their experiences as a mentor, what they hoped to learn from the PLC, and what their personal goals were for the year. Because they were all working with preservice teachers who were completing a full year residency program, the mentors were required to have some previous experience working with preservice teachers, but the six teachers' experience varied from only one previous semester working with a preservice teacher to over 10 years. The teacher leadership PLC continued to meet monthly over the course of the school year. In addition, the university supervisor met with each individual participant on a monthly basis to focus on her specific professional goals related to mentoring. As part of their commitment to the leadership PLC, each participant enacted their goals in the classroom based on literature read in the PLC, and then reported their experiences—both challenges and successes—at the PLC meetings. The mentors determined the agenda for each meeting based on their conversations, experiences, and interests. The university supervisor typically located resources for the mentors to review prior to each meeting, but as the year progressed the mentors themselves shared materials with each other and with the university supervisor. At these meetings, the mentor was prepared to share her progress towards her goals, and ask questions about next steps. The intern joined her mentor at these meetings so that the triad could discuss how the mentor's progress was supporting the development of the intern.

Each PLC and individual meeting was videotaped. In addition, the supervisor maintained a researcher's journal at the end of each PLC and individual meeting. Transcripts of each meeting (both PLC and individual) were analyzed using inductive analysis (Hatch, 2002). Inductive analysis is an approach in which data are coded multiple times, progressing from specific patterns of meaning to general statements about phenomena under investigation. The researcher journal was used to clarify or elaborate the transcripts. In addition, the supervisor shared the findings with the six mentors midyear and after the final analysis was complete, and asked for their feedback regarding the findings and their experiences.

Thomas Elementary

Thomas Elementary is a birth to Grade 8 charter school educating over 800 children in a large metropolitan school district. Situated in a historically Hispanic neighborhood, the demographics of the K–8 student population of Thomas Elementary reveal a diverse student body: 42% Caucasian, 40% Hispanic, 12% African American, 4% multiracial, and 2% Asian American. The charter of Thomas Elementary centers on the philosophical underpinnings of the Bank Street School for Children. Key tenets include an emphasis on developmentally appropriate instruction, parent engagement, and child-centered instruction. A primary focus of administration at Thomas Elementary is collaboration with local universities. Each teacher is expected to complete the clinical educator training required for supervising preservice teachers, and it is likely that classroom teachers will have multiple interns across a school year. Teachers, administration, and parents perceive teacher education as a central part of the school's mission.

While Thomas Elementary has a long history of collaboration with the university in terms of field placements, the move towards a more robust, reciprocal partnership began in earnest in 2011. This included frequent meetings of all stakeholders, collaboration on initiatives at both Thomas Elementary (e.g., incorporation of a social justice curricular focus; construction of a new preschool) and the university (e.g. move to year-long residency; shift to inquiry focused field experiences). Additionally, several teachers taught courses at the university and faculty from the university frequently held seminars at the school site. It was not uncommon for university faculty to structure coursework with embedded field observations and experiences at Thomas Elementary. Administrators at Thomas frequently called upon university faculty for leadership in school governance and guidance in curriculum and instruction decisions. In a given semester, it was likely that each teacher in the school would host a preservice teacher in some form of internship ranging from initial observations to final internships.

Moving from collaboration to partnership necessitated a shift in the nature of the relationships of triad members (preservice teachers, university supervisors, and collaborating teachers). In order to move from a hierarchical approach with shifting alliances (Bullough & Draper, 2004), the university supervisor sought to create opportunities for reciprocal mentorship among members of the triad and across triads.

Together, seven collaborating teachers, seven preservice teachers, and the university supervisor established bimonthly seminar meetings. The purpose of these seminars was to create an atmosphere that valued the voices of each stakeholder and provided opportunities for reciprocal mentorship. The professional development goals of the preservice teachers, established in collaboration with their teachers, served as an overarching frame for the content of the seminars. Additionally, seminar agendas were shaped by shared readings, mutual planning, and opportunities for structured dialogues based on the needs of the group.

The university supervisor collected field notes during each meeting. These double column field notes included verbatim comments made by the participants as well as postmeeting reflections of the university supervisor. Following the final seminar meeting, each collaborating teacher completed a brief open-ended survey of their perceptions of mentoring experiences across the semester. Documents (meeting agendas, e-mails, collaborating teacher and university supervisor feedback via coaching/evaluation cycles with interns) also served as critical archival data. Survey responses, field notes, and archival data were analyzed using inductive analysis (Hatch, 2002.

FINDINGS

While the contexts of our attempts at creating opportunities for reciprocal mentorship are distinct, several key findings emerged across these experiences. First, we learned that participation, and therefore learning, are developmental. Different group members (school administrators, university faculty, and classroom teachers) develop understandings about mentoring differently over time. For example, Emily, a teacher at Watkins observed, "My team has a different view of this than I do, I think. I see my intern as an asset in my classroom—another knowledgeable adult to work with the students. But, my team members just seem to view their intern as more work." In Emily's situation, every teacher on her team was working with a preservice teacher, but they shared vastly different approaches to working with an intern. For Emily working in the PLC with five other teachers who shared her views about the value added with an intern in the room was instrumental in her development as a mentor.

Varying levels of experience and readiness for engaging in mentoring roles also informed collaborating teachers' understanding of reciprocal mentorship. In part, our a priori assumption of this shaped our rationale for our approaches to working with collaborating teachers. Allison, a new collaborating teacher at Thomas reflected, "Being my first year with an intern, I felt very supported. I became cognizant of the natural tendencies in the classroom to discuss with the intern. (The structure) reaffirmed the choices I make and brought a new perspective to collaborative roundtable discussions." Veteran mentor teachers described their learning with a different lens. Heather noted, "I always enjoy being given the opportunity to learn from others. I am constantly reevaluating myself and reflecting on my personal goals, strengths, areas I would like to improve upon." Because of this, their ability to infuse their learning into mentoring experiences also develops differently for each mentor, over varying periods of time.

Philosophies of mentorship appeared consistent across contexts. In other words, for individuals, their philosophies for mentoring interns closely mirrored their philosophies for mentoring colleagues. For example, Jane, a veteran collaborating teacher at Thomas, stated that her philosophy for mentioning interns centered on "providing an environment where they feel comfortable enough to take risks and where they can gain the confidence needed to grow." Similarly, she felt mentoring her colleagues necessitated "a nonjudgmental environment where they felt comfortable and successful." Cathy, also at Thomas, reflected her internship mentoring goals were to "provide a safe and encouraging place for all of my interns to learn." In terms of mentoring colleagues, she hoped to "be an example of what it means and looks like to be a teacher."

From our work we learned that mentorship development begins with the ability to articulate a philosophy about mentoring, which often mirrored that of the professional development offered at the school. For example, Allison at Thomas noted, "I feel that it is important to provide the intern with the most applicable experience.... Learning by experience with guidance rather than being 'told' what to do and allowing the intern to figure out what works best for his/her teaching style is much more valuable." Heather, a Thomas teacher, noted that her philosophy of mentoring began with consideration of the "strengths and needs of the intern." Both of these reflected the overarching philosophy behind Thomas Charter School— that children's developmental needs drive instruction and learning is an active, engaged process. Similarly, a teacher at Watkins noted, "I believe a new teacher can learn to teach anywhere if they have the right mentor. Part of my job is helping my intern understand how what they've learned here at [Watkins] can work in practice at another school."

Once articulated, elements of the philosophy were enacted—some successfully and some not—which led to a newly articulated philosophy. The articulation and implementation of a mentoring philosophy was an iterative process for all group members, though some required more iterations than others before determining a mentoring philosophy that could be enacted in their specific context. In their final reflections and discussions, mentors suggested they struggle with overwhelming interns and providing clear guidance. This may be in part due to the differences inherent in individuals in mentoring relationships. Cathy suggested, "figuring out where they are and pushing them to their edge" is time intensive work. Tensions between when to push for new learning and when to layer additional support structures also emerged. For example, on one hand, Heather noted she was "surprised at how easy it was to turn over the classroom" and "trust them to take charge and learn from their failings." Simultaneously, they expressed concerns about testing and parent communication and hesitancy in "letting them go and be on the hook." Jennifer, a teacher at Watkins, described a tension between the high-stakes environment in the school and her role as a mentor, "In third grade, kids can fail if they don't pass the test. That's a lot of pressure on all of us. I don't always know how to support [my intern] in learning the curriculum and make sure our students learn what they need to learn to pass the test."

Although the focus of the PLC was developing the mentor's knowledge, each of the six mentors at Watkins and the seven at Thomas commented on how their participation supported their intern. Emily expressed this at one of the PLC meetings, "I don't know about all of you, but I feel so much more comfortable talking to [my intern] about her growth because I can relate it to my own. And, I can ask her if the way I am mentoring her is helpful or not, because she knows I am learning how to be a better teacher to her. It's really changed our relationship."

Building the capacity for mentoring takes time and consistent opportunities to develop structures for meaningful professional development. In both studies, the longevity of the job-embedded professional development allowed for all groups to develop and implement philosophies about mentoring that worked for them, as well as those they mentored. Logistical issues such as time and structure were also important. For example, Heather noted meetings related to mentorship were "convenient and did not interfere with other responsibilities." Several others felt the expectations of bimonthly meetings at Thomas were too much, even when the content and participation furthered their professional development. Joe stated, "Having on-site meetings made complete sense. It was nice and convenient and I enjoyed being a part of the development of the topics we discussed. I would suggest that teachers only need to be present once a month."

Finally, the iterative approach to developing a mentoring philosophy, which was supported through consistent professional development, created reciprocal mentoring relationship between members of all groups. This allowed for deeper understanding of each group member's role in the successful development of preservice teachers. Mentorship engaged the mentors in reciprocal learning. They valued establishing life long friendships through mentoring experiences. Mentors learned from "two professionals working together" and releasing interns to "see what they could come up with." Allison felt reciprocal mentoring shaped her professional development by "reaffirming the choices I make in my classroom and (bringing) in a new perspective to collaborative roundtable discussions.

LESSONS LEARNED

As we reflect on the outcomes of our studies of reciprocal mentorship, we must also highlight our learning as stakeholders in the process. First and foremost, reciprocal mentorship is possible only when all stakeholders play a role in creating space for it. At both Watkins and Thomas, school administrators prioritized the learning experiences of mentors, and recognized the importance of learning to develop preservice teachers in order to strengthen the field. Although the administrators did not often participate in the mentor meetings, the importance they placed on these experiences offered teachers room to learn and grow with the university supervisors. Thus, it is essential to work closely with school administration to establish space for mentors and supervisors to learn about supporting the development of interns.

Second, once space has been created, it must be carefully nurtured and maintained. It is incumbent upon all to work to create a community that values and fosters professional development and supports honest conversations. Developing a shared understanding of roles and responsibilities is contingent upon all parties feeling empowered, that they have a voice in the discussion about working with interns (Rikard & Veal, 1998; Stanulis, 1995). In both contexts, we endured difficult conversations about past experiences working with interns, current confusion and communication issues, and maintaining positive relationships in the future. Nurturing relationships amongst triad members and across the mentor meetings was essential in maintaining the forward progress of the experiences.

Within this space it is also essential that all stakeholders value time. For all stakeholders, the mentoring of preservice teachers is one facet of their job. While an important one, it must be understood that many other facets make up the whole of their positions. Therefore, respecting the time commitment required of mentors, university supervisors, and administrators in creating supportive structures is important. Likewise, it is important to recognize that this work does require time, and all stakeholders will need to support this development with the time needed to make meaningful progress (Koehler, 1988; Slick, 1998).

Reciprocal mentorship requires that all stakeholders (supervisor, administrator, collaborating teacher, preservice teacher) view themselves as learners. Collaborative discussions will empower teachers to develop their philosophy of mentoring, an essential finding in our work. Also important in these discussions is the acknowledgment that these philosophies may be enacted differently depending on the context and the mentor's experiences. We believe it is essential for faculty, rather than adjunct instructors and/or graduate assistants, to be at the table with the school-based stakeholders. Faculty have programmatic knowledge, as well as deep understandings of the theory driving practice within programs, which will serve to alleviate the tensions felt by many preservice teachers as they implement theories learned within the university classroom as practices within the K–5 classroom (Derrick, 1971).

Through these experiences, each group of leaders—school administrators, university faculty, and classroom teachers—mentored the other groups. All groups were influenced in meaningful ways, which allowed each group to develop into mentors with a shared, but explicit knowledge related to teaching and learning. This development takes significant time. But, to develop the "educative mentoring" (Norman & Feiman-Nemser, 2005) that is essential to simultaneous renewal (Goodlad, 1994), making the time to engage in the work is necessary. Developing as mentors also requires consistency within the professional development structures, and support from school administrators and university faculty in building those structures. These structures reposition classroom teachers, and frame all groups as learners with contributable expertise.

REFERENCES

Bullough, R. V. J., & Draper, R. J. (2004). Making sense of a failed triad: Mentors, university supervisors, and positioning theory. *Journal of Teacher Education, 55*, 407–420.

Derrick, T. (1971). Teacher training and school practice. Educational Researcher, 13, 106–112.

DuFour, R., & Mattos, M. (2013). How do principals really improve schools? *Educational Leadership, 70*(7), 34–40.

Feiman-Nemser, S., & Buchmann, M. (1985). Pitfalls of experience in teacher preparation. *Teachers College Record, 87,* 255–273.

Goodlad, J. I. (1994). *Access to knowledge: The continuing agenda for our nation's schools.* New York, NY: College Entrance Examination Board.

Hamel, F. L., & Jaasko-Fisher, H. A. (2011). Hidden labor in the mentoring of preservice teachers: Notes from a mentor teacher advisory council. *Teaching and Teacher Education, 27,* 434–442.

Hatch, J. A. (2002). *Doing qualitative research in education settings.* Albany, NY: State University of New York.

Koehler, V. (1988). Barriers to the effective supervision of student teaching: A field study. *Journal of Teacher Education, 39*(2), 28–34.

Labaree., D. (2004). *The trouble with education schools.* New Haven, CT: Yale University Press.

Norman, P. J., & Feiman-Nemser, S. (2005). Mind activity in teaching and mentoring. *Teaching and Teacher Education, 21*, 679–697.

Rikard, L., & Veal, M. (1996). Cooperating teachers: Insight into their preparation, beliefs, and practices. *Journal of Teaching in Physical Education, 15*(3). 279–296.

Rikard, L., & Veal, M. L., (1998). Cooperating teachers' perspectives on the student teaching triad. *Journal of Teacher Education, 49*(2), 108–119.

Shipman, M. D. (1967). Theory and practice in the education of teachers. Educational Researcher, *9*(3), 208–212.

Slick, S. K., (1998). The university supervisor: A disenfranchised outsider. *Teaching and Teacher Education, 14*, 821–834.

Stanulis, R. N. (1995). Classroom teachers as mentors: Possibilities for participation in a Professional Development School context. *Teaching & Teacher Education, 11*(4), 331–344.

Valencia, S. W., Martin, S. D., Place, N. A., & Grossman, P. (2009). Complex interactions in student teaching: Lost opportunities for learning. *Journal of Teacher Education, 60*(3), 304–322.

Vick, M. (2006). It's a difficult matter: Historical perspectives on the enduring problem of the practicum in teacher preparation. *Asia-Pacific Journal of Teacher Education, 34*, 181–198.

Waring, H. Z. (2013). Two mentor practices that generate teacher reflection without explicit solicitations: Some preliminary considerations. *RELC Journal, 44*(1), 103–119.

CHAPTER 3

IMPACTFUL MENTORING WITHIN A STATEWIDE, COMPREHENSIVE

Amanda R. Bozack and Amy Nicole Salvaggio

INTRODUCTION

In the United States, more students than ever before are being taught by beginning teachers. Thirty years ago, teachers most frequently reported having 15 years of classroom experience, while today they most frequently report having *one* year of classroom experience. During the same time period, teachers who report having spent five or fewer years in the classroom has increased from 17% to 28% (Carroll & Foster, 2010; Ingersoll, Merrill, & Consortium for Policy Research in Education, 2012).

The retirement of baby boomers and the persistence of teacher churn—nearly 50% of new teachers leaving the profession within five years—simultaneously contribute to this phenomenon, which has the potential to detrimentally effect an entire generation of American school children (Alliance for Excellent Education, 2004; Ingersoll & Perda, 2012; Ronfeldt, Loeb, & Wyckoff, 2012). Research has shown that beginning teachers are generally less effective than their more seasoned counterparts

Best Practices in Mentoring for Teacher and Leader Development, pp. 31–55
Copyright © 2016 by Information Age Publishing

31

(Hanushek, Kain, O'Brien, & Rivkin, 2005), but that high-quality induction programs can increase the rate of instructional improvement and student achievement for beginning teachers while reducing rates of attrition (DeAngelis, Wall, & Che, 2013; Ingersoll & Strong, 2011; Lopez, Lash, Schaffner, Shields, & Wagner, 2004).

This chapter describes the role of mentoring within the framework of one statewide, comprehensive induction program. It explores how mentors and beginning teachers in the program focused on their work together and how they perceived this work to contribute to the development of their own learning and teaching practice.

Comprehensive Teacher Induction

Induction describes various support structures created to assist beginning teachers as they assimilate into their professional culture. Induction is enacted in one of two ways—informally or comprehensively (Glazerman et al., 2010). The aim of *informal* induction is usually to provide temporary support for beginning teachers' transition into the school setting, but without specific goals and outcomes. It is characterized by a limited set of actions, such as an introductory meeting or periodically checking in with new teachers. Informal induction practices are likely to be in place when no state policy for induction exists, or when a policy exists, but is unfunded. The variability among local districts' ability to fund informal induction is reflected by the sparse and often imbalanced induction experienced by beginning teachers from one district or school to another.

In contrast, *comprehensive* teacher induction is characterized by its structure, intensity, and sequential nature. It is deliberately executed, with training for mentors, beginning teacher orientation sessions, professional development, classroom observations, and feedback to the beginning teachers (Glazerman et al., 2010). Programs with these characteristics have been shown to contribute to beginning teachers' sense of efficacy and professional growth (Wechsler, Caspary, Humphrey, & Matsko, 2012) while fostering systemic changes within school cultures through reduced teacher isolation and the development of a school community that is supportive of continuous learning for all teachers, promotion of effective teaching practices, and a focus on reducing the achievement gap where it exists (Feiman-Nemser, 2012).

Mentoring is widely accepted as a critical component of comprehensive teacher induction; when beginning teachers have a helpful mentoring experience, they are more likely to report positive feelings about their teaching experience and report a greater likelihood of staying in the field (Kapadia, Coca, & Easton, 2004; Smith & Ingersoll, 2004, as cited in Feiman-Nemser & Carver, 2012]). Researchers have also found that an additional benefit to mentoring is the potential positive outcome it can have for mentors. For example, Eby and colleagues (2006) found that workplace-mentoring can improve mentors' work attitudes and intentions to mentor again in the future.

The success of comprehensive induction policies is entwined with necessary funding support at the state level; it is not enough to expect school districts to reallocate already limited resources, or to engage in such intensive work without pecuniary support. A 2012 report by the New Teacher Center on exemplary induction models in the United States noted that "new teacher induction and mentoring is an area where the means are critically important in order to get us to the desired ends, such as more effective teaching and greater student learning" (p. v).

The New Teacher Center, in their review of state policies on teacher induction, found that, in 2012, twenty-seven states required some form of induction or support for new teachers, but only three states—Connecticut, Delaware, and Iowa—required multiyear induction support tied to licensure and provided dedicated state induction funding to the program. The following section describes Connecticut's induction program and, specifically, the role of mentoring within the program.

TEACHER INDUCTION IN CONNECTICUT

Comprehensive induction has been in place in Connecticut since the late 1980s. The state's original and oft cited Beginning Educator Support and Training [BEST] program was largely grounded in the evaluation of a standards-based performance outcome with mentoring situated as a peripheral component within the program. In the fall of 2009, the Connecticut General Assembly passed Public Act 09-6, which included the establishment of a new induction program, the Teacher Education and Mentoring [TEAM] Program, to replace the BEST program (PA 09-6, Sec. 37). Connecticut began funding the revised teacher induction program in July 2010, with an annual allocation of just over $4.3 million.

The two-year program is largely focused on developmental, process-oriented activities that promote reflective practice in teaching. Using the state's foundational teaching standards as a guide, beginning teachers engage in reflective practice by identifying aspects of their teaching that they want to develop and, with the help of a TEAM-trained, assigned mentor teacher, take steps to develop, enact, and reflect on their new learning.

The mission of the program is to "promote excellence, equity and high achievement for Connecticut students by engaging teachers in purposeful exploration of professional practice through guided support and personal reflection" (ctteam.org). The program is nonevaluative, such that the TEAM process is removed from the formal, contract renewal evaluations that take place within school systems. Thus, the activities in which beginning teachers engage with the TEAM program are independent from the administrative reappointment process and focused solely on professional growth. However, the State of Connecticut uses the successful completion of TEAM requirements to transition beginning teachers from an initial educator teaching certificate (three year duration) to a provisional teaching certificate.

The TEAM program provides structure, support, and training for administrators, mentors and reflection reviewers, but the implementation process is designed to be district-driven. Districts create implementation timelines, training plans, mentor requirements, and reflection-paper reviewer requirements. Districts are responsible for identifying mentors and reflection-paper reviewers, who are sent to a three-day training developed by TEAM program representatives and administered by one of the state's regional educational service centers (RESCs) to ensure training conformity. Consultants from the TEAM program office work in collaboration with RESC staff to support TEAM implementation across the state.

TEAM Mentors

In Connecticut, districts reported using a variety of methods to nominate mentors for the TEAM induction program. Most frequently they cited nominations by a building principal, inviting teachers who have been identified as being highly effective in improving students' performance, and committee review of mentor self-nominated applications. Just over half of participating districts reported that they always match beginning teachers and mentors based on placement in the same building, but about three-quarters reported usually making the match based on grade and content alignment. Mentors indicated that they generally spent 1 to 2 hours per week meeting with their beginning teacher to focus on induction-related activities and that they were very confident in their ability to be an effective mentor.

Within the TEAM program, mentors are expected to provide assistance to their assigned beginning teacher(s) throughout the year, with the expectation that they will complete approximately 40 contact hours with each beginning teacher throughout the two-year program. The expectation is that roughly 10 hours of mentoring support (one hour per week) will be provided per TEAM module completed by the beginning teacher(s). Mentors are also expected to coordinate additional support for the beginning teacher, such as setting up observations, providing instructional feedback, facilitating reflective conversation, providing materials, helping the beginning teacher understand policies and school culture, modeling reflection and effective teaching, coaching the beginning teacher to further professional growth, and assisting with preparation of TEAM requirements.

Structure of TEAM

Beginning teachers complete modules pertaining to five teaching domains: classroom environment, planning, instruction, assessment, and professional responsibilities. The modules were developed using the Connecticut Common Core of Teaching (CCT, 2010) standards as the point of focus. Generally, beginning teachers complete the classroom environment and planning modules during year one and the instruction and assessment modules during year two. The professional responsibilities module can be completed in either year and is structured differently from the other modules. Any modules not successfully completed in years one or two may be completed without penalty in year three.

Modules 1 through 4 consist of a four-step process engaged in by the beginning teacher and the mentor: (1) Identifying a need or opportunity for professional growth; (2) Developing a professional growth action plan; (3) Implementing the action plan to develop and apply new learning; and (4) Reflection on and documenting the module process in a reflection paper. The process is recorded by hours logged and by completing a journal on the TEAM website.

During step one, the beginning teacher and mentor review the CCT to identify a focus area for professional growth. For instance, when engaged in the classroom environment module, the beginning teacher and mentor would examine the list of skills identified in the CCT related to promoting a positive classroom environment. Together, the mentor and beginning teacher would identify one skill that they believe could be improved—for example, maximizing the amount of time spent on learning by effectively managing routines and transitions.

Step two requires the mentor and beginning teacher to jointly develop a professional growth action plan by identifying activities and resources that will support growth in the identified area. They then determine an 8- to 10-week timeline for completion and set any necessary meeting dates. Using the previous scenario, the mentor and beginning teacher may identify activities such as observing each other with a focus on how they each approach classroom routines and transitions, or having the beginning teacher observe other teachers identified by the mentor; the mentor may recommend a book, chapter, or article related to transitions within the classroom. They may schedule meetings to talk about what they saw during their observations or discuss insights from the reading.

Step three is the implementation of new learning—how ideas and insights from the learning are implemented or applied, and their effects on student learning. This step is primarily the work of the new teacher, though the mentor may offer some guidance as necessary. Evidence of positive impact on students is collected through anecdotal data, numeric data, quotations, or anticipated outcomes. For example, in this scenario, the beginning teacher may implement a new routine for assigning and turning in homework. The teacher may have noted that it usually took 10 minutes at the beginning of each class to collect homework, and that she often ran out of time to assign homework at the end of class. With the new strategy in place, the teacher may note that homework collection is reduced to two minutes, and that writing the following night's homework on the board reduces the chance of students missing an assignment.

Step four is the documentation of steps one through three and a reflection on how the beginning teacher's practice has improved and the impact seen on student learning or, for the planning module, the anticipated impact on student learning. Reflection papers must address the growth goal that was identified, the professional growth action plan that was developed, how the beginning teacher's new learning developed, the impact of new learning on teacher practice, and the impact of changes in teaching practice on students. This step is primarily the work of the beginning teacher, with the expectation that the mentor will read and comment on drafts of the paper.

A trained reviewer reads each reflection paper. If all areas of the reflection paper meet the criteria for (1) development of new learning, (2) impact on practice, and (3) student outcomes, the reviewer will identify the module completion successful, and the beginning teacher may move on to the next module. If the reviewer identifies the reflection as being deficient in one or more of the above-mentioned areas, the reflection paper is deemed unsuccessful. The reviewer may select suggestions from a predetermined list of feedback statements designed to help beginning teachers make revisions to their reflection papers. Once beginning teachers revise their reflection paper, it is resubmitted and a different reviewer reads the revised paper. This continues until the paper is deemed successful. It is noteworthy that the success of a paper is not determined by a beginning teacher's ability to demonstrate change in their students (though that is a desired outcome); rather, it is determined by their demonstration of an ability to engage in the process of reflective practice—even if it is to determine that a strategy did not work as anticipated and why that may have occurred.

Module 5 requires districts to facilitate discussions focused on professional responsibilities within the field of education. The TEAM Program provides a list of case studies that the districts can use to facilitate discussion. A variety of cases are provided so that districts may select cases that reflect authentic dilemmas encountered within the district. Facilitated conversations are designed to take place within a two-hour session. Districts may choose how to structure the conversations, including whether to invite all school staff, mentors and beginning teachers only, or just beginning teachers. This module only requires beginning teachers' attendance and participation in discussion, and completion of an online survey after the discussion; it does not require a written reflection paper.

AN EVALUATION STUDY OF
THE TEAM STATEWIDE INDUCTION PROGRAM

An evaluation study of the TEAM statewide induction program was conducted in 2012. The study involved collecting data about specific actions that beginning teachers and mentors described as being particularly helpful in developing beginning teachers' skills and new learning, and in having a positive impact on students. The study also explored how mentors were affected by their role in the induction program. Such information, we believe, is important for districts and states that are developing their own induction programs. By identifying the actions that are most impactful for beginning teachers, induction can be crafted to ensure their inclusion. To that end, the evaluation study data was further analyzed to develop a deeper understanding of the role of mentoring within the TEAM induction program.

Research Questions

Specifically, the research addressed the following four questions:

1. Was the TEAM induction program perceived as helpful in the development of beginning teachers?
2. Within the TEAM induction program, what activities do mentors and beginning teachers cite as being most helpful in developing new learning in beginning teachers?
3. When working together, what activities do mentors and beginning teachers cite as having a positive impact on beginning teachers' teaching practice, students' academic outcomes, and students' non-academic outcomes?
4. What changes in their own practice do mentors report, as a result of their role in the TEAM program?

METHOD

We worked with the Connecticut State Education Department as part of a larger project to develop an on-line questionnaire assessing various aspects of the TEAM program. Questionnaire items were drawn from previous TEAM evaluation surveys and suggestions provided by select stakeholders during pilot testing. Multiple stakeholder groups were asked for input during questionnaire development, including beginning teachers, mentors, district facilitators of the program, and administrators. While the final survey covered a wide range of topics about TEAM, for the purposes of this chapter, the focus is on only those questions related to mentoring and to the four research questions.

The State Education Department sent an e-mail with a link to the on-line questionnaire to 6,538 TEAM stakeholders identified from State records. Although the questionnaire was sent to several stakeholder groups, the research focuses on responses from beginning teachers and mentors only.

Usable responses were received from 962 beginning teachers (response rate = 31.1%) and 1,292 mentors (response rate = 41.8%). Participating beginning teachers either recently completed two years of TEAM induction ($n = 159$) or were in their second year of TEAM induction ($n = 804$). Only mentors who worked with a beginning teacher in the 2011–2012 academic year were included in the study, since that year reflected the overlap of beginning teachers in their first and second year of the TEAM induction program. Since the data were collected in the fall of 2012, beginning teachers in their first year of teaching were excluded from the sample because they had limited exposure to the program. New mentors were excluded from the sample for the same reason.

It is important to note that the results presented below are from self-report data for beginning teachers and mentors. This provides a limited perspective of the induction experience—one of personal perception rather than evidence. This is especially important when interpreting the results of the questions that asked teachers and mentors about how their work together affected students' academic and nonacademic outcomes. No student data were collected, and thus the responses are only a reflection of teachers' perceptions and personal experience, not based on actual test score results or other artifacts. The strong response rate and the representativeness of teachers from across the state increase the generalizability of the overall findings, however. Another important consideration is the relationship between the researchers and the State. The researchers were contracted to conduct this study on behalf of the State, and thus were limited in the types of questions to be asked as well as the types of data collected. This type of relationship puts inherent constraints on the research; however, we believe that it is important for states engaging in beginning teacher support practices to see researchers as a valuable part of the process, and that building a mutual foundation of respect is a worthwhile endeavor, even with constraints.

RESULTS

Was the TEAM induction Program Perceived as Helpful in the Development Of Beginning Teachers?

Beginning teachers and mentors responded to several statements about how the work of the TEAM module process affected beginning teachers' practice by indicating their level of agreement with each of a series of statements (see Tables 3.1 and 3.2). The statements were selected based on their ability, as part of the larger survey, to contribute to the determination the usefulness of the induction program.

Table 3.1.   Question: My (Beginning Teacher) Work in the Team Module Process

Answer Options	Percent of Respondents									
	Strongly Disagree		Disagree		Neither Agree Nor Disagree		Agree		Strongly Agree	
	BT	M	BT	M	BT	M	BT	M	BT	M
made me/BT a more effective teacher.	4.2	1.2	5.6	1.2	15.9	11.5	58.9	59.0	15.4	26.6
was directly connected to my/ BT needs/teaching assignment.	4.3	1.1	5.3	1.1	15.7	7.7	56.4	60.1	18.5	29.9
resulted in improved student performance.	3.4	1.5	5.5	3.2	21.8	15.6	54.8	55.5	14.6	24.2
made me/BT more reflective about my/ BT teaching.	3.9	1.3	4.0	1.9	9.9	21.0	49.0	56.0	33.1	19.7
aligned with my district's goals.	3.0	1.1	3.0	0.7	19.6	4.6	55.7	46.6	18.7	47.1
helped me/BT recognize the link between new learning and the impact on students' learning.	3.8	1.7	4.1	2.7	13.7	19.0	57.9	55.1	20.4	21.5

Note. BT = Beginning teachers; M = Mentors. Ratings were made on the following scale: 1 = Strongly disagree, 2 = Disagree, 3 = Neither agree nor disagree, 4 = Agree, 5 = Strongly agree

**Table 3.2.   Question: My (Beginning Teacher) Work in
the Team Module Process**

	Beginning Teachers	Mentors
Made me a more effective teacher.*	3.76	4.08
Was directly connected to my needs/teaching assignment.*	3.79	4.17
Resulted in improved student performance.*	3.72	3.98
Made me more reflective about my teaching.*	4.03	3.91
Aligned with my district's goals.*	3.84	4.38
Helped me recognize the link between my new learning and the impact on my students' learning.	3.87	3.92

Note. Ratings were made on the following scale: 1 = Strongly disagree, 2 = Disagree, 3 = Neither agree nor disagree, 4 = Agree, 5 = Strongly agree

*Mean ratings for the mentors' and beginning teachers' are significantly different.

Beginning teachers' reported that they believed participating in the TEAM induction program was beneficial to them; they most frequently "agreed" that it made them a more effective teacher and helped them recognize the relationship between teaching and learning. They believed that the program was directly related to their needs, contributed to improved student outcomes, and that it helped them become a more reflective practitioner. They also perceived that the program aligned with their districts' goals. Mentors too indicated that they believed beginning teachers' participation in the TEAM induction program was beneficial to beginning teachers, but they were significantly more likely to rate the effects of participation higher ("strongly agree") than beginning teachers did ($F(1, 2035) = 56.69, p < .001$). See Table 3.1 for the percentages and Table 3.2 for the mean scores. The activities that contributed to this response pattern are explored in the responses to the next research question.

Within the TEAM Induction Program, What Activities Do Mentors and Beginning Teachers Cite as Being Most Helpful in Developing New Learning in Beginning Teachers?

Beginning teachers rated the helpfulness of 13 different induction activities, three of which ("Observing my mentor teaching," "Being observed by my mentor," and "Engaging in learning-focused conversations with my mentor") directly involved the mentor. Use of the term "learning-focused" was meant to help differentiate between conversation for the purpose of discussing student learning and other casual personal or professional conversations that often occur within a mentoring relationship. Teachers first indicated if they completed each activity during induction, and then how helpful the activity was for developing new learning on a scale of 1 ("Not at all helpful") to 3 ("Very helpful"). The frequency of each response is shown in Table 3.3 and the helpfulness ratings are shown in Table 3.4.

Table 3.3.   Beginning Teachers: How Helpful Were the Following Activities in Developing Your New Learning?

		Percent of Respondents				
	Activity	Not At All Helpful	Somewhat Helpful	Very Helpful	I Did Not Do This	Average
1.	*Observing my mentor teaching	3.5	14.4	43.8	38.2	2.7
2.	*Being observed by my mentor	3.0	20.4	52.0	24.7	2.7
3.	Observing other colleagues	0.9	20.5	66.0	12.6	2.7
4.	*Engaging in learning-focused conversations with my mentor	2.4	19.3	77.1	1.1	2.8
5.	Assessing and reflecting on my practice	2.4	19.3	77.1	0.9	2.8
6.	Reading relevant educational articles or texts	4.1	41.3	53.4	1.3	2.5
7.	Conducting an Internet search	6.3	45.6	37.7	10.5	2.4
8.	Attending professional development workshops provided by my district	8.2	32.9	42.9	16.0	2.4
9.	Revisiting materials from previous professional development or coursework	5.4	40.0	41.6	13.1	2.4
10.	Participating in data teams	11.5	30.6	29.7	28.1	2.3
11.	Collecting data from my class	4.0	27.6	65.2	3.2	2.6
12.	Analyzing student work	1.4	21.2	74.8	2.6	2.8
13.	Getting additional support from the principal	4.4	24.9	36.4	34.3	2.5

Table 3.4.   Average Helpfulness Ratings by Induction Activity

Activity	Average Helpfulness Rating
Assessing and reflecting on my practice	2.79
*Engaging in learning-focused conversations with my mentor	2.76
Analyzing student work	2.75
Observing other colleagues	2.75
*Observing my mentor teaching	2.65
*Being observed by my mentor	2.65
Collecting data from my class	2.63
Reading relevant educational articles or texts	2.50
Getting additional support from the principal	2.49
Revisiting materials from previous professional development or coursework	2.42
Attending professional development workshop(s) provided by my district	2.41
Conducting an Internet search	2.35
Participating in data teams	2.25

Note. Ratings were made on the following scale: 1 = Not at all helpful, 2 = Somewhat helpful, 3 = Very helpful

*Mentor-related activity

The helpfulness ratings were examined by activity, particularly to see if activities with the mentor were seen as more helpful than the other induction activities. The distribution of the helpfulness ratings were first examined for both sets of activities. The distribution of helpfulness ratings was significantly different for the mentor-related activities (χ^2 (2) = 156.9, $p < .05$), meaning that the difference in these helpfulness rating is probably not due to chance. The average helpfulness rating for the three mentor-related activities was 2.7, compared to 2.5 for all the other activities, suggesting that beginning teachers found the activities they engaged in with their mentor more helpful than activities that did not involve their mentor.

Observations

Observations are frequently cited as an important aspect of teacher development in mentoring and induction programs. In this study, 75% of beginning teachers indicated that they were observed by their mentor teacher as part of the TEAM program, but only 62% of responding beginning teachers reported observing their mentor teacher in practice. A χ^2 test for specific proportions found that the number of beginning teachers who did not observe their mentor was higher than what would be expected by chance (i.e., 25%) (χ^2 (3) = 388.3, $p < .01$). Similarly, the number of beginning teachers who were not observed by their mentors was also higher than expected (χ^2 (3) = 435.4, $p < .01$).

Mentor-beginning teacher observations were not widely endorsed as being impactful. Observations by mentors were only reported as being "very helpful" by 44% of beginning teachers. Similarly, less than 45% of mentors reported that having their beginning teacher observe them in practice was "very useful" in developing beginning teacher new learning, and only 57% indicated that observation of their beginning teacher was "very useful" in developing beginning teachers' new learning.

Nearly 88% of beginning teachers reported observing colleagues other than their mentor. The proportion of beginning teachers who observe a colleague was significantly different from those observing or being observed by a mentor (χ^2 (3) = 129.3, $p < .01$). Beginning teachers also more frequently reported observations of colleagues other than their mentor as being "very helpful" in developing their new learning (67%). Like beginning teachers, mentors acknowledged that observing other colleagues could be "very helpful" (58%). Across the observation questions, 95% or more of beginning teachers found observing and being observed as "somewhat helpful" or "very helpful," suggesting that it is a useful tool in the development of new learning.

Conversations

Beginning teachers were more likely to report engaging in learning-focused conversations with their mentors; nearly 99% reported doing so. They frequently cited conversations with their mentor teachers as being "very helpful" (77%) or "somewhat helpful" (19%) in developing their new learning. Mentors also reported that they engaged in ongoing reflective conversations with their beginning teachers about their effectiveness in the classroom (60%), and they believed that such conversations with themselves (72%) or other colleagues (65%) were "very helpful" in developing new teachers' learning.

Developing New Learning Summary

The results from beginning teachers suggest that while most of the induction activities were helpful for developing new learning, those involving the mentor were seen as especially beneficial and not due to chance. Observing and being observed were seen as helpful for developing new learning, but teachers more frequently reported observing a colleague other than their mentor for practical reasons. Qualitative comments from the beginning teachers suggest that this occurred for number of reasons, including conflicting schedules with the mentor, a mentor not being in the same grade-level or content area, or the development of a relationship with someone other than the assigned mentor. Further, both the mentors and the beginning teachers noted the frequency and importance they placed on engaging in learning-focused conversations in relationship to the development of beginning teachers' learning.

When Working Together, What Activities Do Mentors and Beginning Teachers Cite as Having a Positive Impact on Beginning Teachers' Teaching Practice, Students' Academic Outcomes, and Students' Nonacademic Outcomes?

Of 11 activities inquired about related to the induction program, mentors and beginning teachers reported that most had a "strong impact" on the development of beginning teachers' teaching practice, perceived student academic outcomes, and student nonacademic outcomes. The majority of mentors "agreed" or "strongly agreed" that their contributions positively impacted their beginning teachers' practice regarding classroom management, lesson development, instructional strategies, using assessment data, and use of important resources. Mentors also reported that they spent the most time working with their beginning teachers on activities related to developing or revising lesson plans, discussing classroom behavior issues and strategies for creating a safe classroom environment, discussing student assessment data for the purpose of instructional decision-making, reflecting together on the effectiveness of teaching, and aligning the TEAM program to district initiatives. And, although impact on student outcomes is solely based on teachers' and mentors' perceptions, not on student data, the perceived positive effect on students can be a strong external motivator for teacher buy-in for comprehensive induction programs. Further, the statistically significant differences in how favorably activities were reported suggest that the perceptions of activity effect on student outcomes were not randomly distributed.

Activities that Impact Teaching Practice

Beginning teachers rated nine different activities with their mentor in terms of impact on their teaching practice (1 = "No impact" to 3 = "Strong impact"). The frequency of these responses is shown in Table 3.5. Overall, beginning teachers indicated that each of the nine activities with the mentor had "some" or a "strong" impact on their teaching practice.

Table 3.5. Beginning Teachers: To What Degree Did The Following Activities With Your Mentor Positively Impact Your...

	Percent of Respondents								
	Teaching Practice			*Students' Academic Achievement*			*Students' Nonacademic Achievement*		
Answer Options	*No Impact*	*Some Impact*	*Strong Impact*	*No Impact*	*Some Impact*	*Strong Impact*	*No Impact*	*Some Impact*	*Strong Impact*
1. Completing the Professional Growth Action Plan (PGAP).	15.7	46.5	37.8	27.5	46.9	25.58	34.9	43.2	21.2
2. Developing learning goals.	7.0	36.1	56.9	12.6	41.8	45.54	22.6	45.9	30.6
3. Developing or revising lesson plans.	7.2	37.5	55.3	6.2	36.1	57.72	18.8	49.4	29.3
4. Observing each other's classes to offer feedback and/ or learning strategies.	5.6	30.9	63.5	7.8	41.4	50.81	13.4	41.2	38.7
5. Discussing student assessment data to make decisions about instruction.	5.0	37.2	57.8	5.1	35.8	59.12	19.5	47.3	30.3
6. Analyzing samples of work done by students to plan differentiated lessons.	7.4	34.4	58.3	5.9	36.6	57.51	19.2	48.2	29.6
7. Discussing students or classroom behavioral issues and strategies to help establish a safe and productive classroom.	3.4	23.4	73.2	5.1	29.4	65.51	6.6	30.4	61.7
8. Reflecting together on the effectiveness of my teaching.	2.6	25.5	71.9	3.9	32.3	63.86	8.9	38.1	51.8
9. Aligning TEAM work with school and district initiatives.	10.5	42.7	46.8	15.7	46.4	37.92	27.0	45.2	25.7

Of interest was whether these impact ratings varied significantly by activity. For example, were the impact ratings for "Aligning TEAM work with school and district initiatives" truly different from those for "Reflecting together on the effectiveness of my teaching," or were the differences seen just due to random fluctuations in how the beginning teachers were responding? These questions were examined by analyzing the data using repeated-measures ordered logistic regression. (This analysis is appropriate for data with ordinal outcomes, e.g., "no impact" "some impact" and "strong impact.")

The analysis indicated that beginning teachers rated the nine activities differently in terms of impact on their teaching practice (χ^2 (8) = 310.9, $p < .01$). In particular, beginning teachers rated "Reflecting together on the effectiveness of my teaching," and "Discussing students or classroom behavioral issues" as having more of an impact on their teaching practice than "Completing the Professional Growth Action Plan" and "Aligning TEAM work with school and district initiatives." They perceived the practical immediacy of these activities as more impactful than working toward the broader goals of the induction program.

Activities That Impact Student Outcomes

Beginning teachers rated the same nine activities engaged in with their mentor in terms of impact on students' perceived academic and nonacademic outcomes (1 = "No impact" to 3 = "Strong impact"). The frequency responses for both outcomes are shown in Table 3.5. As with ratings on teaching practice, a repeated-measures ordered logistic regression was used to examine the results further. Beginning teachers did rate the nine mentor activities differently in terms of impact on students' academic outcomes (χ^2 (8) = 344.4, $p < .01$) and nonacademic outcomes (χ^2 (8) = 328.9, $p < .01$). Similar to the ratings about teaching practice, ratings for "Reflecting together on the effectiveness of my teaching," "Discussing students or classroom behavioral issues" had significantly more of an impact on student outcomes than "Completing the Professional Growth Action Plan" and "Aligning TEAM work with school and district initiatives." The consistency in response patterns suggests the value placed on these activities by beginning teachers.

Mentoring Impact on Teaching Practice Versus Student Outcomes

In order to compare the impact of the mentor-beginning teacher relationship by type of outcome (teaching practice, academic outcomes, and nonacademic outcomes), an average impact score was calculated for each activity. These averages are shown in Table 3.6. Although the average ratings are very similar, beginning teachers' response trends suggest that they value talking over their struggles and strategies with the mentor, and see it as most impactful.

Table 3.6.   Average Impact Rating of Mentor Activities on Teaching Practice, Academic Achievement and Nonacademic Achievement

Activity With Mentor	*Teaching Practice*	*Academic Achievement*	*Nonacademic Achievement*
1. Completing the Professional Growth Action Plan (PGAP).	2.22	1.98	1.87
2. Developing learning goals.	2.50	2.33	2.09
3. Developing or revising lesson plans.	2.48	2.52	2.13
4. Observing each other's classes to offer feedback and/or learning strategies.	2.58	2.43	2.32
5. Discussing student assessment data to make decisions about instruction.	2.53	2.54	2.14
6. Analyzing samples of work done by students to plan differentiated lessons.	2.51	2.52	2.13
7. Discussing students or classroom behavioral issues and strategies to help establish a safe and productive classroom.	2.70	2.60	2.56
8. Reflecting together on the effectiveness of my teaching.	2.69	2.60	2.44
9. Aligning TEAM work with school and district initiatives.	2.36	2.22	2.01

Note. Impact ratings were made on the following scale: 1 = No impact, 2 = Some impact, 3 = Strong impact

The impact of "Observing each other's classes to offer feedback and/or learning strategies" varied slightly depending on the outcome being rated. Beginning teachers felt it had a positive impact on their teaching practice ($M = 2.6$), but average ratings for its impact on student academic ($M = 2.4$) and nonacademic outcomes ($M = 2.3$) were slightly lower.

Teaching Practice and Student Outcomes Summary

Overall, beginning teachers indicated that activities with their mentors were positively impactful on their teaching practice, their perceptions of students' academic outcomes, and students' nonacademic outcomes. Closer examination suggests that beginning teachers rated discussing student and classroom behavior issues as having a strong positive impact on all three outcomes. While still generally rated favorably, beginning teachers indicated that administrative tasks associated with the broader induction program, specifically "Completing the Professional Growth Action Plan" and "Aligning TEAM work with school and district initiatives" had comparably less of an impact on their teaching practice or student outcomes.

What Changes in Their Own Practice Do Mentors Report, as a Result of Their Role in the TEAM Program?

Mentors were asked how their work in the TEAM induction program affected their own teaching practice. Their responses indicated that the mentor training process required by the TEAM induction program helped their own teaching practice to "some extent" (70%) or to "a great extent" (18.5%). The survey also listed six possible ways that participating in TEAM could affect mentors' own teaching. Mentors indicated whether or not each item had affected their teaching. Frequency counts of the number of "yes" responses for each item are listed in Table 3.7.

Table 3.7. Frequency Counts

Mentors		
How does your work with your beginning teacher(s) in the TEAM module process contribute to your effectiveness as a teacher? (Select all that apply.)	*Response Percent*	*Frequency Count*
I have modified the way I teach as a result of my work in TEAM.	43.9	481
I am making more purposeful decisions about my instruction and my students.	67.5	740
I am able to see a link between my decisions as a teacher and the impact on the students.	55.2	605
I have gained a deeper understanding of the Connecticut Common Core of Teaching by working in the TEAM module process with my beginning teacher(s).	77.5	849
TEAM further inspired me to continue to develop my skills as an experienced teacher.	68.9	755
My work in TEAM has had a positive impact on my students.	48.7	534
Other (please specify)	5.8	64
Answered question		1,096

Mentors generally indicated that involvement in the TEAM program was beneficial for their own practice. Over half of the mentors reported developing a deeper understanding of the foundational skills used by the state to identify effective teaching practices, making more purposeful decisions about their own instruction and students, and developing a better understanding of the relationship between teacher decisions and impact on students. Nearly 70% indicated that the TEAM program inspired them to continue to develop their own teaching practice, and nearly 50% reported that serving as a mentor in TEAM had a positive impact on their own students.

A repeated measures logistic regression was used to determine if these responses were statistically different from what would be expected by chance — in other words, did mentors endorse a particular option more or less often than would be expected if they were simply responding randomly to the survey (Stokes, Davis & Koch, 2000)? Results of this analysis suggest that the likelihood of endorsing the items differed according to what was asked ($\chi^2(6) = 353.9, p < .001$). In particular, mentors were more likely to say that they "gained a deeper understanding of the Connecticut Common Core of Teaching" ($\chi = 1.17, z = 17.15, p < .001$), that "TEAM further inspired [them] to continue to develop [their] skills as an experienced teacher" ($\chi = 0.86, z = 14.12, p < .001$) and that they were "making more purposeful decisions about [their] instruction and [their] students" ($\chi = 0.82, z = 14.13, p < .001$), as compared to "I have modified the way I teach as a result of my work in TEAM." In other words, it is more likely that participating in TEAM affected how mentors think and understand their teaching practice, rather than motivate them to change their own classroom behavior. Mentors, it is expected, by virtue of selection into the role, should already be strong practitioners. Thus, it is not surprising that they do not report great changes in their classroom behavior. Their responses do suggest that they continue learning in this role—evidenced by their knowledge and skill development in other ways. Their learning is likely to be more nuanced and reflected in thought or subtle action, as is demonstrated across studies of expert learning (Feltovich, Prietula, & Ericsson, 2006; Simon & Chase, 1973).

LESSONS LEARNED

Findings from the study identify beginning teacher-mentor relationships as an important part of Connecticut's TEAM induction program. Responses from the sample suggest that the work being done together is complex and extensive, and that it is a critical support for beginning teachers' success. In addition to the benefits of TEAM for beginning teachers, mentors also found that the TEAM training and the subsequent participation in the program yielded positive outcomes in their own teaching practice. Here, are highlights of the lessons learned from this study and suggestions for how they may have implications for other induction programs.

Mentors Matter

Beginning teachers identified most of their induction-related activities as helpful in their development. However, they perceived the activities that involved their mentor to be more helpful than the activities that did not involve their mentor. Mentors, too, found the process beneficial for their own development.

Implication. This finding supports the development of a robust role for mentors within induction programs. Mentoring should be integrated into many aspects of broader induction programs rather than being an isolated aspect of induction. This may require increased release time or reimbursement for mentors. Mentoring should not be viewed as a responsibility that can be added on to an already full schedule; district and school leaders who select mentors should also work to ensure they can commit the time required by the role—in the short- and long-term. As Schwille (2008) observed, "mentoring, conceptualized as educative practice that depends upon mentors' professional judgment and knowledge of their novices as learners in order to shape experiences that promote novices' learning over time, must be learned over time" (p. 140).

Feiman-Nemser and Carver (2012) also highlighted the need for policies to ensure time for mentoring—through release time and/or common planning time—and to integrate assessment with support to inform mentors' work with beginning teachers and to develop in beginning teachers a process of reflective practice. They also called for continuing support and training for mentor teachers so that, like the beginning teacher, they are not abandoned in their role. The results from this study support these recommendations; in particular, robust training could focus on the development and sustainment of learner-focused conversations, effective observation techniques and practices, and the development of mechanisms for sustainable reflective practice beyond TEAM.

Perceptions of Teaching Observations Vary

In Connecticut, observations of and by beginning teachers are not a required part of the induction program, but it is a tool that TEAM participants are encouraged to use. More than half of beginning teachers reported observing and being observed by their mentors, and indicated that it was helpful in developing their new learning. However, they more frequently reported observing colleagues other than their mentor, and they perceived it to be more beneficial than observing their mentor teacher. Mentors' perceptions of the usefulness of observations varied, but did not heartily endorse the practice as useful for developing new learning.

Implications. If observations are to be a strong tool for developing new learning in beginning teachers, induction programs must develop clearer guidelines and training for their conduct. Teaching and observing are tasks that require some overlapping skills but are fundamentally different. Part of mentor training should include observational training, focusing on varying aspects of the beginning teachers' classroom. We believe beginning teachers should also have some basic training in classroom observation. For example, what elements should be attended to during an observation focusing on classroom environment? How might that observation differ from an observation focused on lesson modification for diverse learners? And importantly, what should the pre- and postobservation discussions focus on? This will help them focus on the areas they identify as most important and strengthen their reflective discussions. A variety of observational strategies are outlined in Schwille's (2008) cross-national study of mentors, which suggests that, within classrooms, observing and coaching instruction is fluid and dependent on the needs of the novice at any given time. We also recommend the use of a basic observation tool and/ or question prompts to ensure focused observations and discussions (e.g., Charlotte Danielson's Framework for Teaching, 2013).

The findings also point to the value of breadth and variety in observations. Schools with beginning teachers would serve them well by creating an environment where observations of and by other colleagues, not limited to their mentor, is endorsed and time to discuss those observations is provided. This is especially important if the mentor assigned to a beginning teacher is in a different grade-level or content area and thus, may have difficulty with observation scheduling or with modeling the grade- or content-skills necessary to help the beginning teacher. Other researchers (e.g., Johnson & Birkeland, 2003) have also described the value of a school environment that is widely-supportive of the development of beginning teachers, particularly as related to teacher retention.

Reflective Dialogue is Valued

Beginning teachers and mentors both agree that reflecting together on the beginning teachers' practice and discussion of student and classroom behavioral issues were the two activities that had the strongest impact on teachers' practice and students' academic and nonacademic outcomes. These interactions were seen as more helpful to beginning teachers than other activities, perhaps because of their timeliness—beginning teachers can take the information from the conversation back into the classroom and immediately apply it—but also perhaps because the cultivation of effective responses to behavioral issues can lead to the development of long-term habits and practices that enhance the learning environment—the type of reflection-as-action described by Schöne (1983).

Implications. It is possible that some activities which may be important in beginning teacher development, but which have less of a primacy affect (such as reading a journal article or a book), may be viewed by beginning teachers as less impactful than activities that provide immediate gratification. "Give me something I can use right now" is a time-honored slogan of beginning teachers everywhere. Because of this, the mentor can play an important role in helping beginning teachers understand the value and importance of slower-growth activities. For example, the development of classroom management techniques that foster a positive learning climate may take time that extends beyond a week or a month or even a year. Or that a cumulative succession of asking "What went well?" and "What will I do differently next time?" can lead to changes that improve student learning without further overwhelming the beginning teacher in their practice.

Mentoring Improves Mentors

Mentors in this study did not report making substantive changes to their teaching, but their responses suggest that involvement with this program impacted the way they think about their practice. In particular, they indicated that participation in the program helped them be more purposeful decision-makers with a greater understanding of how those decisions impact students. They also indicated developing a deeper understanding of the Connecticut's Common Core of Teaching. In effect, they reported improved effectiveness in many of the same areas that TEAM is focused on improving in beginning teachers—making connections between teaching and learning through reflective practice, grounded in the teacher quality framework of the state.

Implications. Other studies have found that midcareer and veteran teachers continue to desire professional support and acknowledgement (e.g., Tschannen-Moran & Woolfolk Hoy, 2007; Parrott, 2008), and that mentoring is one way to recognize the expertise of such teachers. Teachers who serve as mentors have reported feeling renewed by the experience, as well as developing a greater understanding of the broader educational landscape and their role in it (Hansen & Moir, 2008).

Research has also suggested that continued growth opportunities, such as mentoring, for seasoned professionals, may improve the retention of competent educators who might otherwise leave for lack of variety or opportunity for advancement (Margolis, 2008). As our findings demonstrate, mentoring within a formal induction program serves the development of both the mentor and the mentee.

This study complements these earlier findings because it suggests that experienced teachers' thinking changes as they engage in mentoring, and that students in their classrooms may benefit indirectly from the experience as well. If districts and schools truly wish to retain excellent teachers in the classroom, they must provide opportunities for those teachers to continue to grow through leadership opportunities, including mentoring. Further, the growth of the mentor teacher should be a goal of mentoring, not just a fortunate by-product.

ACKNOWLEDGMENTS

We thank the Connecticut State Department of Education (CSDE) Talent Office and the TEAM Program Office for granting us access to this data set. The views expressed in this manuscript are solely those of the authors and do not necessarily reflect the views of the CSDE.

REFERENCES

Alliance for Excellent Education. (2004). *Tapping the potential: Retaining and developing high-quality new teachers.* Washington, DC: Author.

Carroll, T., & Foster, E. (2010). *Who will teach? Experience matters.* Washington, DC: National Commission on Teaching and America's Future.

DeAngelis, K. J., Wall, A. F., & Che, J. (2013). The impact of preservice preparation and early career support on novice teachers' career intentions and decisions. *Journal of Teacher Education, 64*(4), 338–355.

Eby, L. T., Durley, J. R., Evans, S. C., & Ragins, B. R. (2006). The relationship between short-term mentoring benefits and long-term mentor outcomes. *Journal of Vocational Behavior, 69*(3), 424–444.

Feiman-Nemser, S. (2012, May). Beyond solo teaching. *Educational Leadership, 69*(8), 10–16.

Feiman-Nemser, S., & Carver, C. L. (2012). Creating conditions for serious mentoring: Implications for induction policy. In T. M. Smith, L. M. Desimone, & A. Porter (Eds.), *Organization and effectiveness of induction programs for new teachers* the 111th NSEE yearbook (pp. 342–364).

Feltovich, P. J., Prietula, M. J., & Ericsson, K. A. (2006). Studies of expertise from psychological perspectives. In K. A. Ericcson, N. Charness, P. J. Feltovich, & R. R. Hoffman (Eds.), *The Cambridge handbook of expertise and expert performance* (pp. 41–68). Cambridge, England: Cambridge University Press.

Glazerman, S., Isenberg, E., Dolfin, S. Bleeker, M., Johnson, A., Grider, M., & Jacobus, M. (2010). *Impacts of comprehensive teacher induction: Final results from a randomized controlled study*. Washington, DC: Mathematica Policy Research.

Hanson, S., & Moir, E. (2008). Beyond mentoring: Influencing the professional practice and careers of experienced teachers. *Phi Delta Kappan, 89*(6), 453–458.

Hanushek, E., Kain, J. F., O'Brien, D. M., & Rivkin, S. G. (2005). *The market for teacher quality*. NBER Working Paper 11154. National Bureau of Economic Research: Cambridge, MA.

Ingersoll, R. & Strong, M. (2011). The impact of induction and mentoring programs for beginning teachers: A critical review of the research. *Review of Educational Research, 81*(2), 201–233.

Ingersoll, R., Merrill, L., & Consortium for Policy Research in Education. (2012). *Seven trends: The transformation of the teaching force*. Paper presented at the annual meeting of the American Educational Research Association, Vancouver, Canada.

Ingersoll, R., & Perda, D. (2012). *How high is teacher turnover and is it a problem?* Philadelphia, PA: Consortium for Policy Research in Education, University of Pennsylvania.

Johnson, S. M., & Birkeland, S. (2003). Pursuing a "sense of success": New teachers explain their career decisions. *American Educational Research Journal, 40*(3), 581–617.

Kapadia, K., Coca, V., & Easton, J. Q. (2007). *Keeping new teachers: A first look at the influences of induction in the Chicago Public Schools*. Research report by the Consortium on Chicago School Research. Chicago, IL: University of Chicago.

Lopez, A., Lash, A., Schaffner, M., Shields, P., & Wagner, M. (2004). *Review of research on the impact of beginning teacher induction on teacher quality and retention*. Washington, DC: U.S. Department of Education.

Margolis, J. (2008). What will keep today's teachers teaching? Looking for a hook as a new career cycle emerges. *The Teachers College Record, 110*(1), 160–194.

New Teacher Center. (2012). *Review of State policies on teacher induction*. Santa Cruz, CA: New Teacher Center.

Parrott, E. (2008). Evaluation of effectiveness and enthusiasm of veteran high school teachers and recommendations for teacher renewal (Unpublished doctoral dissertation). Northcentral University, Prescott Valley, AZ.

Ronfeldt, M., Loeb, S., & Wyckoff, J. (2012). How teacher turnover harms student achievement. Retrieved July 24, 2012, from http://cepa.stanford.edu/sites/default/files/TchTrnStAch%20AERJ%20RR%20not%20blind.pdf

Schöne, D. A. (1983). *The reflective practitioner*. New York, NY: Basic Books.

Schwille, S. A. (2008). The professional practice of mentoring. *American Journal of Education, 115*(1), 139–167.

Simon, H. A., & Chase, W. G. (1973). Skill in chess. *American Scientist, 61*, 394–403.

Smith, T. M., & Ingersoll, R. M. (2004). What are the effects of induction and mentoring on beginning teacher turnover? *American Educational Research Journal, 41*, 681–714.

Stokes, M. E., Davis, C. S., & Koch, G. G. (2000). *Data analysis using the SAS system*, 2/e. Cary, NC: SAS Institute.

Tschannen-Moran, M., & Woolfolk Hoy, A. (2007). The differential antecedents of self-efficacy beliefs of novice and experienced teachers. *Teaching and Teacher Education*, *23*, 944–954.

Wechsler, M. E., Caspary, K., Humphrey, D. C., & Matsko, K. K. (2012). Examining the effects of new teacher induction. In T. M. Smith, L. M. Desimone, & A. Porter (Eds.). *Organization and effectiveness of induction programs for new teachers*. The 111th NSEE yearbook (pp. 387–416).

CHAPTER 4

REFLECTION ROUNDS IN THE CONTEXT OF VIRTUAL MENTORING

Carmen Gloria Núñez, Verónica López, Bryan González, Carola Rojas, Evelyn Mujica, Evelyn Palma, and Cristina Julio

INTRODUCTION

This chapter presents original findings from a study aimed at describing and analyzing a pioneer online mentoring program for beginning in-service teachers developed in Chile. The virtual mentoring program was designed by a University (Pontificia Universidad Católica de Valparaíso [PUCV]) in association with the Organization of Ibero-American States (Organización de Estados Iberoamericanos [OEI]), as a means of developing a cost-effective method of mentoring that could be replicated throughout the country. The cost-effectiveness of the program was especially relevant in a context where, during the last five years, public policies were initially supported by President Bachelet's administration, but were later dropped by President Piñera's administration. Face-to-face mentoring programs between certified mentors (senior teachers qualified as teachers

Best Practices in Mentoring for Teacher and Leader Development, pp. 57–71

of excellence by the national teacher assessment system) and beginning teachers were thus left without funding.

This chapter first describes the program, its goals and procedures, as well as the theoretical underpinnings that justify an online mentoring system. Next, the chapter describes the strengths and weaknesses of the program. The strengths relate to the possibility of reaching out to teachers in hard-to-reach places, and combining asynchronous and synchronous encounters between mentors and novices, while the weaknesses deal more with the progressive decline in the frequency of weekly encounters, and the higher risk of disengaging from the mentoring experience, both virtually and emotionally.

To further explicate the issues related to emotional disengagement, we present a practice previously used by our research group in real-time mentoring school development programs. We named this practice "Reflection Rounds" (*Círculos de Reflexión*), based on Paulo Freire's dialogical works (Freire, 2002). Reflection Rounds are instances of group dialogs among the mentors and novices separately. This practice proved to be a turning point in the experience of virtual mentoring, both for mentors as well as novices. Mentors were able to better understand the nature and goals of their intervention, and to develop a sense of community between them. For the novices, the Reflection Rounds allowed them to share their experience as beginning teachers as well as concerning their personal experience in the mentor program.

Mentoring From a Dialogic Perspective

We understand mentoring as a system in which a mentor—defined as a qualified teacher with years of in-service experience and willingness to share his/her experience with beginning teachers—works along an inexperienced teacher during his/her induction into the educational system. This type of work requires specific knowledge and skills, which means that mentors need to be intentionally prepared in structured programs where mentors are trained systematically, by providing them with specific professional competencies for the task. In Chile, these kinds of programs are provided only by universities.

Mentor training performed by PUCV uses the *Narrative Model of Development* (Orland-Barak, 2006), which focuses on the inexperienced teacher and his/her personal and professional experience. The program is centered on the improvement of learning and on professional development that includes reflecting on teaching practices that build a stronger professional teacher. Learning occurs through dialogic communication as the mentor and novice reflect on teaching, talk through teaching situations, and resolve conflicts.

Available evidence shows that once dialogic mentoring takes place, mentors and novices develop trust and confidence. Mentors and novices exhibit more autonomy, develop professional competencies and are more critical and reflective about their work. Novices evolve from marginal to full participants (Lave, 1991) in their schools, and have more positive experiences during their induction period as they become enculturated in the school and its culture. This leads to an enhanced sense of self-reliance and autonomy (Fierro, 1999).

During the development of teaching practices, novices go through comprehensive and transformational moments that they can use to reflect critically and "to recognize contradictions, mistakes and good choices, to understand, analyze and review the scope of attitudes and their own actions" (Fierro, 1999, p. 26). This means confronting ideas in ways that will lead to change, since it helps the novice understand teaching practice and ways to transform it.

This type of change requires assistance. Mentoring helps teachers evolve from being students to becoming teaching professionals. It helps novices analyze their perspectives and expectations with respect to the new environment and role. Mentoring promotes continuity in the formative process to advance from peripheral to full participation and from a minimum to a maximum degree of professional autonomy.

Understood this way, mentoring is based on a sociocultural learning perspective. According to Rogoff (1997), such sociocultural learning holds that mentoring is a social activity in which people join and "that is culturally organized in which beginners turn into more responsible participants" (p. 114).

The challenge for novices is to become integrated in an educational unit and a school system that has its own culture. Mentors, on the other hand, face the challenge of being able to foster such an integration so that novices turn into self-confident, responsible and autonomous professionals.

Therefore, this learning approach relates to *participation*. In this chapter, participation is understood as a process developed at both the social and individual level, since it implies understanding the activity performed by members of the community and their contribution to building a collective body, both within the school community as well as between peers (Julio, 2010). According to Wenger (2001), taking part in community *practices* not only shapes what we do, but also helps us to configure our own identity.

The sociocultural learning approach (Rogoff, 1993, 1997) contributes to the conceptualization of mentoring as the process by which "each one configures his/her *learning pathway*, understood as an itinerary in the biographical route of each individual" (Julio, 2010, p. 11). The first years as a professional determine the future development of the novice in school contexts. The experiences they live through, or do not, become obstacles or facilitators in their learning and developmental pathways.

Based on Pasquali (1990) we can state that (a) communication is a feature reserved only for human dialogic relationships or between ethically autonomous individuals, and (b) it is only possible if there is self-awareness and space for otherness. Thus, "authentic communication is based on symmetrical relationships, on paired conditions ... and on the possibility to hear one another or to lend ears to one another (Heidegger), as a reciprocal will to understand each other. This last condition is a basic and insuppressible feature of what we call dialog" (p. 50).

Therefore, dialog is at the core of mentoring from a dialogical perspective, allowing participants to weave common meanings as long as the relationships are fair and collaborative. We understand dialog as the center of the human communication experience, as meant by Freire (2003) in Chapter 3 of *Pedagogy of the Oppressed*. According to Freire (2003), dialog is the *encounter* of individuals mediated by the world. Communication in the pedagogical process "relates with my own self, with my past, with current interactions, and with the future" (Prieto, 1999).

The PUCV Online Mentoring Program

The online mentoring program that we describe and analyze in this chapter was inspired by the Ibero-American States for Education, Science and Culture (Organización de Estados Iberoamericanos, OEI), an institution with established alliances of continuity on this topic with Pontificia Universidad Católica de Valparaíso, and in particular with teams from the School of Psychology and School of Education. This pilot program involved the design and implementation of a virtual space for mentoring from a dialogic and reflective perspective.

The virtual mentoring process included the same participants involved in the face-to-face program (Figure 4.1). First, it considered the relationship between mentor and novice, who established a virtual communication sustained in time where they could engage both synchronously and asynchronously in relevant conversations. Second, virtual mentoring also involved the participation of a tutor, who was part of the back-up intervention Program at PUCV and who interacted directly with the mentors, although some interactions also occurred between tutors and novices.

In our model, the process of mentoring occurred mainly between the mentor and the novice and involved four recursive stages. The first phase involved building a working relationship between the mentor and the novice based on their own expectations. The second stage involved

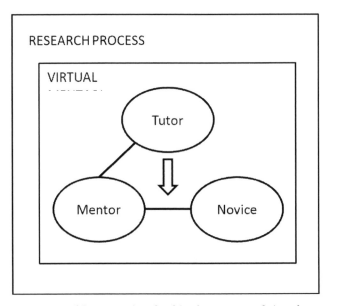

Figure 4.1.   Actors and instances involved in the process of virtual mentoring.

a diagnostic phase, in which mentors were expected to conduct a needs-diagnosis of the novice teacher based on his/her strengths and weaknesses. In the third phase, mentor and novice started constructing an action plan aimed at strengthening the novice's teaching practice, which often involved modifying his/her systems of beliefs and expectations. We considered this third stage as central to the process. The fourth and final phase was an evaluation that allowed for a critical review of the novice's development.

Within this framework, OEI representatives asked PUCV to design and implement a virtual space (platform). In response to this request, a Moodle platform was selected and proposed, and was designed using synchronous (chat, videoconferencing) and asynchronous (forums) tools as dialogical meeting spaces for mentors and novices.

After teams from OEI and PUCV evaluated the options, a change of scope and format was agreed upon, and two online communication media were defined. OEI's institutional platform, operated from Spain, was selected for sharing, evaluating, and reflecting on the mentoring process since it included a forum feature, while open-access social-web 2.0 tools were selected among others for the induction process between mentors and novices, because they allowed for synchronous and asynchronous meetings. These means of communication became the central means of mentoring.

The tools available under web 2.0 for synchronous and asynchronous communication became a common meeting place for mentors and novices, who valued the timeliness in response patterns, the ability to overcome time and space barriers and to shorten physical distance in face-to-face meetings using tools such as Skype.

In general, the novices were more familiar with digital and virtual environments than mentors. This allowed them to be more readily available to solve problems such as installing Skype or other technological difficulties that arose in the dialog with their mentor. Mentors, on the other hand, were often handicapped in terms of the use of synchronous and asynchronous tools, because they had to adjust and adopt practices with which they were unfamiliar. Nonetheless, most of the mentors overcame these problems and barriers by initially communicating with university tutors and novices via e-mail and telephone. Once they became more familiar with social networks like Skype, Facebook, and chat features on Moodle, these became the primary forms of communication between mentors and novices.

An important part of the virtual mentoring process is the mentor-novice relationship. This relationship is directly between the two actors and follows the same communication patterns as in face-to-face mentor-novice relationships. The role of the university tutor is to act as a facilitator of the mentoring process at a meta-analytic level. As a facilitator to the mentor-novice relationship, the tutor promotes critical reflection on the analysis that the mentor develops in accordance with his/her role. The tutor also seeks to enhance critical analyses on the relationship built between the mentor and the novice. These analyses are understood as an essential part of the critical and reflective practice of mentoring.

The following is what we refer to as the "Research Process" that describes the study of the development of the program. This study was guided by the overall objective of systematizing what happened during the process of virtual mentoring, as well as identifying the emerging needs of new teachers in the process.

The Challenges of Online Dialogic Mentoring

We understand online mentoring as a virtual space to accompany novice teachers, one that assumes a formal induction model of narrative development. From this perspective, virtual communication environments become a technological support that allows holding meetings that overcome geographical barriers and the cost involved in real face-to-face meetings in hard-to-reach places. The availability of technology as a way to interact becomes an opportunity to overcome those difficulties. Hence, the term *virtual context* emerges, meaning those features of interactions that frame the conditions under which the global scale of actions take place (Barberá, 2004). In this sense, spaces that are built in the absence of real face-to-face encounters, in the virtual synchronic and asynchronic scenarios, power the dialogic interactions, experiences and meetings and are able to create value-oriented awareness for all participating individuals (Duart, 2003). According to Gros (2008), these kinds of communication environments become technological stages that facilitate alternative formation processes to those that take place on-site.

For the sake of conceptual precision, García and García (2001) propose that *e-learning* is conceived as a space for off-site formation which, by means of technology, allows and increases the flexibility of access and the timing of the reflection and learning process, adjusting to the ability, needs and availability of each of the participants and making sure that learning environments are indeed collaborative. In this sense, the online mentoring program becomes an opportunity to generate meetings and communication geared to strengthen the autonomous professional development of the novice and to analyze the problems associated with the social praxis in his/her school contexts. In this way, these meeting spaces assume a paradigm centered on reciprocal learning, where the knowledge is built through the dialog during virtual encounters. This dialog provides the mentor and novice opportunities to connect and exchange beliefs, opinions, experiences from a bidirectional process that seeks to instill in the novice teacher reflective practices, that are both critical and purposeful. This relationship of reciprocity and collaboration serves to strengthen the novice's professional identity and improve teaching practice.

For the purpose of the project, the technology used to create dialog and professional meetings, such as the OEI platform and web-based social networks like Skype, Facebook, chat, and videoconferencing made it possible to build a relationship between the novice and the mentor that included communication, interaction and analysis. It provided a space to share opinions and reflection, a place where collaboration networks were established, particularly in the social web.

As Chiappe (2003) points out, the ubiquity, accessibility, functionality and adaptability of technology are distinctive features that make communicative instances possible, which take the shape of synchronous and asynchronous meetings. In effect, in the online mentoring process, virtual communication tools generate dialogic spaces for analysis and participation, particularly by the systematic use of the synchronous and asynchronous tools of Web 2.0, which makes it possible to advance the construction of the professional identity and in particular a self-managed novice, who in his/her relationship with his/her mentor manages to establish a dynamic line of communication in which the novice reflects on his/her experiences.

Technical difficulties arise mainly at the beginning of the online mentoring process. This change from being present to becoming a virtual subject requires familiarity as well as digital familiarity. Although informational technology (IT) fosters the creation of these professional or learning community networks (Marcelo, 2002), the paradigmatic change generates some resistance, particularly among mentors, because of the tradition to assist novices through face-to-face interactions. Mentors need to adapt to a system that is not usually familiar to them. In almost all cases, novices were not as resistant. This might be due to two reasons: first, novices typically display more digital familiarity due to the generational gap in technology; and second, novices first encountered mentoring as a virtual communicational space and not as a face-to-face one, and therefore have not experienced another form of mentoring.

Reflection Rounds: A Dialogical Proposal for Helping Mentors Reflect on the Process of Becoming Mentors

The Reflection Rounds are designed as interactions where conditions are set so as to allow the weaving of shared meanings. The leader of the reflection round must keep the symmetry across relationships, level the field for sharing, foster recognition and respect for one another and, make sure there is a climate of warmth and mutual respect.

In this practice, a tutor who mediates the round is defined as someone who promotes and facilitates the participation and interaction among participating actors. The tutor's role is to foster reflexive dialog and decision making. For each of the Reflection Rounds, the research team defines questions and counseling topics and establishes the communication mechanisms to ensure the participation of all parties. In this way, each Reflection Round epistemologically facilitates the construction of knowledge from both a personal reflection perspective and the collective analysis of the events that took place during the mentoring process, thus contributing new perspectives and experiences that add value to reflection.

Therefore, we define Reflection Rounds as systematic synchronic encounters (face-to-face or virtual), where everyone is able to attend and can see each other's faces. Reflection Rounds are held between mentors or between novices. In both types of Reflection Rounds, with mentors and novices, both face-to-face as well as through virtual synchronous encounters, the topic is previously defined by tutors, according to the diagnosis of the process of induction of novice teachers. The tutor also accompanies the process. The tutor generates individual and collective reflections, based on questioning, pinpointing problematic issues, and framing key questions. During the Reflection Rounds, the mentor allows time for individual narratives and for collective feedback. Hence, Reflection Rounds with mentors are a means to reshape and construct new meanings related to the process of mentoring. They are designed to enhance reflective processes that allow mentors and novices to analyze and transform practices through continuous feedback from participants, constituting virtuous circles of collaborative learning.

Technological Aspects of Virtual Reflection Rounds

Technologically, this was accomplished using the Google-enabled videoconferencing tool Hangout, accessed through its social network in Google+. This allowed participants to communicate and "see" one another simultaneously from different geographical locations. Technical conditions required mentors and mentees to count with—and count on—Internet and a camera. In order to establishing synchronous communication, each participant was assisted by a professional in charge of orienting mentors and novices by explaining to them the steps needed to create the technical conditions necessary for communication to take place.

Thus, and in order to overcome the difficulties described above, we set up a new means to communicate synchronously in order to generate meetings between novices, mentors and tutors, allowing them to overcome the geographical dispersion that got in the way of face-to-face meetings. For this process, we designed three Virtual Reflection Rounds. These synchronous meetings allowed mentors and novices to have synchronous face-to-face contact, adding a new dimension to the relationship. Initially, the virtual platform was utilized as a way to review and evaluate the mentoring process, but it quickly became apparent that virtual Reflection Rounds added to and even enhanced the mentoring process.

Two Reflection Rounds were held among the mentors and one held among the novices. Online data were collected before and after these rounds and were used as data gathering techniques for research purposes. The Reflection Rounds were taped and transcribed verbatim. The mentorship partnerships were automatically saved as text. A qualitative approach was used for analysis, using categorical content analysis (Vázquez, 1994) as the data analysis tool. Our purpose was to analyze both the content of what mentors and novices were communicating, as well as analyzing the process of virtual dialogical communication between novices and mentors, in terms of its possibilities, strengths, and challenges.

Main Findings: Relevant Themes That Emerged From the Analysis of the Reflection Rounds

The main findings derived from the analysis of the data showed there were different styles and different ways of understanding the process of mentoring. While some mentors were focused on the novice and his/her stance as a teacher, most mentors were "handing out recipes" to novices based on their own experiences. These "recipes" were pretty much tied to technical aspects of pedagogy, such as classroom discipline.

We soon realized that mentors were using different strategies and materials to meet the needs of their individual mentees. While some pairs of mentor-mentees based their discussions on slides predefined and prepared by the mentor, others reviewed and discussed recorded lectures. Still others jointly read articles, while some mentors assigned tasks to their mentees. The differences in materials and strategies used was not an issue in itself, but rather, our analysis showed that some mentors were adopting a position of expert by using almost exclusively top-down strategies such as preparing a PowerPoint presentation and then "teaching" the mentee a specific topic (such as how to get along with school leaders). This finding led us to create the first Virtual Reflection Rounds with mentors, for the purpose of helping us and the participants to further understand the different styles of mentoring. We also wanted to create dialogue in terms of the deeper sense of mentoring. Therefore, the Reflection Rounds, from a dialogical perspective, were introduced as an opportunity for mentors to revise their epistemological stances, to reflect and become aware of the implications of their own and others' styles, senses, and methodological strategies.

Hence, Reflection Rounds allowed us to understand the different styles of mentors which are based on their own training and professional experience. The mentoring process initially stems from the personal/professional experience of mentors, as well as from their epistemological understanding of mentoring. Therefore, mentoring itself may take different roads depending on the epistemological stances and methodological styles of the mentor. We were able to identify different and diverse interests in mentors, not only between mentors but also within mentors. There were times when the focus of mentoring was based on the needs of novice. These needs include very practical, everyday issues considered to be "problems" faced by novices either at the classroom level, at a relational level (between peer teachers), or at the emotional (personal) level.

This focus on the problems is closely related to an approach of mentoring, which is defined as a space used by mentors to convey to novices very practical and directive "strategies." This type of mentoring was discussed in the first Reflection Round. Tutors discussed with mentors how paradoxical this "cookbook" style of transmitting strategies turned out to be, when the aim was promoting and strengthening the autonomy of novices in their professional practice.

Others mentors, on the other hand, adopted more bottom-up approaches, such as viewing a recorded lesson of the mentee teaching in the classroom, and then asking the mentee what he/she wanted to talk about with respect to that lesson. This allowed them to adopt more horizontal interactions with their mentees.

Thus, our conclusion was that there are some mentors—a minority of them—who see their role as helping to facilitate reflection and the construction of a professional identity. In practice, this type of mentoring, which was closest to our expectations as tutors, was reported by mentors as having little acceptance by novices, who sought practical and very concrete strategies. Therefore, mentors are faced with a very strong dilemma: do they follow the dialogical approach that focuses on the long-term development of the professional, or do they give in and comply with the novices' seeking for practical, direct advice?

Another aspect that was revealed from the Reflection Rounds, and that relates to the role of the mentor who caters to the "problems" of the novice, was that mentors complained when their subject area was different from the subject area of their novice (i.e., math versus science). This aspect is relevant since it reveals that mentoring is assumed to be a process for improving teaching practice in a specific discipline or subject area, and not necessarily as a space for reflection on the role and identity of teachers, independent of the specific subject area.

Mentoring aimed at helping beginning teachers navigate daily job-related problems required the mentor to analyze the situation, assess the teacher's needs and implement materials and strategies to help the teacher develop ways to solve daily problems. In this type of mentoring, *self-distrust* was seen as a novice trait. A direct consequence that we were able to observe was that mentoring initially involved "consultancy," where the experience of the mentor was validated by assigning the novice the label of inexperienced, thus fostering a *vertical relationship*. In other words, consultancy was a natural part of assisting a new teacher and was not necessarily negative in and of itself, but rather often had the unintended outcome of steering the work in a direction that was opposite to the goals proposed by this process, which were the facilitation of reflection and autonomy of novice teachers.

This analysis, together with the reflective discussions of our research group, revealed three additional findings on the effects of incorporating the Reflection Rounds in the mentoring process: (1) a sense of higher emotional engagement in beginning teachers, (2) a greater sense of community between mentors, and (3) the reenactment of the dialogical approach that theoretically sustained our model of mentoring.

Although the online platform brought mentors and novices face-to-face, mentors expressed concern regarding the disengagement they were seeing from their protégés, such as the decrease in the frequency of online encounters, the length of these encounters, and the depth of analysis in them. We believe that virtual disengagement was related to emotional disengagement. Mentors expressed a need to emotionally engage their protégés and themselves in the experience. During Reflective Rounds, mentors talked about their mentoring practice with the university tutors and one another. These sessions proved to have a positive effect on the emotional engagement of the mentors themselves, with the mentees, and with the mentoring program itself. One mentor expressed: "To me, it was very good to be able to count on this meeting space. It allowed us to feel involved and committed to the challenge we face." Mentors benefited from sharing their worries and successes, face-to-face with other mentors, who understood their challenges and could offer support.

Participants also expressed a higher *sense of community* after the Reflection Rounds. Mentors expressed a feeling of bonding that they had not felt before, and that strengthened their commitment to the e-mentoring program: "This instance takes us closer as mentors. It allows us to share from the reflection, the processes that we are living and to commit ourselves to our task."

Finally, during these Reflection Rounds, tutors from the university research group explicitly expressed their doubts about the contents of the asynchronous encounters between mentors and protégés when a vertical, expert-novice approach was used. The *dialogical approach* was reviewed and contrasted with data gathered from the e-encounters. Reflective processes were held about the role of mentors within a dialogical approach, and about the need to regard the protégé as a legitimate other.

Discussion: Lessons Learned

As we have described, after the Reflection Rounds mentors were able to identify, in hindsight, the moments in their interventions where they tended to "give recipes" by instilling a logic of vertical consultancy, rather than engaging in a dialogical encounter with the other. Our research group had previously designed and implemented Reflection Rounds as part of nonvirtual mentoring processes in a previous project (Rojas et al., 2011), but they were not originally included in the online mentoring program. However, as a result of our initial evaluation of the e-mentoring, we decided to include them to help overcome the limitations of vertical, consultancy-type relationships that allow for little reflection or conversation about school context. Reflective rounds enhanced the mentoring experience because they allowed novices to take more ownership of their learning by reflecting on their emerging practice and building a deeper understanding of the school context and the role that they played both, personally and professionally within that school system.

Our analysis revealed that these Reflection Rounds proved to be a turning point for mentors, both in terms of their greater commitment to the mentoring process and through a shift in the relationships they were building with their novices, which evolved from consultancy to capacity-building and from daily problem-solving to questioning and probing about broader issues related to teaching. In this way, mentors helped their protégés develop long-term habits and skills.

Another positive result from the Reflective Rounds was that the university-based tutors were able to analyze the effectiveness of the program, based on the mentors' conversations and adjust their approach midstream. This illustrates one of the potential benefits that can result from university/school partnerships and supports our argument for changing the mentor-protégée relationship from expert-novice to dialogical advisory.

We contend that synchronous encounters are an important part of online a-synchronic encounters in mentoring programs. These results suggest that in order to be effective, online mentoring partnerships need to engage mentorship partners emotionally, something that proved to be difficult using only asynchronous encounters, but that was greatly facilitated as the mentors developed their own practice as mentors during Reflection Rounds. Virtual Reflective Rounds became a space for discussion and sharing that was highly valued by mentors, novices, and tutors and in the end allowed for the e-mentoring to be as effective as the typical face-to-face approach. Thus, the social web tools and the videoconference were recognized as meeting rooms that mentors, novices, the PUCV and OEI teams valued because they provide the opportunity to talk collaboratively and learn from one another about their practices

While we understand that reflective rounds do not completely overcome all obstacles, we believe that they have the potential to generate reflective habits, which involve participants in analyzing the process in the midst of the process itself. In other words, reflection becomes part of the mentoring and ultimately the teaching. Reflection Rounds as a practice tool can also help maintain the foundations of dialogical mentoring, by producing and facilitating moments for meta-analyzing mentor's own power-related positions, and mentor-mentee interactions. However, it does not depend exclusively on the project coordination team, but rather includes all participants, by necessity.

We conclude that asynchronous e-mentoring processes are highly strengthened by synchronous e-mentoring moments, which when properly designed, can have positive effects. The design of these synchronous meetings should include tutors who are able to guide the process, address issues of emotional engagement and build a sense of community among the members in ways that will strengthen their identities as mentors.

The Organization of Ibero-American States (OEI), who funded this e-mentoring pilot program, is considering implementing e-mentoring programs in other countries of Latin America. We hope the findings from this study will help illuminate decision-making processes. Specifically, we suggest incorporating Reflection Rounds as part of e-mentoring programs.

ACKNOWLEDGMENT

We would like to thank Dr. Adolfo López for the English edition of this chapter.

REFERENCES

Barberá, E. (2004). *La educación en la red. Actividades virtuales de enseñanza y aprendizaje* [The education in the network. Virtual activities of teaching and learning]. Barcelona, Spain: Paidós.

García, F. J., & García C. J. (2001). *Los espacios virtuales educativos en el ámbito de Internet. Un refuerzo a la formación tradicional, teoría de la educación. Educación y cultura en la sociedad de la información* [The virtual educational spaces in the Internet area. A reinforcement to the traditional training, theory of the education. Education and culture in the society of the information]. Retrieved April 15, from http://www3.usal.es/~teoriaeducacion/rev_numero_03/n3_art_garcia-garcia.htm

Chiape, A. (2003). *La virtualidad como estrategia educativa* [The virtuality as an educational strategy]. Manizales, SiC editorial.

Gros, B. (2008). *Aprendizajes, conexiones y artefactos: la producción colaborativa del conocimiento* [Learnings, connections and appliances: The collaborative production of the knowledge]. Barcelona, Spain: Gedisa.

Duart, J. M. (2003). Educar en Valores por medio de la red [To educate in values by the web]. In J. M. Duart & A. Sangrà (Eds.), *Learning in the virtuality.* Barcelona, Spain: Gedisa-Ediuoc.

Fierro, C., B. Fortoul, & L. Rosas (1999). *Transformando la práctica docente. Una propuesta basada en la investigación-acción* [Transforming the teaching practice. An offer based on the research-action] México: Ed. Paidós.

Freire, P. (2002). *Pedagogía de la esperanza* [Pedagogy of hope]. Editorial Siglo XXI, Buenos Aires; Argentina. (5ta ed.).

Freire, P. (2003). *Pedagogía del oprimido* [Pedagogy of the ipressed]. Argentina: Siglo XXI Editores.

Julio, C. (2010, Julu). Legítimos aprendices: recuperando al sujeto en el proceso educativo [Legitimate apprentices: Recovering to the subject in the educational process]. *Diversia N°2, CIDPA Valparaíso*, pp. 19–43. Retrieved from http://www.cidpa.cl/diversia2.htm

Lave, J. (1991). *Cognición en la práctica* [Cognition in the practice]. Barcelona, Spain: Paidós. New York, NY: Cambridge University Press.

Marcelo, C. (2002). *E-learning. Teleformación* [E-learning. TV training]. Barcelona, Spain: Gestión 2000.

Maushak, N. J., & Ellis, K. A (2003). Attitudes of graduate students toward mixed-medium distance education. *Quarterly Review of Distance Education, 4*(2), 129–141

Orland-Barak, L. (2006). Convergent, divergent and parallel dialogues in mentors' professional conversations. *Teachers and Teaching: Theory and Practice, 12*(1), 13–33.

Pedró, F. (2006). *The new millennium learners: Challenging our views on ICT and learning.* OECD-CERI.

Pasquali, A. (1990). *Comunicación y cultura de masas* (6th ed.) [Communication and mass culture]. Caracas, Venezuela: Ed.Monte Avila.

Prieto, D. (1999). *Comunicación y educación* [Communication and education]. Buenos Aires, Argentina: Editorial Ciccus La Crujia.

Rogoff, B. (1993). *Aprendices del pensamiento: Desarrollo cognitivo en el contexto social* [Apprentices of thought: Cognitive development in social context.] Buenos Aires, Argentina: Paidós.

Rogoff, B. (1997). Los tres planos de la actividad sociocultural: Apropiación participativa, participación guiada y aprendizaje [The three planes of the socio-cultural activity: participative ownership, guided participation and learning.] In J. V. Wertsch, P. del Río, & A. Alvarez Fund (Eds.), *La mente sociocultural: Aproximaciones teóricas y aplicadas* [The socio-cultural mind: Theoretical and applied approaches.] Madrid, Spain: Fundación Infancia y Aprendizaje.

Rojas, C., Julio, C., Lopez, V., Nuñez, C., Espinosa, B., Mujica, E., Lopez, C., & Palma, E. (2011). Estudio exploratorio: Experiencias de inserción profesional de docentes con y sin acompañamiento de mentores formales [Experiences of teachers' professional insertion with and without accompaniment of formal menthors]. Madrid, Spain: Organización de Estados Iberoamericanos.

Vázquez, F. (1994). *Análisis de contenido categorial: El análisis temático* [Categorical content analysis: Thematic analysis] Barcelona, Spain: Unitat de Psicología Social. Universitat Autónoma de Barcelona.

Watzlawick, J. H. (1984). *Teoría de la comunicación humana* [Theory of human communication] Spain: Ed. Herder.

Wenger, E. (2001). *Comunidades de práctica: Aprendizaje, significado e identidad* [Communities of practice: Learning, meaning and identity.] Barcelona, Spain: Paidós.

CHAPTER 5

FACE-TO-FACE, ONLINE, AND HYBRID MGENTORING IN A PROFESSIONAL DEVELOPMENT PROGRAM

Ya-Wen Cheng, Deborah L. Hanuscin, and Mark J. Volkmann

INTRODUCTION

Teachers are a critical component to successful educational reform, but in order for them to help transform schools, teachers "need to be offered expanded and enriched professional development experiences that should be tied directly to the emerging student performance standards and be continuous, site-based, job-embedded, teacher designed, and organizationally focused" (Dilworth & Imig, 1995, p. 5). Effective professional development that leads to change helps teachers develop content knowledge, pedagogical content knowledge, and skills they need to succeed in their classroom as well as build or strengthen their learning community (Loucks-Horsley, Stiles, & Hewson, 1996; Vrasidas & Zembylas, 2004).

However, too often professional development consists of one-time learning opportunities with limited impact on teaching and learning

Best Practices in Mentoring for Teacher and Leader Development, pp. 73–92
Copyright © 2016 by Information Age Publishing
73

(Loucks-Horsley et al., 1996). After a short period of time in face-to-face professional development, teachers are left on their own in terms of determining when and how to implement these new ideas from professional development (Collins & Clark, 2008; Opfer & Pedder, 2011). High quality professional development programs, in contrast, are designed to provide ongoing support that includes mentoring. Mentoring, as a supportive mechanism, has been used to assist preservice and in-service teachers to gain content knowledge and pedagogical skills (Gutke & Albion, 2008; Schneider, 2008). The inclusion of mentors, or "experienced teachers with more content knowledge or experience in using a particular program or teaching practice" (Loucks-Horsley, Love, Stiles, Mundry, & Hewson, 2003, p. 219), is becoming increasingly common in teacher professional development programs. Successful professional development for K–12 teachers relies on high quality mentoring programs.

Unfortunately, high quality is often synonymous with high cost. In the past, mentoring has been a face-to-face endeavor. However, as the price of meeting space, teacher time, substitute pay, and travel increases, professional developers have begun to use a variety of online communication tools (e.g., e-mail, Googlechat, Sakai, Wimba, etc.) to reduce costs associated with mentoring. With the advent of new technologies, there are increasing opportunities for professional development activities, such as mentoring, to be carried out virtually (Gentry, Denton, & Kurz, 2008). However, fully online mentoring has limitations. Within online mentoring, for example, it can be difficult to establish relationships between mentor and mentee (DuBois & Karcher, 2005). As an alternative, professional developers have sought to create "hybrid" forms of professional development that combine both face-to-face and online interactions (Cheng & Hanuscin, 2012). Learners have the flexibility to meet virtually, without time and location constraints in the hybrid environment (Single & Muller, 1999). Given the newness of these hybrid models, there is currently a lack of shared language regarding design principles for hybrid professional development and a lack of research that explores the relative effectiveness of various models and mentoring environments (Cheng & Hanuscin, 2012). The purpose of this chapter is to describe recent research that examines the nature of three different mentoring environments. We are particularly interested in understanding about the learning opportunities afforded by face-to-face, online, and hybrid mentoring environments. This chapter addresses this question by examining two subquestions:

1. What do teachers perceive as essential for effective mentoring in a professional development program?
2. In what ways do various mentoring environments (face-to-face, online, and hybrid) support effective mentoring and teacher learning?

THEORETICAL FRAMEWORK

Learning is a social behavior, where individuals learn through interaction with others (Vygotsky, 1978). Mentoring is one type of social interaction that enhances opportunities for learning. Given this view, we framed our research within the theory of social constructivism, which focuses on how individuals construct knowledge through meaningful social interactions, discourse, and negotiation. Social constructivism explains the processes of learning in terms of three key concepts: zone of proximal development (ZPD), intersubjectivity, and enculturation (Woo & Reeves, 2007).

The zone of proximal development is "the region of activity that learners can navigate with aid from a supporting context, including but not limited to people" (Vygotsky, 1986, cited in Brown et al., 1993, p. 5). The ZPD is "the distance between the actual developmental level, as determined by independent problem solving, and the level of potential development, as determined through problem solving under adult guidance, or in collaboration with more capable peers" (Vygotsky, 1978, p. 86). The zone of proximal development is "constantly changing with the learner's increasing independent competence at each successive level" (Brown et al., 1993, p. 35), with the assistance of a more capable peer, who is someone with better skills, understanding, or ability, such as a mentor. Intersubjectivity is the mutual understanding that people share through meaningful interaction and communication (Gauvain, 2001; Woo & Reeves, 2007). Mentoring is an activity that "creates intersubjectivity among the participants, thus transmitting meaning, values, affect, motivation, and indeed the planes of consciousness of mentors and entire cultures" (Gallimore, John-Steiner, & Tharp, 1992, p. 15). Enculturation is the process whereby individuals acquire values that are appropriate or necessary in that particular culture (Kottak, 2007) and through this process, the individual is accepted by the community or culture. As long as the individual remains in that context, the process of enculturation continues to shape the individual's learning, values, and beliefs as the culture changes. "Learning occurs through the process of intersubjectivity in the enculturalized zone of proximal development" (Woo & Reeves, 2007, p. 19). Therefore, understanding how different mentoring designs support meaningful discourse and social interaction is important for understanding how mentoring can be an effective component of professional development.

METHODOLOGY

Context of the Study

The context of the study is a five-year professional development project funded by the National Science Foundation Math and Science Partnerships

(MSP) program. A TIME for Physics First (PF-MSP) focuses on supporting ninth grade science teachers to become teacher leaders and build their physics content knowledge through an approach that integrates inquiry, modeling and technology. Teachers who participated in PF-MSP were divided into two cohorts and all attended summer academies and academic year follow-up sessions (face to face), as well as participating in a year-long course on teacher leadership and interactions via a members-only online portal. With respect to mentoring, across the five years Cohort 1 teachers received face-to-face mentoring, whereas Cohort 2 teachers only received online mentoring. In order to distinguish between Cohort 1 and 2 mentors, the program refers to the mentors provided to Cohort 1 participants as "coaches" and to Cohort 2 as "mentors."

Online mentoring took place through Sakai (www.sakaiproject.org), which is an online learning management system that provides interactive functions for users. For example, Sakai includes an e-conferencing tool called Wimba (http://vcrp.wimba.com/) to support online meetings. Coaches, mentors, and teacher-participants were assigned to different professional learning communities (PLCs). Each PLC was led by a coach (Cohort 1) or a mentor (Cohort 2). Coaches and mentors were trained through Cognitive Coaching (Costa & Garmston, 2002). One of the key concepts of Cognitive Coaching (Costa & Garmston, 2002) is that coaches/mentors must remain nonjudgmental throughout the mentoring process, help the mentee identify the problem, reflect on the problem, and solve the problem (Costa & Garmston, 2002).

Face-to-Face, Online, and Hybrid Learning Environments

The primary role of coaches and mentors in this program was to assist teacher-participants as they implemented a ninth-grade physics curriculum. The face-to-face mentoring for Cohort 1 included monthly preobservation discussions, classroom observations and postobservation discussions (see Figure 5.1). The preobservation discussion provided opportunities for coaches to understand broader issues related to the mentee's progress and teaching practice, in addition to better understanding the classroom context and specific lesson about to be taught and observed.

During the classroom observation, coaches observed the actual implementation of the curriculum and teacher-student interactions in the classroom, taking observational notes for later discussion. After the observation, coaches and teachers identified and discussed successes and challenges related to the implementation of the curriculum. Coaches also participated in PLC meetings (face-to-face) during which teachers shared resources, discussed successes, and strategized ways to overcome

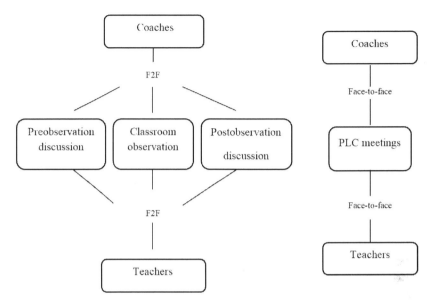

Figure 5.1. Cohort 1 Coaching Design.

difficulties. In the PLC meetings, coaches acted as facilitators, assisting teachers in identifying problems and strategizing ways to improve their teaching and student learning.

The mentoring of Cohort 2 teachers, which had no face-to-face component, included a monthly reflection form and online discussion with mentors (see Figure 5.2). Because mentors in this case did not observe in teachers' classrooms, there was no preobservation form. Rather, teachers completed a postteaching reflection prior to meeting with their mentors. On the form, teachers provided details of a lesson s/he has implemented by responding to several self-evaluation questions and then providing additional comments about the lesson. Within 48 hours, mentor and teacher virtually discussed the form using Wimba. The PLC meetings for Cohort 2 also took place virtually, through Wimba.

The hybrid mentoring model (Figure 5.3 and Figure 5.4) emerged during implementation of the PF-MSP, and involved a subset of Cohort 1 and Cohort 2 teachers. The hybrid mentoring model involved both face-to-face and online learning environments, in that teachers still had face-to-face preobservation discussions and classroom observations. However, the postobservation discussions with mentors was held online. Additionally, mentors attended PLC meetings online instead of face-to-face, while teachers met as a PLC group in both online and face-to-face environments.

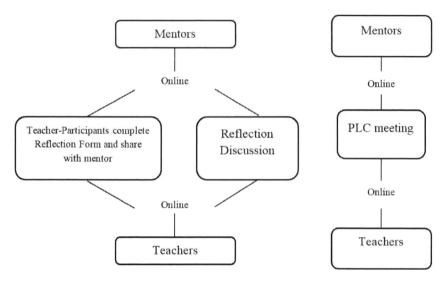

Figure 5.2.   Cohort 2 Mentoring Design.

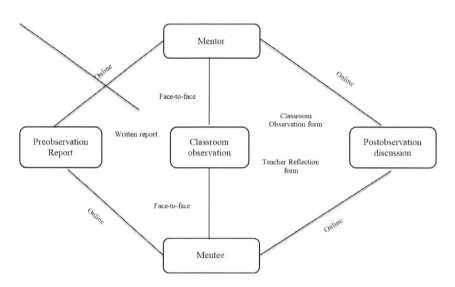

Figure 5.3.   Hybrid Mentoring.

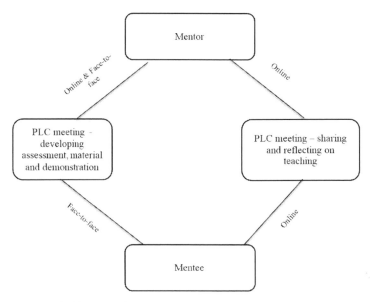

Figure 5.4.   Hybrid Mentoring.

Participants

A total of 12 participants were purposefully selected and consented to participate in the study. According to Patton (2002), purposeful sampling focuses on in-depth understanding of the case. Our sampling was intended to provide robust examples of the three different mentoring models occurring in the professional development: face-to-face, online, and hybrid. We selected mentors/coaches and their mentees based on their full participation (both frequency and quality) in monthly classroom visits/mentoring sessions, online discussions, and PLC activities. The final group included four of the 36 teachers from Cohort 1 and five from the 34 teachers in Cohort 2, along with their three coaches/mentors (from a total of 10).

Cohort 1 participants. A total of four teachers—Henry, Bella, Andy and Emma—and two coaches—John and Ken—from two PLC groups participated in the study. Henry and Bella taught in the same school and shared the same coach, John. Andy and Emma shared the same coach, Ken. However, they taught in different school districts and were in different PLC groups.

Henry had taught science subjects for nineteen years. He taught earth science four years before teaching physical science at the high school level. This was his first time to teach the Physics First curriculum. His school supports the Physics First curriculum and Henry, Bella, and another Physics

First participant teacher were the only teachers who taught the Physics First curriculum in their school. Bella had 10 years of teaching high school level science subjects but no experience teaching physics. She planned to improve student engagement and motivation by implementing the Physics First curriculum. She also thought that joining the Physics First program would have great impact on her teaching and student learning.

Andy, who had been teaching freshman physics for three years, had attended another Physics First professional development at Arizona State University prior to his participation in this program. Thus, he believed he had a deep understanding of the Physics First curriculum. He also received support from his school since they had adopted Physics First concept as their curriculum. Emma had 13 years of experience but was teaching freshman physics for the first time. However, according to Emma, her physics content knowledge was relatively weak. As the only science teacher in her school teaching the Physics First curriculum, Emma had no other person with whom to discuss her implementation of the Physics First curriculum. Thus, she valued having a coach observe and discuss her implementation, because she really wanted to help students understand the physics concepts.

Table 5.1 shows the demographic information of the teachers of the two C1 groups. Of note, only Andy had prior experience teaching the Physics First curriculum and Emma was the only teacher who utilized hybrid mentoring.

Table 5.1.   Demographic Data of C1 Teachers

Coaches	Teachers by PLC	Prior PF Experience	School District Demographic	Years of Physics Teaching Experience	Years of Teaching Experience
John	Henry	N	Urban	1	17
	Bella	N	Urban	1	10
Ken	Andy	Y	Urban	3	9
	Emma	N	Rural	3	13

Note: Y means yes; N means no

Cohort 2 participants. Becky had taught science subjects for seven years and was the only science teacher in her school. She was an experienced freshman physics teacher and her primary goal for participating in the professional development program was to communicate and collaborate with other science teachers. She also wanted to improve the implementation of white boarding. Amber had five years of experience teaching high school science. She was the only science teacher in her rural area school and therefore was concerned about the implementation and pacing of the curriculum materials.

Katy has been teaching science subjects for 20 years. Katy and the other two teachers in her PLC (Alisa and Ted), taught in the same urban school district. As an experienced teacher, she was confident in her content knowledge. One of her freshman classes had a majority of students with learning disabilities. For this reason, her primary concern was with implementing the curriculum for students with learning problems. Alisa has been teaching science subjects for 16 years. She wanted to learn new instructional strategies to help students learn physics concepts. She also focused on student learning and the modification of curriculum to satisfy learning needs. Ted has 11 years of experience of teaching science subjects. He has experience teaching the freshman physics curriculum and was familiar with the "Physics First" concept. Since he also had special needs students in his class, he focused on learning progress and engagement for these students. In should be noted that Katy, Alisa, and Ted utilized hybrid mentoring environment.

Ken was a retired physics teacher who had experience teaching the Physics First curriculum. Ken worked as both coach and mentor, giving him experience with both professional development designs. John was a physics professor in a Midwest University. Before he became a professor, he taught physics at the high school level for many years. Finally, Ryan was a former high school physics teacher and had experience teaching freshman physics. He had been a coach and mentor in the program since 2008 when it first received funding as a state Math and Science Partnership.

Table 5.2.   Demographic Data of C2 Teachers

Mentors	Teachers by PLC	Prior PF Experience	School District Demographic	Years of Physics Teaching Experience	Years of Teaching Experience
Ryan	Becky	Y	Rural	2.5	7
	Amber	N	Rural	1	5
Ken	Katy	Y	Urban	6	20
	Alisa	Y	Urban	4	16
	Ted	Y	Urban	6	11

Note: Y means yes; N means no

Data Sources and Analysis

We utilized a qualitative case study research method in which each mentoring model served as a case (Yin, 2009). Data sources included semistructured interviews, coach observation forms, mentor reflection forms, as well as artifacts and field notes over a six-month period. Interviews were conducted at the beginning and end of the academic semester. Field notes were recorded during coaches' classroom visits and online mentoring sessions. Additionally, artifacts were collected from teacher-participants, including lesson plans, assessments and classroom handouts. We adapted cross-case analysis and open coding technique to analyze the data (Strauss & Corbin, 1990; Yin, 2009). All the data were openly coded and separately coded by two researchers to avoid bias and increase interrater reliability. Similar data were categorized and labeled during the open coding process. Then, we identified the themes that emerged from the data to address our research questions, which were:

RQ1: What did teachers view as essential to effective mentoring?

RQ2: In what ways do various learning environments (face-to-face, online, and hybrid) support effective mentoring and teacher learning?

FINDINGS

In this section, we organize our discussion of research findings based on order of the research questions. We first discuss the teachers' views on essential elements of effective mentoring. Then, we elaborate the benefits and limitations of face-to-face, online and hybrid learning environments.

Essential Elements of Effective Mentoring

All of the teachers in this study discussed the importance of receiving support and mentoring from the professional development project. Three distinct elements of mentoring emerged from our analysis of the data from teachers' perspectives: Reflection, Feedback and Observation.

Opportunities for reflection. Both Cohort 1 and 2 teachers mentioned the importance of reflection in terms of improving teaching and implementation of the curriculum. Specifically, teachers reported appreciating the *opportunities* to reflect on teaching practice and implementation of the curriculum. With their busy schedules and teaching loads, teachers did not have time built into their workday to reflect on their teaching practice. Amber, a Cohort 2 teacher, described how the mentoring offered in the program encouraged her to reflect on her teaching:

> When you're busy, it is good to have a reason to stop and reflect.... [When you] have a mentor give you a set time when you're going to meet, of course

you stop and reflect. The most effective part is having the ability to have time set aside where [a mentor] can help you guide your reflection and give you feedback and ideas on how to improve your ... since I am the only teacher in my school that teaches [freshman physics].... It's really great to have some else to talk to that familiar with the curriculum and in teaching, they can give me additional ideas. (C2: Amber)

Specific feedback. Teachers valued specific feedback on their actual teaching practices. Yet, only the Cohort 1 coaches observed teachers' actual classroom implementation of the curriculum. Therefore, Cohort 1 teachers were better able to address their concerns and ask for specific feedback on their lesson implementation from coaches. For example, Andy stated:

I do like to ask him to watch how I am asking questions. I want to make sure that I am focusing on students, not doing "call and response" We have several conversations. In that respect, it's just nice to hear—gentle criticism is a good thing to have. *You could have done a little bit better job if you could have done those kinds of things* [from your coach]. (C1: Andy)

The support for Cohort 2 did not include classroom observations, thus, Cohort 2 teachers were tasked with providing their own account of their lesson implementation to mentors. While this allowed them to request specific feedback, these accounts were filtered by teachers in that they were limited by their own awareness of problems in their implementation of the curriculum. If teachers did not address recognized issues, mentors had no way of knowing whether there were issues.

Some teachers recognized this, and expressed a need for feedback on related to problems that a mentor might identify. For instance, Becky, a Cohort 2 teacher, had experienced face-to-face mentoring in an earlier program, and found the online mentoring did not fulfill her needs:

So, the first time I had my coach visit my classroom, I have to say that was more useful to me at that time because I'd never taught [the curriculum] before. So, it was really good to have someone watch my teaching. The biggest difference to me is now *nobody watches me teach* and I'd like to have that feedback. (C2: Becky)

Thus, there was a greater value placed on feedback provided based on observations in the classroom.

Observations of teaching. Many teachers reported that direct observations of their teaching created opportunities to improve their teaching practice. As alluded to above, having coaches observe the actual implementation of a lesson was essential for teachers. However, the online-only mentoring design lacked this mechanism. Without the observation, teachers could potentially receive inaccurate feedback from mentors. For example, Alisa would send her reflection form with details of her classroom setting and interactions to her mentor before they met online. Sometimes, her mentor misinterpreted the situation, and Alisa felt as a result that she did not always receive the help that she needed:

> Most of the difficulty [is] just that my mentor does not know my classroom, so he does not know how it is set up or designed. I have to use my own descriptive narration to provide him an understanding of what is happening. And I could see that at the time, he would ask me questions, and I would not be as clear—or he would not—[so] he would misinterpret what I was saying because he had not seen the classroom. So, that occasionally [that] is a problem. (C2: Alisa)

On the other hand, Cohort 1 teachers had a different experience within the face-to-face design. Emma talked about the effectiveness of classroom visits and discussions in terms of supporting her teaching and learning.

> For him [Ken] to actually observe my class and then to talk about how he thinks it went and how I think it went. We couldn't really talk about anything unless he actually saw my class and if he just watched my class and gave me observations, I don't think that will be as effective either. So I am thinking both things, both the observation and the chance to talk about these observations are the most important. (C1: Emma)

In summary, teachers identified the essential elements of effective mentoring as (1) having the opportunities to reflect on teaching practice and the implementation of the curriculum, (2) receiving specific feedback on their actual implementation of teaching practices, and (3) having direct observations of classroom instruction. The structure of each of the three support models required teachers to reflect on their teaching. From teachers' experience in receiving face-to-face and online mentoring, we found that both the face-to-face and online mentoring designs provided teachers opportunities to reflect and also promoted learning and teaching. Although some teachers in the study had a great deal of experience with the curriculum, they still needed the type of support provided by the observation/feedback combination. Research questions two and three focus on the benefits and limitations of each support model. In the next section, we discuss our findings by highlighting the advantages of each model. We also include a discussion of how these advantages and limitations impact the effectiveness of mentoring.

Analyzing Various Learning Environments

Face-to-face, online and hybrid learning environments offer various ways to support mentoring. Overall, we found that all three learning environments provided an opportunity for teachers to "step back" from being in the moment of teaching to reflect on their practice, making this a part of their learning. Reflecting on teaching makes teachers aware of how they teach, as well as how students learn. Finding time for reflection is not easy for teachers, however, because of busy schedules and heavy workloads. Thus, reflection is not always a priority for teachers, despite its value. Mentoring can help address that. Andy, a Cohort 1 teacher explained:

> The biggest thing is it made—forced me—to reflect and think about why I teach and how I teach.... If I am not going to be watched, if I am not going to get feedback, I probably won't think twice about it at all; but if I am going to be watched, it makes me reflect before I have to do the lesson. (C1: Andy)

Yet, despite the similarities, there were unique benefits and limitations to each of the models, as we describe below.

Face-to-face learning environment. The face-to-face learning environment provided mentors opportunities to address immediate concerns —both in the moment and in postobservation sessions after the lesson —and held teachers more accountable for their teaching and learning. Face-to-face mentoring allows mentors to provide feedback "in the moment" that mentors helps teachers recognize the mistakes they make. Bella, for example, stated "I remember I was doing something on the board; he [the mentor said] *Hey come here. You flipped it; you did it backwards.*" (C1: Bella). Since Bella was in her first semester of teaching the curriculum, receiving just-in-time feedback was important because it helped her correct errors in her own understanding of the content and implement the curriculum more effectively. Mentors also addressed immediate concerns regarding teaching and learning during postobservation discussions. Andy talked about this in regards to his postvisit discussion.

> My coach (Ken) observed the lesson and took notes. Then we sat down and talked about how the lesson went, different things I did, different things that I would like to change in the future, and things that I changed during the lesson. We also talked about things like "thinking like your kids" so we can adapt [our lessons] better for students. (C1: Andy)

In this sense, the face-to-face interaction held teachers accountable for their teaching and learning. As Henry explained:

It's having a professional in your room that is observing what you do. I think that holds you a little more accountable and makes you, you know, kind of want to do your best for that person. It's just nice to be able to go to that person with questions, and if I need clarification on either pedagogy or content, I have that available. (C1: Henry)

Some elements of the face-to-face learning environment, however, limited the effectiveness of mentoring. This was primarily related to mentors and mentees not having enough time for pre- and postobservation discussions. These discussions are critical because they are designed to foster reflection and provide feedback. However, because of class schedules, which often leave just a few minutes between classes, teachers and coaches do not always have enough time immediately afterwards to discuss the observations. All four teachers in the face-to-face mentoring case had to teach other courses and/or had school duties after the observations. Usually, coaches and teachers only had 5 to 10 minutes for the postobservation discussions. The time was too short for in-depth discussions that were associated with the teaching. For example, Andy lamented, "I guess the biggest, the hardest part of that is just having time to do it (reflection) quickly and get quick feedback" (C1: Andy).

Online learning environment. In contrast to the face-to-face learning environment, the online learning environment provided ample opportunities for teachers and mentors to have meetings to discuss their teaching practice. Meeting online helped teachers overcome location constraints (enabling teachers to meet with their mentors without concern for travel to and from distant locations) and better utilize time (enabling teachers to meet when it was convenient and for longer chunks of time). Because it was easy to set up online meetings, mentors and teachers met more frequently. Cohort 2 teachers, for example, had more than one mentoring meeting a month, because of this flexibility and some coaches, like Ryan, met weekly with their teachers. The online venue also led to a reduction in time wasted. For instance, Amber taught in a rural area and was the only science teacher in the school building. As she explained:

I think it is great because when you teach in a small school—it is 80 minutes for me to [get to] town. The folks in my PLC—we are all at least an hour apart. It would really take more of my time if we all needed to drive to different locations to have our PLC meeting. I think we'd have a lot fewer PLC meetings. Same goes for meeting with my mentor; it is a lot easier and you can have more meetings if there is no travel involved. (C2: Amber)

Many of our coaches and teachers found that the online learning environment removed the barriers posed by time and money, but raised new problems associated with the absence of classroom observations. As mentioned earlier, not having a mentor observe an actual lesson led to misunderstandings, especially when trying to learn to enact a new curriculum and new pedagogy. Overall, the online learning environment offered synchronous communication while eliminating travel and time expenses.

Hybrid learning environment. The hybrid learning environment, which consisted of a combination of in-person and virtual contact with mentors, provided both the benefit of flexibility with the potential for enhanced collegiality. Debriefing after an observation is valuable in terms of improving teaching, but in the face-to-face model this was often shortened. The hybrid learning environment allowed for this important step in the mentoring process to occur when it might otherwise not happen. Teachers who were not able to debrief with their coach immediately after a classroom observation were able to do it online. For example, Emma, a Cohort 1 teacher, is the only science teacher in her school building. Thus, she has a heavy workload with lots of responsibilities. Since she was not able to debrief with her coach after his visits, they decided to use Wimba to hold their postobservation discussion. Emma talked about her experience with the hybrid learning environment:

> The two things most important are 1) for him to actually observe my class and then to talk about how he thinks it went and how I think it went. 2) After the class, the classes he watches, he has a reflection sheet that he asks me to fill out and I email it to him and then we discuss. And he sends his observations, he emails them to me and so we talk about his observation and my reflection on Wimba. So since we use Wimba, we can talk back and forth. I think in our case that does help the face-to-face visit. Because otherwise, we wouldn't be able to talk about the lesson after it happened. (C1: Emma)

Teachers also utilized the hybrid learning environment in additional ways to collaborate with other teachers to learn, share ideas, and develop teaching materials (e.g., lesson plans and lab equipment). For example, Katy, Alisa and Ted met regularly in online and face-to-face environments. As a group, they utilized different environments to achieve different goals. The flexibility of the hybrid learning environment offered opportunities to work together to develop classroom materials, as well as improve instructional strategies. For example, Alisa, a Cohort 2 participant, talked about how they utilized the hybrid learning environment.

> We get a lot out of that face-to-face [meetings] but also having the flexibility to meet online or meet in person—whatever meets our needs. I kind of like it being a mix, right now. This semester, in my PLC, everybody is really busy, so we've been really grateful that we can do online meetings instead of face-to-face meetings. It just makes it more manageable for everyone. (C2: Alisa)

Katy also explained the differences between the two environments and the benefits of utilizing a hybrid learning environment.

We schedule [meetings] once a week, and it's either a one-hour online Wimba session or 1–2 hour session in somebody's classroom. My PLC meets online part of the time as well, and we get a lot out of those meetings. But, we can't do the physical things—like creating lab equipment—there's lots of things for Physics First labs that we make. The other thing that's nice about face-to-face is that we take turns meeting in different classrooms. So, when we're in one person's classroom, we can see all the different things they are teaching that are different from our own classroom and we get more ideas. (C2: Katy)

When reflecting on the PLC meetings, Katy compared the face-to-face to the online environment. She recognized that teachers could do the physical work such as creating lab materials in the face-to-face environment, but not in the online environment. Accordingly, her PLC utilized the two venues to fit their schedule and needs. When they met face-to-face (in each other's classroom), they could see the classroom setting and see how and what materials and equipment were used in supporting the implementation of the curriculum. This helped teachers share ideas with one another to improve their implementation.

Overall, the face-to-face and online learning environments had both benefits and limitations in supporting face-to-face and online mentoring. In the face-to-face learning environment, teachers received in-the-moment feedback, had an opportunity to address immediate concerns, and were held more accountable for their teaching and learning. But the face-to-face learning environment limited the opportunity for reflective discussion due to the inflexibility of schedules. The online model enabled frequent meetings and the better utilization of time. Moreover, the online learning environment gave teachers time to reflect and elaborate on teaching practice and learning.

However, the absence of classroom observations in the online model often resulted in misunderstandings between teachers and mentors, who had only an incomplete picture of the lesson. In the hybrid case, teachers were able to utilize both face-to-face and online environments to support their needs. Having access to both forms of communication enhanced the mentoring process. For example, teachers developed teaching materials in the face-to-face environment and met online to share their successful and challenging experiences. Having the ability to meet either face-to-face or online for PLC meetings increased the meeting frequency and resulted in an increase in the strength of the relationship and teaching practice.

CONCLUSION

Prior research has focused on teachers' comfort with technology as a possible barrier to their participation and learning in online and hybrid professional development (Al-Senaidi, Lin, & Poirot, 2009; Sujo de Montes & Gonzales, 2000). Our results indicate mentoring, in some situations, might be best addressed using a hybrid approach that combines both in-person and virtual support. There is currently a lack of research on what pedagogical challenges are best addressed through hybrid mentoring and how mentors and mentees construct knowledge through hybrid mentoring.

From our study, we identified many essential elements of effective mentoring that align with current literature, including the ability to reflect (Rudney & Guillaume, 2003), receive feedback (Donnelly & McSweeney, 2011), share experience/understanding (Jaffe, Moir, Swanson, & Wheeler, 2006) and develop accountability (Rikard & Banville, 2010). Three support models provided teachers an opportunity to reflect on practice and help them to become better teachers. We also found some differences among the three environments. In the face-to-face learning environment, teachers received immediate feedback specific to teaching practice.

Additionally, because coaches observed the teaching and interactions in the classroom they are able to provide accurate and timely feedback. As stated in the previous sections, classroom observation and reflection discussion are essential components for an effective mentoring. Both components aim at providing social interaction, discourse, and collaboration opportunities for mentors and mentees. Therefore, hybrid learning environments allow for ZPDs to develop and mentors and mentees to share the intersubjectivity. Also, teachers were held accountable for their teaching because coaches were present in the classroom. An online learning environment enabled participants to communicate frequently because conversations were not limited to specific days/times. In our study, many of our participants taught in rural areas or far away from other PLC members. The online learning environment helped them connect and communicate with mentors and other teachers. In this way, teachers in remote locations could receive the support they needed without the extra expense and time associated with face-to-face mentoring. A hybrid learning environment offered a more flexible learning environment and increased collegiality. This is also an important component to promote enculturated intersubjectivity so that mentors and mentees can continue to learn, share values, and beliefs as the learning environment changes. For instance, teachers utilized the online environment for discussion and brainstorming and the face-to-face environment to develop materials or lab equipment to support their teaching. Our findings parallel work in higher education by Vaughan and Garrison (2006) which suggests that hybrids of online and face-to-face—or "blended" approaches—"create a flexible and accessible environment for faculty to engage in sustained critical reflection and discourse about their teaching practice" (p. 150).

In this economy, teacher educators and funding agencies face enormous challenges to continue providing high quality teacher professional development. The online learning environment is recognized as a cost-effective option that can reduce the cost associated with face-to-face meetings. However, based on our findings, it is evident that that online mentoring is not an equivalent replacement for face-to-face mentoring. The face-to-face learning environment has advantages for meeting the needs of teachers in a way that an online environment cannot provide. We observed our participants mixing different modes of learning environments. Hybrid learning environments integrate face-to-face and online learning environment so that they complement and support one another to fulfill the learning and teaching needs of teachers. Our study provides valuable insights into learning environment and mentoring designs for teacher educators and professional development designers by providing a better understanding of teachers' needs and the ways that different learning environments can support professional development, teacher learning, and mentoring.

REFERENCES

Al-Senaidi, S., Lin, L., & Poirot, J. (2009). Barriers to adopting technology for teaching and learning in Oman. *Computers & Education, 53*(3), 575–590.

Brown, A. L., Ash, D., Rutherford, M., Nakagawa, K., Gordon, A., & Campione, J. C. (1993). Distributed expertise in the classroom. In G. Salomon (Ed.), *Distributed cognitions* (pp. 188–228). New York, NY: Cambridge University Press.

Cheng, Y.-W., & Hanuscin, D. (2012, January). *The taxonomy of characteristics of hybrid teacher professional development* (pp. 1–22). Presentation at the annual meeting of the Association for Science Teacher Education. Clearwater Beach, FL.

Collins, S., & Clark, A. (2008). Activity frames and complexity thinking: Honouring both public and personal agendas in an emergent curriculum. *Teaching and Teacher Education, 24*, 1003–1014.

Costa, A., & Garmston, R. (2002). *Cognitive coaching: A foundation for Renaissance schools* (2nd ed.). Norwood, MA: Christopher-Gordon.

Dilworth, M. E., & Imig, D. G. (1995). Professional teacher development. *The ERIC Review, 3*(3), 5–11.

Donnelly, R., & McSweeney, F. (2011). From humble beginnings: evolving mentoring within professional development for academic staff. *Professional Development in Education, 37*(2), 259–274.

DuBois, D. L., & Karcher, M. J. (2005). Youth mentoring: Theory, research, and practice. In D. L. DuBois & M. J. Karcher (Eds.), *Handbook of youth mentoring* (pp. 2–11). Thousand Oaks, CA: Sage.

Gallimore, R., John-Steiner, V. P., & Tharp, R. G. (1992). *The developmental and psychological foundations of mentoring*. New York, NY: Institute for Urban and Minority Education, Teachers College, Columbia University.

Gauvain, M. (2001). *The social context of cognitive development.* New York, NY: Guilford.

Gentry, L. B., Denton, C. A., & Kurz, T. (2008). Technologically-based mentoring provided to teachers: A synthesis of the literature. *Journal of Technology and Teacher Education, 16*(3), 339–373.

Gutke, H. J., & Albion, P. R. (2008). Exploring the worth of online communities and e-mentoring programs for beginning teachers. In K. McFerrin, R. Weber, R. Carlsen & D. A. Willis (Eds.), *Proceedings of the 19th International Conference of the Society for Information Technology &Teacher Education* (pp. 1416–1423). Las Vegas, NV.

Jaffe, R., Moir, E., Swanson, E., & Wheeler, G. (2006). E-mentoring for student success: Online mentoring and professional development for new science teachers. In C. Dede (Ed.), *Online professional development for teachers: Emerging models and methods* (pp. 89–116). Cambridge, MA: Harvard Education Press.

Kottak, C. P. (2007). *Window on humanity: A concise introduction to anthropology.* Boston, MA: McGraw-Hill Higher Education.

Loucks-Horsley, S., Love, N., Stiles, K. E., Mundry, S., & Hewson, P. W. (2003). *Designing professional development for teachers of science and mathematics education* (2nd ed.). Thousand Oaks, CA: Corwin.

Loucks-Horsley, S., Stiles, S., & Hewson, P. (1996). Principles of effective professional development for mathematics and science education: A synthesis of standards. *NISE Brief, 1*(1).

Patton, M. Q. (2002). *Qualitative research and evaluation methods.* Thousand Oaks, CA: Sage.

Opfer, D., & Pedder, D. (2011). Conceptualizing teacher professional learning. *Review of Educational Research, 81*(3), 376–407.

Rikard, G. L., & Banville, D. (2010). Effective mentoring: Critical to the professional development of first year physical educators. *Journal of Teaching in Physical Education, 29*, 245–261.

Rudney, G. L., & Guillaume, A. M. (2003). *Maximum mentoring: An action guide for teacher trainers and cooperating teachers.* Thousand Oaks, CA: Corwin.

Schneider, R. (2008). Mentoring new mentors: Learning to mentor preservice teachers. *Journal of Science Teacher Education, 19*, 113-116.

Single, P. B., & Muller, C. B. (1999). Electronic mentoring: Issues to advance research and practice. *International Mentoring Association Annual Meeting Proceedings* (pp. 234–250). Atlanta, GA.

Strauss, A., & Corbin, J. (1990). *Basics of qualitative research: Grounded theory procedures and techniques.* Newbury Park, CA: Sage.

Sujo de Montes L. E., & Gonzales C. L. (2000). Been there, done that: Reaching teachers through distance education. *Journal of Technology and Teacher Education, 8*, 351–371.

Vaughan, N., & Garrison, D. R. (2006). How blended learning can support a faculty development community of inquiry. *Journal of Asynchronous Learning Networks, 10*(4), 139–152.

Vrasidas, C., & Zembylas, M. (2004). Online professional development lessons from the field. *Education and Training, 46*, 326–334.

Vygotsky, L. S. (1978). *Mind in society.* Cambridge, MA: Harvard University Press.

Woo, Y., & Reeves, T. (2007). Meaningful interaction in web-based learning: A social constructivist interpretation. *The Internet and Higher Education, 10*(1), 15–25.

Yin, R. K. (2009). *Case study research: Design and methods* (4th ed.). Thousand Oaks: Sage.

CHAPTER 6

EMPOWERING TEACHERS THROUGH MENTORING

**Elizabeth Doone, Karen Colucci,
Laura Von Staden, and Dominique Thompson**

ONE STORY OF BEGINNING TEACHER SUPPORT AND MENTOR EMPOWERMENT

Mentee's Story: From Distress to Success

It was not until late in my college career that I discovered that I wanted to teach students with disabilities. During my third semester of my Masters of Arts in Teaching (MAT) in Special Education, the difficulty of the coursework and projects increased exponentially. The time in our practicum increased from two full days to five half days each week. I would not have survived without the other members of my cohort and my Professional Practice Partner (PPP)/mentor. What was more intimidating was the grade level and content area: middle school math and science! I was terrified, but my mentor welcomed me, introduced me to other school staff. She encouraged me and nurtured my development by allowing me to work directly with the students to build relationships prior to teaching lessons in her classroom. By asking thoughtful questions of me after observing her

Best Practices in Mentoring for Teacher and Leader Development, pp. 93–108
Copyright © 2016 by Information Age Publishing
93

teach, my mentor increased my ability to reflect. This reflective process ensured that I understood why she did what she did, and how and why she altered plans mid-lesson. We discussed her lessons at the end of each day; these were valuable times in which she continued to probe, forcing me to process and develop my own understandings. When I noticed a behavior problem during lessons, I requested her assistance, but she assured me I could handle the situation myself. She was able to turn my lack of confidence into the development of my own behavior management system. My mentor later inquired about the linked assignments and pressed me to develop time-management structures to stay on track, offering her time and resources to ensure my success. Despite my mentor's persistence, I began to decline assistance because I was overwhelmed, and I did not know where to start. I was able to pull together lessons at the last minute, but they were not coherent and more often than not, did not go well. My mentor often had to pick up the pieces of a lesson gone awry to ensure our students did not suffer from my lack of organization and preparation. By the end of the practicum, it was clear and my mentor's/PPP's evaluations reflected that I exhibited major weaknesses in the areas of standards-based lesson planning, punctuality, dependability, organization and time management skills. As a result, and despite her hard work and our growing positive bond, my PPP was obligated to fail me.

Despite my failure, my PPP continued to work with me and like an effective teacher, she was able to analyze the program expectations and help me prioritize. She continued to have difficult conversation with me while letting me know she was confident in my development: "You are missing major skills necessary for success, but they are skills you can develop. Once you get them, you will be a phenomenal teacher, but you will need to invest extra time and effort to get there." At the time, I did not consider the additional time and effort required of my PPP. I responded, "What's the point? I suck so much at this. Look at my scores!" As an evaluator my PPP was able to pinpoint my skills and areas of needed growth, and as my mentor she encouraged me by assuring me we could work on my weaknesses. My PPP and I worked together daily on specific skills as we utilized a variety of tools to assess, promote and document my development. We videotaped weekly, utilized Danielson's (2011) Framework of Teaching Rubric and set incremental goals to scaffold my growth without discouraging me, all the while shifting the responsibility to me to monitor my own development. My mentor spent endless hours analyzing videotaped lessons and providing emotional support when I was frustrated. Had it not been for my PPP who went above and beyond to provide specific, targeted instruction based on my needs, I would not be an educator now. I would not have changed the lives I have, and I would not be the educational leader I have become.

Mentor's Story

After teaching for a few years, I was ready for the next challenge: I applied to become a Professional Practice Partner (PPP), was accepted, completed the PPP course, and was assigned my first mentee. My first mentee was very organized and really had it all together. While she was new to teaching and needed some advice and help with strategies, she was very easy to mentor. Although I did not realize it at the time, I grew from this experience, both as a teacher and a mentor, albeit to a small degree compared to the growth that has followed. Due to the university's trust in me, since then I have been assigned mentees with increasing challenges requiring me to stretch and grow even more as mentor and teacher. The mentee who probably resulted in my most rapid growth phase was a young lady who lacked the maturity, professional skills and confidence necessary to be successful. These skills included time management, organization, punctuality, and goal and priority setting. One of the hardest issues that I faced in this relationship was my desire for her to be successful, despite knowing that she did not yet possess the necessary skills. When she failed her first practicum with me, I was sure that I had failed the University and that they would never ask me to mentor again! Thankfully, this did not prove to be true, as I have continued to mentor for the university and my input is continually sought.

Throughout this experience, I received the full support of the university faculty, who were as patient with my inexperience as a mentor as they were with my mentee's, who subsequently has transformed from a struggling preprofessional educator into a phenomenal teacher who recently was awarded Teacher of the Month at her school, and who is an asset to the teaching profession. Again, I did not notice it at first, but I was slowly transforming who I was as well. Faculty guidance and support of my mentoring skills, time spent reflecting deeply, and focusing on what I expected of my mentee have all caused me to raise the expectations for myself and improve my own practice. Due to this and subsequent mentoring experiences, I have become a much more insightful mentor and teacher leader.

I began videotaping my classes in an effort to help my mentee. I disliked this strategy at first because I felt since I was the mentor, I was supposed to do things right and be the role model. I did not like seeing myself do something I felt could have been done better, while my mentee was watching. I was afraid if the university knew I wasn't "all that"—that I was modeling mistakes as well as good teaching—hat they might not want me to be a mentor, which was a role I was quickly coming to love and that was unintentionally improving my own practice and increasing my passion for both teaching and mentoring. The decision to expose my shortfalls to both my mentee and eventually the university faculty proved, much to my surprise, to be beneficial. As a result, I have dramatically improved my ability to reflect on my teaching and best practices, help other mentees, and better bridge the theory to practice gap. I am able to critically review and constantly revamp my teaching, and teach mentees how to continually improve their own practice. I feel vibrant and passionate as a teacher, not ready to burn out despite all the demands placed on today's teachers, because I am still growing due to my role as a mentor.

Mentoring is not for the weak-hearted. I have had to learn to turn over my classroom to a mentee, who does not have much experience. This is particularly stressful in this age of accountability, as I am still responsible for my students' learning and my evaluations are based on their success. I have had to learn to live through the tough times of growing a new educator from times of dissonance to times of great success. I have worked hard and put in many hours as a mentor with only very modest financial compensation, but it has been an experience I would not trade for anything. Mentoring has given me the opportunity to continue to grow and increase my passion for education. Empowering teachers to mentor the next generation of educators is one of the greatest contributions that can be made to the teaching profession; it is a win-win-win.

INTRODUCTION

Special educators, like the teacher above, have a unique role in educating students with various learning and behavioral challenges. The role requires using complex and varied skills to meet the learning needs of students and is compounded by the growing demands of newly enacted legislation. Schools typically employ a handful of Exceptional Student Education (ESE) teachers whose duties and functions range from behavior specialist to coteacher to support facilitator. Although ESE class sizes are mandated to be smaller, in reality the ESE teacher's class sizes, caseloads and additional responsibilities are extensive—from Individual Education Plan (IEP) development and monitoring, to Response to Intervention (RTI) data collection, to coteaching with multiple teachers and multiple course preparations, in addition to the typical responsibilities faced by all teachers (duties, etc.). As a result of this wide range of responsibilities, all of the accompanying paperwork required of special educators, and the challenges involved with teaching diverse and complex students with extensive needs, ESE teachers tend to burnout at a faster rate than other teachers (Billingsley, 2004a; Fore, Martin, & Bender, 2002). In large urban districts such factors can create a swinging door effect with special educators moving in and out of positions faster than new teachers can be effectively prepared (Ingersol & Kralik, 2004). Therefore, creating a system of support for retaining new

ESE teachers is as critical as ensuring teacher candidates are appropriately educated and trained (Billingsley, 2004b).

With this in mind University faculty examined the traditional triad model of teacher candidate supervision and found it to be no longer adequate and efficient in meeting the programs' needs. University faculty supervisors were assigned to supervise many students across large urban-rural districts, often with only one ESE teacher candidate at a school (due to the limited number of ESE placements at each school). Spread thin with limited time, quality mentoring suffered and became an additional task in the myriad of responsibilities for faculty working towards tenure. Fortunately, an untapped resource existed in the schools—competent teachers passionate about their profession and willing to work hard to ensure the next generation of teachers was well-prepared. Quality mentoring has well-documented support in teacher preparation and teacher retention (Billingsley 2004b; Feiman-Nemser, 2012; Ingersol & Kralik, 2004), particularity mentoring that focuses on the development of quality teaching practices (Bay & Parker-Katz, 2009).

Therefore, a teacher preparation model featuring a system of support by qualified and effective teacher mentors was developed. The model also addressed teacher retention by empowering both mentors and teacher candidates through professional development and teacher leadership opportunities. The role of the PPP, or teacher mentor, was created to tap into the expertise and willingness of the teachers to engage with the university as partners (Epanchin & Colucci, 2002). PPPs act as both the cooperating teacher and the university supervisor, mentoring and supervising teacher candidates during early field placements and the final internship. PPPs mentor and supervise within their own classrooms and are credentialed for this new role after completing a graduate course in mentoring.

Professional Practice Partner Model

Implementation of the model began with a partnership with two local school districts. Building on that partnership, the University and the districts established partnership guidelines for the new model and then identified and trained mentor teachers. A memorandum of understanding with the university and local districts gave the university input into field placement decisions and selection of PPPs and districts' opportunities to partner in mentor training. Teacher buy-in was established through the understanding that the unique PPP role created a true partnership in the professional development of teacher candidates, creating a model where they were valued and respected.

PPPs acknowledged commitment and ownership in the partnership and understood their role was valued; this led to their expression of empowerment and a reason to remain in the classroom.

> No one lets us make decisions about education. We are not used to having someone have confidence in us and our abilities. (PPP data, 2002)

> I like the trust. Our professional knowledge is valued. It makes me feel good about our teaching. (PPP data, 2002)

[Response to the Triad Model]

> The 20 minutes every two weeks is not a fair observation by the university supervisor. We see the intern every day. This is our responsibility now. (PPP data, 2002)

> I felt useless. I think sometimes my recommendations were ignored. I had concerns and if the university supervisor didn't see them, the intern passed anyway. (PPP data, 2002)

Selection of PPPs

District supervisors and principals recommended their best teachers for the PPP model. Qualifications for PPPs include a minimum of three years exemplary teaching, some mentoring experience, a desire to guide the development and nurture the growth of teacher candidates, and a principal's recommendation. One hundred and twenty five teachers were identified and trained in the first PPP course. This was thought to be a significant pool of teachers which would sustain the model. However, in choosing the best and the brightest, the PPP pool soon diminished as PPPs were promoted to positions such as behavior specialist, assistant principals, district mentors and administrators creating a need for ongoing PPP recruitment and training. Twelve years later, over 400 PPPs have been trained and the university continues to recruit and train teachers willing to take on the additional responsibilities required of a PPP.

PPP Course

To ensure the newly selected PPPs are well prepared for their role as mentor and supervisor, they are required to take a graduate course titled *Mentoring Novice Teachers* created in collaboration with the partnering districts. The course outlines PPP responsibilities, and helps them negotiate the space between being an encouraging and supportive mentor while holding high standards as an evaluator (Yusko & Feiman-Nemser, 2008). The course is comprised of five modules (see Table 6.1) and is offered free of charge and at times convenient to teachers. The unique requirements of the PPP's dual role of mentor/evaluator are clearly woven throughout the five modules.

Table 6.1.   PPP Course Modules

Module	Topic	References
1	Mentor-Mentee Relationships • developing trust and communication • identifying and understanding communication styles, conflict resolution • outlining the university program of study for both initial teacher certification programs (BS and MAT)	Hobson, Ashby, Malderez, & Tomlinson (2008)
2	Teacher Development • outlining the stages of teacher development • understanding supports to move the pre-professional educator to the next level • revealing good teachers do not automatically make good mentors	Eros (2011); Feiman-Nemser (2012); Levin (2003); Watzke (2007)
3	Issues of Diversity and Cultural Competence • holding high expectations for all educators and K–12 students • reviewing materials critically to ensure understanding of students' backgrounds in classroom and lesson development to ensure success • checking bias and assumptions to ensure fairness and equity	Cartledge & Kourea (2008); Gay & Kirkland (2003); Tatum (1992); Villegas & Lucas (2002);
4	Teacher Inquiry • reviewing the benefits and requirements of Action Research for teacher-candidates • providing resources for support and questioning strategies • developing ideas to collaborate with mentee in project	Babkie & Provost, (2004); Ponte, Ax, Beijaard, & Wubbels (2004); Ryan (2009, 2013)

(Table continues on next page)

Table 6.1. (Continued)

Module	Topic	References
5	• Development of Professional Education Goals	Danielson (1996, 2007, 2011);
	• immersing mentors in Danielson's model—begin with a review of the four Domains of Practice and a self-assessment in each	Danielson (2013)
	• developing fidelity in rating, utilizing Danielson's Framework for Teaching	
	• generating ideas to utilize the Framework for teaching with teacher-candidates to support their growth and development throughout the program of study (including ongoing goal setting based on areas of weakness)	

The purpose of the course is not to didactically convey information about mentoring, but rather to engage the PPPs in a dynamic process (case scenario discussions, video processing and analysis, and ongoing reflection) to help them build an understanding of the role of the mentor, the developmental nature of learning to teach, and how to develop a mentoring relationship that effectively bridges the gap between their level of experience/knowledge and the inexperience of teacher candidates. The course also focuses on communication skills and styles, effective ways of giving feedback, conducting conferences with interns, having difficult conversations when teacher candidates do not perform to expectations, observational skills, evaluation tools and content that facilitates cultural competence. Case studies and vignettes highlight these issues, providing real life scenarios to introduce PPPs to the variety of situations they may encounter and providing an opportunity to problem solve difficult situations.

Throughout each module of the PPP course the importance of self-reflection, making teacher thinking explicit and modeling are emphasized. Self-reflection is critical to growth and an important attribute for an effective teacher to model (Etscheidt, Curran, & Sawyer 2012; Gay & Kirkland, 2003). After learning about Danielson's (1996) *A Framework for Teaching*, PPPs complete a self-evaluation using a modified Framework for Teaching rubric which they will ultimately use to evaluate their teacher candidates (Danielson, 1996, 2007, 2011). This facilitates an understanding of the process expected of the teacher candidate, while ensuring PPPs focus on their own professional development and model a "life-long" learner philosophy (Furtado & Anderson, 2012). PPPs then utilize the same process with the teacher candidates to promote goal setting and reflection. This ongoing iterative process ultimately develops self-efficacy and empowerment when goals are achieved—developing a critically important skill contributing to teacher retention and professional growth (Hoy & Spero, 2005; Tschannen-Moran, & Hoy, 2007).

Completing the PPP course certifies the PPP to take on the dual role of university supervisor/in addition to the cooperating teacher and makes them eligible to be assigned a mentee (teacher candidate). The placement process requires input from both University faculty and teacher candidate. The teacher candidates provide input by selecting from options regarding district, grade level (elementary, middle or high school), and setting (i.e. inclusion classroom, self-contained, etc.). Teacher candidates desiring specialized placements must demonstrate competence in the area (early childhood, autism, etc.). University faculty discuss candidates' strengths and professional development learning needs and match them with the PPP most suited to meet those needs. Recognizing some students require additional support, faculty ensure that veteran PPPs are matched with those teacher candidates with the greatest developmental needs. Principals provide final approval for all suggested placements.

PPPs receive a stipend from the University for the additional responsibilities required of their dual role. This money was previously paid to university supervisors; therefore, there is no additional cost to sustain the PPP model, only a shift in student credit-hour-generated funds. While the stipend is minimal, the PPPs appreciate the validation of the legitimacy of their role and the increased recognition as a leader in the school associated with their role.

Programmatic Support for Professional Practice Partners

Due to their dual roles, a variety of supports are available for PPPs during the semesters they mentor/supervisor a teacher candidate. Monthly mentor meetings are the first support and provide the PPPs with an opportunity to remain connected with the university faculty, ask questions, submit evaluations and other required documents, as well as discuss the teacher candidate's progress. Ongoing contact with the university ensures an awareness of the university requirements, but more importantly ensures that the university requirements are relevant. Furthermore, these meetings allow PPPs to collaborate, problem-solve and discuss issues with colleagues in the field who are also mentoring. PPPs share their experiences and provide insights on ways to scaffold experiences to support their teacher candidate's growth, often generating a range of new strategies to try. PPPs also enjoy cross-district discussions comparing differences related to curriculum, policies, procedures, and teacher evaluations. Monthly meetings also provide university faculty with an insider's view on the trends, issues, and challenges facing in-service teachers in each district. Open communication and continuous dialog with PPPs and university faculty create a more cohesive program in which both sides are truly invested in the teacher candidates' growth and development.

Each semester, these meetings are hosted by a faculty member who serves as the University liaison. This faculty member works closely with the teacher candidates and has an understanding of the teacher candidates' development in the program. Beyond organizing and facilitating monthly meetings, the university liaison provides a second layer of support to the PPPs. Between monthly meetings, PPPs with concerns about their teacher candidate contact the University liaison directly. As needed, the University liaison visits schools and classrooms and together the PPP, liaison, and teacher candidate review the issue at hand. Then the team works to develop a plan that will support the teacher candidate's growth. The University liaison facilitates the development and monitoring of the growth plan while the PPP and teacher candidate provide weekly updates on the teacher candidate's progress. The University liaison continues to communicate with the PPP and the teacher candidate throughout the implementation and completion of the growth plan; ensuring the PPP and the teacher candidate have the support and resources needed. By working together to problem solve, develop action plans, and provide difficult feedback, the model helps PPPs grow as mentors and teacher leaders. The goal is to ensure PPPs are empowered and supported in their role in making decisions about a teacher candidate's development and teaching dispositions.

Sustainability of the PPP Model

Twelve years and several hundred trained mentor teachers later, the PPP program is viable and has resulted in positive outcomes for both teacher candidates, mentor teachers and the teacher preparation program. PPPs have reported during focus groups that as a result of their responsibility as the sole evaluator of their intern, they have become better teachers as they feel compelled to not only improve their practice, but also practice what they preach.

> I cannot even begin to express just how much I've grown as a result of my experiences with each and every one of my interns. If I was to pick just one example I would have to use my most recent intern, who brought to my classroom technology to monitor, mold, and track behavior over time. He also utilized a student-centered goal setting technique, which not only do I continue to use to this day, but I also incorporated into one of the trainings I present district-wide and I now teach other teachers how to use it when work-

ing within certain curricula. I so look forward to each new intern experience for the growth professionally it provides to me and the benefits it gives my students. (PPP data, 2014)

[Reflection on first mentee]

> When I was first asked to be a USF Professional Practice Partner I felt confident that I would be able to help my mentee in all phases of her transformation into an exceptional education classroom. After all, I had over 20 years of classroom experience, and I was just named the Florida Exceptional Education Teacher of the Year by the Council of Exceptional Children. Somehow in my myopic view of how I thought the relationship would be, I envisioned imparting all types of wisdom and knowledge upon my new protégé on a one-way street of knowledge disbursement. Upon my first meeting with my mentee she asked me for help ... and I quickly realized she knew far more about accessing computer programs than I did.... I then realized that our relationship would be a two-way street of sharing knowledge. And so it has continued in various aspects of exceptional student education for the past 10 years between the two of us. Accepting the challenge of being a Professional Practice Partner was one of the best decisions of the later part of my teaching career. (PPP data, 2014)

As teachers change positions and move from one school or district to another they choose to continue their roles as PPPs within the partnership. Since the partnership is with the district and the PPP (not a specific school), this creates stability and sustainability in the model. The cadre of PPPs form a learning community of dedicated mentors committed to their own professional development and the development of future teachers. Monthly meetings are essential during the semester mentoring a teacher candidate, and annual meetings sustain the community of PPPs and provide for a social and intellectual community and opportunities for professional development.

Teacher candidates provide feedback on the PPP model as they evaluate their program of study upon graduation. Exiting the program, teacher candidates ranked their field placements as one of the most important components of their teacher education program (mean of 4.6 on a 5.0 scale). The data was taken from teacher candidates' program evaluations upon exit from the program between 2005 and 2009 ($N = 89$). Teacher candidates' comments often focus on their learning gains while working with their PPP.

> My PPP was wonderful. I learned so much from her. She helped me learn to critique myself and figure out where I went wrong. (Teacher Candidate exit data, 2009)

I don't know who matched me with my PPP but it was a perfect fit. I could not have asked for a better experience! (Teacher Candidate exit data, 2009)

Teacher candidates' recognition of the value of their experience with their PPP is substantiated by the number of program graduates who express a desire to become PPPs themselves. In a typical Mentoring Novice Teacher Course, half of the PPPs selected are graduates of one of the Department of Special Education's teacher preparation programs.

Targeting Growth and Increasing Reflection

Beginning with the first field placement and in each subsequent field placements, PPPs provide feedback to teacher candidates using the modified *A Framework for Teaching* rubric. This rubric is used throughout the teacher candidate's program with increasing expectations each semester to facilitate their growth in meeting the professional standards (Danielson, 2013). The teacher candidates, together with guidance from their PPP, use the feedback from the rubric and identify specific goals to work towards every two weeks. Teacher candidates' ongoing self-evaluation of progress towards their goals, scaffolded with ongoing mentor feedback and support contributes to the teacher candidate's increased sense of self-efficacy (Hoy & Spero, 2005). Areas of success are celebrated and problem areas are addressed with next steps and are then reevaluated in another two weeks.

Monthly documentation ensures both teacher candidate and PPP remain focused on the areas of growth identified utilizing the *A Framework for Teaching* rubric (Danielson, 2013). Teachers' schedules are tight and therefore requiring tangible documentation ensures that time is spent focused on the facilitation of skill development prior to the evaluation of their teacher candidate. This proactive approach helps our teacher candidates continue to make progress in their program of study, focus on issues of concern before they become a problem, and develop critical skills in goal setting and reflection. Furthermore, the process provides PPPs an opportunity to model their own reflection and self-evaluation process.

The investment by the PPPs of their own time, efforts and resources in working outside of their classrooms with the University was contrary to what the districts expected. District officials were not sure if teachers would have time, or the willingness to commit to additional outside duties. However the PPPs expressed a strong commitment to participate, seeing value in molding colleagues. Additionally, the PPPs responded to the increased trust by taking responsibility for making decisions about their interns' future in the profession more seriously.

Capitalizing on PPP Expertise

Trust and respect have been the foundation on which relationships have been built with the PPPs. Their expertise is valued and they are viewed as partners in the incredibly challenging, yet important work of teacher preparation. PPPs expressing a desire to take on leadership roles have been invited to collaborate with the University on a number of projects. PPPs have been instrumental in providing specific feedback at a variety of levels: input on course content, program restructuring, and program improvement. Prior to resubmitting our degree programs for state continuing approval, we solicited input from PPPs on course content, course sequencing, field placement requirements, programmatic assessments, and the rubric's alignment with Exceptional Student Education Standards. The partnership between University faculty and PPPs working together to improve course content and practicum requirements provides the context for such critical feedback; this dynamic process also increases the PPPs effectiveness as mentors.

During monthly meetings with University faculty, PPPs were asked how prepared their teacher candidates were prior to the final field placement and what additional experiences would benefit the teacher candidates. PPP's ongoing practice utilizing the modified *A Framework of Teaching* rubric facilitated their expertise in identifying experiences which would build competency for the teacher candidates. Since Danielson's work was not developed specifically for ESE teachers, some indicators within the rubric were adapted to ensure the ESE teacher candidates were able to meet the highest rating on the rubric. PPPs have also helped faculty revise key projects/assessments within the program, which with their input, are better suited to meet the realities encountered in our schools. We tapped into the content-specific expertise of PPPs as we worked with them to prepare online modules that facilitate teacher candidates' learning prior to a specialized placement (early childhood or autism setting). Additionally, PPPs provided valuable input that helped ensure the programmatic performance and evaluation rubrics provided incremental progress towards best practices. Increased time mentoring in the program and the PPPs evolving relationship with the University increases their self-efficacy and empowerment, which has led to seasoned PPPs eagerly volunteering to coteach or guest lecture on specific topics of expertise within our courses. Their contextual knowledge about district policies and wealth of current resources shared with our teacher candidates augments the theory practice continuum. Working closely with the PPPs, we were able to easily update them regarding any changes in the linked course field assignments and the associated goals or expectations for teacher candidates, and they in turn understood and reciprocated the open communication by contacting us at any time with questions or to provide feedback.

An interesting outcome of the PPP model has been the gradual change over time in the PPPs' thought processes about their roles in their teacher candidates' development. For example, during focus groups PPPs stated they realize the benefit of "molding a colleague" versus training an intern. Over time teacher candidates have been hired on at the schools in which the PPPs teach; therefore, PPPs came to realize the benefits of modeling a conscientious, competent, teacher candidate who could become a colleague.

> I think it's important to pass the torch and train new teachers. I've been teaching for 30 years and I want to foster the same passion in new teachers that I still have. The passion for our work is what sustains us. (PPP data, 2001)

CONCLUSIONS

The PPP model grew out of the needs of a teacher preparation program and the surrounding school districts to better utilize shared resources to more effectively meet the needs of teacher candidates. In meeting the needs of the program, a model evolved which has proven to empower mentor teachers and strengthen the mentoring process. PPPs are more invested in their teacher candidates' growth and more knowledgeable about university practices. This has created a space for mentors to increase their level of professionalism as demonstrated by the PPP's story at the beginning of the chapter. Her ongoing evaluation of her teacher candidate has not only increased her teacher candidate's reflective processes and problem solving, but hers as well. It is no surprise that this PPP continues to engage in professional development opportunities and has been awarded a variety of leadership roles in both her school and at the district level. It is also important to note that the mentoring relationship often continues beyond the internship, particularly when the teacher candidate is hired on at the PPPs school as was the case of the PPP and the teacher candidate featured at the beginning of the chapter. Together, they find greater satisfaction in their roles as classroom teachers, inevitably impacting the collaboration retention of quality teachers in the field.

REFERENCES

Babkie, A., & Provost, M. C. (2004). Teachers as researcher. *Intervention School and Clinic, 39*(5), 260–268.

Bay, M., & Parker-Katz, M. (2009). Perspectives on induction of beginning special educators research summary, key program features, and the state of state-level policies. *Teacher Education and Special Education, 32*(17), 17–32. doi:10.1177/0888406408330871

Billingsley, B. S. (2004a). Special education teacher retention and attrition: A critical analysis of the research literature. *Journal of Special Education, 38*(1), 39–55. doi:10.1177/00224669040380010401

Billingsley, B. S. (2004b). Promoting teacher quality and retention in special education. *Journal of Learning Disabilities, 37*(3), 370–376. doi:10.1177/0022219 4040370050101

Cartledge, G., & Kourea, L. (2008). Culturally responsive classrooms for culturally diverse students with and at risk for disabilities. *Exceptional Children, 74*(3), 351–371.

Danielson, C. (1996). *Enhancing professional practice: A framework for teaching*. Alexandria VA: ASCD.

Danielson, C. (2007). *Enhancing professional practice: A framework for teaching*. Alexandria VA: ASCD. (further defined and renamed individual components)

Danielson, C. (2011). *Enhancing professional practice: A framework for teaching*. Alexandria VA: ASCD. (Response to MET provided clearer language for distinction at each level).

Danielson, C. (2013). *The framework for teaching evaluation instrument*. Alexandria VA: ASCD. (Added connection to CCSS)

Epanchin, B. C., & Colucci, K. (2002). The professional development school without walls: A partnership between a university and two school districts. *Remedial and Special Education, 23*(6), 349–358.

Etscheidt, S., Curran, C. M., & Sawyer, C. M. (2012). Promoting reflection in teacher preparation programs: A multilevel model. *Teacher Education and Special Education 35*(1), 7–26. doi:10.1177/0888406411420887

Eros, J. (2011). The career cycle and the second stage of teaching: Implications for policy and professional development. *Arts Education Policy Review, 112*, 65–70.

Feiman-Nemser, S. (2012). Beyond solo teaching. *Educational Leadership, 69*(8), 10–16.

Fore, C., Martin, C., & Bender, W. (2002). Teacher burnout in special education: The causes and the recommended solutions. *The High School Journal, 86*(1), 36–44.

Furtado, L., & Anderson, D. (2012). The reflective teacher leader: An action research model. *Journal of School Leadership, 22*, 531–568.

Gay, G., & Kirkland, K. (2003). Developing cultural critical consciousness and self-reflection in preservice teacher education. *Theory Into Practice, 42*(3), 181–187. doi:10.1207/s15430421tip4203_3

Hobson, A. J., Ashby, P., Malderez, A., & Tomlinson, P. D. (2008) Mentoring beginning teachers: What we know and what we don't. *Teaching and Teacher Education, 25*, 207–216.

Hoy, A. W., & Spero, R. B. (2005). Changes in teacher efficacy during the early years of teaching: A comparison of four measures. *Teaching and Teacher Education, 21*(6), 343–356.

Ingersol, R. M., & Kralik, J. M. (2004). The impact of mentoring on teacher retention: What the research says. *Research Review Teaching Quality* (Education Commission of the States).

Levin, B. (2003). *Case studies of teacher development: An in-depth look at how thinking about pedagogy develops over time*. Mahwah, NJ: Lerlbaum Associates.

Ponte, P., Ax, J., Beijaard, D., & Wubbels, T. (2004). Teachers' development of professional knowledge through action research and the facilitation of this by teacher educators. *Teaching and Teacher Education, 20*(6), 571–588.

Ryan, T. G. (2009). The emerging educator as leader and action researcher. *International Electronic Journal of Elementary Education, 1*(3), 202–217.

Ryan, T G. (2013). The scholarship of teaching and learning within action research: Promise and possibilities. *I.E.: Inquiry in Education, 4*(2), 1–17. Retrieved from http://digitalcommons.nl.edu/ie/vol4/iss2/3

Tatum, B. D. (1992). Talking about race, learning about racism: The application of racial identity development theory in the classroom. *Harvard Educational Review, 62*(1), 1–24.

Tschannen-Moran, M., & Hoy, A. W. (2007). The differential antecedents of self-efficacy beliefs of novice and experienced teachers. *Teaching and Teacher Education, 23*(6), 944–956. doi:10.1016/j.tate.2006.05.003

Villegas, A. M., & Lucas, T. (2002). *Educating culturally responsive teachers: A coherent approach*. Albany, NY: State University of New York Press.

Watzke, J. L. (2007). Longitudinal research on beginning teacher development: Complexity as a challenge to concerns-based stage theory. *Teaching and Teacher Education, 23*(1), 106–122.

Yusko, B., & Feiman-Nemser, S. (2008). Embracing contraries: Combining assistance and assessment in new teacher induction. *The Teachers College Record, 110*(5), 923–953.

CHAPTER 7

CROSSING BORDERS ON THE BORDER

Implementation of a Mentoring Network

Etta Kralovec and Laura Gail Lunsford

INTRODUCTION

Schools on the U.S.-Mexico border are some of the most challenging environments for teachers in the U.S. Low teacher pay, the isolation of rural life, regressive state policies in regards to English language learners and students who cross the border each day to attend school are commonplace in border schools. The lack of qualified teachers in border schools contributes to the enormous achievement gap between students in border schools and those in the rest of state (McRobbie & Villegas, 2004).

Schools struggle to find teachers; in fact, some of our partner schools now import teachers from the Philippines and India. Among these teachers, a language barrier exists to such an extent that some parents in these schools will not allow their children to be the classrooms of these teachers. In some schools, teachers commute 70 miles to teach on the border and

Best Practices in Mentoring for Teacher and Leader Development, pp. 109–124
Copyright © 2016 by Information Age Publishing

return home at night; these teachers have little connection to community life on the border.

In this chapter, we discuss the development of a unique mentor network, designed to address the specific challenges faced by rural, border communities when it comes to recruiting, preparing and retaining STEM teachers. Philosophically we framed the mentoring network around four ideas: (a) developmental networks and educative mentoring; (b) growth mindset; (c) developing strengths, including self-awareness and reflection; and (d) the importance of understanding the unique cultures along the border and revising course curriculum that addressed this uniqueness. We developed a mentoring program to achieve three goals:

1. Recruit and place STEM teachers in schools in Title 1 school districts, the federal designation of poverty level school communities.
2. Develop academic coursework leading to a master's in secondary education that is closely aligned with the needs and challenges in partner schools, with an emphasis on culturally responsive teaching techniques and focus on the uniqueness of communities.
3. Retain new teachers for three years.

This chapter contributes to the literature by highlighting innovations in developing and implementing a cross-disciplinary mentor network for new math and science teachers in high-need schools on the U.S./Mexico border in Arizona. The program design included components that have been identified as essential characteristics of good mentoring. We drew on the mentoring literature in teacher education, as well as in psychology and organizational leadership. This cross-disciplinary approach moved beyond the limitations of mentoring designs, such as a focus on one-to-one relationships, commonly found in teacher education.

CONCEPTUAL UNDERPINNINGS

Literature from teacher education, psychology and organizational leadership informed the design of the mentor network. A review of the literature on mentoring new teachers highlights three areas where research-based, program development may benefit from such an interdisciplinary approach. First, numerous studies suggest mentoring is associated with mentee and mentor benefits; however, much of this work is self-report, survey research (Hobson, Ashby, Malderez, & Tomlinson, 2009). Second, mentoring in teacher education focuses on two core activities: task assistance and emotional support. Yet, this second aspect is often left out of both research reports and widely-used mentoring standards (Marable & Raimondi,

2007; Moir & Hanson, 2008). Finally, literature on mentoring in teacher education is isolated from research on mentoring in the organizational or psychological literature, which may have relevant findings. There is remarkably little research on what comprise effective practices or content for mentoring programs and activities. Below we discuss only the literature that informed the development of our mentoring network for new teachers.

Teacher Education

The preparation of new teachers consists of two phases of mentoring: (a) during student teaching, and (b) during their early years as a new teacher. In the student teaching phase of preparation, classroom teachers, often called cooperating teachers, supervise student teachers as they learn to teach. Graham (2006), in her study of cooperating teachers, found that mentoring typically falls into two categories, "maestros" and "mentors." Maestros encouraged student teachers to mimic their expert practices; while mentors, "viewed teaching and the process of learning to teach as multidimensional and recursive" (p. 1126). Graham called for a transformative mentoring model, based on social construction of learning models, or what is called, "educative mentoring" (Norman & Feinman-Nemser, 2005). In this model, mentoring moves beyond technical and emotional support to shape novice teachers' conceptualization about the teaching and learning process.

The second phase of mentoring occurs for new teachers as they enter their first job. When new teachers enter a school, they are often assigned to a mentor, as per state/federal recommendations under NCLB (Johnson & The Project on the Next Generation of Teachers, 2004). During the years of 1990–2000, eighty percent of new teachers reported having a mentor (Blasé, 2009). Yet, these mentor relationships work only as well as the district administration's commitment to their importance and the principal's willingness to carve time out of the school day for mentors and new teachers to meet. Researchers suggest that new teachers who work in hard-to-staff content areas and low-income schools are "less likely to have even three conversations with their mentors by the spring of their first year about any of the core tasks of teaching" (Kardos & Johnson, 2010, p. 3).

Studies on teacher mentoring suggest that the mentoring relationship must go beyond technical and emotional support by demanding that mentors treat mentees as learners who critically construct and reconstruct their teaching around students' ways of knowing and learning in *specific contexts* (Blasé, 2009; Murrell, 2001). This conception of teacher mentoring highlights the importance of specific contexts in which learning takes place.

This idea of learning to teach in specific contexts had strong resonance for our Design Team. The importance of the unique border culture into which our new teachers were entering became a central focus of our work and led us to draw on a theoretical perspective not common in teacher education, Bronfenbrenner's ecological system approach that is described in the next section.

Psychology: Ecological Systems and Psychological Strengths

Our school partners were faced with multiple challenges such as poverty, poor student performance on state tests, and teacher and administrator attrition. In addition, there were a high number of English Language Learner students in our partner schools and a state ban on bilingual education, which made serving this population of students difficult. However, 40 years of focusing on problems in school reform activities have done little to ameliorate them (Rappaport & Seidman, 1986).

Much of the research on teacher mentoring focuses on the individual. However, individuals learn through interaction with others in various settings. The characteristics of the setting or "place" matter. Thus, the design and implementation of the mentor network was framed using an ecological systems perspective (Bronfenbrenner, 1979), which acknowledged the role of place. This perspective highlighted the importance of the systems that influence individuals. One-on-one interactions, for example between a mentor and mentee or between a student and a teacher, take place in a microsystem. A mesosystem consists of multiple microsystems, for example, a mentee-mentor dyad and a mentee-coach dyad. Individuals are influenced indirectly by the exosystem, which includes people with whom they do not have direct interactions but who make decisions that influence them. A school board's decision to fund a mentoring program would be an example of an exosystem's influence on mentoring. The macrosystem includes the cultural values and norms that influence all of the systems.

Some researchers redefine problems as opportunities (Sarason, 1986). We decided to work from that perspective. For example, at the micro- and mesosystem levels an emphasis on individual and community strengths might build resiliency. Community (Perkins, Hughey, & Speer, 2002) and positive psychology (Seligman & Csikszentmihalyi, 2000) researchers have suggested that building on strengths is one way to build important psychological traits like empowerment, resiliency, and optimism (Garmezy, 1991; Seligman, 2011). Further, these traits have been associated with a reduction in teacher attrition, an increase in student achievement (Masten & Coatsworth, 1998), and greater wellbeing (Seligman, 2011). Therefore, activities to assess and build psychological strength were included in the design of the mentor network. For example, we assessed optimism with the Optimism Test freely available at the University of Pennsylvania Authentic Happiness website (https://www.authentichappiness.sas.upenn.edu/). During the Mentoring Institute, we discussed what the scores meant and used role playing to teach a new cognitive framework to increase optimism when faced with challenging events (Seligman, 2011).

Student and teacher beliefs about learning have been associated with student progress (Dweck, 2008). Dweck's (2008) work suggests that beliefs about learning, called learning orientation, influence individuals' ability to persist when encountering difficulties. She refers to these beliefs as a *mindset*. A person who focuses on the outcome, for example, a grade or winning a competition, has a fixed mindset. These individuals believe their success is based on their performance. In contrast, a person who focuses on their effort, for example, learns from an experience or relishes a challenge, has a growth mindset. Consider a student who failed a math quiz. A student with a fixed mindset might say, "I'm not good at math" and cease to try to learn the material. A student with a growth mindset might say, "That was a difficult concept for me and I need to review it again." Teachers who have their own fixed or growth mindsets can influence student mindsets. Beliefs about learning are themselves learned. Our goal was to help teachers promote growth mindset among their students. This construct was built into mentoring network activities.

Organizations: Developmental Networks and Leadership Development

Organizational researchers have moved beyond focusing on one-on-one relationships to examining developmental networks. There is evidence that most mentored individuals are embedded in a network of supporters, also known as developers. For example, Lunsford (2012) found that most doctoral students reported having more than one person who provided career mentoring. These developmental networks may vary in their degree of closeness and in their number of developers (Higgins & Kram, 2001). This idea connects well with the notion of community of practice in the education literature and highlights the importance of developing a network of support for new teachers.

Leadership has been well studied by organizational researchers, but this work rarely permeates the education literature. There is an increasing emphasis for universities to develop "Teacher Leaders" (Muijs & Harris, 2003; Taylor, Yates, Meyer, & Kinsella, 2011). The work on leadership suggests increasing self-awareness is one way to develop leaders (Padilla,

2013). Activities to increase self-awareness include taking and discussing inventories on personality, communication styles and other personal tendencies. Thus, activities to increase self-awareness were included in the mentor network.

PROJECT DESIGN AND DESCRIPTION

This project was supported by Transition to Teaching (TTT) funds administered by the U.S. Department of Education. This work was completed in the first two years of a five-year grant. Over the five years of the grant we hope to prepare about 100 new science and math teachers to work in 12 partner school along the U.S./Mexico border.

At the close of the first year of grant activities, seven teachers, called TTT Fellows, were teaching in partner schools and 14 mentors and content coaches were prepared to mentor these new teachers. Course content in required multicultural and educational technology classes were significantly altered to reflect the cultural realities and technology needs of our partner schools. On the recommendation of mentors and mentees, the second-year course content in the Classroom Management and Methods of Teaching courses will extend more fully into the monthly work of the mentor network. This will provide space for mentors to engage in current thinking on "educative mentoring" (Norman & Feinman-Nemser, 2005). This work will include common planning time for mentors and mentees to develop lesson and classroom management plans.

Design of the Mentor Network

Faculty from the education and psychology departments collaborated with the mentor Design Team, which included local teachers, in the design of the mentor network. This group met monthly over nine months to brainstorm and provide guidance on the design of program elements and workshop schedules.

The team acknowledged the need to provide new teachers with in-depth knowledge of partner communities. Thus, four high schools were selected as sites for in-depth study. Undergraduates, from the local communities and under the guidance of one of the authors, collected data using multiple methods, including focus groups, eco-mapping, school data analysis, student and community stakeholder interviews and surveys, and photo documentation. This aspect of the project was important because it resulted in profiles of the schools for incoming TTT Fellows, mentors and coaches. Most of the TTT Fellows were not from the border area and the profiles helped them learn about the schools they were about to enter as teachers. These in-depth studies uncovered core elements of life in our partner communities: the importance of community and family; student motivation to learn, give back and be a part of their communities; the level of teacher motivation for professional growth; and the centrality of schools in rural communities.

From our initial examination of these four sites, we identified disconnects in the following areas: (a) in terms of student and teacher cultural backgrounds, (b) a digital divide relative to available technology and use of existing or new technology, and (c) geographical distance challenges relative to scheduling professional development programming.

Description of the Mentor Network

Mentors were selected from recommendations by school principals; content coaches from the local community college were selected upon recommendations from the dean of math and science. The selection process provided opportunities for building relationships across institutions and provided a way to inform our partners of the vision and work of the grant. At the end of the application process, 14 mentors and content coaches agreed to join the network, of which 13 completed the first year and 12 will return for year two. These mentors were provided a $3,000 yearly stipend, funded from the grant, for their work with the network.

The mentor network activities consisted of a 2-day Mentoring Institute, seven "Super Saturdays," an eMentoring community, and six teaching observations conducted by the mentors. The Mentoring Institute focused on self-awareness, including building psychological strengths, increasing resiliency and identity development in teachers (Palmer, 2007). Participants took four inventories that were used as tools to increase their self-awareness. Two inventories (available at http://www.authentichappiness.sas.upenn.edu/) were the Virtues in Action with 240 items (Seligman, 2011) and the Optimism Test with 32 items (Seligman, 2011). The Big Five Personality Test with 55 items was available at http://similarminds.com/cgi-bin/newbig5.pl. The Learning Orientation Inventory consisted of 14 items (Godshalk & Sosik, 2003) and was provided in a Word document with scoring instructions. Participants recorded their scores online in a survey and their results were aggregated and shared for discussion during the Mentoring Institute. The four inventories were free (see Table 7.1).

The Super Saturdays were six-hour workshops, intended to provide professional development opportunities around mentoring and teaching math and science. The morning session usually focused on mentoring or related psychological concepts and the afternoon sessions were focused on aspects of teaching, like developing lesson plans, and aligning curriculum with the Common Core standards. The November session was devoted to using technology in the classroom.

Table 7.1.   Inventories Used to Assess Psychological Strengths and Promote Discussion

Inventory	Psychological Strength	Activity
Virtues in Action	Resiliency	Design work day to draw on strengths
Optimism	Optimism & Resiliency	Role play handling challenging events
Big Five Personality	Self Awareness	Discussion about identity and reputation
Learning Orientation	Growth Mindset	Role play how to respond to failure.

The eMentoring community was developed in Google sites and provided materials, resources, and a discussion board. The observations were typical of teacher education programs, except the coaches, community college faculty (content experts), conducted the observations rather than the mentors. We used free-flow observations and provided content-based prompts in our monthly meetings. Mentors were asked to post on the discussion board twice a month. Prompts posted by mentors, versus program administrators, generated more participation on the discussion board. However, mentors often felt this was just one more thing on their "to-do" list, so we now do not require mentors to post monthly. This decision has increased their participation on the site.

IMPLEMENTATION AND ASSESSMENT

The network was implemented in August, 2012. We used surveys and focus groups to solicit formative assessment data throughout the year that was used to inform ongoing program redesign. In addition, the Design Team served as a sounding board for proposed changes.

FINDINGS

Super Saturday Workshops

The first workshop was in September and included a session to discuss further Dweck's notion of growth mindset. At the end of the workshop participants describe what worked well. Over half of the 22 participants ($n = 12$) answered by describing the discussion related to a growth learning orientation. Further, most ($n = 15$) respondents valued the time to work in small groups, that is, mentee, mentor and coach. A representative response was, "Getting together and beginning the work on the book Mindset—I liked to hear how to change from fixed to growth."

The second workshop, in October, included a session on the difference between hierarchal and developmental mentoring. This session was only for mentors and coaches, while the mentees met with another faculty member about their courses. There were five coaches and seven mentors in attendance. Two coaches and six mentors noted that the opportunity to discuss and to reflect on mentoring worked well. Two coaches and one mentor noted that an opportunity to review mentoring activities worked well. A representative comment was, "The mentoring aspect was useful because this is my first time mentoring and I haven't had a mentor to help me along." There was an afternoon session where the mentees, mentors, and coaches worked together on lesson planning. Most of the respondents ($n = 15$) noted that this time together worked well. A representative comment was, "I liked us evaluating our instruction and being able to compare with other groups."

During the fourth workshop, held in January, mentees presented their ideas for an action research project in their classrooms. Mentors and coaches provided feedback on the proposed projects. The evaluation of this workshop indicated that participants valued the content with an average 3.4/4 rating, and that they learned 3.54/4 (average).

The fifth workshop focused on culture and teaching. This topic was selected as a result of informal mentee feedback in the fall term suggested there might be a need to learn more about culture and teaching. We surveyed the participants before and after the workshop to assess their views on culture. In addition, we conducted a focus group on culture with mentees, mentors, and coaches (see Lunsford & Ochoa, in press, for detailed results). The surveys and focus groups indicated that most mentees wanted to know more about their students' culture but did not know how to gain this information; that mentors were aware of culture but only some used that information to enhance their teaching; and that culture was not a topic of any their mentoring conversations.

January Formative Assessment

In January participants were asked to describe how they wanted to connect with one another in an online environment and they wished to engage in the network in future years, for example, become a mentor, lurk on the site. A facilitator wrote responses on a flip chart. Four themes emerged from their comments. First, participants desired more information about their roles and the activities, including (a) "clarity" about how often they should interact, (b) a year-long calendar with key dates, and (c) earlier communication about workshop content. Second, they wanted high quality, online resources, for example, videos of "good classrooms" or examples of teachers using a growth mindset. Third, participants desired easier access and navigation to materials in the online community established in Google groups. For example, they found it challenging to navigate the "permissions" to access information and mentees found it challenging to access a separate course management system. There were few comments posted on the discussion board, which backed up this point. Fourth, mentees wanted to share information with the next cohort of mentees. The mentors and coaches wanted to attend the same Mentoring Institute again to focus more on mindset as they felt they would learn more from it after their experience mentoring new teachers.

LESSONS LEARNED

Our work uncovered five aspects of learning to teach that both have profound impacts for the further development of this Mentoring Network and for designing mentor support systems for new teachers more broadly. In addition, we believe that some of these insights and lessons point teacher education in new directions.

First, teachers want to feel competent in their mentoring skills and that participating as a member of a community of learners fostered new mentors learning how to mentor. Interestingly, not only did the mentors reflect on their desire to work with colleagues to develop their mentor skills, but mentees expressed a strong interest in mentoring incoming TTT Fellows. This desire to mentor, on the part of the mentees, illustrates how participation in a mentor network can build, among first year teachers, a sense of professionalism and desire to be part of a community of learners.

Second, the strong desire among participants for access to good recordings of classrooms highlights the desire, of even expert teachers, to have the opportunity to see how it is "done right." During one Super Saturday, the participants viewed online teaching recordings, and everyone agreed that the recordings appeared staged and didn't really "look like" their classrooms. Thus, in the coming year we hope to record classrooms of participants in our Network. The field of teacher education could benefit from a rich library of *authentic* classroom videos, capturing teaching in all its richness and messiness. Beyond the notion of "best practices," viewing recorded classroom episodes has the potential to provide mentors and new teachers rich subject matter for discussion in professional learning communities and builds the opportunity for educative mentoring.

Dweck's (2008) work spoke strongly to the members of our network. Thus, our third lesson learned is that we needed to spend more time developing a growth mindset in our mentors and new teachers. Beyond reading Dweck and revisiting her work periodically during the year, we hope to embed the idea of growth mindset into lesson plan formats used by the mentees and to include a section on demonstrations of growth mindset in the observation forms used in the classroom.

Fourth, the matter of culture remains a difficult topic. Mentors and content coaches varied in their understandings and approach to the role of culture in teaching. Fellows had taken one multicultural education class but still felt a lack in their own understanding of their students' cultures. This was particularly problematic given that only one Fellow was from the border area and most were Anglo. This "culture" gap between teachers and students is widely known and discussed in the field of teacher education. The view of Murrell and others suggest that teacher preparation *must* prepare teachers to teach in particular communities that they know well (Blasé, 2009; Levine, 2010; Murrell, 2001). This remains a challenge for us and for the field of teacher education at large.

Fifth, we identified important areas where teacher education was disconnected from what teachers need in order to be successful. We found evidence of the two worlds Norman and Feiman-Nemser (2005) discuss. The disconnect between the "culture" of the university and the culture of schools presents the greatest challenge to building mentor networks that operate across institutional boundaries. The increasing calls for embedding teacher education in school sites sounds good in theory (Levine, 2010). However, there are profound cultural differences and turf battles that these kinds of cross border and cross institutional initiatives challenge. For example, many of our partner schools had existing mentor programs, some in name only. Connecting the work of our mentor network to existing school-based mentor networks has yet to occur. Invitations to merge the work of the network and the mentor programs in partner schools went unanswered and at times outright rejected. This was due in part to an unwillingness on the part of district leadership to require existing mentors to participate. We have developed close working relations with 5 of our 11 partner school districts. Yet even with these close relations, linking existing mentor programs in schools and our mentor network is a ways off.

Further, there are degrees as to what "embeddedness" means. Many universities hold classes in public schools as a way to make their program more embedded in clinical sites, but often these classes are isolated from the daily work in schools. The degree of embeddedness that we are striving for is that advocated by Levine and others (Levine, 2010; Zeichner, 2010) who describe the importance of a close *partnership* between schools and teacher preparation programs. Developing these kinds of close partnerships and rethinking the work of preparing teachers is slow tedious work to which few of our school partners could commit. Few school leaders have embraced the idea that preparing new teachers is *part* of the work of schools and until this idea becomes part of the preparation for school leaders, building the kind of robust partnerships that embedded, clinically-based teacher education requires will be a long way off.

Teacher education programs must respond to both university requirements and state and federal teacher education mandates. Navigating these diverse requirements has long been a challenge for teacher education programs. In the case of building a robust mentor network, these mandates can become barriers. For example, coursework at the graduate level offered by the university must have faculty who have terminal degrees. Yet feedback from the mentor network indicated that much of the university coursework graduate students must take was not authentically connected to the work students were doing in school classrooms. This was first evident in the disconnect between life in classrooms and the academic course work in educational technology and cultural diversity classes. Over the course of the year, it was clear that the work of the mentor network should include the *content* of coursework in these areas as well as coursework in classroom management and teaching methods. In the coming year, the content of the monthly seminars will focus more directly on these areas but can only count as internship credits, not academic credit. University faculty are protective of "their" courses and moving academic coursework into clinical work in schools remains a distant dream. In addition, our academic courses are online and the university course management system is closed to nonstudents, so mentors could not participate in online course discussions.

There is an important place for the role of university coursework in the preparation of teachers. University classes are often the only place where students can engage in critical thinking about teaching and learning. We have found that teachers in our mentor network were great "cheerleaders" for their schools. However, as Zeichner (2010) has reported, we too found they were unwilling at times to critically look at student data and what that might mean for teaching in their schools. Thus, teachers were sometimes disconnected from the reality of student achievement in their schools.

Another disconnect was in our effort to develop an online community. The use of the eMentor Network was hindered by uneven technological resources available in the partner schools. We began with a Google group site for communications between mentors and mentees, but soon found that many schools block this site, even though many schools use Google apps.

A key goal of the mentor network was to more closely link partner school protocols and schedules with the work of the network. Typically, schools of education use their own evaluation protocols and lesson plan formats that do not align with protocols used in schools. Working across 11 school districts, all on somewhat different calendars, using different teacher evaluation tools and lesson plan formats meant that finding common ground on these important aspects of learning to teach was impossible. This was especially evident when we attempted to link the observation forms used by the mentors and content coaches with the evaluation forms used by principals in our partner schools. We found our schools partners used 10 different classroom observation forms and the teacher education program used an entirely different form. Apart from the confusion that this was causing our new teachers, who were very unclear about what they were being observed on, it demonstrates an essential problem in teacher education. Observation forms are essentially a catalog of what are considered to be good teacher characteristics. If the characteristics on observations forms that are used by universities differ from those used in schools, the gap between schools and teacher education programs cannot be bridged.

Additionally, national frameworks like Marzano and Danielson do not address fully the specific needs of bilingual students on the border (Heilig, López, & Torre, 2013). Mentors have worked to design a context-specific tool appropriate for border schools that incorporates national InTASC Model Core Teaching Standards, while strengthening the focus on instructional strategies for English Language Learners. As we use this tool for the first time, we will monitor its usefulness and appropriateness as measured by feedback from principals, mentors and fellows.

SUMMARY

The lessons we learned were grounded in our conceptual and philosophical orientation described early in the chapter (see Table 7.2). First, the mentoring program promoted self-awareness and leadership by using personality inventories to initiate the mentoring relationships between student teachers and expert teachers (Dweck, 2008; Palmer, 2013). This focus on self, a strong aspect of mentoring in fields other than teacher education, provided a new framework for a mentor network. Second, the mentor network was designed to be sustained by a robust eMentoring environment. Third, the project involved collaboration between outstanding math and science teachers from a local community college and expert teachers from middle and high schools. In the design phase, this cross-disciplinary, cross-institutional partnership seemed necessary. Research on teacher education indicates that teacher preparation needs to occur in learning communities that are clinically-based and place-specific (Cochran-Smith & Lytle, 1999; Levine, 2010). Involving clinicians in the design phase of the mentor network ensured that the program was aligned with the realities of public school partners. The inclusion of community college faculty as content coaches, to support new teacher learning, was a unique but important collaboration.

Our project suggests the importance of a cross-disciplinary approach to the development of the mentor network. In the field of teacher education, the literature on mentoring is focused primarily on details of teaching, leaving aside what many consider to be the core of learning to teach, which is the new identity development necessary to become a teacher. Broadening the Design Team to include mentoring standards from across other disciplines meant that the mentoring process began with an exploration of self-knowledge, not typical of mentoring literature in teacher education. This early focus on self set new parameters for mentor/mentee discussions. Further, in the just completed third year of the program we successfully transitioned to having local teachers, one of whom is Hispanic, run the Mentoring Institute. These changes help to sustain the work and recognize the importance of place and context in mentoring teachers. Our mentors and coaches helped to revise our online community to make it more user friendly and we continue to embed the coursework in our eNetwork site. The partnerships with the different school districts continues to take attention and work but we hope that those relationships will also become easier as the program continues to produce successful STEM teachers for our region.

ACKNOWLEDGMENT

We thank Inger McGee for her useful comments on a draft and mentor network participants for their input and feedback.

REFERENCES

Blasé, J. (2009). The role of mentors of preservice and inservice teachers. In *International handbook of research on teachers and teaching* (pp. 171–181). New York, NY: Springer.

Bronfenbrenner, U. (1979). *The ecology of human behavior.* Cambridge, MA: Harvard University Press.

Cochran-Smith, M., & Lytle, S. L. (1999). Relationship of knowledge and practice: Teacher learning in communities. *Review of Research in Education, 24,* 249–306. Washington, DC: American Educational Research Association.

Dweck, C. (2008). *Mindset: The new psychology of success.* New York: Ballentine Books.

Garmezy, N. (1991). Resiliency and vulnerability to adverse developmental outcomes associated with poverty. *American Behavioral Scientist, 34,* 416.

Godshalk, V. M., & Sosik, J. J. (2003). Aiming for career success: The role of learning goal orientation in mentoring relationships. *Journal of Vocational Behavior, 63*(3), 417–437.

Graham, B. (2006). Conditions for successful field experiences: Perceptions of cooperating teachers. *Teaching and Teacher Education, 22*(8), 1118–1129.

Heilig, J., López, F., & Torre, D. (2013). Examining ELL teacher quality, educational policy, and evolving political contexts in Latina/o growth states. In C. M. Wilson & S. D. Horsford (Eds.), *Advancing equity and achievement in diverse U.S. schools.* New York, NY: Routledge.

Higgins, M. C., & Kram, K. E. (2001). Reconceptualizing mentoring at work: A developmental network perspective. *Academy of Management Review, 26*(2), 264–288.

Hobson, A. J., Ashby, P. Malderez, A., & Tomlinson, P. D. (2009). Mentoring beginning teachers: What we know and what we don't. *Teaching and Teacher Education, 25,* 207–216.

Johnson, S. M., & The Project on The Next Generation of Teachers. (2004) *Finders and keepers: Helping new teachers survive and thrive in schools.* San Francisco, CA: Jossey-Bass.

Kardos, S. M., & Johnson, S. M. (2010). New teachers' experiences of mentoring: The good, the bad, and the inequity. *Journal of Educational Change, 11*(1), 23-44.

Levine, M. (2010). *Developing principals for clinically-based teacher education.* Commissioned by the National Council for the Accreditation of Teacher Education for the Blue Ribbon Panel on Clinical Preparation and Partnerships for Improved Student Learning.

Lunsford, L. G. (2012). Doctoral advising or mentoring: Effects on student outcomes. *Mentoring & Tutoring: Partnership in Learning, 20*(2), 251–270.

Lunsford, L. G., & Ochoa, E. (in press). Culture and mentoring: Teacher preparation in the U.S.–Mexico borderland. In L. Searby & S. Brondyk (Eds.), *Best practices in mentoring for K–12 teacher and leader development* (Volume 4). Perspectives in Mentoring Series. Information Age Publishing: Charlotte, NC.

Marable, M. A., & Raimondi, S. L. (2007). Teachers' perceptions of what was most (and least) supportive during their first year of teaching. *Mentoring & Tutoring: Partnerships in Learning, 15*(1), 25–37.

Masten, A. S., & Coatsworth, J. D. (1998). The development of competence in favorable and unfavorable environments: Lessons from research on successful children. *American Psychologist, 53*(2), 205.

McRobbie, J., & Villegas, M. (2004*). La Fronters: Challenges and opportunities for improving education along the U.S.–Mexico border.* San Francisco: WestEd.

Moir, E., & Hanson, S. (2008). A learning community for teacher induction. In A. Samaras, A. R. Freese, C. Kosnik, & C. Beck (Eds.), *Learning communities in practice* (pp. 155–163). New York, NY: Springer Science.

Muijs, D., & Harris, A. (2003). Teacher leadership—Improvement through empowerment? An overview of the literature. *Educational Management Administration & Leadership, 31*(4), 437–448.

Murrell, P. C. (2001). *The community teacher: A new framework for effective urban teaching.* New York, NY: Teachers College Press.

Norman, P. J., & Feiman-Nemser, S. (2005). Mind activity in teaching and mentoring. *Teaching and Teacher Education, 21*(6), 679–697.

Padilla, A. (2013). *Leadership: Leaders, followers, environments.* Hoboken, NJ: Wiley & Sons.

Palmer, P. (1997). The heart of a teacher. *Change Magazine, 29*(6), 14–21.

Perkins, D. D., Hughey, J., & Speer, P. W. (2002). Community psychology perspectives on social capital theory and community development practice. *Community Development, 33*(1), 33–52.

Rappaport, J., & Seidman, E. (1986). Framing the issues. In E. Seidman & J. Rappaport (Eds.), *Redefining social problems* (pp. 1–8). New York, NY: Plenum Press.

Sarason, S. (1986). Chapter 2, The nature of social problem solving in action. In J. Rappaport, & E. Seidman (Eds.), *Redefining social problems* (pp. 9–28). New York, NY: Plenum Press.

Seligman, M. E. (2011). *Learned optimism: How to change your mind and your life.* Random House LLC.

Seligman, M. E., & Csikszentmihalyi, M. (2000). Positive psychology: An introduction. *American Psychologist, 55*(1), 5–11.

Taylor, M., Yates, A., Meyer, L. H., & Kinsella, P. (2011). Teacher professional leadership in support of teacher professional development. *Teaching and Teacher Education, 27*(1), 85–94.

Zeichner, K (2010). Rethinking the connections between campus courses and field experiences in college and university-based teacher education. *Journal of Teacher Education, 61*(1–2), 89–99.

CHAPTER 8

BUILDING INDUCTION CAPACITY

Collaboration, Formative Assessment, and Systems Thinking

Lara H. Hebert and Elizabeth A. Wilkins

INTRODUCTION

School induction programs are most effective when they are designed to provide support so that beginning teachers can learn to navigate the complexities and demands of teaching (Feiman-Nemser, 2012; Strong, 2009). Designing induction in this way aligns with Gold's (1996) definition of induction as a *comprehensive program of support* that provides both instructional and psychological support, and "embraces the principle of "totality of experience." This principle recognizes that beginning teachers are affected by the impact of all elements in their environment" (p. 589). Other researchers have extended this same idea and contend that school context exerts great influence on beginning teachers' success (e.g., supportive school leadership, good collegial relationships, adequate supplies

Best Practices in Mentoring for Teacher and Leader Development, pp. 125–149
Copyright © 2016 by Information Age Publishing

and materials, opportunities for planning and learning, and a reasonable workload) (Flores, 2010; Wechsler, Caspary, Humphrey, & Matsko, 2010). Unfortunately, these approaches to induction programming are different from what beginning teachers traditionally receive. Instead, support is often piecemeal and inconsistent.

As districts and schools work to identify the best ways to support their beginning teachers, we believe there needs to be a move toward more broad-based, systemic support aimed at strengthening school wide instructional practices and student achievement. That is, coordinating services can benefit beginning teachers more than when they only receive isolated support from their school or district. This approach to induction and mentoring supports people at all levels, from induction leaders to beginning teachers. In order for these collaborative structures to be successful, though, there has to be a shared vision for the work that is clearly communicated to, and even defined by, all involved. Participants at each level must understand their role and work together to create supportive environments both within individual schools/districts and across support networks (e.g., regional service agencies, consortium). This also entails coordinating with other teacher learning initiatives—more at a systems level. With that goal in mind, greater emphasis is on professional development as well as support by and for all stakeholders (Feiman-Nemser, 2012). Fullan (2009) refers to this as "coherence making"—the alignment of all initiatives toward a common purpose. In order to move toward induction support and mentoring in this way, change is needed along with understanding the inherent challenges in doing so.

This chapter will draw from three different studies conducted by the authors to examine school mentoring and induction programs when collaboration, systems thinking, and policymaking are taken into consideration. These studies give voice to the perspectives of beginning teachers, mentors, administrators, and regional service agency leaders working within complex school contexts in varied geographic settings. First, the background context for how and why Illinois took a more collaborative, systemic approach with regard to induction and mentoring is provided. Next, each study is briefly described followed by a synthesis of the findings. Finally, the lens of capacity-building practices and structures is used to illustrate how induction programs are typically out-of-synch with practices that ultimately lead to strong and sustainable learning environments for beginning teachers.

Background

Our research and experience with induction and mentoring programming stems from a shared history of involvement with the Illinois New

Teacher Collaborative (INTC). It is through this state-wide, collaborative partnership of concerned stakeholders that we have seen the benefits and challenges of coordinating a network of services and resources to support beginning teachers, rather than programming based on a single school, district, or regional service agency.

In 2004, the creation of the INTC demonstrated a paradigm shift in how programming and support could occur (Brady et al., 2011; Wilkins & Clift, 2006). A major impetus for the shift was caused by state-wide educational stakeholders feeling that beginning teachers' needs were not being consistently well served. The collaborative was also formed at a time when federal funding sources were no longer available, and there was no identifiable, dependable source of funds on which districts could rely. The situation in Illinois was similar to many states experiencing budget restrictions coupled with attrition in schools that are traditionally difficult to staff with high quality teachers. Across the 850+ school districts in Illinois there were districts and buildings in which educators were willing and able to provide new teachers with some form of support, but not all districts had sufficient funding to do so. Also, there was no coordination across efforts, no systematic way to provide coordination and advice, and no guarantee that resources of any type would be available.

Given this need and lack of coordination, the INTC was created as a grass-roots effort to develop a network of services to support induction and mentoring programs from across the state. The partnership included representatives from stakeholder groups such as the state board of education, teachers unions, principals association, regional offices of education, superintendents, induction coordinators, mentors, beginning teachers, and universities. Since its inception, the INTC has accomplished the following: (a) an annual state-wide conference focused on induction/mentoring; (b) a web presence; (c) regional support personnel and initiatives; (d) a summer beginning-teacher conference; (e) an established working and positive relationship with the State Board of Education; (f) state policy which resulted in induction standards and a continuum to assess quality of programming; and (g) ongoing research about induction/mentoring focused on the various stakeholder groups and geographic settings (urban, suburban, and rural).

THREE EMPIRICAL STUDIES

During our decade-long relationship with the INTC, we purposely studied the influence of a more systemic approach to induction and mentoring. In addition to multiple descriptive studies that came out of INTC's internal research initiatives, we, the authors, also coordinated three individual studies within this context. What follows is a brief introduction to these three studies with Table 8.1 containing specifics about each study's design and outcomes, followed by a brief synthesis of each study's findings. The evidence revealed implications related to collaboration and systems thinking.

Table 8.1. Research Design, Research Questions, Methods, and Major Findings Per Study

	EdCentral RSA Study	Rural Study	Funded Program Study
Design	Case Study	Mixed Method	Mixed Method
Research Questions	1. In what ways do participants' perspectives of, and experiences with, the Regional Service Agency's (RSA) initiatives differ by role (coordinator, district superintendent, principal, mentor, and beginning teacher)? 2. How are participants' experiences within this induction program impacted by levels of economic and human capital available in the districts and at the RSA? 3. How does the RSA's regional work align with individual district, school, and teacher needs?	1. What induction supports do rural school beginning teachers receive? 2. What induction supports do rural school administrators make available to beginning teachers? 3. What do rural school beginning teachers and administrators value as support strategies? 4. What kind of mentoring support do rural school teachers receive?	1. What kind of mentoring do beginning teachers receive in state-supported ISBE induction programs? 2. What kinds of supports are provided to beginning teachers other than mentoring in state-supported ISBE induction programs? 3. How do beginning teachers describe teacher professional community/ school context in state-supported ISBE induction programs? 3. How do beginning teachers describe teacher professional community/ school context in state-supported ISBE induction programs?

(Table continues on next page)

Table 8.1.   (Continued)

	EdCentral RSA Study	Rural Study	Funded Program Study
Design	Case Study	Mixed Method	Mixed Method
Research Questions			4. What are the requirements for mentor selection, training, and accountability in state-supported ISBE induction programs?
Population	Regional Offices of Education ($n = 3$) School Districts ($n = 9$)	Regional Offices of Education ($n = 6$) School Districts ($n = 86$)	State-supported Illinois State Board of Education (ISBE) induction programs ($n = 39$)
Participants	Administrators ($n = 5$) Mentors ($n = 67$) Beginning Teachers ($n = 26$) Induction Program Coordinators ($n = 2$)	Administrators ($n = 131$) Beginning Teachers ($n = 297$)	Beginning Teachers ($n = 1,973$) Mentors ($n = 1,323$)
Methods	Surveys Interviews Observations	Surveys Interviews	Survey
Data Analysis	Descriptive Open, Axial, Selective Coding	Descriptive and Nonparametric Open, Axial, Selective Coding	Descriptive and Regression Open, Axial, Selective Coding
Major Findings	• The RSA provided mentor training and beginning teacher professional development for multiple districts.	• The most common induction support provided in rural settings was "regular communication with the administrator." Frequent administrator interactions with their beginning teachers was viewed as a form of informal mentoring.	• Beginning teachers desired more professional development focused on teaching in diverse classrooms and working with English Language Learners.

(Table continues on next page)

Table 8.1.   (Continued)

	EdCentral RSA Study	Rural Study	Funded Program Study
Design	*Case Study*	*Mixed Method*	*Mixed Method*
Major Findings	• Administrators viewed the RSA role and the use of technology as means to providing beginning teachers with a peer network. However, they were limited in their understanding about the RSA's induction coordinator and efforts to use technology to overcome barriers of time and limited financial and human capital • Administrators played a critical role in implementing support strategies at the district level. • Beginning teachers reported wanting more direct curricular assistance because those needs were often not met through the district-assigned mentor.	• Administrators needed to be more aware of and provide more opportunity for mentors and beginning teachers to demonstrate lessons, analyze student work, conduct classroom observations, and attend workshops together (i.e., activities least experienced but with high potential for improving instructional practice). • Beginning teachers valued the time provided for joint planning with colleagues, however that type of collaboration was not highly valued by administrators. • Lifelines to professional and personal relationships benefited the beginning teachers (e.g., a mentor, fellow teacher, friend, administrator, family member, professor, or staff member).	• Greater attention needed to be given to when mentors are provided initial training, how long that training takes place, and how often ongoing mentor training occurs throughout the school year. • Effective professional learning occurred best through interaction and in collaboration with peers. • Criteria needed to be reexamined with regard to mentor/mentee selection, location, match based on grade level/content area. •There were infrequent meetings between some mentor and beginning teacher pairs that resulted in "less-than-expected-contact time" as well as the inability to complete 60 total hours of contact time per school year (a state requirement).

(Table continues on next page)

Table 8.1.   (Continued)

	EdCentral RSA Study	Rural Study	Funded Program Study
Design	Case Study	Mixed Method	Mixed Method
Major Findings	• Beginning teachers did not understand that distance mentoring involved having a mentor to assist with curricular needs, rather they viewed distance mentoring as unnecessary since they already had an onsite mentor.	• Beginning teachers wanted to advocate for their own needs, and nurture their ability to become part of, or work toward the creation of, a community of collaborative learners.	• Induction coordinators need to probe to find out why orientation programs do not meet the perceived needs of half of the new teachers indicating a need to redesign.

OVERVIEW OF STUDIES

EdCentral Regional Service Agency (RSA) Study. This yearlong case study drew from observations, interviews, and surveys to better understand the process of change as a regional induction program introduced virtual supports as a means of supplementing the face-to-face components already provided for beginning teachers (Hebert, 2012). Robin was the focal participant in this study. She coordinated the region-wide induction activities that served nine school districts across 14 rural counties. EdCentral's induction activities supplemented the mentoring and other supports that were provided at the district level. While the district provided a trained mentor for each new teacher, the region provided mentor training and monthly Just-in-Time workshops for the beginning teachers. These Just-in-Time sessions had always been face-to-face, but Robin wanted to offer virtual opportunities using web conferencing software during the winter months so that the weather would not interfere with their ability to meet. In addition, she wanted to offer beginning teachers a chance to have a content-matched mentor from a different district if the small school was unable to establish this level of a mentor-match. Skype would be used to allow this content mentor to observe and meet with the beginning teacher from a different district.

Throughout the year, Robin struggled to maintain participation in the program's initiatives. Despite this, interviews and survey responses indicated strong support from administrators, mentors, and beginning teachers for EdCentral's professional development work, as well as for the intended use of technology. The findings from this study illustrated a set of four important elements that influenced EdCentral's ability to meet the needs of those being served: shared purpose, relationships & communication, and resource allocation.

Participants' held differing views of the program's purpose depending on the person's role in the program. Where administrators expected cross-district networking, the coordinator expected increased pedagogical and content-pedagogical knowledge.

Relationships and communication proved to be critical issues influencing the successes and the challenges experienced by participants in EdCentral's induction program. District administrators and district mentors reported being unaware of Robin's attempts to implement a distance mentoring program through the use of Skype. The few who were aware of this project often had misconceptions of the intended purpose and of the procedural logistics. In addition, Robin's lack of network connections to district administrators and mentors presented challenges in recruiting participants for EdCentral's induction initiatives.

Access to resources was the final element of influence. Limited fiscal resources meant unmet professional learning needs for the participants, and this included unmet needs for the beginning teachers, the mentors, and for Robin, the program's coordinator. EdCentral lost its funding from the state's grant during the year of this study. As a result, Robin's time on this project was significantly decreased. While trying to provide more support via technology for the new teachers in the region, she also found herself in a steep learning curve, particularly with the process of integrating technology tools she was unfamiliar with prior to this initiative and coordination of a project that spanned multiple school districts.

Rural Study, This statewide study focused on beginning teachers and building administrators from 86 unit school districts (Wilkins, 2011). Data from online surveys and interviews revealed that rather than limited induction supports being received, an abundance of support was provided but was valued differently, based on each element's perceived usefulness. The most common supports provided were (a) regular communication with the administrator, (b) a special orientation at the beginning of the school year, (c) general professional development, not just for beginning teacher, and (d) working with an assigned mentor.

Dichotomous differences existed in what beginning teachers and administrators reported concerning supports received. For example, with regard to "constructive feedback based on nonevaluative classroom observations," only 40% of beginning teachers reported receiving this support whereas 73% of administrators said this support was received. Also, the "opportunity to observe other teachers" was reported by only 36% of beginning teachers, while administrators stated this occurred 66% of the time. The beginning teachers also found "common planning time with colleagues" to be highly valued; however, it was not highly ranked by the administrators. In contrast, the administrators placed a higher value on "working with an assigned mentor," "observing other teachers," and "taking part in informal meetings of groups of beginning teachers for peer support."

Two qualitative themes emerged not previously found in induction studies related to supports: *relationships are key* and *getting involved is critical*. Whether professional or personal, lifelines to relationships benefited the beginning teachers (e.g., a mentor, fellow teacher, friend, administrator, family member, professor, or staff member could be a person they relied on for the bulk of their support). Beginning teachers also felt they needed to advocate for their own needs, and nurture their own ability to become part of, or work toward the creation of, a community of learners.

Funded Programs Study Beginning. Teachers and mentors from 39 state-funded induction programs from varied settings (i.e., urban, suburban, and rural) as well as configurations (e.g., community unit districts; single school districts; and consortiums, partnerships through regional offices of education and universities) were the focus of this study (Wilkins, Holt, Nelson, Quinzio-Zafran, & Wells, 2012). The survey data revealed that nearly all mentors (96%) received professional development to prepare for their role and responsibilities. Of those, only 67% received training before they met their beginning teacher. Even less (58%) received ongoing professional development throughout the school year to support their mentee. Limited requirements were used to hold mentors accountable (e.g., logging of mentoring hours (49%) and summaries of mentoring meetings (36%).

The most common mentoring activity included discussing instructional issues and problems followed by talking about the strengths and/or needs of specific students. Most beginning teachers never had the opportunity to see their mentors demonstrate lessons, observe their mentor's teaching, jointly plan lessons, analyze student work, or attend a workshop together. This suggests a lack of mentor/mentee activities with high potential for improving instructional practice.

Of the 71% of beginning teachers who attended an orientation at the start of the school year, only half reported this support to be moderately or extremely valuable. They found a more valued support to be a professional network that occurred in their respective buildings due to collaborative school environments. This organic professional network provided camaraderie as well as a forum for the beginning teachers to share instructional ideas, voice successes, and share fears. Over 80% of the beginning teachers worked in a school where they could seek and share advice about instructional issues. In addition, over half of the beginning teachers reported opportunities to work together to develop materials and lessons as well as discuss assessment data—growth caused by collaboration. The mentors also saw development in their own practice because of their role/responsibilities (i.e., increase in their own professional growth and desire to support their mentees by having more time to plan, collaborate, and observe).

DISCUSSION OF CROSS-STUDY PATTERNS

Careful examination of these findings reveals implications related to the need for broad-based collaboration and systems thinking. Experts in the field of educational change tell us that efforts to affect instructional change or organizational change will fail without sufficient time and without collaboration and partnerships across all stakeholders (Fullan, 2007, 2009; Hargreaves, 1994). In a comprehensive review of literature around effective induction and school cultures, Flores (2010) concluded, "Support programs for new teachers need to be embedded and nurtured within contexts comprising supportive, collaborative, and learning-oriented school cultures (p. 52). These structures, we believe, are as relevant to affecting the instructional practices of beginning teachers, as they are to the process of designing and implementing an impactful induction program. When looking across our three studies, we find evidence of induction program practices that are out-of-synch with practices that ultimately build capacity for strong and sustainable learning environments in schools. We discuss these patterns using the National Center for Literacy Education's (NCLE) Framework for Building Capacity (Nelson, Hill, Palmisano, Hebert, & Roth, 2012), comprised of six domains that build the collective capacity necessary for lasting change (Table 8.2).

Table 2.2.   Domains of the Framework for Building Capacity

Domain	Description
Deprivatizing Practice	Participants make their tacit knowledge visible to others.
Creating Collaborative Culture	In an environment that balances safety and rigor, individuals trust and respect one another and engage in hard conversations about strengthening professional practices.
Maintaining an Inquiry Stance	Participants engage in an iterative process of questioning, acting, assessing, and reflecting around problems or questions of practice.
Using Evidence Effectively	Participants use various forms of data to inform the inquiry cycle and professional practice.
Enacting Shared Agreements	Participants share a vision, and hold one another accountable for taking action in alignment with shared beliefs.
Supporting Collaboration Systemically	System leaders demonstrate support of the above practices by engaging in collaboration alongside staff and providing the resources necessary for effective implementation.

In the sections that follow, we use the lens of these research-based, capacity-building practices and structures to highlight emerging patterns that cross these three studies. The data tell a story of why it is important to pay attention to relationship and organizational structures when going about the business of supporting beginning teachers. By looking across the three studies, we noticed issues and experiences that were present for each level of induction experience—beginning teacher, mentor, or induction program coordinators.

Deprivatizing Practice and Collaborative Cultures

Tacit knowledge of professional practice becomes more visible when it is openly shared with others, whether this occurs through conversation, observation, or presentation. As with Lave and Wenger's (1991) apprenticeship model of sociocultural learning within a community of practice (CoP), observation and interaction with others leads to new knowledge. For example, doctors deprivatize their practices when they participate in medical rounds, sharing patient cases with a small group of peers for feedback regarding diagnosis and treatment decisions. In teacher preparation programs, field placements along with feedback based on observation are used to discuss and reflect on pedagogical decision making and delivery often with the cooperating teacher, university supervisor, and peers (Gall & Acheson, 2011). However, for inservice teachers, observation and feedback is typically tied to evaluation processes rather than professional development. In addition, making practices more visible through observation and the sharing of stories requires access to safe and trusting environments that are made available.

Safety and trust are key components of a collaborative culture. School climate factors such as these have been shown to have an impact on the retention of new teachers (Johnson & Kardos, 2008). An external evaluation of the funded induction programs during the first full year of implementation revealed school context was a significant predictor of teacher growth, self-efficacy, and retention (Wechsler et al., 2010).

While typically measured at the school level, Wechsler, et al. (2010) argued that microcultures within different grade levels and departments are likely just as relevant to decisions about staying or leaving. Ingersoll (2006) also found that collaborative cultures played important roles in teacher retention where the beginning teachers with multiple support networks exhibited significantly higher rates of retention than those without.

Beginning teachers. Evidence across Illinois induction studies reveal instances where the domains of Deprivatizing Practice and Collaborative Culture were clearly present, as well as instances where they were prominently absent.

On a Wednesday evening, after a full day in the classroom and for some, a drive of 30 minutes to an hour, 21 first year teachers from across EdCentral's six rural counties gathered for their September Just-in-Time session titled "Classroom Management and Parent Interactions." The region's induction program coordinator, Robin, invited the teachers to share their initial experiences with the parents of their students, first with a partner and then with the large group. One pair of young beginning teachers who had grown up in suburban, middle-class settings, discussed their surprise during fall open house to see dads arriving in stained, white t-shirts, and a mom who was clearly intoxicated. Another young teacher shared her challenge of trying to connect with parents who did not have working phones or e-mail. In a post-session reflection, Robin wondered aloud whether these teachers would have felt comfortable discussing these issues with the staff in their home-school settings, or if the cross-district environment of the Just-in-Time sessions provided a safer place for them to discuss sensitive issues openly.

The Funded Programs study indicated that over 80% of the participating new teachers worked in a school where they could seek and share advice about instructional issues. A key component of a collaborative culture is the ability to experiment with practice and to discuss questions openly without fear of repercussions. Opportunities to share and discuss their experiences with one another repeatedly received the highest satisfaction ratings on EdCentral's session feedback forms. Beginning teachers were most engaged during small group and paired activities, and written comments often indicated a preference for interaction. The beginning teachers needed opportunities to hear that they were not alone in their struggles, and they appreciated opportunities where they could share their experiences.

The Funded Program study and the Rural study also found that this professional network was a valued support. In the Funded Program study, time to interact with other teachers was the most frequently experienced support for beginning teachers in addition to having a mentor, and this support was considered to be moderately to extremely valuable by 80% of them. The program leaders reported increased camaraderie among beginning teachers who used these forums to share instructional ideas, voice successes, and share fears.

Unfortunately, less than a quarter of the beginning teachers in Illinois' most rural areas have the opportunity to participate in conversations like the one that occurred at EdCentral. The survey of beginning teachers in rural contexts indicated that only 24% of the participants were provided with workshops specifically designed for beginning teachers and even fewer (21%) took part in informal meetings with other beginning teachers for peer support. Even among the programs that received supplemental funds from the state, only 27% of participating beginning teachers reported having access to workshops or seminars specifically for beginning teachers. Less than half (41%) of the funded program beginning teachers reported having opportunities to observe their mentor's instructional practices. Even fewer rural school beginning teachers (36%) were provided opportunities to observe other teachers in practice.

Despite the limited access to formal networking opportunities, 239 beginning teacher respondents to the Rural study's survey indicated that relationships were key to helping them be successful, whether that person was a mentor, colleague, friend, family, supervisor, or a professor. In the EdCentral RSA study, new teachers in smaller districts often described a system of support that extended beyond the induction program and compensated for the lack of a mentor who shared the same content-area of expertise. Mike, an elementary school PE teacher, was connected to other PE teachers who had ties to the district and that he met through his role as a high school coach. Similarly, a fifth grade teacher in a rural K–12 school described meeting and swapping contact information with the teacher he was replacing.

Mentors. In the EdCentral study, mentors also described drawing from their own relationships and professional networks to better serve their mentees, in addition to describing an interest in having opportunities to troubleshoot the challenges of mentoring with one another. A mentor from a small, rural high school described challenges of being a science teacher and trying to mentor a novice driver's education teacher. The mentor felt that the best service he provided to his mentee was to introduce him to a retiree who had formerly been the driver's education teacher.

Opportunities for mentors to observe and share their practices with one another were impacted by resource availability. For example, of the funded programs, 58% of mentors reported having access to ongoing opportunities for mentors to discuss their practices with one another. This stands in stark contrast to only 21% of unfunded programs that were able to provide monthly opportunities for mentors to meet (Sikma, 2012).

Program Leaders. Relationships are important for administrators and program coordinators just as for beginning teachers and mentors. In EdCentral's attempts to implement a distance mentoring option that would connect content-like teachers across district boundaries, the initiative did not make it beyond its initial pilot phase. Despite having a volunteer beginning teacher who wanted to be mentored via Skype, Robin was unable to locate a mentor with a content-area match. She did not know the district staff well enough to determine who might meet the qualifications. Instead, she worked in isolation with only an occasional opportunity to discuss her work with her supervisor and colleague. Robin also struggled to recruit participation in her online sessions for district mentors. She found that because two other staff members in the RSA were the primary facilitators of mentor training sessions and other regional workshops, many mentors and administrators did not recognize Robin's connection to their induction work.

Collaborative connections, though, made a difference within individual induction programs and schools, as well as across programs. For example, as part of INTC's regional support for induction programs, Professional Learning and Networking (PLaN) sessions were offered each semester for the leadership of the state's grant-funded induction programs along with occasional web conferences. Robin described how these opportunities to learn with and from other program leaders inspired her to try new things. Additionally, in a paper presented at the American Educational Research Association's annual meeting, INTC researchers noted that many of the funded program leaders "reported that learning from one another, across programs, enabled continuous improvement. The networking allowed people to share strategies, tools, and concerns" (Clift et al., 2010, p. 5). These discussions were examples of program leaders deprivatizing their practices by discussing the ongoing process of strengthening their induction programs. Looking across three years of annual reports, the researchers noted evidence of these programs becoming more coherent, with increasing clarity of individual program expectations and increasing differentiation of professional development, for both beginning teachers and mentors. INTC attributed this evidence of growth, at least in part, to the opportunities INTC provided for program leaders to network and to share their progress with one another.

The importance of reducing isolation and increasing collaboration stretches beyond its impact on the educators involved. Leana and Pil (2006) conducted a series of empirical studies using value-added methods of measuring student achievement gains, and found that the frequency and strength of knowledge-sharing interactions with other educators was a stronger predictor of student achievement gains than an individual teacher's knowledge and experience. They found that teachers with lower levels of experience and knowledge performed on par with average teachers in the same building when they were well connected to other educators (Leana, 2011). Given findings related to the important role of professional community, the National Commission on Teaching and America's Future argues that an increased focus on building collaborative environments is vital for strengthening beginning teacher development and retention (Fulton, Yoon, & Lee, 2005).

Inquiry Stance and Using Evidence

When professional learning is job embedded, relevant, ongoing, and collaborative, the impacts on instruction and on student learning are greatest (Desimone, 2009). Also, as these professional learning qualities become a regular part of the school context, the domains of "inquiry" and "use of evidence" are strengthened. These two domains are difficult to untangle since use of evidence is a vital component of the inquiry process. Inquiry is the cycle of defining a key question, developing and acting on a plan to address that question, and collecting evidence along the way to inform the question. The outcome is typically a new question, and the cycle continues. This model for professional learning honors the expertise of those closest to the work, recognizing them as best able to define their own learning needs and outcomes. A formative assessment cycle or professional growth plans fall neatly into both domains.

Beginning teachers. When done well, the formative assessment process or professional growth plans provide opportunities for mentors and beginning teachers to jointly establish standards-based goals for strengthening instruction. They develop plans for achieving the goals, and then gather and analyze evidence to inform next steps (Gless, 2004). INTC researchers found funded programs to be much more likely to require these types of processes for beginning teachers (83%) than did unfunded programs (43%) (Sikma, 2012). The Funded Programs study also found that over time, the percentage of mentor/mentee pairs who discuss assessment data together had increased by 9%.

Mentors. Developmental theorists describe expected differences between experts and novices to be the quantity of skills that become automated over time and with experience (Berliner, 1986; Livingston & Borko, 1989). It takes time before a novice teacher begins to easily supplement, augment, or rewrite lessons to fit the needs of individual students. A similar learning curve applies to the practice of being a mentor and facilitating professional learning. For the mentors within the EdCentral RSA districts, nearly all of them had received initial training but very few participated in ongoing professional learning relative to strengthening their mentoring skills. In one district, a lead mentor was given the opportunity to repeat the initial training as a refresher course prior to taking on a greater leadership role in the district's program. This mentor described how incredibly beneficial that opportunity was for her. She described how her experiences of putting mentoring into practice brought a new lens to what she was learning, and she was able to simultaneously be a voice of experience for those who were taking the training for the first time. For herself, she was able to focus more intentionally on the areas of mentoring that she wanted to strengthen. The Funded Programs study also noted limitations in the level of ongoing, job-embedded support for mentors that occurred after the initial training. While 96% of mentors attended initial mentor training sessions, only 58% received ongoing support.

Program leaders. Rarely do we consider the inquiry process, or development of a professional growth plan as being important for induction coordinator development. When looking across the years of state funding for induction, INTC staff noticed increasing quantity and sophistication in the use of evidence to inform induction practices (Clift et al., 2010). In the Funded Programs study, programmatic collection of evidence, such as Log of mentoring hours and Summaries of mentoring meetings had increased by 14% and 8% respectively.

However, making use of the data collected is also a learning curve that requires attention in the development of program leaders. Just as teachers need time to practice using student data to make instructional decisions, the same is true of program leaders.

> Robin took her part-time position as coordinator of EdCentral's induction program after five years of retirement. The training she received for this position was the same as that provided to the mentors in the region. While she had experience with new teacher support while working with a Professional Development School (PDS) in the region, coordinating within a regional context was new. Her Just-in-Time sessions followed designated themes according to the time-of-year as designated by the training she had received from well-known trainers in the state. This predesignation of topics was grounded in research regarding the needs of beginning teachers (Breaux & Wong, 2003; Veenman, 1984). In addition, Robin reduced the amount of time spent in peer-to-peer conversation because end-of-year feedback from the previous had indicated dissatisfaction with the collaboration time. However, feedback forms collected after each Just-in-Time workshop during the year of this study revealed that EdCentral's new teachers rated opportunities for sharing with their peers as most favored. Yet, Robin did not make use of this feedback to inform how time would be spent in subsequent sessions.

Robin hypothesized that decreasing attendance at EdCentral sessions was due to lack of compensation, but available evidence indicated a mismatch between what was provided and what was of interest to the beginning teachers. Survey results from the nationally sampled 2003-2004 Schools and Staffing Survey Follow-up Teacher Questionnaire indicated a stronger preference among teachers for content-related learning opportunities than other topics (Darling-Hammond, Wei, Andree, Richardson, & Orphanos, 2009), and interviews with EdCentral participants indicated that this was an unmet need of the beginning teachers, especially those with mentors from other grades or disciplines. While Robin was using year-end-data to inform decisions about the following year, she had not taken this skill to the next level of using formative assessments throughout the year to inform daily decisions of program leadership. This is part of the learning curve that ongoing inquiry can address. Remembering, also, Robin's isolation in these practices, one has to wonder how her own learning curve might have been impacted if she had had someone to share program leadership with. Across the three years where state funding was available for induction grants in Illinois, annual interview and survey data indicated that programs with collaborative leadership tended to develop more rapidly and exhibit stronger induction practices such as formal mentor selection processes and use of evidence to inform program changes (Clift et. al., 2010).

Shared Agreements and Systemic Support

Whereas all four of the previous domains focused on the practices of participants and leaders within induction programs, these final two domains look across roles and beyond the boundaries of the induction program to assess the system's supports that are necessary for the effective professional learning outcomes that are the foundation of the Capacity Building Framework. These two domains ask us to consider the alignment of beliefs and goals among the induction program participants, as well as among those outside of the program whose decisions and policies impact the ability to enact shared visions. Change theorists argue that deep and sustained change occurs best when all stakeholders are working toward a common purpose, and that decision making at all levels of the system are aimed toward enacting that shared purpose—specifically that of student learning (Fullan, 2009; Kotter & Cohen, 2002). Similarly, effective induction programs are grounded in a shared vision of effective teaching and learning, and program decisions are enacted with this vision at the core (Wood & Stanulis, 2010). The Enacting Shared Agreements domain encompasses ideas such as sharing a common instructional framework or a common goal, but even more important is that participants hold one another accountable for acting on this shared purpose. Student learning standards, teaching standards, and even induction program standards fall squarely in the realm of shared visions, but only if these are used to inform decisions and actions. As Fullan (2009) describes, alignment of purpose has little impact on change if decision-making about resource allocation does not reflect a commitment to these shared purposes. Below, we consider patterns evident in the Illinois studies that are relevant to these domains both within the induction program and to the context in which the induction programs were situated.

Internal alignment and structures. Lack of alignment and shared agreements was evident in the Rural study when looking across the perspectives of study participants. Where common planning time with colleagues ranked in the top five of beginning teachers' most valued supports, administrators did not list it as valuable at all. In contrast, the administrators ranked working with an assigned mentor, observing other teachers, and taking part in informal meetings of groups of beginning teachers for peer support as more valuable than the beginning teachers did. Similar differences were evident in the EdCentral program.

> EdCentral's induction coordinator, Robin, focused her attentions on two primary purposes. Her first objective was to provide participating new teachers with instruction in general pedagogy and professional practices, such as classroom management, parent communication, and instructional strategies, all of which fell squarely within the Illinois Professional Teaching Standards. However, only a few administrators in the participating districts expressed appreciation to EdCentral for covering the just-in-time topics of classroom management and parent engagement. The most prominent reason provided by district leaders for their new teachers to participate in the EdCentral programming was for the purpose of interacting with other beginning teachers from across the region, a practice that Robin was doing less of than in the previous year. Robin's secondary objective was to provide distance mentoring opportunities for new teachers whose district supports did not provide for content area or grade level needs. This second objective aligned well with the Illinois Induction Program Standards in the area of effective mentor selection, which is typically a challenging standard for small, rural schools to meet. Robin expressed frustration over insufficient time and compensation for learning about and planning for use of the technology in this new way. In addition, the majority of administrators reported being unaware of Robin's efforts to provide distance mentoring. While official programmatic documentation from participating districts described EdCentral's Just-in-Time sessions as a component of their induction programs, there was no clear expectation from district administrators or regional leaders for the new teachers to attend. Attendance at EdCentral's Just-in-Time sessions steadily declined throughout the year, with 21 beginning teachers attending in September to just two beginning teachers attending in January.

While program leaders at the district and regional levels described their belief in the importance of induction, their views about important components did not align with one another. The rural study illustrated an additional example of misaligned understandings between administrators and their beginning teachers. Administrators (78%) reported that they assigned a mentor to each beginning teacher, whereas only 59% of the beginning teachers reported being provided with one. This difference is most likely attributed to a lack of shared vision about the "formality" of the mentoring component (i.e., buddy program vs. formal mentor assignment).

The Funded Programs study also illustrated the misalignment between beliefs about effective induction practices and resource allocation. A large percentage of new teachers reported rarely having opportunities to observe other teachers or to collaborate with colleagues. Mentors also describe challenges related to resources. Time was the most often mentioned barrier to becoming a successful mentor. One mentor wrote, "When you teach in a full-time position and then have to plan for your own classroom and meet with the others, it does become overwhelming." In order for induction to make a difference in teacher effectiveness, retention, or student achievement, mentors and new teachers need dedicated time allocated for discussions about instructional practice (Ingersoll & Strong, 2011; Strong, 2009).

INTC studies of state-funded programs have documented unique challenges associated with accountability and implementation when coordinating across multiple districts (Clift et al., 2010). Program leaders serving multiple districts described challenges associated with lack of administrator involvement and the inability to require attendance, feeling that their hands were tied when it came to the accountability of mentor and beginning teacher participation (Roegge et al., 2009). Both the Rural study and EdCentral's case study indicated that administrators might be more involved in induction than represented in these studies. Both beginning teachers and administrators in the Rural study reported that regular communication with the building administrator is the most prominent support available for beginning teachers, and it was ranked most valuable by both the beginning teachers (91%) and administrators (96%). In addition, many principals in the EdCentral region reported direct involvement in the district-level mentoring of new teachers. Many coordinated the district's mentoring program. However, these principals were not connected directly to EdCentral's induction work. EdCentral leaders expressed frustration about limited administrator involvement, but these rural studies suggested that a larger issue might have been limited communication and lack of shared understandings about induction practices between district leaders and the consortia leaders.

External alignment and structures. As we have noted in the sections above, state-funded and previously funded induction programs in Illinois exhibit higher proportions of ongoing learning opportunities for mentors, more formal requirements for interaction time and observations of mentee, and a greater use of formative assessment processes and data use than in programs that have not been part of the funded programs cohorts (Sikma, 2012). As the grant's rules changed and funding decreased, the largest proportions of programs choosing to not apply for renewed state funds were the newest programs to the cohort and the multidistrict programs that often served in rural settings. The new rules placed obligations on these programs that they could not effectively meet. The one-size-fits-all requirements for induction left some programs unable to participate, and inequitably impacted the new teachers being served in these contexts.

> EdCentral made the hard decision to not reapply for continued funding for their regional induction program because new state rules connected to the grant became more restrictive, specifying where the funds could be spent and how mentoring was to be structured. Stipend funds were no longer

available for beginning teachers who attended the Just-in-Time sessions and assistance to the districts for mentor stipends also disappeared. EdCentral staff felt that without the money, they had no means to hold new teachers, mentors, or administrators accountable for participation. Economic capital affected decisions about time allocation. One principal commented about how it seemed that EdCentral was unable to plan ahead due to the state's funding uncertainties. To the surprise of the EdCentral's leaders, all but one district continued providing their beginning teachers with mentor support. However, barely more than a quarter of the mentors participating in this study reported having release time to meet with their beginning teachers. Instead, their interactions occurred before or after school, during lunch, or during planning time.

The policy context plays a strong role in systemic supports that impact the effectiveness of induction implementation. Fullan (2009) lists "tri-level development" as one of eight key forces behind effective change, and this includes programmatic decisions related to the development of teachers as they transition into the classroom. This means alignment of goals and decisions across three tiers of the organizations simultaneously: the school, the district, and the state. The rural studies discussed in this chapter, however, call for simultaneous attention to a fourth level. The regional service agency is often responsible for meeting professional learning needs for the rural schools and districts in the region including induction supports and services, and this is often true in states with larger, rural populations.

RECOMMENDATIONS

Based on our decade-long experience observing and studying the benefits and challenges of coordinating a network of services and resources to support beginning teachers, we know that broad-based collaboration and systems thinking are possible, but doing so is complex. We close by offering the following recommendations divided by various stakeholders related to policy, practice, and research to better support new teachers.

Policymakers and System Leaders

- **Know the process of educational change, especially when services and resources are networked through large-scale collaboration.** Although policymakers want proof that induction programs impact new teachers, especially in the area of student achievement, they need to be reminded that initiatives in the early stages of development are too unstable to provide reliable data. Change takes time (Fullan, 2009).

• **Allocate economic and human capital based on a comprehensive, broad-based, systemic approach to professional learning**. Given the complexities and demands of teaching, all teachers, not just new teachers, need financial support to survive and thrive in the classroom. In taking this approach with policymakers/funding agencies, emphasis is on professional learning for all stakeholders involved.

• **Provide opportunities for induction leaders to collaborate and evaluate.** State and regional organizations need to provide opportunities for induction leaders to collaborate and to formatively assess their programs' impact and implementation. Similar to the outreach provided by the INTC, opportunities need to be provided for leaders from across multiple induction programs to learn with and from one another. Isolation and communication issues can be greatly reduced when induction programs are led by a representative committee rather than an individual.

Induction Program Leaders and Professional Developers

• **Continue to educate administrators about their role and responsibilities.** Administrators play a more critical role than they realize in understanding, supporting, and helping deliver induction and mentoring programs. They are in the best position to impact the school context and to establish an environment that supports a systemic and comprehensive program of ongoing professional learning.

• **Integrate technology as a robust form of support, but with sufficient resources to support leaders and participants through the learning curve.** Internet-based technology provides a means for establishing extended professional networks and expanded professional learning opportunities. New teachers and those who support them need consistent access to up-to-date technology; but even more importantly, sufficient time and resources are needed for effective implementation.

• **Understand that professional learning occurs best through interaction and in collaboration with peers.** Professional learning entails creating, valuing, and sustaining a community of collaboration. Professional learning opportunities such as these require considerations of time and resources (e.g., joint planning with colleagues, peer observations, opportunities for curricular assistance). Also, remember that the program's mentors are learners, too, and need ongoing collaborative learning opportunities as well.

- **Address disconnected views that stakeholders hold about induction and mentoring by bringing everyone together, face-to-face, to develop a shared vision.** Disconnected views are often the result of faulty communication. In order to effectively coordinate a network of services and resources to support beginning teachers, all stakeholders need to coordinate decision-making about policy and resource allocation in alignment with shared purpose.

- **Apply an evidence-based, inquiry stance to program leadership.** Establish a routine practice of asking the important questions that will lead to induction program improvement and leadership improvement. Devise a plan for addressing these questions. Most importantly, use evidence to determine the questions of greatest importance, and use evidence to assess the impact of new strategies as they are implemented.

Mentors and Beginning Teachers

- **Seek a network of others.** Do not wait for the induction program leadership to provide a learning community. Seek other teachers and mentors to be thought partners and costrategists. Such a network provides opportunities for discourse about both challenges and successes related to teaching and mentoring practices.

- **Apply an evidence-based, inquiry stance to the practice of teaching and learning.** Establish a formal plan for strengthening practices of teaching and learning. If the induction program and school system does not include this in their programming, advocate to get it started or take the initiative to start this on your own. Use evidence to define the most important questions or issues of practice, devise a plan for tackling these issues, and use evidence to test the impact of the things you try.

Researchers

- **Gain a better understanding of the impact of context on induction and mentoring.** The majority of past research has focused on induction program effectiveness and initiatives in mostly urban and suburban schools or districts. Future studies are needed that focus specifically on capacity building practices that cross multiple districts, the program structure most often implemented in rural contexts. More data is needed to better understand induction/mentoring networks that are successful and those that fail to thrive.

- **Continue to examine induction/mentoring challenges and benefits associated with collaborative structures and systems thinking.** In order to build induction program capacity using this broad-based approach, more empirical studies are needed. In particular, attention should be given to the stakeholders: beginning teachers, mentors, administrators, and regional service agency leaders working within complex school contexts in varied geographic settings. The lens of capacity-building practices and structures could then be used to illustrate if or how induction programs are out-of-synch with practices that ultimately lead to strong and sustainable learning environments for beginning teachers.

More than anything else, we need to begin building bridges between the many silos that exist in education. No longer can we be content to allow induction and mentoring to function separately from other school improvement initiatives. Individual teachers should no longer have to wrestle with instructional dilemmas alone, but should be able to do so in collaboration with a safe yet enriching circle of peers. And let us not forget the need for shared and collaborative learning opportunities for mentors and for induction program leaders. Programs across the tiers of reform should work more closely to align their initiatives and to consider the impact of decisions on all stakeholders, whether they are from rural, urban, or suburban settings, high income or low.

REFERENCES

Berliner, D. C. (1986). In pursuit of the expert pedagogue. *Educational Researcher, 15*(7), 5–13. doi:10.3102/0013189X015007007

Brady, P., Hebert, L., Barnish, M. E., Kohmstedt, J., Welsh, H., & Clift. R. T. (2011). Induction new teachers in Illinois: Challenges and response. *Action in Teacher Education, 33*(4), 329–342.

Breaux, A. L., & Wong, H. K. (2003). *New teacher induction: How to train, support, and retain new teachers.* Mountain View, CA: Authors.

Clift, R. T., Hebert, L., Brady, P., Barnish, M. E., Kohmstedt, K., & Johnson, N. (2010, May). New teacher program implementation in a time of uncertainty. In S. J. Odell (Chair), *Methods for assessing the impact of teacher induction programs: possibilities and limitations.* Symposium conducted at the meeting of the American Educational Research Association, Denver, Colorado.

Darling-Hammond, L., Wei, R., Andree, A., Richardson, N., & Orphanos, S. (2009). *Professional learning in the learning profession: A status report on teacher development in the United States and abroad.* Retrieved from the Learning Forward website: http://www.learningforward.org/docs/pdf/nsdcstudy2009.pdf

Desimone, L. M. (2009). Improving impact studies of teachers' professional development: Toward better conceptualizations and measures. *Educational Researcher, 38*(3), 181–199. doi:10.3102/0013189X08331140

Feiman-Nemser, S. (2012). Beyond solo teaching. *Educational Leadership, 69*(8), 10–16.

Flores, M. A. (2010). School cultures and organizations and teacher induction. In J. Wang, S. J. O'Dell, & R. T. Clift (Eds.), *Past, present, and future research on teacher induction: An Anthology for researchers, policy makers, and practitioners* (pp. 45–56), Lanham, MD: Rowman & Littlefield Education.

Fullan, M. (2007). *The new meaning of educational change* (4th ed.). New York, NY: Teachers College Press.

Fullan, M. (Ed.). (2009). *The challenge of change: Start school improvement now.* Thousand Oaks, CA: Corwin.

Fulton, K., Yoon, I., & Lee, C. (2005). *Induction into learning communities.* Retrieved from the National Commission on Teaching and America's Future website: http://nctaf.org/wp-content/uploads/2012/01/NCTAF_Induction_Paper_2005.pdf

Gall, M., & Acheson, K. (2011). *Clinical supervision and teacher development: Preservice and inservice applications* (6th ed). New York, NY: John Wiley & Sons.

Gless, J. (Fall 2004). The role of formative assessment in induction. *Reflections, 7*(2), 2–3, 15.

Gold, Y. (1996). Beginning teacher support: Attrition, mentoring, and induction. In J. Sikula, T. J. Buttery, & E. Guyton (Eds.), *Handbook of research on teacher education* (2nd ed., pp. 548–594). New York, NY: Macmillan.

Hargreaves, A. (1994). *Changing teachers, changing time: Teacher's work and culture.* London, England: Cassell.

Hebert, L. (2012). *Challenges of communication and participation in supporting new teachers using technology across six rural counties* (Doctoral dissertation). Retrieved from Illinois Digital Environment for Access to Learning and Scholarship. http://hdl.handle.net/2142/30979

Ingersoll, R. M. (2006). *Does teacher induction matter?* Presentation given at the Illinois New Teacher Collaborative Conference, Springfield, IL.

Ingersoll, R. M., & Strong, M. (2011). The impact on induction and mentoring programs for beginning teachers: A critical review of the research, *Review of Educational Research, 81*(2), 201–233.

Johnson, S. M., & Kardos, S. M. (2008). The next generation of teachers: Who enters, who stays, and why. In M. Cochran-Smith, S. Feiman-Nemser, & D. J. McIntyre (Eds.), *Handbook of research on teacher education* (3rd ed., pp. 445–467). New York, NY: Routledge.

Kotter, J. P., & Cohen, D. S. (2002). *The heart of change: real-life stories of how people change their organizations.* Boston, MA: Harvard Business School Press.

Lave, J., & Wenger, E. (1991). *Situated learning: Legitimate peripheral participation.* Cambridge, England: Cambridge University Press.

Leana, C. R. (2011). The missing link in school reform. *Stanford Social Innovation Review, 9*(4), 30–35. Retrieved from http://www.ssireview.org/issue/fall_2011

Leana, C., & Pil, F. (2006). Social capital and organizational performance: Evidence from urban public schools. *Organization Science, 17*, 1–14. doi:10.1287/orsc.1060.0191

Livingston, C., & Borko, H. (1989). Expert-novice differences in teaching: A cognitive analysis and implications for teacher education. *Journal of Teacher Education, 40*(4), 36–42. doi:10.1177/002248718904000407

Nelson, C., Hill, R., Palmisano, M., Hebert, L., & Roth, S. (2012). *Framework for capacity building: Conditions and practices that support effective collaboration and impact student learning.* Urbana, IL: National Center for Literacy Education/National Council of Teachers of English. Retrieved from http://www.literacyinlearningexchange.org/sites/default/files/capacitybuildingframework_0.pdf

Roegge, C., Barnish, M. E., Brady, P., Hebert, L., Kohmstedt, J., Murphy-Lucas, C., & Welsh, H. (2009, November). State-funded induction and mentoring programs in Illinois report. Retrieved from Illinois New Teacher Collaborative website: http://intc.education.illinois.edu/resource/rod/state-funded-induction-and-mentoringprograms-illinois-report-november-2009

Sikma, L. (Fall, 2012). *INTC Report on Previously Funded Programs.* Retrieved from http://intc.education.illinois.edu/resource/rod/intc-report-previously-funded-programs-fall-2012

Strong, M. (2009). *Effective teacher induction and mentoring: Assessing the evidence.* New York, NY: Teachers College Press.

Veenman, S. (1984). Perceived problems of beginning teachers. *Review of Educational Research, 54*(2), 143–178.

Wechsler, M. E., Caspary, K., Humphrey, D. C., & Matsko, K. K. (2010). *Examining the effects of new teacher induction.* Menlo Park, CA: SRI International

Wilkins, E. (2011). *A mixed method examination of beginning teacher induction and mentoring programs in rural schools.* Paper presented at the 2011 Mid-western Educational Research Association, St. Louis, MO.

Wilkins, E., & Clift, R. (2006). Building a network of support for new teachers. *Action in Teacher Education, 28*(4), 25–35.

Wilkins, E. A., Holt, J., Nelson, C., Quinzio-Zafran, A., & Wells, C. (2012). *State-funded Illinois induction and mentoring programs: 2011 survey research results.* Retrieved from http://intc.education.illinois.edu/sites/default/files/State-Funded%20Illinois%20Induction%20and%20Mentoring%20Programs%202011%20Results%20FINAL.pdf

Wood, A. L. & Stanulis, R. (2010). Components of 1997-2008 teacher induction programs: Reflections on comprehensive induction programs. In J. Wang, S. J. O'Dell, & R. T. Clift (Eds.), *Past, present, and future research on teacher induction: An Anthology for researchers, policy makers, and practitioners* (pp. 135–149), Lanham, MD: Rowman & Littlefield Education.

CHAPTER 9

PROMISING PRACTICES FOR DEVELOPING TEACHER LEADERS IN HIGH SCHOOLS

The Principal's Role

**Tricia Browne-Ferrigno,
Amanda Perry Ellis, and Matthew Douglas Thompson**

Leadership of contemporary K–12 schools has become too complex for a single person to accomplish alone (Leithwood & Louis, 2012; Mangin & Stoelinga, 2010). Rather, it requires relationships and interdependence among individuals within a school and its local community who work together to improve educator practice and enhance student learning (Green, 2010; The Wallace Foundation, 2012). Literature about shared leadership and organizational learning in schools places significant emphasis on contributions by teachers and others (Angelle & Schmid, 2007; Collinson & Cook, 2007) who share with the principal "responsibility and mutual accountability toward a common goal or goals" (Arnold, 2004, p. 5).

Best Practices in Mentoring for Teacher and Leader Development, pp. 151–171
Copyright © 2016 by Information Age Publishing

Collective leadership, conceptualized as "a form of distributed influence and control" (Leithwood & Mascall, 2008, p. 532), has the potential to transform school structures by changing roles, responsibilities, and relationships through community building (DuFour & Marzano, 2011; McBeth, 2008; Spillane, 2006). Such change, however, can be integrated effectively into school cultures only where ownership of the initiative is widely dispersed and human concerns are addressed (Demarest, 2010; Fullan, 1993; Lambert, 2003). Successful change integration requires teachers to assume leadership responsibilities and work with their principals, peers, and other community members to achieve shared goals (Birky, Shelton, & Headley, 2006; Boyer, 1995; Moller & Pankake, 2006). Unfortunately, the organizational structures of American high schools (e.g., hierarchal leadership, academic departments) often limit opportunities for interdisciplinary collaboration among teachers, which in turn also impacts student learning and engagement in school activities (Cohen, 2001; Goodlad, 1984; Sizer & Sizer, 1999).

This chapter presents key findings that emerged from evaluation of a funded project to develop broad-based leadership teams within high-need rural schools that needed to improve their performance and increase student achievement. The project's theory of action was reconceptualization of instructional leadership as a collective responsibility accomplished by a high-performing team focused on addressing student learning issues (Bellamy, Fulmer, Murphy, & Muth, 2007; Chance & Segura, 2009; Cotton, 2003). Although the overarching goal was to assist the high schools in meeting their improvement goals, evaluation of its impact revealed two unanticipated, but important findings—development of teacher leaders and principals' new awareness of their role in facilitating teacher leadership (Katzenmeyer & Moller, 2009; Mullen, Gordon, Greenlee, & Anderson, 2002; Mullen & Lick, 1999). This chapter thus begins with an overview of the project design, participants, and other relevant information about the context. Key findings are presented through commentary provided by teachers and principals in the four participating high schools at the project's conclusion. It closes with a discussion about unanticipated outcomes and promising practices for developing teacher leaders.

PROJECT DESIGN AND PARTICIPANTS, EVALUATION METHODOLOGY, CHALLENGES

To achieve the project goal, broad-based leadership teams representing diverse stakeholder groups were used to overcome stumbling blocks to successful innovation in high schools (Cohen, 2001; Giancola & Hutchison, 2005; Huffman & Hipp, 2003). Each team identified an authentic issue related to student learning, developed and implemented an action plan to address the issue, and assessed initial implementation impact through action research.

Participating High Schools

The one-year project was partially funded by the U.S. Department of Education Improving Teacher Quality State Grants Program, which required at least one school district to meet U.S. poverty rates for classification as a high-need local education agency. Districts paid portions of project expenses (e.g., personnel travel, supplies, refreshments), and a partnering community college provided no-cost use of meeting rooms throughout the implementation year. The four high schools were selected by district administrators because leadership development was a priority in their improvement plans at the time project was proposed. Table 9.1 displays school data; all district and school names are pseudonyms.

Table 9.1.   Participating High School Data

School (District)	Grades Served	Approximate Enrollment	Poverty Rate[a]	Average Experience[b] (Range)[c]	Teacher Education[d]
Evans High School (Bristol)	9–12	700	62%	13.5 years (10–17 years)	51%
Foster High School (Tazwell)	9–12	600	58%	12 years (5–10 years)	60%
Jackson High School (Wayne)	9–12	1,000	66%	12 years (5–19 years)	50%
Pickens High School (Bristol)	7–12	450	70%	10 years (1–22 years)	27%

[a] Percent of students eligible for federal free or reduced price lunch program

[b] Average years teaching experience among all faculty at school

[c] Range of teaching experience among faculty serving on project-created leadership team

[d] Percent of teaching staff holding graduate degree

Evans High School (EHS) was established in 2000 when three smaller schools were merged into the largest and newest facility in Bristol County. When EHS failed over consecutive years to achieve its performance goal, the Kentucky Department of Education (KDE) sent an accountability audit team to identify conditions contributing to student underachievement. The audit team reported that (a) leadership beliefs and practices were not consistently demonstrated, (b) school personnel rarely used self-reflection or evaluation to assess student learning, (c) few teachers or staff members participated in decision making, and (d) professional development was sporadic and not job embedded. Although not enthusiastic about the invitation, the veteran principal who opened EHS agreed to form a leadership team and participate in the project.

Foster High School (FHS) is located in the largest town of Tazwell County and has the largest student body among the district's four high schools. Prior to participating in the project, FHS had made little progress toward its state-assigned accountability goals, evidenced by significant percentages of students achieving below acceptable levels in all core content areas. Transforming the learning environment (i.e., developing a school culture conducive to learning and teaching, communicating with all stakeholder groups) and improving school efficiency (i.e., developing a focused vision, setting higher performance expectations, restructuring organization) were priority needs identified by the district review team in their report. The principal and staff agreed to participate because the project addressed the school's priority needs.

Jackson High School (JHS), the only high school in Wayne County, had the largest student body of the four participating high schools. One year after the veteran principal assumed leadership, JHS achieved its state accountability goal for the first time. The principal and staff enthusiastically accepted the invitation to participate in the project because they hoped to learn ways to reduce barriers to learning by (a) improving the organization of resources, (b) providing self-improvement and career information to students, and (c) providing more support to students in all subpopulations.

Pickens (PHS) was the smallest, most isolated high school in Bristol County and among those participating in the project. Shortly after a new principal assumed leadership in 1998, the school board announced that PHS would be closed if it did not improve its overall performance. Because the high school serves as the community center for the small town of Pickens and surrounding region, the principal and school staff worked diligently to improve academic programs and extracurricular experiences for students. PHS surpassed its accountability goal in 2002 and narrowly missed achieving its 2014 goal in 2006, earning it recognition as a *pacesetter school* by the Kentucky Department of Education. The invitation to participate was accepted immediately because teachers wanted to collaborate in refining, implementing, and evaluating their new plan to improve student learning through increased engagement in school activities.

Project Participants

Each participating high school assembled a 10-member team composed of the principal, at least three teachers, a guidance counselor, one student leader from Grade 10 and one from Grade 11, a parent or community representative, and two additional individuals determined by the principal. The method used for member selection was left to the discretion of each principal, but those selected had to commit to participating in all project activities throughout a calendar year. Superintendents approved the final team composition to assure principals, teachers, and students were released from work or class to participate in school-based monthly team meetings with the project mentor. The leadership teams' work had to complement or support initiatives established by the state-mandated, school-based governance councils at each site. Thus, it was recommended that at least one council member (i.e., an elected teacher or parent representative) be included on the leadership team.

A professor of educational leadership studies at the University of Kentucky (lead author of this chapter) served as the principal investigator and grant administrator. A retired superintendent, who collaborated with the professor on another grant-funded leadership development project, served as the project coordinator and on-site coach and mentor. District administrators collaborated on project design, and paid consultants provided training support during project events.

Leadership Development Activities

Learning activities were delivered over a calendar year through a coordinated mix of three 3-day summer institutes and a fall weekend workshop, team-conducted action research in each school, and monthly on-site coaching and mentoring. The curricular framework incorporated recommendations for shared leadership and school improvement, many specifically for high schools. Assigned readings and seminar activities focused on changing perceptions about student failure (Blankstein, 2004; National Association of Secondary School Principals, 2004), creating school cultures supportive of continuous improvement (Sullivan & Glanz, 2006; Zmuda, Kuklis, & Kline, 2004), conducting schoolwide action research (Sagor, 2004), making data-informed decisions (Bernhardt, 2002), and sharing accountability for student learning (Blank, Hale, & Harkavy, 2005; Institute for Educational Leadership, 2000). Team-building efforts included identifying individual strengths (Buckingham, 2005), developing trusting relationships (Kochanek, 2005), and reflecting on the impact of individual behaviors and group actions (York-Barr, Sommers, Ghere, & Montie, 2001).

School Improvement Projects

Each team determined its unique school improvement initiative based on a review of school and student performance data. Table 9.2 displays key elements of the four projects designed, implemented, and assessed through action research during the project.

Table 9.2.   Leadership Team School Improvement Projects

High School	Project Key Elements
Evans High School	• Launch a school-within-a-school "Evans U" freshman academy
	• Ensure freshmen experience successful transition into high school by focusing on attendance and literacy
Foster High School	• Improve school culture by creating professional learning communities focused on student success
	• Align instructional program by creating curriculum maps, units of studies, standard course syllabi, and unified lessons for all subjects
	• Improve communication throughout the school and broader community
Jackson High School	• Improve schoolwide attendance and enhance student ownership of the school
	• Implement schoolwide incentive program developed collaboratively by and for teachers and students
	• Add 10 minutes of noninstructional time at the beginning of each day to provide time for improving teacher-student rapport
Pickens High School	• Design and implement schoolwide initiative focused on increasing student engagement to improve their achievement
	• Identify students at risk of failing or dropping out of school and engage them in "Connecting with Kids" buddy groups to help them feel more connected to school
	• Increase extracurricular options for all students

Project Evaluation Methodology

A qualitative case-study design was used to conduct formative and summative evaluation of the project (Creswell, 2003; Davidson, 2005; Merriam, 1998; Stake, 1995). Data collection began during the first session of the first summer institute and closed eight months after conclusion of project-sponsored activities. Data sources included (a) participant responses to questionnaires after each training session, (b) reports prepared by the project director following each school visit, (c) participant comments during group interviews conducted during the final summer institute, (d) teacher and resource specialist responses to a survey administered online eight months after the project closed, (e) district administrators and high school principal reflections within electronic mail messages exchanged with the principal investigator, and (f) content within documents (e.g., team reports of improvement efforts, school report cards posted on state department of education web site). This chapter reports findings from the analysis of interview transcriptions and postproject assessments.

Unanticipated Challenges

Events during project implementation influenced goal achievement, exemplifying how change is a fragile process (Fullan, 2003; Hall & Hord, 2006). These disruptions affected two resources critical to change: *stable leadership* and *sufficient time*.

The appointment of a new superintendent for Bristol School District shortly after project launch triggered a series of other leadership changes. The PHS principal accepted a position outside the district, and the EHS principal became the district's new director of personnel. Their replacements were not announced until late September, which halted progress on the team-planned initiatives at those two schools for two months. The appointment of the new PHS principal was handled quickly with widespread approval. Selection of the new EHS principal, however, generated conflict within the school and community because both assistant principals, who were project participants, applied for the open principalship. Support for their appointment was split equally inside and outside the school community. When the governance council chose one of the assistant principals, the other disengaged from the project.

All four high schools were closed multiple days during the spring semester of project implementation due to widespread illness, severe winter weather, utility outages, and flooding in the region. Three teams thus had to minimize or cancel portions of their school-improvement initiatives, and a project-sponsored weekend workshop during the spring was cancelled.

PROJECT EVALUATION FINDINGS

During the final summer institute, team members participated in three group interviews conducted by the principal investigator. School principals participated in one interview, while teachers and resource specialists were interviewed in two groups with balanced representation across all four high schools in each group. Due to conflicting schedules, the JHS principal was not able to attend the final seminar; thus, the assistant principal participated in the principal's interview.

Reconceptualized School Leadership

Because the project goal was reconceptualization of school leadership as a function, not a responsibility vested solely in the principalship, the first question posed during all three group interviews was, *What is school leadership?* The assistant principal at JHS immediately responded that it involves "a group of people aiming in the same direction for the same cause and that is student success." He mentioned reading a book about leadership, distributed to each high school the previous summer, which helped him realize that "to be an effective leader, people have to want to follow you." The new principal of EHS posited that school leadership means a principal has "to be a leader of leaders," but he discovered that is difficult to do when one works in a "very tough situation" like he did during his first year. The new PHS principal, who as a teacher had been actively involved in previous school improvement efforts, perceived school leadership as a collaborative effort.

> If you're going to be successful, you've got to have input from your faculty and community, and you've got to allow your students to have some say. Everybody has to have the same vision: This is where we want to go, let's all go in the same direction.

He added that school leadership is "a group of people" and that a principal needs to use the "strengths from all of them."

The veteran principal at FHS learned from participating in the project that "a lot goes into decision making." He now realizes that it is better to "get the perspective of the people in my building before I just shoot from the hip and make some decision [without understanding] how it's going to impact the teachers." He also asserted that it is important to have "more than one person making decisions" because the "old style of one guy at the top and everybody else doing what he says is over."

During their interviews, several teachers used the word "principal" in their responses to the question, *What is school leadership?* For example, the arts and humanities teacher at JHS stated that participating in the project "changed the way that I viewed the things that [the principal and assistant principal] were doing" and "made it more obvious that we're all one team going in the same direction." Her school colleague who taught English admitted that she did not understand "the extent of what [a principal's] duties were" before serving as a team member.

The literacy coach at PHS realized her school's faculty and staff are composed of individuals with "diverse personalities" and that her principal must "deal with all of these personalities" every day. Before participating in the project, she dealt with students, parents, and occasionally teachers. Working as a team member, she learned that principals must deal with "people under them" and "people over them." She now has greater empathy for her principal because she understands better the demands placed on him: "I can't imagine dealing with that on a daily basis. It's just overwhelming."

An English teacher from EHS, who served on several district and state initiatives and holds a master's degree in school administration, stated that participating in the project reinforced her belief that a principal needs to "know who he or she is" and "have a good handle on the school's vision to stay focused." Because principals have "people coming at them" every day, she thinks "it's very important that [they] are not 'wishy washy.'" If principals do not "know what they want, what that school wants and needs" and are not able "to follow through with it," then their schools will be "in trouble." She was one of the teachers who transferred to another school in the district due to the upheaval at EHS the previous year.

Other teachers perceived school leadership as a function, which was a project goal. For example, a science teacher at JHS stated, "School leadership is anything an individual in a school does to [achieve] its mission to improve the school and to improve student performance. And it can be anybody, from the principal on down." Although students are often ignored as leaders, he perceived that they were "some of our best leaders" on their team and thought "involving students" in school improvement efforts at JHS was very effective.

The EHS counselor posited that school leadership "is not necessarily people that we appoint." Instead, leaders "just stand up and take charge without being told to do so," which she asserted was important to remember because "those are the ones that usually get things going." An English teacher on the FHS leadership team, which experienced the greatest membership instability, supported that perspective.

> If we had to form another leadership team, I'm not so sure that it would be the original people that we had. Our team kind of grew. We had people who joined on their own free will. They would say to us, "This is a great thing you all are doing." "What do you think about this?" There was a lot of neat sharing.

Her teammate defined school leadership as an action that "provides direction for the school." Being a school leader is much more than just "someone who tells you what to do," but instead requires "taking the time to gather input, making everybody feel valuable, inviting contributions, and then providing direction" to accomplish goals.

Collective School Leadership

During the group interview with school administrators, the veteran principal at FHS admitted that he used a top-down leadership style prior to participating in the project. He reported that shared-leadership responsibilities among team members was, however, misunderstood by some individuals within the school community—and even created "a little bit of jealousy." Some teachers could not understand why he was "letting [the team] make all the decisions," and one asked bluntly, "What kind of principal does that?" Near the end of his reflection, he posited that teachers who have worked for "25 to 30 years probably need to go to the farm [i.e. retire]." His opinion may have emerged from working with teachers on the leadership team who had considerably less experience (5–10 years) compared with most members of the school faculty.

The previous PHS principal formed the leadership team for the project, which the new principal thought "has actually been a plus." At first he did not perceive leadership potential in several individuals and admitted he probably would not have selected them. During the year "some of them surprised" him by their "work commitment and willingness to be engaged in school leadership." He plans to "give them a little bit more to do" in the future and to ask "other people in the building" to participate in leadership. He also admitted a few "have let me down."

The principal's comment about being surprised and disappointed by others was echoed in the words of the Spanish teacher at FHS. During the early stages of project implementation, two teachers "did not want to fulfill their responsibilities." This surprised her because they were individuals she considered to be teacher leaders, yet they "did not want to put forth the necessary time and the effort" toward the school improvement project. Other teachers "ended up stepping in" to assist. Although at first disappointed by the actions of two original team members, she discovered "it was kind of neat to see the changes" that happened after they quit.

Teacher Engagement and Development

All four principals reported that teachers on their teams displayed leadership through their involvement in the project. The JHS assistant principal stated that his principal announced the project to the entire faculty and invited them to self-nominate as potential team members, rather than selecting teacher leaders already involved in school activities. This action provided opportunities for the principal to "see what kind of leaders [the teachers on the team] were when put in situations," which the assistant principal claimed was "one of the biggest positives" for his school. The veteran principal at FHS asserted that teachers on his team now "feel like they have ownership" of the school and "tend to stand up and do the right thing." They are "more outspoken" and "try to keep folks that stir up [issues] in their place ... so the culture is beginning to change." He was hopeful that "some [teachers] on this team ... will be able to keep seeing positives" and thus make a greater difference over time.

Most teachers described how working with their peers and principals made them aware of their unique leadership strengths, while others shared that they honed already developed skills. For example, although an elected teacher representative on the EHS school-governance council, a veteran mathematics teacher reported that participating in the project provided her with new insights about her leadership.

> I have strengths that I can offer my school, other teachers, and students. I won't say that they're like an administrator's strengths, but I'm willing to say, "OK, here I am. What do you need me to do?" And I will do my best to do that. And if I can't do that, then I'll work with somebody else that can do that.

The novice mathematics teacher at PHS participating in the same group interview spoke next.

> Everybody has some style or something they do really well. And I think everybody together is what makes a team good. [Team members] have different styles of leadership, and everybody gets to sell an idea.... I think everyone on our team is a leader. Everybody on every team was a leader in some way.

The notion of shared leadership, empowerment, and diverse strengths was described by an English teacher on the JHS team: "Our team had complementary strengths. [For] something that I'm probably better at doing, there would be someone who could pick up something that I was not strong in."

Teachers' reactions to discovering their "inner leader" through project activities and situated learning were strong. When asked if they had grown professionally through participating in the project, all interviewed teachers responded, "Yes." When asked if participating in the project improved their professional practice, all likewise responded, "Yes." To support their affirmative responses, they reported conducting "classroom observations of other teachers" and working with peers in other disciplines to address student learning issues. Rather than immediately contacting parents about student-learning matters, they "took care of issues [themselves] through their [new] relationships." Through expanded collegiality, they discovered they could "do the work to get things accomplished," rather than always relying on administrators or guidance counselors to recommend actions.

Transformed teacher leadership within the high schools also resulted in changed relationships with others. According to a JHS team member, the teachers' collaborative actions inspired students to feel "more comfortable coming to us and sharing their ideas about what they would like to see happen in the school." The PHS band director described how the leadership team's initiative changed the school culture.

> The kids really didn't have pride in our school except for our test scores. That's the only thing they cared about. And now they want to [participate in] this club or that club, and they want to be part of [the school improvement] team. So it's really changed [our students], and our attendance has gotten better because of it.

An English teacher at FHS reported developing a different relationship with her principal.

> We have spent all this time together, working on this leadership stuff and … it's not all been peachy. I mean we've had some "knock down-drag outs" with people getting up and walking out of the room because we've not agreed on things. But still I feel [that the principal's] door is open. If I have an idea, if it's silly, he's just going to say, "That's crazy." But you know we're at that level now because of the leadership team where we can have open discussions. I think more productive things will come from that.

Eight months after the leadership development project closed, teachers and resource specialists were invited to complete an online survey administered by the principal investigator to assess project's impact. The responses to four prompts (see Table 9.3) indicated they perceived that participating in the project changed their perceptions about leadership and improved professional practice.

UNPLANNED PROJECT OUTCOMES

The overarching goal of the leadership-development project described in this chapter was to change instructional leadership within high schools—from positional responsibility vested solely in the principalship to leadership shared among administrators, teachers, and other members of the school community—in order to improve school performance and enhance student learning. As participants' comments above reveal, leading high schools cannot be solely attributable to status, authority, or position of one person

Table 9.3.   Teacher Perceptions of Their Professional Growth

Survey Prompt	Strongly Disagree	Disagree	Agree	Strongly Agree	Total Responses
The project changed my mind about leadership.	0	2	11 (65%)	4 (24%)	17
Because of the project, I know I am a leader.	0	3	11 (65%)	3 (18%)	17
Now that I've had this experience, I am a better teacher.	0	0	12 (71%)	5 (29%)	17
I would participate if another opportunity like this was available.	0	1	11 (65%)	5 (29%)	17

but rather collective responsibility—"an *emergent property* that arises from individuals joining their expertise in ways that allow the group or collective to accomplish more than an individual could alone" (Chrispeels, 2004, p. 5). Shared leadership requires mutual openness and trust, individual and group commitment to organizational purposes, and a common vision of desired goals that are reinforced through shared experiences and action (Donaldson, 2006; Kochanek, 2005; Louis, 2006).

Teacher Leadership Developed

Through engagement in communities of practice (Lave & Wenger, 1991; Wenger, 1998) and job-embedded professional development (Croft, Coggshall, Dolan, & Powers, 2010), teachers learned to navigate through tensions that arise when working collaboratively. Through those experiences, most teachers experienced a role-identify transformation—from being a teacher to being a teacher leader. They developed trusting relationships with their principals and peers (Lieberman, Hanson, & Gless, 2012), and they experienced reciprocal mentoring through the synergy created while working together to achieve their school's goals (Mullen & Lick, 1999). Teachers in two high schools discovered that peers can disappoint by failing to keep promises or by becoming embroiled in political machinations—yet despite professional differences colleagues can also amaze by volunteering to complete needed tasks or by collaborating to address student issues. Although not a project goal, teacher leadership was developed and practiced in all four participating high schools (Institute for Educational Leadership, 2008; Katzenmeyer & Moller, 2009), despite the stumbling blocks to its creation that typically exist in secondary schools (Ellis, 2013).

Principals Learned About Developing Teacher Leaders

Through engaging in job-embedded leadership activities (Browne-Ferrigno & Muth, 2004, 2006; Crow & Matthews, 1998; Mullen & Lick, 1999; Thompson, 2013), novice and veteran principals learned to reframe their professional perceptions about and practices of shared instructional leadership (Copland & Boatright, 2006; Hansen & Matthews, 2002). Recall that a veteran principal admitted he now realizes that "the old style of one guy at the top and everybody else doing what he says is over," a lesson learned through his engaging regularly with teachers throughout the project year. The principal's transformative thinking also yielded positive results according to the director of instruction for Tazwell School District. In his response to an email message sent by the principal investigator eight months after project closure, he reported that FHS was "the most improved high school on the state assessment" in the district that year and attributed this improvement to "the development of leadership and the leadership team." Principals discovered latent leadership within teachers who served on the leadership teams, which was "one of the biggest positives" for participating schools according to another principal. They also learned to navigate through issues created by teachers' professional jealousy, misconceptions about shared leadership, and failure to fulfill commitments.

New Optimism Emerged for Developing Teacher Leaders/Shared Leadership

Without question, traditional structures within the participating high schools posed challenges to innovation (Cohen, 2001; Goodlad, 1984, Green, 2010). Nonetheless, teachers and principals voiced optimism about shared instructional leadership and through their combined efforts evidenced that high schools can transform. This is a key finding because eastern Kentucky's culture, mountainous terrain, and economic conditions impede the inward migration of new residents. School districts seldom receive applications for open positions from educators outside the region because few are willing to relocate to an economically depressed location; those that do often leave within a year or two. Because outsiders are often not readily accepted by residents in some remote areas, districts must develop instructional leaders among local educators who can achieve required school and student performance requirements (Browne-Ferrigno & Allen, 2006). Despite events external to the project (e.g., administrator changes, school closings), new leadership models were implemented within high schools and student learning issues were addressed. As a result of this study, we have identified several promising practices for developing teacher leadership, all centered around the roles that principals play in facilitating this development.

TEACHER LEADERSHIP DEVELOPMENT: PROMISING PRACTICES

According to York-Barr and Duke (2004), little is known about how teacher leaders are formally prepared—yet for decades, teachers working in K–12 schools have nonetheless assumed diverse leadership roles (Danielson, 2006; Harrison & Killion, 2007). The roles may be formal (e.g., school-governance committee member, department chair, grade-level team leader) or informal (e.g., curriculum-design team member, instructional model, peer mentor). Although actively engaged teacher leaders build organizational capacity and create sustainable change within a school culture (Angelle & Schmid, 2007; Lieberman & Miller, 2004; Stone & Cuper, 2006), their actions are often counter to deeply ingrained school and teacher norms (Frost & Harris, 2003; Huggins, Klar, Hammonds, & Buskey, 2013; Lieberman & Fredrich, 2010).

Although the project described in this chapter focused on developing team-based instructional leadership, several promising practices for developing teacher leaders emerged. According to Derrington (2013), "Context is an influential leadership factor" (p. 2). Thus, it is important to note that these promising practices—emerging from teachers' situated learning and job-embedded work within K–12 schools—require the support of principals. Three important principal behaviors for fostering teacher leadership emerged from our data.

The Principal Must Encourage Teachers to Lead in Authentic Ways

Each participating principal became a "leader of instructional leaders" (Glickman, 1989, p. 6) who actively engaged with teachers in supervising curriculum development and instruction, assessing student-learning progress regularly, implementing school improvement initiatives and monitoring impact (Marks & Nance, 2007; Marks & Printy, 2003; Marzano, Waters, & McNulty, 2005). This learning-centered leadership enacted collaboratively by administrators and teachers relied on "complex, organic interrelationships" (Murphy, Elliot, Goldring, & Porter, 2006, p. 1) as well as shared responsibility and reciprocal accountability for outcomes (Demarest, 2010; McCombs & Miller, 2007). Relationships between principals and teachers changed. Although the principals retained "positional power"

(Katzenmeyer & Moller, 2009, p. 128), the teachers were supported in using their personal power and influence to engage peers in addressing the identified student-learning issues. The transformed leadership within the high schools created a structure supportive of teacher leadership, which is essential.

The Principal Must Participate in Continued Professional Growth Alongside Teachers

All members of the broad-based leadership teams participated together in two 3-day summer institutes at the beginning of project implementation. The group-development activities facilitated by experienced leadership-development consultants were guided by such questions as, *Why are we here? Is leadership a position or a function? How do we become teams? What are our individual strengths? How can our individual strengths be used in our work? How does change impact people? What roles and behaviors are helpful for school leaders who want to encourage positive change? How do we handle conflict?* The purpose for their teamwork was explicitly stated, and team members practiced newly learned skills within risk-safe learning environments. Following each guided practice, they reflected on their performance by collaboratively answering four questions: *What went well? What did not go so well and how can it be fixed? What did we learn about ourselves and teams? How can this information be used by our team?* The organizational commitment made by principals, evidenced by their participation in the leadership-development activities, generated relational trust with teachers and other team members (Kochanek, 2005; York-Barr & Duke, 2004) and created strategies for conflict management (Hord & Sommers, 2008). The principals' engagement in these activities affirmed the importance of continuous professional growth, which is another essential component of developing and sustaining teacher leadership.

The Principal Must Foster, Value, and Prioritize Teacher-Led Communities of Practice

Collective leadership practices—*setting directions, developing people, redesigning the organization, improving the instructional program* (Leithwood & Louis, 2012, p. 59)—were enacted in the high schools. Teachers serving on the teams modeled collective instructional leadership through building relationships among their peers, breaking down barriers that inhibit collegial collaboration, and sharing resources to improve instruction (Blasé & Blasé, 2006; Wilmore, 2007). In some high schools, teachers observed classrooms informally and afterwards met privately with their peers to talk about learning and teaching (Danielson, 2009). These collegial relationships fostered reciprocal learning and created communities of practice in which steadily improving role performance was the ultimate goal (Mullen et al., 2002; Mullen & Lick, 1999). This situated learning involved the "embodied, delicate, active, social, negotiated, complex process of participation" (Wenger, 1998, p. 49) that occurs in teacher-led professional learning communities, which is the third requirement for developing and sustaining teacher leadership.

CONCLUSION

This chapter described how educators in four high-need, rural Kentucky high schools expanded leadership capacity and addressed school-improvement expectations through participation in a yearlong leadership development project. The overarching project goal was reconceptualization of instructional leadership as a collective function of broad-based instructional leadership teams, rather than a responsibility vested solely in the principalship. Two unanticipated outcomes emerged from the project: the development of teacher leaders and principals' new awareness of their role in facilitating teacher leadership. Although the project was implemented in Central Appalachia, findings suggest promising practices, supported by research literature, for principals elsewhere who would desire to develop teacher leaders in their schools. First, the principal must encourage and empower teachers to lead in authentic situations in the school. Secondly, the principal must also invest in and participate in continued professional growth opportunities *with* the teachers. And finally, the principal must value and prioritize teacher-led communities of practice. The principal's diligence in enacting these behaviors will result in shared instructional leadership of a school that is truly transformative.

REFERENCES

Angelle, P. & Schmid, J. (2007). School structure and the identity of teacher leaders: Perspectives of principals and teachers. *Journal of School Leadership, 17*(6), 771–799.

Arnold, M. (2004). *Guiding rural schools and districts: A research agenda.* Aurora, CO: Mid-continent Research for Education and Learning.

Bellamy, T., Fulmer, C., Murphy, M., & Muth, R. (2007). *Principal accomplishments: How school leaders succeed.* New York, NY: Teachers College Press.

Bernhardt, V. L. (2002). *The school portfolio toolkit: A planning, implementation, and evaluation guide for continuous school improvement.* Larchmont, NY: Eye on Education.

Birky, V., Shelton, M., & Headley, S. (2006). An administrator's challenge: Encouraging teachers to be leaders. *NASSP Bulletin, 90*(2), 87–101.

Blank, M. J., Hale, B., & Harkavy, I. (2005, Summer). Engaging all leaders. *Threshold,* 16–17. Retrieved from http://www.ciconline.org/thresholdsummer05

Blankstein, A. M. (2004). *Failure is not an option: Six principles that guide student achievement in high-performing schools.* Thousand Oaks, CA: Corwin Press.

Blasé, J., & Blasé, J. (2006). *Teachers bringing out the best in teachers: A guide to peer consultation for administrators and teachers.* Thousand Oaks, CA: Corwin Press.

Boyer, E. L. (1995). *The basic school. A community for learning.* Princeton, NJ: The Carnegie Foundation for the Advancement of Teaching.

Browne-Ferrigno, T., & Allen, L. W. (2006). Preparing principals for high-need rural schools: A central office perspective about collaborative efforts to transform school leadership. *Journal of Research in Rural Education, 21*(1), 1–16. Retrieved from http://www.jrre.psu.edu/articles/21-1.pdf

Browne-Ferrigno, T., & Muth, R. (2004). Leadership mentoring in clinical practice: Role socialization, professional development, and capacity building. *Educational Administration Quarterly, 40*(4), 468–494.

Browne-Ferrigno, T., & Muth, R. (2006). Leadership mentoring and situated learning: Catalysts for principal readiness and lifelong mentoring. *Mentoring & Tutoring: Partnership in Learning, 14*(3), 275–295.

Buckingham, M. (2005). *The one thing you need to know ... about great managing, great leading, and sustained individual success.* New York, NY: Free Press.

Chance, P. L., & Segura, S. N. (2009). A rural high school's collaborative approach to school improvement. *Journal of Research in Rural Education, 24*(5), 1–11. Retrieved from http://www.jrre.psu.edu/articles/24-5.pdf

Chrispeels, J. H. (Ed.). (2004). *Learning to lead together: The promise and challenges of sharing leadership.* Thousand Oaks, CA: Sage.

Cohen, M. (2001). *Transforming the American high school.* Washington, DC: Aspen Institute.

Collinson, V., & Cook, T. F. (2007). *Organizational learning: Improving learning, teaching, and leading in school systems.* Thousand Oaks, CA: Sage.

Copland, M. A., & Boatright, E. (2006, December). *Leadership for transforming high schools.* Seattle. WA: University of Washington, Center for the Study of Teaching and Policy. Retrieved from http://depts.washington.edu/ctpmail/PDFs/HighSchool-Dec13.pdf

Cotton, K. (2003). *Principals and student achievement: What the research says.* Alexandria, VA: Association for Supervision and Curriculum Development.

Creswell, J. W. (2003). *Research design: Qualitative, quantitative, and mixed methods approaches* (2nd ed.). Thousand Oaks, CA: Sage.

Croft, A., Coggshall, J. C., Dolan, M., Powers, E., with Killion, J. (2010, April). *Job-embedded professional development: What it is, who is responsible, and how to get it done well.* [Issue brief]. Washington, DC: National Comprehensive Center for Teacher Quality. Retrieved from http://www.tqsource.org/publications/JEPD%20Issue%20Brief.pdf

Crow, G. M., & Matthews, L. J. (1998). *Finding one's way: How mentoring can lead to dynamic leadership.* Newbury Park, CA: Corwin Press.

Danielson, C. (2006). *Teacher leadership that strengthens professional practice.* Alexandria, VA: ASCD.

Danielson, C. (2009). *Talk about teaching! Leading professional conversations.* Thousand Oaks, CA: Corwin.

Davidson, J. E. (2005). *Evaluation methodology basics: The nuts and bolts of sound evaluation.* Thousand Oaks, CA: Sage.

Demarest, E. J. (2010). *A learning-centered framework for education.* New York, NY: Teachers College Press.

Derrington, M. L. (2013, November). *Implementing teacher evaluation: Lattice of leadership.* Paper presented at the annual meeting of the University Council for Educational Administration, Indianapolis, IN.

Donaldson, G. A., Jr. (2006). *Cultivating leadership in schools: Connecting people, purpose, and practice* (2nd ed.). New York, NY: Teachers College Press.

DuFour, R., & Marzano, R. J. (2011). *Leaders of learning: How district, school, and classroom leaders improve student achievement.* Bloomington, IN: Solution Tree Press.

Ellis, A. P. (2013, November). *Principal and teacher perceptions on the role of teacher leadership in K–12 schools.* Paper presented at the annual meeting of the University Council for Educational Administration, Indianapolis, IN.

Frost, D., & Harris, A. (2003). Teacher leadership: towards a research agenda. *Cambridge Journal of Education, 33*(3), 479–498.

Fullan, M. (1993). *Change forces: Probing the depths of educational reform.* London, England: Falmer Press.

Giancola, J. M., & Hutchison, J. K. (2005). *Transforming the culture of school leadership.* Thousand Oaks, CA: Corwin Press.

Glickman, C. (1989). Has Sam and Samantha's time come at last? *Educational Leadership, 46*(8), 4–9.

Goodlad, J. I. (1984). *A place called school: Prospects for the future.* New York, NY: McGraw-Hill.

Green, R. L. (2010). *The four dimensions of principal leadership: A framework for leading 21st century schools.* Boston, MA: Allyn & Bacon.

Hall, G., & Hord, S. (2006). *Implementing change: Patterns, principles and potholes* (2nd ed.). Boston, MA: Allyn & Bacon.

Hansen, J. M., & Matthews, J. (2002). The power of more than one. *Principal Leadership, 3*(2), 30–33.

Harrison, C., & Killion, J. (2007). Ten roles for teacher leaders. *Educational Leadership, 65*(1), 74–77.

Hord, S. M., & Sommers, W. A. (2008). *Leading professional learning communities: Voices from research and practice.* Thousand Oaks, CA: Corwin Press.

Huffman, J. B., & Hipp, K. K. (2003). *Reculturing schools as professional learning communities.* Lanham, MD: Scarecrow Education.

Huggins, K. S., Klar, H. W., Hammonds, H. L., & Buskey, F. C. (2013, November). *Becoming a teacher leader: A study of leadership development in three high schools.* Paper presented at the annual meeting of the University Council for Educational Administration, Indianapolis, IN.

Institute for Educational Leadership. (2000, October). *Leadership for student learning: Reinventing the principalship.* Washington, DC: Author. Retrieved from http://www.iel.org/programs/21st/reports/principal.pdf

Institute for Educational Leadership. (2008). *Teacher leadership in high schools: How principals encourage it, how teachers practice it.* Washington, DC: Author. Retrieved from http://www.iel.org/pubs/metlife_teacher_report.pdf

Katzenmeyer, M., & Moller, G. (2009). *Awakening the sleeping giant: Helping teachers develop as leaders* (3rd ed.). Thousand Oaks, CA: Corwin Press.

Kochanek, J. R. (2005). *Building trust for better schools: Research-based practices.* Thousand Oaks, CA: Corwin Press.

Lambert, L. (2003). *Leadership capacity for lasting school improvement.* Alexandria, VA: Association for Supervision and Curriculum Development.

Lave, J., & Wenger, E. (1991). *Situated learning: Legitimate peripheral participation.* Cambridge, United Kingdom: Cambridge University Press.

Leithwood, K., & Louis, K. S. (2012). *Linking leadership to student learning.* San Francisco, CA: Jossey-Bass.

Leithwood, K., & Mascall, B. (2008). Collective leadership effects on student achievement. *Educational Administration Quarterly, 44*(4), 529–561.

Lieberman, A., & Fredrich, L. D. (2010). *How teachers become leaders: Learning from practice and research.* New York, NY: Teachers College Press.

Lieberman, A., Hanson, S., & Gless, J. (2012). *Mentoring teachers: Navigating the real-world tensions.* San Francisco, CA: Jossey-Bass.

Lieberman, A., & Miller, L. (2004). What research says about teacher leadership. In R. Ackerman & S. Mackenzie (Eds.), *Uncovering teacher leadership* (pp. 37–48). Thousand Oaks, CA: Corwin Press.

Louis, K. S. (2006). Changing the culture of schools: Professional community, organizational learning, and trust. *Journal of School Leadership, 16*(4), 477–489.

Mangin, M., & Stoelinga, S. R. (2010). The future of instructional leader roles. *The Educational Forum, 74,* 49–62.

Marks, H. M., & Nance, J. P. (2007). Contexts of accountability under systemic reform: Implications for principal influence on instruction and supervision. *Educational Administration Quarterly, 43*(1), 3–37.

Marks, H. M., & Printy, S. M. (2003). Principal leadership and school performance: An integration of transformational and instructional leadership. *Educational Administration Quarterly, 39*(3), 370–397.

Marzano, R. J., Waters, T., & McNulty, B. S. (2005). *School leadership that works: From research to results.* Alexandria, VA: Association for Supervision and Curriculum Development.

McBeth, M. E. (2008). *The distributed leadership toolbox: Essential practices for successful schools.* Thousand Oaks, CA: Corwin Press.

McCombs, B. L., & Miller, L. (2007). *Learner-centered classroom practices and assessments: Maximizing student motivation, learning, and achievement.* Thousand Oaks, CA: Corwin Press.

Merriam, S. B. (1998). *Qualitative research and case study applications in education.* San Francisco, CA: Jossey-Bass.

Moller, G. & Pankake, A. (2006). *Lead with me: A principal's guide to teacher leadership.* Larchmont, NY: Eye on Education.

Mullen, C. A., Gordon, S. P., Greenlee, B. J., & Anderson, R. H. (2002). Capacities for school leadership: Emerging trends in the literature. *International Journal of Educational Reform, 11*(2), 158–198.

Mullen, C. A., & Lick, D. W. (Eds.). (1999). *New directions in mentoring: Creating a culture of synergy.* London, England: Falmer Press.

Murphy, J., Elliott, S. N., Goldring, E., & Porter, A. D. (2006, August). *Learning-centered leadership: A conceptual foundation* [Report prepared for The Wallace Foundation]. Nashville, TN: Vanderbilt University.

National Association of Secondary School Principals. (2004). *Breaking ranks II: Strategies for leading high school reform.* Reston, VA: Author.

Sagor, R. (2004). *The action research guidebook: A four-step process for educators and school teams.* Thousand Oaks, CA: Corwin Press.

Sizer, T. R., & Sizer, N. F. (1999). *The students are watching: Schools and the moral contract.* Boston, MA: Beacon Press.

Spillane, J. P. (2006). *Distributed leadership.* San Francisco, CA: Jossey-Bass.

Stake, R. E. (1995). *The art of case study research.* Thousand Oaks, CA: Sage.

Stone, R., & Cuper, P. (2006). *Best practices for teacher leadership: What award-winning teachers do for their professional learning communities.* Thousand Oaks, CA: Corwin Press.

Sullivan, S., & Glanz, J. (2006). *Building effective learning communities: Strategies for leadership, learning, and collaboration.* Thousand Oaks, CA: Corwin Press.

Thompson, M. D. (2013, November). *Principals' perceptions of experiences that helped improve their practice as instructional leaders.* Paper presented at the annual meeting of the University Council for Educational Administration, Indianapolis, IN.

Wallace Foundation. (2012, January). *The school principal as leader: Guiding schools to better teaching and learning.* New York, NY: Author

Wenger, E. (1998). *Communities of practice: Learning, meaning, and identity.* Cambridge, United Kingdom: Cambridge University Press.

Wilmore, E. (2007). *Teacher leadership: Improving teaching and learning from inside the classroom.* Thousand Oaks, CA: Corwin Press.

York-Barr, J., & Duke, K. (2004). What do we know about teacher leadership? Findings from two decades of scholarship. *Review of Educational Research, 74*(3), 255–316.

York-Barr, J., Sommers, W. A., Ghere, G. S., & Montie, J. (2001). *Reflective practice to improve schools: An action guide for educators.* Thousand Oaks, CA: Corwin Press.

Zmuda, A., Kuklis, R., & Kline, E. (2004). *Transforming schools: Creating a culture of continuous improvement.* Alexandria, VA: Association for Supervision and Curriculum Development.

CHAPTER 10

HOW AN ASSISTANT PRINCIPALS' ACADEMY EVOLVED INTO DYNAMIC GROUP AND PEER MENTORING EXPERIENCES

D. K. Gurley and L. Anast-May

Recently, school leadership experts have begun to focus on instructional leadership skills as essential to the success of school principals in the 21st century (Fusarelli, Militello, Alsbury, Price, & Warren, 2010; Nettles & Herrington, 2007; Schoen & Fusarelli, 2008). Accountability policies are requiring more comprehensive systems of principal and teacher evaluation and are raising expectations in terms of standards of instructional performance and student achievement (Leithwood, 2001). This evolution in policy has transformed instructional leadership from an option into a necessity for school administrators (Silva, White, & Yoshida, 2011).

Researchers affirm that sustainable school improvement is rarely accomplished without skillful instructional leadership from principals (Hallinger, 2011; Hallinger & Heck, 2010; Leithwood, Harris, & Hopkins, 2008) and that instructional leadership must be firmly entrenched into the

Best Practices in Mentoring for Teacher and Leader Development, pp. 173–195
Copyright © 2016 by Information Age Publishing
All rights of reproduction in any form reserved.

professional practice of today's school leaders (Hallinger, 2011; Hallinger & Murphy, 2013; Leithwood & Jantzi, 2005; Robinson, Lloyd, & Rowe, 2008; Witziers, Bosker, & Kruger, 2003).

In response to this increasing demand for high quality instructional leadership from school administrators, some school leaders are beginning to take a closer look at the human resources that may be available, within current school personnel structures, where instructional leadership skills may be developed. Leadership scholars have begun to acknowledge that, though the principal of a school remains the primary leader for learning (Hallinger, 2011), instructional leadership may come from a wide variety of sources, including teacher leaders, curriculum coordinators, and assistant principals (Austen, 2010; Crowther, Ferguson, & Hann, 2009; Roby, 2011). Smith and Addison (2013) reported on the initiative in one school district in Mississippi to proactively develop key instructional leadership skills among preservice principal candidates (i.e., classroom teachers and other nonadministrative school leaders). Such an intervention helped the district bolster data-driven decision making and shared leadership in the process of examining student performance and plan for interventions to improve student achievement across the district.

Scholars also have begun to take a second look at the role and function of the assistant principal in school settings across the United States (Drago-Severson & Aravena, 2011; Glanz, 2004; Lovely, 2004; Oliver, 2003, 2005). Though the position of assistant principal has become commonplace in U.S. schools since the 1930s (Glanz, 1994), these school leaders have traditionally been relegated to a supportive, operational role, usually having their practice confined to such managerial functions as oversight of student discipline, scheduling, management of instructional resources (e.g., counting and dolling out textbooks), and keeping the school cafeteria under control. District leaders and principals have more recently begun to ask, "Have we overlooked the assistant principal as a potential key player in enhancing instructional leadership in schools?" (Drago-Severson & Aravena, 2011; Glanz, 2004; Lovely, 2004; Oliver, 2003, 2005).

Background

During the fall of 2009, the superintendent of Horry County Schools in South Carolina collaborated with a member of the educational leadership faculty at Coastal Carolina University to design a two-year Assistant Principals' (AP) Academy, a professional development program for practicing APs. The superintendent had become concerned about a developing pattern of assistant principals interviewing for principal openings in the district, but falling short of district expectations for their knowledge base and experience in instructional leadership. The superintendent and university faculty team designed the Academy to develop APs' skills in instructional leadership and opened it to all APs throughout the district. The superintendent anticipated multiple retirements of school principals in the near future; thus the plan for the AP Academy was to grow a cadre of APs who had the expertise to step into the principal's role as the primary leader of learning in the school.

The results of a qualitative analysis of AP Academy leaders' and participants' perceptions of academy effectiveness have been reported elsewhere (Gurley, Anast-May, & Lee, 2013). During the first year of the AP Academy, 53 assistant principals voluntarily enrolled and remained in the program throughout its first year of implementation. In the second year, there were 33 assistant principals enrolled, because eight of the original group had been promoted to principal positions, and 12 had withdrawn for reasons such as assuming different roles in the district, moving out of the district, or retiring. The original case study project included several qualitative data collection strategies, including: (a) observations from a participant-observer, (b) individual interviews with academy graduates and district leaders, (c) surveys of remaining academy participants, and (d) document review. All data collection was conducted after the close of the second year of the two-year Academy.

The focus of this chapter, however, will be on an element of the Academy that emerged as an unplanned process, but one that we believe can be labeled as a *best practice* for leader development. While interviewing and observing participants during the follow-up study, the authors noticed a strong, and serendipitous dynamic that occurred as a by-product of the Academy. That is, what started out as fairly prescribed, content-specific, ongoing professional development for APs evolved into a rich and powerful experience of group and peer mentoring for participants. In this chapter, we explore pertinent elements of effective mentoring in general (Finkelstein & Poteet, 2007), and in group and peer mentoring programs specifically, that manifested themselves in the lived experiences of AP Academy participants. We describe APs' experiences relative to these mentoring elements. The chapter concludes with a discussion of how educators, designing professional development programs for leaders, might be more deliberate in planning for adult learning to include these best practices in mentoring, enhancing participant experiences and deepening their learning.

Elements of Effective Mentoring

Daresh (2004) articulated the role of mentor as, "someone willing to assume the challenge of assisting another in the formation of ideas and patterns of thinking" (p. 497). Mentoring is often thought of as a one-on-one relationship between protégé and mentor centered on the professional and personal development of the former. Daresh, however, among other mentoring experts, suggested a different conceptualization of the mentoring relationship, at times referred to as *collaborative mentoring* (Mullen, 2000) or *developmental networks* (Higgins & Kram, 2001) wherein both individuals and entire systems benefit from a more comprehensive mentoring structure. Such a mentoring structure may include professional interaction between multiple mentors and multiple protégés, all learning collaboratively from one another. But whether the mentoring relationship is an intense, one-on-one collaboration, or a more fluid, open collaboration involving multiple mentors and protégés, several best practices and key elements of effective mentoring have been identified in the literature (Finkelstein & Poteet, 2007) and were manifested in the AP Academy.

Throughout this chapter, we explore several of the many benefits resultant from group mentoring and peer mentoring practices in schools and other organizations. We first address general elements or best practices of effective mentoring drawn from mentoring literature. Next, we explore group mentoring and peer mentoring individually. After each mentoring element is presented, it is followed by a brief description of how the assistant principals experienced that element of mentoring as a result of participation in the AP Academy.

Organizational support for mentoring programs. The first of several general mentoring best practices is organizational support. Organization-wide support for a mentoring program is positively correlated with increased levels of employee job satisfaction and longevity (Rhoades & Eisenberger, 2002). In terms of support for mentoring programs specifically, Finkelstein and Poteet (2007) stated that, through a combination of communication and upper-management involvement, organizational support can catalyze a mentoring program and contribute to its success. Specific organizational actions, such as including management personnel in the mentoring process and providing work time release for mentors and protégés to participate in the mentoring program, have been identified as conducive to mentoring program success (Phillips-Jones, 1983; Tyler, 1998).

The AP Academy established in Horry County Schools enjoyed the highest level of organizational support from its inception. When the superintendent conceived of the idea, she shared her plan with members of the local Board of Education who applauded the initiative as a proactive plan for leadership succession. Further, members of the district-level leadership team were also supportive, as evidenced by executive director volunteering to serve as the Academy coordinator and primary administrator. All APs in the district were invited and encouraged to participate, and were given release time from their daily duties to attend the half-day Academy sessions each month.

Establishing clear mentoring program objectives. Essential to effective mentoring programs is the establishment of clear program objectives from the outset. These objectives, stemming from a formal or informal needs assessment at the organizational level, serve to guide decision making processes and the identification of program participants. Eddy, Tannenbaum, Alliger, D'Abate, and Givens (2001) identified several primary objectives for a mentoring program, including leadership succession and development of employee skills.

AP Academy objectives sprang from a perceived need to develop instructional leadership skills among the current cadre of APs in the school district. From the earliest phase of Academy planning, the goal of providing high-quality, focused training for APs in instructional leadership was established. Detailed planning for each session of the Academy ensued. All session content was centered on a clear objective of helping APs develop their skill base in acting as instructional leaders in their schools, more fully preparing the APs to assume the role of principal. Further, the fact that there was a single, district-level administrator acting as facilitator for the Academy likely contributed to the program retaining a clear and singular focus throughout the two-year timeframe.

Selection of mentoring program participants. In identifying suitable mentors, organizations use a variety of strategies, depending on the desired outcomes of the program. Experts identified some of the most common criteria for mentor selection, including: (a) level of expertise, (b) demonstrated skill and success in a targeted area of organizational function, and (c) a strong desire or motivation to serve as a mentor (Burke & McKeen, 1989; Catalyst, 1993; Messmer, 2001; Phillips-Jones, 1983).

Protégés may also be identified in a variety of ways, depending on program objectives. Finkelstein and Poteet (2007) identified two common themes for the selection of protégés, including: (a) identification of an overall group of targeted employees, and (b) identification of specific individuals within that overall group who should be invited to participate (p. 349). While most organizations allow potential protégés to volunteer for participation in mentoring programs, several authors have stressed that protégé identification strategies be transparent and widely communicated in order for potential protégés to be treated fairly (Eddy et al., 2001; Finkelstein & Poteet, 2007).

Because the AP Academy was not conceived as a mentoring program, per se, attention was not given to specific processes of mentor and protégé identification. Nevertheless, Academy session presenters (i.e., mentors) were identified based upon their expertise in leadership education (e.g., university educational leadership faculty) and upon experience and expertise in supporting the teaching and learning processes at the school district level. For example, university faculty members with experience teaching graduate level courses in instructional supervision were tapped to structure sessions on conducting teacher observations and providing feedback. District experts in Special Education, Technology Integration, and Support Services were also invited to share their knowledge.

The population of would-be "protégés" was defined as all APs in the district. All APs were openly invited to participate in the Academy, with no formal selection process established. Only individuals, however, who were currently serving as APs in the district were invited to attend. In essence, all APs who wished to join in order to develop their instructional leadership skills were welcome to participate, and participation was totally voluntary.

Matching mentors to protégés. The mentoring research is inconclusive as to whether or not mentors and/or protégés should have input into selecting one another for a mentoring relationship, and if so, what type of input and how much (Allen, Eby, & Lentz, 2006; Finkelstein & Poteet, 2007; Ragins, Cotton, & Miller, 2000; Viator, 1999). Eddy et al. (2001) concluded that many formal mentoring programs allow participants a wide range of freedom in the mentoring-protégé selection process, maintaining that a more organic, natural process of selection, based upon mutual attraction and interest, results in a more successful and dynamic mentoring experience for mentors and protégés alike. Allowing some degree of choice by participants in the mentor match-making process is generally accepted and likely most preferable, given the context and culture of the sponsoring organization and mentoring program goals.

Again, because the AP Academy was never designed as a mentoring program, no efforts were made to match mentors to protégés. Any such relationships that may have developed were strictly informal and entirely spontaneous. Relationships of this nature did, however, emerge, even in the early stages of the Academy, as APs began to interact with one another on a regular basis, either face-to-face during Academy sessions, or via email or social media outlets (e.g., Twitter) between sessions. Connections spontaneously ensued between APs and their would-be mentors from the university and from the district-level administration, as APs became familiar with one another and began to learn to whom they should turn in the district for needed information and resources.

Structuring mentoring relationships. Often, formal mentoring programs explicitly structure program procedures and define parameters for mentoring content, mentor-protégé relationships and interaction, and duration of the mentoring relationship (Finkelstein & Poteet, 2007). Clearly defined goals and expectations also support success in mentoring programs and between mentors and protégés, especially if participants play a role in establishing these goals and receive feedback regarding their progress toward the goals (Zachary, 2012). Some mentoring experts recommended that mentors and protégés go through a process of "assumption hunting" prior to entering the mentoring relationship. Assumption hunting means formally identifying, examining, and discussing assumptions that each party may consciously or subconsciously bring to the mentoring relationship in order to increase the likelihood of success (Searby, 2013; Zachary 2012).

In the AP Academy, a clear timeframe and session structure was established before the Academy began. Academy sessions were scheduled for the participants to meet one half day per month, but due to the size of enrollment, two sections of the academy were established, one in the morning, and a second in the afternoon of the same day. Monthly sessions were scheduled to extend over two academic school years. Procedures were informal within the sessions themselves, but attendance at each session was expected and closely monitored by district leaders. Sessions were carefully planned to include content relevant to developing instructional leadership skills, including, among other topics, conducting classroom observations, facilitating pre- and postconferences with teachers, and using technology to enhance the instructional supervision process and communication.

Monitoring and evaluating the mentoring program. The final general mentoring element involves regular monitoring and evaluation of the program. Most organizations implement a formal or informal monitoring procedure in order to check in on the development of the mentor-protégé relationship and progress toward program goals (Catalyst, 1993; Eddy et al., 2001; Kochan & Trimble, 2000). Formal and informal evaluation of a mentoring program may take any of several forms, including interviews with participants, questionnaires, and written program reports (Finkelstein & Poteet, 2007). Program elements subject to evaluation, however, will be a function of the specific mentoring program targeted outcomes. Eddy et al.(2001) noted that at the organizational level the two most frequently evaluated program elements were employee retention and improvement in succession planning. Mentors' level of satisfaction at helping their protégés is often evaluated. And for protégés, increased levels of job skills and increased networking are often evaluated (Eddy et al., 2001).

After each Academy session, participants completed a short evaluation survey, offering their perspective of the quality and practical value of the session as well as providing input for future topics to be presented. District and university personnel reviewed these evaluation surveys regularly, using the data gleaned to guide planning and in order to better respond to participants' learning needs.

Elements of Group and Peer Mentoring

In the following two sections of the chapter, we provide details regarding group mentoring and peer mentoring. While similar, in that they are both variations of possible mentoring structures, group mentoring and peer mentoring are distinct from one another in the ways that individuals participating in a mentoring program may interact. Again, after identifying each element of group or peer mentoring, we provide a description of how each of these best practices in mentoring, though not intentionally designed, were manifested within the context of the AP Academy.

Group mentoring. Kram (1985, 2004) first identified group mentoring as a process distinct from a traditional, one-on-one mentoring structure. Group mentoring may be structured in at least four different ways, including: (a) one-to-many mentoring, (b) many-to-one mentoring, (c) many-to-many (i.e., "group") mentoring, and (d) peer group mentoring (Huizing, 2010).

Many-to-many, or group mentoring, is becoming an increasingly popular response to addressing the learning needs of adults in schools and other organizations (Zachary, 2012). Zasloff and Okurowski (2011) defined group mentoring as "a group of individuals who engage in a mentoring relationship to achieve specific learning goals" (p. 1). Group mentoring may be designed to include two or more protégés who share similar learning needs or goals. Protégés may share a desire for greater integration into a new workplace culture, aspirations for networking and career advancement, enhancement of specific work-related skills, or increased exposure to institutional culture, norms, and expectations.

Further, as Huizing (2010) mentioned, multiple mentors may also be involved in a group mentoring design. Zachary (2012) wrote, "In group mentoring, individuals ... rely on one or more individuals to facilitate the learning of a group of mentees" (p. 73). Group mentors may be selected or they may volunteer for participation because of the mentor's tenure, demonstrated expertise or success in a specific area, or merely due to the mentor's desire to help further the careers of others within the organization. In effective group mentoring contexts, however, multiple perspectives from mentors and protégés coalesce into rich learning experiences for all involved, learning which often surpasses that which is achieved in a more traditional, one-on-one mentoring dyad (Ledford, Peel, Good, Greene, & O'Connor, 2006).

Diverse perspectives. Mentoring experts have identified many benefits resulting from an effective, group mentoring process. Among the most powerful of these benefits is the introduction of multiple and diverse perspectives from the various members of the group mentoring experience (Ambrose, 2003; Kamler, 2007; Ledford et al., 2006; Zasloff & Okurowski, 2011). Zasloff and Okurowski wrote, "Group mentoring facilitated access to diverse views and capabilities with exchanges among multiple mentees and mentors" (p. 2). The introduction of multiple perspectives and experiences into a group mentoring process can result in a pooling of energy and expertise from mentors and protégés alike (Ambrose, 2003).

Diversity in AP Academy. The AP Academy provided a group mentoring experience rich with diversity for participants. Academy planners deliberately assigned academy participants to heterogeneous groups. This insured that APs from elementary, middle, and high schools, as well as specialty schools (e.g., technical schools, magnet schools), were represented in each section. Academy participants were also diverse relative to gender, ethnicity, years of experience, age, school size, school setting (e.g., rural or suburban), and socioeconomic status of the students they served. Although some participants questioned the mixing of school levels at first, at the end of their two-year experience, several APs reported that they gained many important insights into the role of the school district as a system through interacting with job-alike colleagues from many different contexts and perspectives. One AP wrote, "The ability to network with other assistant principals at different levels (elementary, middle, high) is a great professional development tool." Another AP claimed, "The ideas and relationships I have gained through participating in the AP Academy have helped me see farther than just my own little box and to grow personally and professionally." Designing the sections to represent this level of diversity was intentional, and resulted in a rich learning experience for the academy participants. Table 10.1 presents an overview of Academy participant demographic information.

Table 10.1. Demographics of Participants at Conclusion of AP Academy

	N	*M Age*	*Male*	*Female*	*M Years Taught*	*M Years as AP*	*Elem*	*Middle*	*High*
							School Level		
Assistant Principals	24	43	8	16	9.8	6.3	7	11	7
Principals	6	41	1	5	8.0	4.8	3	1	2

In terms of mentor diversity, district administrators and school district leaders from multiple roles invested their time and energy to foster the personal and professional development of APs. For example, several university educational leadership faculty members presented topics such as (a) developing a vision for instructional supervision, (b) providing effective feedback to teachers, (c) research on best practices in teacher observation, and (d) developing professional learning communities. One middle school AP claimed, "The opportunity to have conversations regarding instructional vision has been a tremendous resource in collaborative and collegial exchanges."

District-level leaders also presented information regarding (a) curriculum alignment and assessment practices, (b) the integration of technology into supervisory practice, (c) specific district-wide initiatives relative to teaching and learning, and (d) the analysis and interpretation of student achievement data. One district administrator volunteered to serve as the AP Academy facilitator and lead mentor. Because of his background as an assistant principal, building principal, and district-level director of middle school education, the lead mentor had a clear understanding that the APs did not have the instructional leadership background necessary to lead schools, but also recognized that the academy could not be a "one size fits all" venture. Each AP was unique and brought with him or her a variety of different experiences. Likewise, each mentor brought his or her own, unique expertise to the table, providing APs multiple and diverse perspectives regarding the norms, values, and functions of the school district.

Additionally, in order to broaden the base of mentor expertise, a partnership was developed between the school district and the educational leadership faculty members at Coastal Carolina University. Armstrong (2010) particularly advocated for this type of partnership when she stated, "Coordinated, cooperative partnerships between professional qualifications providers and regulatory bodies are needed to provide early and ongoing scaffolding that supports opportunities for new administrators to learn and practice new skills in emotionally and physically safe environments" (p. 710). University faculty members served as presenters, facilitators, and mentors to academy participants. One university faculty member actually assisted in the original design and implementation of the academy. When reflecting about her involvement in the planning and implementation of the Academy, this university faculty member stated, "I was so excited to work collaboratively with the school district from the beginning stages of planning, implementing, participating in every session, and delivering instructional topics to AP Academy participants for two years. I became a mentor to many of them and helped guide them to think differently about their future roles as instructional leaders. By the end of the two years, I had the golden opportunity to see these assistant principals gain wisdom and act with increased confidence and competence. This is rewarding in itself." Including university faculty mentors in the design and delivery of the Academy added additional dynamics to the group process. The faculty members focused on various ways to assist APs frame their thinking about the new learning they gained in the Academy. The perspectives provided by university faculty members made a valuable contribution to the quality of AP learning in the Academy.

Enhancing organizational goals. Another benefit from group mentoring lies in the potential of enhancing organizational goals and procedures. Mullen (2005) stated that benefits can accrue to an organization through the group mentoring process due to the fact that group mentoring is driven by organizational as well as individual learning needs and objectives. Zasloff and Okurowski (2011) further noted that group mentoring may increase organizational consistency and service delivery, result in increased efficiency in communicating organizational goals and objectives, and bring new organizational members into the culture of the organization.

Enhancing organizational goals in AP Academy. Clearly, the AP Academy, as a professional development program, met its goals of increasing APs' skills and knowledge in instructional leadership and in initiating a leadership succession plan for the school district. Reflecting on the success of the Academy, the superintendent stated,

> It's not that we tap individuals necessarily, but we know that there's a group that can succeed any leader we have in the district. And that is comforting to the Board [of Education], it's comforting to me because, well, it's just like a baseball team when you have plenty of strength on the bench to come and win the game.

We asked another district level administrator how successful the Academy had been at achieving the established goals. He emphatically responded, "Very! … After completing the second year of the program, we had already promoted seven of the academy participants to principal positions in the district. I see this as a great success."

An added and unplanned-for benefit, however, arose through the informal, group mentoring process. Many of the AP Academy participants commented that the interaction with multiple mentors (i.e., district and university school leaders) who possessed many different areas of expertise helped them develop a much broader and clearer understanding of the functions, initiatives, and goals of the school district as a system, expanding their perspectives on the role the school district played in the community and the roles that they as APs fulfilled within the district.

One respondent stated that participating in the academy, "Gave me a better understanding of what is going on in the district. I am now able to find out what is working in other schools. I am constantly gaining new ideas from other people." Another wrote, "I believe I am much more knowledgeable of district initiatives which in turn helps me help my school keep up with current items of concern or focus." As a result of the serendipitous group mentoring evolution, the school district realized not only its professional development goals, but also a greater sensitivity and awareness among academy participants of the district goals, initiatives, structure, support systems, expectations, and resources.

Wider sharing of expertise. Further, through group mentoring, mentors who possess particular expertise and knowledge have the opportunity to share that expertise with a wider range of individuals. Kram (1985, 2004) claimed that protégés in a group mentoring context can expand their exposure to a wide network of mentors, thus having a more powerful influence on organizational learning. In describing the benefits realized through a group mentoring program initiated at the National Security Agency, Zasloff and Okurowski (2011) stated, "Our approach maximized senior [mentor] sharing and minimized time commitment" (p. 3).

Sharing of expertise in AP Academy. School district leaders also acted as mentors for the group of AP Academy participants. One example of this wider sharing of expertise demonstrated by district leaders was in the incorporation of the use of technology into the AP's daily professional practice. District administrators purchased a mini-laptop for each academy participant and established an expectation that each AP begin using this technology in his or her daily routines of observing teachers, taking notes in meetings, analyzing data, and providing feedback to teachers. District technology mentors and experts presented training during academy sessions in the use of the devices and of multiple software applications. One respondent shared, "The use of technology helped me make better use of my time and complete my regular responsibilities as well as for curriculum and instruction across the board."

Academy participants worked closely with group mentors in a relationship built on positive risk-taking, trust, and support. Mentors acted as guides to help APs think differently about their role as a future principal. Browne-Ferrigno (2003) concluded:

> Role socialization for aspiring principals is an intricate process of learning and reflection that requires working closely with leadership mentors in authentic field-based experiences, developing confidence through engaging in leadership activities and administrative tasks, and assuming a new professional self-concept grounded in confidence about leading schools. (p. 471)

This is precisely the type of activity that the AP Academy participants engaged in and found to be helpful.

Peer mentoring. Related to, but distinct from group mentoring, is peer mentoring. Zachary (2012) stated "in peer mentoring one peer may mentor another peer, or both peers might mentor each other. They share some level of commonality" (p. 70). Peer mentoring is different from group mentoring in that peers self-organize and self-manage the mentoring experience, rather than having a mentor or group of mentors set an agenda for the protégés. Further, peer mentors may share a similar job function, learning agenda, or organizationally-specific needs. Bryant and Terborg (2008) speculated that the recent rise in popularity of peer mentoring structures may be due in part to a general flattening of organizational hierarchies and an increase in the use of work teams. Several key elements of peer mentoring are described below.

Protégé input on learning agenda. The literature on peer mentoring coalesces around the concept that learners participating in this type of mentoring structure should, and often do, have considerable input into setting the learning agenda (Grogan, 2000, 2002; Newcomb, 2011; O'Neil & Marsick, 2009). Newcomb (2011) stated explicitly that "the mentoring relationship should be centered around the mentee's desires and goals" (p. 15). In their description of an Active Learning Conversation structure including peer coaching and mentoring, O'Neil and Marsick (2009) noted that "the mentee participants [were] able to frame their own issues and the help they wanted" (p. 23). Due to the fact that peers often encounter similar job situations, facilitating peer mentors' and mentees' (protégés) involvement in defining learning goals is critical to the authenticity and overall success of the peer mentoring process.

Protégé input in AP Academy. According to Hansen and Matthews (2002), "Peer mentoring encourages individuals with similar assignments and expectations to collaborate and explore problems and situations. Peer mentors are allies for change and risk-taking. In peer mentoring relationships, collegial cooperation and professional growth are the desired outcomes" (p. 21). Though the original intent of the AP Academy was not to design a mentoring program, per se, peer mentoring, such as that described by Hansen and Matthews, definitely occurred within and as a result of the AP Academy. In describing their most valuable learning resulting from their participation in the Academy, one middle school AP wrote, "Collaboration with and support from other assistant principals was very valuable to me," while another stated,

> I have come to rely on my colleagues and learn from their individual, unique situations. It is easy to feel isolated, but I have a network to fall back on when needed which allows me to be focused on providing the best possible leadership I can in my school.

Academy participants served as collaborative, peer mentors to one another throughout and beyond academy sessions.

APs reported the desire for the balance between content and process. Problem simulation learning; individualized learning; facilitated groups, cases, and brainstorming were mentioned by a few as preferred formats for learning. Professional development activities and sessions were customized and designed in response to these suggested delivery preferences. However, regardless of gender, school-level, or years of AP experience, all APs mentioned collegial discussion and informal networking as processes that provided them with material for practical applications. Collaborating with peers, working together, sharing ownership in what was accomplished and finding resource people who could offer information and support appeared vital to these APs. A district leader commented:

> Our greatest success goes back to the process. If you have an assistant principal with the greatest degree of sophistication in learning styles, that assistant principal can serve as a mentor and share experiences with other participants. Group dynamics are critical for us.

Increased collaboration and decreased isolation. Newcomb (2011) stated that peer mentoring activities can help to develop a sense of collaborative organizational community and acculturation. The power of peers sharing information and learning from one another within the context of their current working situation is a recurring theme in the literature (Browne-Ferrigno, 2003; Browne-Ferrigno & Muth, 2004; Bryant & Terborg, 2008; O'Brien & Llamas, 2012; O'Neil & Marsick, 2009). Kram and Higgins (2008) agreed, stating that peer mentoring relationships "have a high degree of mutual learning and trust in which [peers] give and receive various kinds of informational, emotional, and strategic support" (p. 2).

Increased collaboration in AP Academy. Several peer mentoring collaborative teams emerged spontaneously during the academy. One type of collaborative team that formed was a colleague team (Hansen & Matthews, 2002). Illustrating the powerful connections academy participants made, one principal, who had been promoted after her first year in the academy, described the formation of a small group of academy participants/colleagues whom she called a "true, mini professional community." These APs began to meet on their own time to extend their discussions of academy content. Members of this professional community shared readings, problem-solved together, visited one another's schools, and finally chose to conduct a small action research project together to further explore the impact of their increased skills in providing feedback to teachers regarding instructional practice. The AP stated, "We worked together to increase our knowledge of the world of education. That helped me grow as an administrator." This principal (a former AP Academy participant) further reported that the teachers in her building responded very positively to the increased feedback on their instruction, and that their practice as classroom teachers improved.

Another type of peer mentoring collaboration that transpired was mentoring teams (Hansen & Matthews, 2002). Several APs bonded closely with another AP who acted as a resource person to them. If an AP was struggling with a difficult situation or problem at his/her school, the other AP acted as an ally, or as a collaborative peer mentor, who provided support and insight in dealing with the problem. According to Hansen and Matthews (2002),

"Both team members are learning from each other and helping each other develop and become more capable" (p. 32). Emphasizing how the academy helped participants improve in their current jobs, one respondent wrote, "I feel like I can call on anyone in this group to talk to if I need help with something."

Decreased isolation in AP Academy. Collaborative teams of several types developed as a result of the AP Academy (Hansen & Matthews, 2002). Respondents noted that, due to the large geographical area of the school district, and due to the isolated nature of their positions as APs, opportunities for APs to collaborate with other professionals who hold similar positions in other schools, were nearly nonexistent prior to the academy. One assistant principal stated, "As assistants we typically have no peers in a school, so it's nice to get a chance to meet monthly at the academy and share what is going on at our schools ... everyone has so many different things happening!" Peers assisted peers when working on a specific issue or assignment. For example, after participants received training in a formal evaluation process that involved feedback and conferencing, they were to conduct an observation, provide feedback to the observed teacher, and utilize their conferencing skills in the process. APs called upon one another as they completed the specific assignment, often via the new technology, to discuss their progress and address questions and concerns. The collaborative teams validated each other's strengths and helped collaboratively address identified areas of improvement.

Goal-sharing teams also emerged (Hansen & Matthews, 2002). These goal-sharing teams of APs met to discuss their goals for their own professional learning, and the goals they established for improving their instructional leadership skills in the contexts of their daily work. The goal-sharing teams of APs worked together to define their vision and purpose in what they were doing as instructional leaders in their schools. For example, one peer mentoring elementary school AP developed a calendar for the year with the team's vision and purpose statements on it and shared it with her team for input and advice. She believed that sharing and reviewing her vision and purpose with her AP Academy teammates assisted her (and other members of her team) in maintaining focus on the most important aspects of their work with teachers, for example, improving instruction and student learning.

APs indicated that the AP Academy made them feel as if they belonged. The fact that group mentors and peer mentors engaged in behavior that signaled caring relationships about another's personal and professional well-being let the AP know that he/she would be taken care of in the school district. As one AP told the interviewer, "The AP Academy is a safe, encouraging place where I know that I can make mistakes but that is OK because people care for me and my success."

Increased opportunities for networking. A related benefit resulting from a peer mentoring structure is the increased opportunities that participants have to network with one another and with others within and outside of the district for support as they continue to develop workplace skills. Though traditional, one-on-one mentoring offers similar networking opportunities, Kram and Higgins (2008) describe the process and benefits of including peers, as well as more senior organizational leaders, in a developmental network to whom protégés may turn for help, knowledge, and advice. These authors stated:

> A better approach [than in traditional, one-on-one mentoring] is to create and cultivate a developmental network—a small group of people to whom you can turn for regular mentoring support and who have a genuine interest in your learning and development. (p. 1)

Kram and Higgins (2008) expounded on the benefits of creating a developmental network from participating in a peer mentoring process. Rather than being a single individual, the mentor role in a developmental network is actually performed by the group itself. The mentor role, then, results in "co-learners, sharing knowledge" (p. 3). The relationships within a developmental network are both hierarchical and peer-based, but are fluid, and can be formed both inside and outside of the organization. Learning accrues on both an individual and an organizational level, resulting in enhanced performance, self-awareness, retention, innovation, and leadership capacity (Kram & Higgins, 2008).

Developmental networks in AP Academy. Perhaps the most powerful outcome of the Academy was the establishment of developmental networks between and among program participants over the two years of implementation. Networking is a key benefit to administrative mentoring. Well-designed mentoring programs help protégés to develop networks for potential job openings, gain friendships with other administrators, provide visibility among administrative peers, and provide an extended cadre of potential mentors in specialized arenas (Crow & Matthews, 1998; Reyes, 2003). APs commented that one of the most valuable outcomes of their participation in the AP Academy was having the ability to network with other personnel from other schools in the district for practice advice and information, brainstorming, and problem solving. Virtually all respondents mentioned, on some level, how much the collegial discussions and informal networking meant to them in providing support for the practical application of their new learning and in the performance of their daily duties as school leaders.

The evolution of building developmental networks was particularly noteworthy inasmuch as it relates to the isolation that principals and assistant principals often report in the performance of their duties (Price, 2012; Spillane & Lee, 2013). A district administrator shared that the power of developmental networking has been a positive outcome of the academy. She stated, "The networking has been so positive, not only for sharing information, but also in making connections, mentoring, and peer support." Clearly, development of collaboration and communication was a strong and positive, albeit unanticipated, outcome.

APs engaged in peer mentoring that enabled their schools and district to become professional learning communities. Networking, communication, support alliances, and professional learning became a means of reform and renewal. According to Hansen and Matthews (2002), "Peer mentoring has opened a way of renewing and strengthening the principal. It is a demonstrated means of dealing with change and problems and it is a partnership for growth and improvement" (p. 33).

Discussion

Assistant principals, like principals, seldom have an opportunity to interact with other, like-job professionals concerning personal or professional issues (Barth, 1986). These school leaders often must intentionally seek out colleagues in other schools in order to gain the support and professional stimulation they need to perform their jobs more effectively. The AP Academy fulfilled this function in a very positive way for participants by regularly bringing together a diverse group of APs from multiple school levels that naturally formed networks with one another resulting in a substantial increase in collaboration regarding the performance of their duties as assistant principals. Principals interviewed concurred, claiming that they carried this network of connections with them as they transitioned into their new roles as principals. Program participants overwhelmingly stated that sharing and interacting with colleagues offered many opportunities for them to grow and develop as professionals. Collaborating, working together, sharing ownership in what is accomplished, and finding resource people who can offer support and information helped program participants refine their craft as leaders.

Although the AP Academy was conceived of and implemented as a professional development initiative, the parallels between professional development and group and peer mentoring are surprising. The AP Academy served the purpose of preparing assistants to be stronger instructional leaders through content delivered in formal academy sessions, but also through the group and peer mentoring experiences of academy participants.

A common goal of mentoring programs is to develop stronger professionals who are better equipped to perform in their individual roles. While this process is frequently accomplished through a one-on-one mentoring relationship, the group mentoring experience, and especially the peer mentoring experience reported in this unique case study, supports the use of effective mentoring programs as a best practice in the development of school leaders.

Browne-Ferrigno and Muth (2004) stated:

> Professional development involves the social construction of professional-practice expectations through mentoring, peer sharing and critique and systematic induction. Carefully constructed and implemented mentoring experiences serve as effective professional development not only for aspiring and novice principals but also for veteran principals. (p. 471)

In terms of their growth as instructional leaders, APs, principals, and district leaders agreed that there was much progress in the development of APs' skills. When asked if participation in the Academy had helped the APs feel more prepared to step into the principalship, one middle school AP replied, "Yes. I feel more confident as an instructional leader. Just the ability to have instructional and visionary dialogue with peers, as opposed to just talking about operations or discipline, has been invaluable." A high school AP responded, "I think that my experience in the AP Academy has been beneficial and has increased my capacity and confidence level to be an effective instructional leader and building principal by providing information on current trends and district initiatives."

One participant, who was hired as a principal after just one year of participation in the Academy, expressed her feelings about how the Academy affected her instructional leadership skills. Stemming from the relationships she built in the Academy, and as a result of an action research project she and her colleagues conducted in response to Academy content, this principal stated, "The Academy was a really good bridge to get [to the principalship]. It has just helped us make our teaching practice stronger in our building." A high school principal, hired after completing two years in the Academy, wrote "[The Academy] enabled me to put on the instructional leader's hat, which is a large part of the principal's job today. No longer are principals simply managers. It allowed me to gain insight for the instructional leadership piece."

Finally, district leaders agreed that APs grew in their instructional leadership skills, primarily evidenced by the fact that, by the end of the two-year Academy, seven APs had been selected to fill key roles in the district as building principals. Designers of the Academy were pleased with the outcomes and with the growth of the APs in instructional leadership skills.

The superintendent stated, "The assistant principals have felt so valued. [We're] building that instructional leadership capacity by valuing them and helping them see that they are important."

Best Practices in Developing School Leaders Through Mentoring

We believe that experts who design and provide professional development for leaders may benefit from reviewing and incorporating some of the best practices in mentoring realized in the AP Academy. These best practices included establishing:

1. Strong organizational support for leader development;
2. Clear mentoring program goals and objectives;
3. Clear guidelines for selection of program participants;
4. Specific procedures to match mentors to protégés;
5. Reasonable structures for mentoring relationships; and
6. Careful and ongoing evaluation of the mentoring program.

Those creating leadership development opportunities through best practices in mentoring would also be well served to explore the many different mentoring program sizes and shapes that could be realized. In the case of the AP Academy, participants clearly benefitted from group mentoring and peer mentoring experiences that included (a) the deliberate design to inclusion of diverse perspectives from which all participants can learn, (b) the focus on and enhancement of organizational (i.e., district) goals, (c) opportunities for individuals to share their expertise with a wide array of others, (d) protégé input into developing the learning agenda, (e) increased opportunities for collaboration to reduce isolation, and (f) increased opportunities for networking with peers and mentors.

Participants in the AP Academy described in this chapter developed collegial and trusting relationships between and among mentors and peers. Participants changed their perspectives about their future role as a principal that resulted in changed professional practices in their current role. Communicating with one another in a risk-safe and open environment that included supportive mentors and peers allowed APs to reflect on and explore their professional practice. Interaction, creativity, and innovation were encouraged between mentors and APs and thus, increased the APs' opportunity for leadership capacity building. Program participants indicated high levels of enthusiasm for their own continued professional learning. One AP stated, "I am so much more prepared to lead my school and staff because of these experiences." Comments such as these were echoed by principals and district level leaders. The superintendent stated, "We're building that leadership capacity by valuing [the assistant principals] and helping them see that they are important and that we do see them as future leaders." District leaders as well as participants believed that the professional development, which resulted in mentoring, improved a culture of school leadership throughout the district. The best practices for mentoring were realized through both formal structures and informal serendipitous interactions among AP Academy participants. Clearly, both served the professional development needs of these assistant principals in the pipeline for senior school leadership.

REFERENCES

Allen, T. D., Eby, L. T., & Lentz, E. (2006). The relationship between formal mentoring program characteristics and perceived program effectiveness. *Personnel Psychology, 59*(1), 125–153.

Ambrose, L. (2003). Multiple mentoring: Discover alternatives to a one-on-one learning relationship. *Healthcare Executive, 18*(4), 58–60.

Armstrong, D. E. (2010). Rites of passage: Coercion, compliance and complicity in the socialization of new vice-principals. *Teachers College Record, 111*(12), 1–21.

Austen, P. (2010). Informal instructional teacher leaders: How principals can support them and their effect on instructional reform. *Academic Leadership, 8*(3), 94–101.

Barth, R. (1986). The principal and the profession of teaching. *The Elementary School Journal, 86*(4), 471–492.

Browne-Ferrigno, T. (2003). Becoming a principal: Role conceptualization, initial socialization, role-identity transformation, purposeful engagement. *Educational Administration Quarterly, 39*(4), 468–503.

Browne-Ferrigno, T., & Muth, R. (2004). Leadership mentoring in clinical practice: Role socialization, professional development, and capacity building. *Educational Administration Quarterly, 40*(4), 468–494.

Bryant, S. E. & Terborg, J. R. (2008). Impact of peer mentor training on creating and sharing organizational knowledge. *Journal of Managerial Issues, 20*(1), 11–29.

Burke, R. J., & McKeen, C. A. (1989). Developing formal mentoring programs in organizations. *Business Quarterly, 53*(3), 76–79.

Catalyst. (1993). *Mentoring: A guide to corporate programs and practices.* New York: Catalyst.

Crow, G., & Matthews, L. (1998). *Finding one's way: How mentoring can lead to dynamic leadership.* Thousand Oaks, CA: Corwin Press.

Crowther, F., Ferguson, M., & Hann, L. (2009). *Developing teacher leaders.* Thousand Oaks, CA: Corwin.

Daresh, J. (2004). Mentoring school leaders: Professional promise or predictable problems? *Educational Administration Quarterly, 40*(4), 495–517. doi:10.1177/0013161X04267114

Drago-Severson, E., & Aravena, J. L. (2011). The power of connectivity. *Journal of Staff Development, 32*(2), 50–53.

Eddy, E., Tannenbaum, S., Alliger, G., D'Abate, C., & Givens, S. (2001). *Mentoring in industry: The top 10 issues when building and supporting a mentoring program.* Technical report prepared for the Naval Air Warfare Center Training Systems Division (Contract No. N61339-99-D-0012).

Finkelstein, L. M., & Poteet, M. L. (2007). Best practices in formal workplace mentoring programs. In T. A. Allen & L. T. Eby (Eds.), *The Blackwell handbook of mentoring: A multiple perspectives approach* (pp. 345–367). Malden, MA: Blackwell Publishing.

Fusarelli, B., Militello, M., Alsbury, T., Price, C. E., & Warren, T. (2010). Translational leadership: New principals and the theory and practice of school leaders in the twenty-first century. In A. Shoho, B., Barnett, & A. Tooms (Eds.), *The challenge of first generation principals in the 21st Century: Developing leadership capabilities through professional support* (pp. 1–27). Charlotte, NC: Information Age Publishing.

Glanz, J. (1994). Redefining the roles and responsibilities of assistant principals. *Clearing House, 67,* 283–287.

Glanz, J. (2004). *The assistant principal's handbook: Strategies for success.* Thousand Oaks, CA: Corwin.

Grogan, M. (2000). Laying the groundwork for a reconception of the superintendency from feminist postmodern perspectives. *Educational Administration Quarterly, 36*(1), 117–142.

Grogan, M. (2002). Influences of the discourse of globalization on mentoring for gender equity and social justice in educational leadership. *Leading and Managing, 8*(2), 124–135.

Gurley, D. K., Anast-May, L., & Lee, H. T. (2013). Developing instructional leaders through assistant principals' academy: A partnership for success. *Education and Urban Society.* Advance online publication. doi: 10.1177/0013124513495272

Hallinger, P. (2011). Leadership for learning: Lessons from 40 years of empirical research. *Journal of Educational Administration, 49*(2), 125–142.

Hallinger, P., & Heck, R. (2010). Collaborative leadership effects on school improvement: Integrating unidirectional- and reciprocal-effects models. *Elementary School Journal, 111*(2), 226–252.

Hallinger, P., & Murphy, J. (2013). Running on empty? Finding the time and capacity to lead learning. *NASSP Bulletin, 97*(1), 5–21.

Hansen, J. M., & Matthews, J. (2002). The power of more than one. *Principal Leadership: High School Edition, 3*(2), 30–33.

Higgins, M. C., & Kram, K. E. (2001). Reconceptualizing mentoring at work: A developmental network perspective. *Academy of Management Review, 26*(2), 264–288.

Huizing, R. L. (2010, October). *Mentoring together: A literature review of group mentoring.* Paper presented at the meeting of the Northeastern Association of Business, Economics, and Technology, State College, PA.

Kamler, E. (2007). The aspiring superintendents' study group: Investigating a mentoring network for school leaders. *Mentoring & Tutoring: Partnership in Learning, 14*(3), 297–316.

Kochan, F. K., & Trimble, S. B. (2000). From mentoring to co-mentoring: Establishing collaborative relationships. *Theory Into Practice, 39*(1), 20–28.

Kram, K. E. (1985). *Mentoring at work: Developmental relationships in organisational life.* Glenview, IL: Scott Foresman.

Kram, K. E. (2004). Forward: The making of a mentor. In D. Clutterbuck, & G. Lane (Eds.), *The situational mentor.* Aldershot: Gower.

Kram, K. E., & Higgins, M. C. (2008). A new approach to mentoring. Retrieved from http://online.wsj.com/article/SB122160063875344843.html

Ledford, C. C., Peel, B. B., Good, A. J., Greene, H. C., & O'Connor, K. A. (2006). Roadmap to success: Multiple perspectives on mentoring. *Delta Kappa Gamma Bulletin, 72*(4), 17–39.

Leithwood, K. (2001). School leadership in the context of accountability policies. *International Journal of Leadership in Education, 4*(3), 217–235.

Leithwood, K., Harris, A., & Hopkins, D. (2008). Seven strong claims about successful leadership. *School Leadership and Management, 28*(1), 27–42.

Leithwood, K., & Jantzi, D. (2005). A review of transformational school leadership research, 1996–2005. *Leadership and Policy in Schools, 4*(3), 177–199.

Lovely, S. (2004). Leadership forecasting. *Leadership, 34*(1), 17–19.

Messmer, M. (2001). *Human resources kit for dummies.* New York, NY: Wiley

Mullen, C. A. (2000). Constructing co-mentoring partnerships: Walkways we must travel. *Theory Into Practice, 39*(1), 4–11.

Mullen, C. A. (2005). *Mentorship primer.* New York, NY: Peter Lang.

Nettles, S. M., & Harrington, C. (2007). Revisiting the importance of the direct effects of school leadership on student achievement: The implications for school improvement policy. *Peabody Journal of Education, 8*(4), 724–736.

Newcomb, W. S. (2011). Planning for successful mentoring. *Educational Planning, 20*(2), 14–21.

O'Brien, M., & Llamas, M. (2012, October). Lessons learned from four years of peer mentoring in a tiered group program within education. *Journal of the Australia and New Zealand Student Services Association, 40,* 7–15.

Oliver, R. (2003). Assistant principal job satisfaction and desire to become principals. *Educational Leadership Review, 4*(2), 38–46.

Oliver, R. (2005). Assistant principal professional growth and development: A matter that cannot be left to chance. *Educational Leadership and Administration, 17,* 89–100.

O'Neil, J., & Marsick, V. J. (2009). Peer mentoring and action learning. *Adult Learning, 20*(1), 19–24.

Phillips-Jones, L. (1983). Establishing a formalized mentoring program. *Training and Development Journal, 2,* 38–42.

Price, H. E. (2012). Principal-teacher interactions: How affective relationships shape principal and teacher attitudes. *Educational Administration Quarterly, 48*(1), 39–85.

Ragins, B. R., Cotton, J. L., & Miller, J. S. (2000). Marginal mentoring: The effects of type of mentor, quality of relationship, and program design on work and career attitudes. *Academy of Management Journal, 43*(6), 1177–1194.

Reyes, A. (2003). The relationship of mentoring to job placement in school administration. *NASSP Bulletin, 57*(635), 45–64.

Rhoades, L, & Eisenberger, R. (2002). Perceived organizational support: A review of the literature. *Journal of Applied Psychology, 87*(3), 698–714.

Robinson, V. M. J., Lloyd, C. A., & Rowe, K. J. (2008). The impact of leadership on student outcomes: An analysis of the differential effects of leadership types, *Educational Administration Quarterly, 44*(5), 635–674.

Roby, D. E. (2011). Teacher leaders impacting school culture. *Education, 131*(4), 782–790.

Schoen, L., & Fusarelli, L. D. (2008). Innovation, NCLB, and the fear factor: The challenge of leading 21st-century schools in an era of accountability, *Educational Policy, 22*(1), 181–204.

Searby, L. J. (2013). Do you have a mentoring mindset? Ten tips to help new principals make the most out of a mentoring relationship. *Principal, 92*(3), 26–29.

Silva, J., White, G., & Yoshida, R. (2011). The direct effects of principal-student discussions on eighth grade students' gains in reading achievement: An experimental study. *Educational Administration Quarterly, 47*(5), 772–793.

Smith, I., & Addison, C. (2013). The "new" school leader: Training instructional leaders for a new generation of teachers and learners. *Academy of Educational Leadership Journal, 17*(2), 135–140.

Spillane, J. P., & Lee, L. C. (2013) Novice school principals' sense of ultimate responsibility: Problems of practice in transitioning to the principal's office. *Educational Administration Quarterly.* Advance online publication. doi:10.1177/0013161X13505290

Tyler, R. (1998). Mentoring programs link employees and experienced executives. *HR Magazine, 43*(5), 98–103.

Viator, R. E. (1999). An analysis of formal mentoring programs and perceived barriers to obtaining a mentor at large public accounting firms. *Accounting Horizons, 13*(1), 37–53.

Witziers, B., Bosker, R. J., & Kruger, M. L. (2003). Educational leadership and student achievement: The elusive search for an association. *Educational Administration Quarterly, 39*(3), 398–425.

Zachary, L. J. (2012). *The mentor's guide: Facilitating effective learning relationships* (2nd ed.). San Francisco: Jossey-Bass.

Zasloff, M., & Okurowski, M. E. (2011). Federal agency finds success in group mentoring program. *Public Manager, 41*(2), 53–56.

CHAPTER 11

MENTORING FOR NEW PRINCIPALS IN URBAN SCHOOL DISTRICTS

One Size Does Not Fit All

Constance Magee and Charles L. Slater

SCENARIO

The call comes late in the afternoon on Tuesday, August 17th, just 21 days before school is scheduled to begin. The district administrator shares the news, hours before the school board will make it official. Karen is the new principal of South Middle School, one of the most challenging schools in the district with low achievement of students and high poverty in the community. She is elated and shocked at the same time. Having spent the last three years as a middle school assistant principal in a similar urban school, she feels she has a vision for improving South, but the job seems overwhelming. Elated and scared, she calls her former boss to share the news. Her mind is reeling with all of the jobs to do: clean out her old office, move into her new office, look at the student schedules, look at the school data, complete the staffing process, and start building a rapport with her new staff. Karen has to get

Best Practices in Mentoring for Teacher and Leader Development, pp. 197–217
Copyright © 2016 by Information Age Publishing
All rights of reproduction in any form reserved.

the keys to her new school, find out what is in place and what she feels are the first things to change, and get ready to meet teachers on September 7th and the students on September 8th.

Karen begins her work as soon as she gets the call. Officially, she does not begin until August 20th, but she knows she needs to start now; every minute is precious. The 14-hour days begin as Karen tries to fully understand her new job and the responsibilities that she previously watched others take care of. Now she must do it all by herself.

This job would be a challenge for any school administrator, but Karen's situation is uniquely challenging considering the time left before school begins. South Middle School has all of the problems of an urban school. It has been in Program Improvement (PI) for the past 10 years. Any school accepting Title I funds and not meeting Annual Yearly Progress (AYP) targets is considered Program Improvement (PI) status. South has been through all 5 years of PI sanctions required under the federal No Child Left Behind Act (NCLB, 2001), and teachers continue to struggle getting students to reach proficiency in math and language arts. Current data shows that 30% of the students are proficient or advanced in math and language arts based on the California Content Standards Test (CST).

Most of the teachers at South are inexperienced, yet energetic, and most have stated that they enjoy collaborating with other educators. Their biggest concern is student discipline because they say "the kids run the school." The list of changes Karen wants to see include: strengthening the uniform policy, creating an ID policy, creating On Campus Suspension (OCS) and detention, tightening daily accountability by checking classrooms, and establishing clear school-wide rules and rewards. Karen also wants to add a "Student of the Month Breakfast" recognition, start a Monday Morning Message via the cable network, calibrate consequences between and among administrators and counselors, and create a point system with rewards and consequences for student behavior.

South's teachers are asking for better student behavior and higher expectations for students. The superintendent is expecting increased student achievement as measured by improved CST scores. The parents expect the school to be a safe and nurturing place where students will gain the skills and habits needed to succeed in high school. The community expects the school to improve test scores and student behavior and get out of PI, which could lead to increased property values near the school.

When all of the expectations are put on one page, the list is overwhelming. Even the most experienced administrator would struggle to complete all of these goals over several years, but South's new principal must implement these changes and succeed within one year.

The job of principal is hard to understand until one imagines what it must be like to be handed the school keys and to be instantly responsible for 1,000 students, 40 teachers, and 35 other staff members. Being principal cannot be learned solely in a university classroom or by observing a principal in action. Schön (1983) made an eloquent case for the necessity of combining reflection with action, and this reflection can likely be aided by conversation with another person such as a mentor. Principals must learn through experience; yet they are expected to have expertise right from the start. There is no forgiveness for error; everyone expects the principal to make the right decision every time (Howley, Adrianaivo, & Perry, 2005; Walker & Qian, 2006; Weindling & Dimmock, 2006). Even unintended mistakes can change the culture of the school.

Given these intense pressures and expectations, one would expect that only experienced principals would be selected for these most challenging schools, but research studies have shown that inexperienced principals often begin their principalship at low performing schools, in areas of poverty, serving minority students (Knapp, Copland, Honig, Plecki, & Portin, 2010). South Middle School, the urban school in the opening vignette, exemplifies a typical low performing school because all of South's students qualify for free or reduced price lunch, and are members of minority subgroups. Leading an urban, low performing school presents great challenges to a new principal.

Nation-wide over 20% of principals of urban schools leave within the first two years. This loss is critical to the school because after losing a principal, schools tend to have lower student achievement (Burkhauser, Gates, Hamilton, & Ikemoto, 2012). Principal support is necessary to reverse this trend and increase the tenure of principals (Alsbury & Hackman, 2006; Crippen, 2004; Daresh, 2007; Davis, Darling-Hammond, LaPointe, & Meyerson, 2005; Knapp et al., 2010; LaPointe, Davis, & Cohen, 2007; Olson, 2007b; Piggot-Irvine, 2004). Unfortunately, many urban principals are called to report to the school with little formal support. Most districts do not have the resources or motivation to create and sustain effective principal support programs (Wallace Foundation, 2007). With or without support, principals must make significant changes in short periods in order to turn around low performing urban schools.

The job of the principal in challenging schools has changed dramatically over the past decade. Good principals used to be those who took care of student discipline and efficiently managed the site. Today's principals must be agents of change, committed to continuous improvement. They must be masters of finance, human resources, instruction, data analysis and politics, while balancing the needs of their students, parents, teachers and district administrators (Wildy & Clarke, 2008; Wohlstetter, Datnow, & Park, 2008). It is no wonder that many view the job of being a principal in an urban school as overwhelming and some question whether one person can effectively accomplish everything that is expected (Olson, 2007a; Walker, 2008).

In this study, we explored the experiences of urban principals as they led their schools during the first year, and the support they received through mentoring. This chapter will begin with a review of literature examining the challenges that urban principals face and the kind of support they receive. Using case study methodology, the experiences of four new school principals in an urban area are presented. The path each leader followed to becoming principal is described and their varied mentoring experiences are explored through narratives. Findings are explained through the themes that emerged from interviews with the new principals. Finally, we discuss recommendations for those responsible for creating mentoring programs for urban principals.

RELEVANT LITERATURE

Competent principals are second only to teachers in affecting student achievement (Leithwood, Louis, Anderson, & Wahlstrom, 2004). Hess and Kelly (2005) argue, "In an era of results-driven school reform, in which principals are asked to take responsibility for student achievement and use data to drive decisions, their skill and knowledge matter more than ever" (p. 2). Because of the connection between principal action and student achievement, investing in programs to help new principals succeed in their increasingly complex jobs would seem to have great merit (Cotton, 2003; Leithwood, Harris, & Stauss, 2010; Leithwood, et al., 2004; Marzano, Waters, & McNulty, 2005).

Alsbury and Hackman (2006) reported that 32 states have passed laws related to administrator support; however, these are primarily for those just entering the profession.

In many other states support is not comprehensive, leaving new principals isolated and overwhelmed in the role of principal. The voices of these new principals and their first hand experiences are only beginning to be heard in the literature (Cowie & Crawford, 2011).

Challenges for Urban Principals

The challenges of urban schools are particularly acute. Portin, Knapp, Dareff, Feldman, Samuelson, and Yeh (2009) summarize that the challenges come from a history of racial segregation and intractable poverty. Law suits in many states have challenged the lack of equity in distribution of resources to urban schools. Principals face intense scrutiny from political and business interests and the federal government has imposed a high stakes accountability system in an effort to overcome long-standing low achievement of students in urban areas (NCLB, 2001). All students are required to be proficient in math and language arts. Schools whose students do not meet this federal target are placed in Program Improvement (PI) and failure to exit PI comes with sanctions that increase in severity including removing the principal, reconstitution of the teaching staff, or closing the school.

Principal responsibilities have changed dramatically in the last 20 years (LaPointe, Meyerson, & Darling-Hammond, 2006). As budgets have shrunk, principal job duties have expanded (Peterson & Kelley, 2001). Principals are often assigned to these challenging urban settings with little time to prepare, given inconsistent support, but still held to the same standards as nonurban schools. Without proper support, principal success is unlikely (Crippen, 2004; Darling-Hammond & Orphanos, 2007; Davis et al., 2005; Piggot-Irvine, 2004; Silver, Lochmiller, Copland, & Tripps, 2009; Wildy & Clarke, 2008). Yet districts continue to assign new principals to urban schools and expect them to flourish, often with little support. What support is offered may not be adequate to meet the unique needs of individual principals and their site-specific issues (LaPointe et al., 2007; Silver et al., 2009).

Mentoring for New Principals

One possibility for supporting new principals and helping them to manage their new challenges is mentoring. Mentoring has been widely used in medicine, law, and business, and has been used extensively in teaching (Neumerski, 2013). Villani (2006) defined mentoring as "support from a more experienced colleague to help a beginner or someone new to a position or school system perform at a high level" (p. 19).

The Wallace Foundation (2007) reported that mentoring programs for principals have varied widely in quality and have had mixed results. The authors of the report cited that mentoring programs often had "vague or unclear goals, insufficient focus on instruction, little training for mentors, insufficient mentoring time, lack of data to assess results, and little funding" (Wallace Foundation, 2007, p. 4). The report concluded that mentoring for new principals should be required by all school districts, and that programs should have clear goals and provide sufficient time and funding for mentoring, as well as conduct regular evaluations of the programs.

Hansford and Ehrich (2006) conducted a meta-analysis of principal mentoring and found several cases in which principals felt increased support and confidence from sharing ideas and solving problems with a mentor. However, they also cited lack of time for mentoring activities and sometimes a mismatch between mentor and mentee. These authors recommended that mentors should focus on giving support, building trust, and offering respect. Mentees valued mentors who were good listeners and kept confidences. They reported that the most successful programs included emphasis on reflection, networking and sharing of ideas.

Daresh (2007) studied 20 mentors in two districts implementing new principal mentoring programs. He found that they were often selected to be mentors because they had solid records of efficient management of their schools, but that these types of mentors were not necessarily the best ones to model instructional leadership for new principals. The mentors were more comfortable helping new leaders adjust to their roles as school administrators, rather than helping them with skills that would improve instruction.

The use of mentoring is most common with individuals who are new to a profession. In educational administration, new principals face multiple challenges that can impact and shape their entire careers (García-Garduño, Slater, & López-Gorosave, 2011). As researchers, we sought to add to the knowledge base about how new principals have experienced mentoring in urban districts through this study. The research questions employed were: What support is provided for new principals in urban districts? To what extent does the support provided meet the needs of new principals in urban districts?

BACKGROUND AND METHODS

A purposeful sampling strategy was used in this study, combining criterion sampling and convenience sampling (Creswell, 2009). The criteria for selection were that the participants be principals in an urban school district who had served in that capacity for less than two years. This resulted in choosing four participants who were principals from two urban districts in California: West Unified and Central Unified. West Unified district has nearly 100 elementary and secondary schools, and serves approximately 80,000 students. Central Unified has approximately 25 middle and elementary schools, and serves approximately 15,000 students. The researcher served as one of the principals in the study and the other three were principals whom the researcher knew.

Although these two districts are clearly not the same size, they offered very similar support programs to their new principals. The two district mentoring programs assigned experienced principals to mentor new principals. A district leadership grant paid the new principals and mentors for time spent collaborating. They were required to meet two times a month and required to call two times a month. There were also required trainings and monthly meetings. This structure lasted for the first two years of each principal's service.

Data Gathering and Analysis

The qualitative method of narrative inquiry was selected because it allowed a focus on the experience of the participants through story telling (Clandinin & Connelly, 2000; Slater, 2011).The main data-gathering instrument was semistructured interviews, conducted with new principal participants. We asked open-ended questions to learn the stories of new principals' experiences with mentoring. There were five interview protocols that were administered over the course of the study. Examples of questions were: Describe how the staff reacted to you as a new principal. What did you spend most of your time on? What do you wish you could have spent more time doing? What challenges were you facing when you first began? Were you offered support after the year began? If so, what types of support were most helpful during this time?

Data analysis was conducted by carefully reading the transcripts to recall the setting and details of each story and to identify significant statements, descriptions, or expressions made by the respondents (Viernes & Guzman, 2005). The data were analyzed after each interview using the method of constant comparison (Lincoln & Guba, 1985). Interviews, memos, e-mails, call logs, and all other data were coded using ATLAS.ti, a qualitative data analysis program. The data were subjected to both within-case and cross-case analyses to find internal coherence and to determine the meaningfulness of the statements (Creswell, 2009; Patton, 2002). Cross-case analysis resulted in the identification of common themes which emerged through condensing the codes from all of the transcripts and documents. We now summarize the new principals' experiences through their narratives.

PARTICIPANTS' NARRATIVES

Four principals were interviewed for this study. The pseudonyms used as the school names were also used as the principals' names in these narratives, as principals identify with their school name and school and community members often see them as synonymous.

Harding

The first narrative is the personal experience of one of the authors of this article when she was a new principal in West Unified. The pseudonym Harding is used to represent the hardening or solidifying of her practice at the school. She believed that the policies, procedures, and curricular practices she initiated when she began five years prior to this study were fully integrated and sustainable school programs, partly due to the mentoring support she received.

Her new principal support started immediately after she was hired in October. She was given the Change of Principal Workshop information that had been created for the prior principal in August. Several pages summarized a school meeting where the staff discussed openly and honestly what they wanted to change and keep from the former principal, like a specific do's and don'ts list for the new principal. In early November, the district assigned her a new principal coach. During this year, West Unified had six other new principals. A principal on special assignment was designated to mentor all six of them. The mentor was in charge of meeting with them at their sites, coordinating monthly support meetings, accessing district resources, and supporting them to ensure their success as new principals. Although she was assigned, Harding felt a rapport with her mentor. She felt that she could trust her to help her and keep her issues confidential. Her mentor made herself available via cell phone and email, and she scheduled monthly meetings in her office.

In addition to her monthly visits, the mentor organized monthly group meetings for all the new principals. She asked what district topics needed to be covered, and then she would arrange for an expert in this area to address the issue or offer individual tutoring. Some of the topics were budgeting, human resource issues, district data systems for finance and students, and staff evaluations. The group meetings also gave the new principals time to network and talk about common new principal issues or problems.

Harding felt supported by her new principal mentor, and the structure put in place during her first year. Her mentor was there to listen and suggest ideas. Many times, she helped process an issue to clarify a plan for action. Harding confided in her when she was having trouble explaining her vision for the school to her boss. Her mentor was a continual voice of reason. She was not there to tell her what to do, but more to ask questions and help her find her own solutions. Harding's mentor could access anyone she needed at the district level. If she wanted to know more about a specific part of the job, her mentor would locate the expert and set up a meeting to learn directly from that person.

Hope

Hope was placed in a particularly tough school in West Unified, in a poor community experiencing an increase in gangs and violence. She started her principalship in the first year of the leadership grant which supported the mentoring program for new principals. She was assigned to her school in mid-August, but did not receive any formal new principal support until mid-October. In October, she was assigned a new principal mentor, but that mentor was promoted and so another mentor was assigned. Several circumstances made it difficult for Hope to connect with her new mentor. Hope's first concern was that she was assigned to someone she did not know. She found it hard to confide in her mentor and had difficulty establishing a level of trust needed to work closely with her. Compounding this issue was the mentor's lack of availability. The mentor was an experienced principal who had just been moved to a new school. Her mentor was overwhelmed with her own list of changes to make and issues to resolve, leaving less time available to meet with Hope. There was also an issue in scheduling meetings. Hope was keeping long hours and wanted to meet at the end of her day at 6:30 or 7:00 P.M. Her mentor wanted to meet at 5:00 P.M. Hope said, "If I meet with her at 5:00, I will have to take a bunch of stuff home and I will be up late getting it all done."

Hope attended the monthly new principal meetings, but said, "The meetings don't cover things I need right now." One monthly meeting, however, was very productive for Hope. The new principals and their coaches were trained to use a system called "Breakthrough Coaching," where they learned how to use the school secretary as a time manager so that they could maximize their time working on curriculum and visiting classrooms. Hope seemed motivated by this system and felt it would help her focus on visiting classrooms and spend less time distracted by paperwork. The program emphasized teaching the principal how to delegate everything possible in order to focus on instruction.

Hope was not without mentoring or support; she just did not connect with her new principal mentor and never developed a relationship or had regular meetings to build rapport. She did get mentoring through the district as a Program Improvement (PI) school principal, and she had informal mentoring from Harding. She said, "I found my own support when I needed it." She called or met with Harding when she had questions or concerns, and she called or met with her PI coach, but she rarely accessed her assigned new principal coach in this way.

To outside observers, Hope had taken on a difficult job and had made significant positive changes in her first seven months as principal. She implemented behavior standards and the uniform policy and started to transform the culture of the school. Students became more respectful and quieter in the halls and classrooms. She set the stage to improve classroom instruction and established a team, getting the teachers to enforce new rules and work to provide student incentives. Hope was later asked by the district leaders to be a paid mentor for aspiring principals, acknowledging her success as a new principal.

Sunrise

Sunrise is also a West Unified principal who was teaching and working on her administrative credential when she was promoted to assistant principal at a neighboring elementary school where she had worked for three years. She was promoted again in August, 2010, to be the senior principal at an elementary school in a quiet neighborhood nearby. The pseudonym Sunrise was selected for her school because she walked into a well performing school. The school had made steady gains in the Academic Performance Index (API) during the previous six years. She worked to keep the effective practices in place but also made improvements to boost the achievement of the English Language Learners, whose lack of growth had originally placed the school in Program Improvement.

Like Hope, Sunrise was also promoted in mid-August, but she was able to select her new principal coach. She was also in West Unified and was part of the leadership grant. For her mentor, she chose the principal she had worked with three years prior to her promotion. She was with him during his first year at the site, and he had kept a binder of everything he had done that year. He had also asked her to keep a similar binder. The binders documented every staff meeting, training, staff development, agenda, and form of communication that he had sent during his first year at the site. He gave her his binder at their first meeting, and she said that the binders and the mentoring from him made her feel very confident about her new position. She said it was, "like having a lesson plan for the school." She said she often referred to the binders to get a sense of what was coming up or what she should do during certain parts of the year. Sunrise described her level of support as very effective. She had great rapport with her new principal mentor with whom she met, emailed, called and saw socially outside of school. He was her friend as well as her mentor. She trusted him to keep confidences and felt she had access to him whenever she needed him, in addition to the scheduled meetings. At times she would ask for suggestions, but most conversations helped her process what she did, or what she was planning to do. She felt prepared for the job, but she just wondered, "Is this going to be fun?"

Another level of support provided to her was the Assistant Superintendent, who called her each Friday for the first few months of the year to check in on her. Sunrise said when the Assistant Superintendent called her she felt cared for, and she was glad she had someone to talk to or answer her questions. She also had monthly group meetings for new principals. These were the same meetings that Hope attended, organized around general district topics like budgeting, human resources, planning, evaluation or other items the district felt were important for new principals to know about. Like Hope, Sunrise expressed some frustration with the monthly group meetings. The one piece she really liked was the "Breakthrough" training, which emphasized prioritizing and delegating as much paperwork as possible. Sunrise was eager to start parts of this process and said it helped encourage her to delete excess email and delegate calls or projects that did not directly impact the classrooms.

She felt the district support met her needs, and she emphasized that she was glad she was able to choose her coach. She said it would have been more difficult if she was forced to work with someone she did not already know personally and professionally.

Fast

The last narrative is the story of Fast, from Central Unified. She was in her second year as principal at the school. The pseudonym of Fast was selected because it seems that things were changing very quickly at her school. The district committed resources to help the school improve which set the stage for dramatic increases in student achievement.

Fast was a middle school principal. What is different about her story is that she was an assistant principal at the same school for two years before being named principal at the start of her third year. She had been brought to the school with the other members of the administrative team after the district heads reconstituted, which was one of the methods used to address schools with low student achievement, transferring some of the administrators and starting with a fresh team. All of the site administrators had been moved to other schools, except the principal. Fast had been a chronically low performing school and had been in Program Improvement for many years. This effort was part of the district's attempt to improve the school and satisfied the Program Improvement requirements for schools that had been in PI for more than four years.

During her first year as principal, Fast said she felt supported. Although the district was smaller than West Unified, it had a comprehensive new principal support program. She was informed in June that she would take over as principal. Fast had all summer to plan, and she had two years of experience at the school which helped guide her vision. During her two years as assistant principal, she worked to strengthen the discipline at the school. During this time, the district also devoted resources to improve the appearance of the campus. New paint, landscaping, gardens, and murals were among the improvements.

Fast described a campus that had looked more like a prison than a school before these improvements. All of the halls were fenced in, and there had been very few plants or green spaces. The On Campus Suspension (OCS) program for student discipline was in a separate building area. It had high cyclone fencing around it, keeping the students inside. This area was completely transformed. All of the fencing was removed and colored picnic tables were placed there with decorative planters and other improvements to the landscaping. This created a space for students to sit and eat during nutrition break. The OCS was moved to a classroom near the office. This classroom was decorated with rules, rewards, and consequence posters. It had information about the school, and directions on how to get to college. It was clean, and bright. This was a big change in the environment and processes that had been in place four years previous.

Fast said she felt supported during her first year. She was assigned a new principal mentor who worked closely with her, she had role models at the district office, and she was in the district new principal monthly support program. During the first semester, her new principal mentor was available at any time to answer questions, meet with her, observe and give feedback, and problem solve with her if she was unsure how to handle an issue. At the end of the first semester, the district had to reassign her mentor to take over a school where the principal had left midyear. After they reassigned her mentor, she was not as comfortable talking about her struggles. She knew the supervisor wanted her to feel comfortable, but she said, "I don't really want my boss to know I am having any struggles at all." Although she may not have shared all of her frustrations with her supervisor, Fast said she still felt supported. When her new principal mentor left, the director of schools filled in as the mentor on-site. Fast attended the monthly district induction meetings, and she had several informal mentors whom she could call or meet with when she needed additional feedback.

FINDINGS

As we examined all of the narratives in a cross-case analysis, we identified four central themes that emerged from the new principal experiences. The four themes were trust, relationships between the principal and the mentor, transformation, and support. These ideas are explained through the principals' words, using exemplars from their transcripts.

Trust: Support Starts with Trusting Each Other

The first theme from the principal narratives was trust. Trust was a key factor in cases where the principals felt supported. Trust was established over time through building relationships with those who offered support. Support came through both formally established relationships and informal ones. Trust was a necessity in the relationships new principals built with those assisting them. They also sought trust through feedback from support providers. Site and union surveys were used to build trust with the staff and to gain valuable feedback about their principal behaviors.

The principals who had a Change of Principal Workshop noted that this process was extremely helpful in establishing priorities and getting a head start on ways to build trust and improve the school, gleaned from the teacher's perspective. The Change of Principal Workshop process was used in West Unified to help the new principals get a feeling for what was working at the school, what teachers wanted to change, and what they wanted to improve. The workshop participants (teachers) also aired any rumors that may have been circulating about the new principal, all before the year began. Sunrise described the support of the workshop this way:

> They talked about it in the morning and then they presented it to me. What was working, what can be improved, thoughts, what they want to know, the rumor mill, all that stuff. That's just been my document that I go on. So that's, I think, really supportive because it kind of gives a new principal a path.

Sunrise described using the Change of Principal feedback as a list of what she should do. Hope described the teacher feedback like this:

> Based on the feedback, even from the Change of Principal Workshop, they just felt kind of just discouraged, I guess. They felt there was lack of communication. They felt like they did not really know things that were going on. There were just a lot of questions, confusion. They sort of felt like they weren't supported, in terms of their curriculum or in terms of dealing with students and parents. They kind of felt like the kids were able to run the show.
>
> So, they were very hopeful, that things would get better. They said things like, well, it cannot get any worse; we really hope that it gets better. And they were very, very positive and never said anything disparaging about the former administration, other than it just did not work. They said the principal was a nice person who had good intentions or a good heart, but it just did not work.

Like Hope and Sunrise, Harding also had the benefit of the Change of Principal Workshop information. The only difference was that the workshop was done for another principal, so there was no information specific to her. She found the list was like reading a teacher's diary about the school. She was immediately privy to insight on what teachers wanted and what they felt their issues were before she stepped onto the campus. For her it was invaluable. She was starting at the end of October and the workshop insight allowed her to jump-start her planning process. So, trusting their mentors and trusting information from teachers on what they desired in their principals emerged as a common theme with the new principals.

Relationship Between Principals and Mentors

The principals who felt the most support were working with mentors who fit the principals' needs and personalities. A "good fit" emerged as a key element of effective support. Principals who selected their mentors, or were matched with someone they respected and got along with, gained the most from their working relationships. New principals felt the need to be paired with someone they already knew so they would not have to develop a new relationship while trying to learn their role. Sunrise expressed it like this:

> I already have a good friendship with my coach (mentor), and if I did not get to choose my coach.... It would've just stressed me out ... the whole thing would have been BS, because I would've had to establish a professional working relationship and I already had that all built up. So thank goodness. I think that was the biggest support because I obviously have his cell phone number. He takes me, we go to eat and ... hang out. He's probably been the biggest support that I've had this year, besides you.

The new principals expressed a need to keep certain conversations confidential. They felt comfortable asking questions about protocol or processes, but some issues were frustrating. They could share their struggles if their mentor was separated from their evaluator, but in some cases, where staffing was decreased, mentors became the new principal's evaluator. Hope and Fast described this feeling in a very similar way:

> Hmm. I hesitate only because I don't know about the emotional part. Like, I do feel that I can talk to them but politically speaking, would I? No. Do I want my boss to know that I am having a hard time doing the job? [No]

Fast developed a very productive relationship through informal mentoring with her union representative. Fast shared that this relationship was a key piece to her success. Fast felt "the union person actually kind of coaches and is another layer of intervention when the principal is concerned about a piece of the school." Fast was also supported by the district mentoring program for new principals and by her new principal coach. Fast described her mentoring this way:

> She would come in, other than the meetings, she would come in once a month and just like shadow me or if I had any questions or concerns or we'd walk around classes and she'd give me feedback. Or if there were things that I was working on that I wanted her input on, so it was flexible for me. You know, sometimes, I would have her come in on a leadership meeting because I wanted her to see how I ran the meeting and give me some outsider feedback on what do I need to work on as a leader. And then sometimes we'd

walk through classrooms and I'd ask for her honest feedback. What do you see are the gaps that maybe I am not seeing? Or things like that.

Transformation: Becoming an Effective and Confident Principal

The theme of transformation describes the changes in the new principals as they transitioned into their role of principal. Daresh (2007) describes career entry as an exercise in survival; however, the principals in this study seemed to be prepared for their positions, essentially skipping the "survival" stage. They were stressed and overwhelmed, but it was not a feeling of helplessness. Rather, it was a feeling that there was just not enough time in each day to accomplish everything they had put on the "to do" list.

At the beginning of their first year, the new principals needed support in the form of someone to talk to, to listen, and to guide them to the resources they needed. Hope explained her district mentor like this:

> My district coach (mentor), yes, he's very open and he's just a great listener. Yeah. You just need someone to listen at the beginning; I had a lot more questions. But still, like, last week, I had a question about the contract for the block schedule because we had to vote. So, he's my go-to person for those kinds of things.

At the beginning of the year, new principals relied on their mentors to help them get off to a strong start. Some mentors helped by modeling an effective process or system. Sunrise described her mentor's help this way:

> In the beginning, I sent them [the staff] all a letter introducing me, giving them their data. Then one thing my coach (mentor) taught me besides sending that letter is everything you do for them that they want you to do, you have to tell them you're doing it. You have to publish it. So I put everything in the bulletin. So now we have like the custodial schedule they were concerned about, that's in the bulletin. The library schedule they were concerned about, that's in the bulletin. The discipline stuff they were concerned about, that's in the bulletin.

The mentor helped Sunrise to model transparency, celebrating, and publishing the good news, so the staff knew that she was working toward the goals they set together. Sunrise said she used her Change of Principal Workshop document like a to-do list. She wanted to make sure the staff felt she was working toward the concerns they had shared with her.

Support

All four new principals were offered formal support from a new principal mentor and monthly group meetings. Three of the four principals felt supported during their first year. Hope did not feel supported because her first mentor was assigned well into the school year and then had to leave when she was promoted to a new position. She did not know the next mentor who was assigned and she was often unavailable for consultation. The other principals met with their coaches frequently and gained confidence through a process of listening, reflecting, and support. Their experiences are aligned with the research on support for new principals. Support must be comprehensive, covering the managerial, financial, political, emotional, and operational needs of the new principal (Knapp et al., 2010).

DISCUSSION

Quality mentoring for new principals includes giving empathy, counseling, sharing ideas, problem solving, offering support, and providing professional development (Hansford & Ehrich, 2006; Wallace Foundation, 2007). The mentoring experiences of the new principals in this study led to them acquiring increased confidence (Hansford & Ehrich, 2006). One new principal (Hope) received less formal support, had little face time with her mentor, and felt a weak connection to her mentor. The Wallace study (2007), *Getting Principal Mentoring Right: Lessons from the Field* described insufficient mentoring time and weak training for mentors as two of the six most common problems in mentoring programs for principals. This, indeed, was demonstrated by Hope's experience.

Other activities that served to support the new principals were networking with other principals, site and union surveys, and reflection time with colleagues and mentors. In Crippen's (2004) study of support for new principals, these activities were among the ten features she outlined as those that provided a safety net for new principals.

Piggot-Irvine (2004) described the value of mentoring for both new and experienced principals. She found that the process of reflection was of greatest value, explaining that through reflection, principals get the chance to acknowledge ongoing change, recognize things that are going well, and celebrate success (Piggot-Irvine, 2004). The findings in the study reported in this chapter confirm the strength of the reflective process. Each new principal mentioned how useful she found the built-in time for reflection in the new principal mentoring program. Some did not see that changes had occurred until they reflected with their mentors.

Mentoring is likely to be helpful to all beginning principals, but the need is particularly pressing for urban principals. Their survival rate is low and their challenges are steep (Burkhauser et al., 2012). Research on the principalship often looks at what leaders need to do, but rarely examines the support they require to achieve success.

This study begins to fill a gap in existing educational leadership literature by reporting what urban principals need. The new principals in this study were open and honest, sharing their successes and struggles as they became more comfortable in the role of principal. The different levels of support from the districts served to meet their needs in most cases. All four felt that the mentoring, both formal and informal, was most beneficial to their success as new principals. They emphasized the need to select their own mentors or be matched with someone with similar experience in that type of school with knowledge of the community and specific school issues. Those who had a Change of Principal Workshop also spoke highly of the experience. Knowing what the staff wanted to keep and change before starting the year helped the new principals plan their work more efficiently.

RECOMMENDATIONS FOR PRACTICE

Districts can take specific actions to help new leaders successfully transition into the role of principal. District action should include improving new principal support by enhancing mentor training, extending the mentoring period, and using new principal input to tailor support to meet new principal needs. New principals are not the only ones who benefit from the mentoring process. Experienced principals improve their own practice as they support new principals (Smith, 2007). This structure could also be used among experienced principals to counteract stagnant practice and focus on continuous improvement.

Mentor Training and Time

Not all successful principals make successful mentors for new principals. As described in this study, each new principal's experience is unique and depends on the context of the school, the timing of the principal placement, and the relationships that have been established on the campus. Training for mentors must address these individual needs, while also supporting the common challenges of being a new principal. Findings from this study and the literature suggest training for mentors should include instruction in: (a) listening, rather than advising; (b) asking reflective questions, rather than giving answers; (c) maintaining frequent contact while

taking responsibility for the communication; and (d) providing encouragement, empathy, and support as opposed to specific content knowledge and
skills (Alsbury & Hackman, 2006).

Mentoring often ends after the new principal's first year. The findings
from this study and the literature on new principals undergird the notion
that mentoring should be a two or three year commitment (Wallace Foundation, 2007). First year principals are learning about their school during
their first year and often make the largest system changes during their
second year. First year mentoring support could focus on encouragement
and empathy, while second year support may transition to helping new
principals improve instruction and school systems. Lengthening the coaching time commitment may also help new principals feel more confidence
and stability during their first two years. In addition to lengthening the
duration of new principal mentoring, districts should consider using full-
time mentors rather than adding this responsibility to working principals.
The literature confirms that time spent with the mentor was a critical part
of new principals feeling supported (Alsbury & Hackman, 2006; LaPointe,
Meyerson, & Darling-Hammond, 2006; Piggot-Irvine, 2004; Silver et al.,
2009; Smith, 2007; Wallace Foundation, 2007). New principals who had
full time mentors had more meetings during the day, at their convenience,
and at their own site, saving the new principal valuable time.

Individualizing Support

The "fit" between principal and mentor was a key finding both in this
study and in the literature on principal support (Alsbury & Hackman,
2006; Wallace Foundation, 2007). New principals need to have rapport with
their mentor, and they need to have confidence in their mentor's expertise
and experience. Districts should try to provide a choice of mentors. New
principals who have had intern-like experiences may likely select the prior
principals to mentor them. Those new to the district could meet several of
the potential mentors and then select the ones with whom they felt they
had the best rapport.

Personalized support was a strong finding confirmed in the literature
on mentoring new principals (Silver et al., 2009). Personalized support is
necessary to address the stress and pressure that new principals experience during their first year. The new principals in this study all admitted
feeling overwhelmed by the amount to do in the short period allotted.
They poured themselves into their jobs mentally and physically, at times
feeling frustration and exhaustion. As they transitioned into their role, they
began finding ways to balance the stress of the job through exercise and
time with family and friends.

Personalized support also helped these principals grow professionally. The new principals benefited from sharing best practice and telling their stories of success and challenge. The principals expressed that the simple act of sharing, listening, and observing each other in action improved practice significantly.

CONCLUSION

The chief lesson learned from this study was that though new urban principals all experience similar stressors when adjusting to their positions, the type and amount of support each needs may differ. Urban district leaders would be wise to remember this when structuring new principal mentoring programs. One size is not likely to fit all. New principals appreciate having some choice in their mentors because trusting relationships are based on compatibility and sharing. If there is any hope of retaining urban principals in their positions long enough for them to make a difference, these elements of new principal mentoring must be implemented.

REFERENCES

Alsbury, T. L., & Hackman, D. G. (2006). Learning from experience: Initial findings of a mentoring/induction program for novice principals and superintendents. *Planning and Changing, 37*(3&4), 169–189.

Burkhauser, S., Gates, S. M., Hamilton, L. S. & Ikemoto, G. S. (2012). *First-year principals in urban school districts: How actions and working conditions relate to outcomes.* Santa Monica, CA: RAND Corporation. Retrieved from http://www.rand.org/pubs/technical_reports/TR1191

Clandinin, D., & Connelly, F. M. (2000). *Narrative inquiry: Experience and story in qualitative research.* San Francisco, CA: Jossey-Bass.

Cotton, K. (2003). *Principals and student achievement: What the research says.* Alexandria, VA: Association for Supervision and Curriculum Development.

Cowie, M., & Crawford, M. (Eds.). (2011). *New primary leaders.* London, England: Continuum.

Creswell, J. W. (2009). *Research design: Qualitative, quantitative, and mixed methods approaches.* Thousand Oaks, CA: Sage.

Crippen, C. (2004). A safety net for new principals: Ten features. *Management in Education, 18*(1), 18–23.

Daresh, J. (2007). Mentoring for beginning principals: Revisiting the past or preparing for the future? *Mid-Western Educational Researcher, 20*(4), 21–27.

Darling-Hammond, L., & Orphanos, S. (2007). *Leadership development in California.* Palo Alto, CA: Stanford University, Institute for Research on Education Policy and Practice.

Davis, S., Darling-Hammond, L., LaPointe, M., & Meyerson, D. (2005). *School leadership study: Developing successful principals*. Standford, CA: Stanford Educational Leadership Institute. Retrieved October 2010, from http://www.wallacefoundation.org

García-Garduño, J. M., Slater, C., & López-Gorosave, G. (2011). Beginning elementary principals around the world. *Management in Education, 25*(3), 101–106.

Hansford, B., & Ehrich, L. (2006). The principalship: How significant is mentoring? *Journal of Education Administration, 44*(1), 36–52.

Hess, F. M., & Kelly, A. P. (2005). In preparing principals, content matters. Retrieved October 5, 2010 from http://www.frederickhess.org/5067/in-preparing-principals-content-matters

Howley, A., Adrianaivo, S., & Perry, J. (2005). The pain outweighs the gain: Why teachers don't want to become principals. *Teachers College Record, 107*(4), 757–782.

Knapp, M. S., Copland, M. A., Honig, M. I., Plecki, M., & Portin, B. (2010). *Learning-focused leadership and leadership support: Meaning and practice in urban systems*. Seattle, WA: Center for the Study of Teaching and Policy, University of Washington. Retrieved October 2010, http://www.wallacefoundation.org

LaPointe, M., Davis, S., & Cohen, C. (2007). *School leadership study: Developing successful principals*. Standford, CA: Stanford Educational Leadership Institute. Retrieved October 2010, from http:// www.wallacefoundation.org

LaPointe, M., Meyerson, D., & Darling-Hammond, L. (2006). *Preparing and supporting effective leadership: Early findings from Stanford's School Leadership Study*. Standford, CA: Stanford University. Retrieved October, 2010, from www.seli.standford.edu

Leithwood, K., Harris, A., & Strauss, T. (2010). *Leading school turn around: How successful leaders transform low-performing schools*. San Francisco, CA: Jossey-Bass.

Leithwood, K. Louis, K. S., Anderson, S., & Wahlstrom, K. (2004). *Review of research: How leadership influences student learning*. Minneapolis, MN: University of Minnesota, Center of Applied Research and Educational Improvement.

Lincoln, Y. S., & Guba, E. G. (1985). *Naturalistic inquiry*. Thousand Oakes, CA: Sage.

Marzano, R. J., Waters, T., & McNulty, B. A. (2005). *School leadership that works: From research to results*. Alexandria, VA: Association for Supervision and Curriculum Development & Aurora: Mid-continent Research for Education Learning.

Neumerski, C. M. (2013). Rethinking instructional leadership, a review: What do we know about principal, teacher, and coach instructional leadership, and where should we go from here? *Educational Administration Quarterly, 49*, 310–347.

No Child Left Behind Act of 2001, Pub. L. No. 107-110, Retrieved June 2010, from http://www2.ed.gov/policy/elsec/leg/esea02/107-110.pdf

Olson, L. (2007a). Policy focus turning to principal quality. *Educational Week, 27*(15), 1–2.

Olson, L. (2007b). Getting serious about preparation. *Educational Week, 27*(3), 3–6.

Patton, M. (2002). *Qualitative research and evaluation methods*. Thousand Oaks, CA: Sage.

Peterson, K., & Kelley, C. (2001). Transforming school leadership. *Leadership, 30*(3), 8–12.

Piggot-Irvine, E. (2004). Growth, development, and a way out of principalship's isolation. *Management in Education, 18*(1), 24–29.

Portin, B. S., Knapp, M. S., Dareff, S., Feldman, S., Russell, F. A., Samuelson, C., & Yeh, T. L. (2009). *Leadership for learning improvement in urban schools.* Seattle, WA. Center for the Study of Teaching and Policy, University of Washington.

Silver, M., Lochmiller, C. R., Copland, M. A., & Tripps, A. M. (2009). Supporting new leaders: Findings from a university-based leadership coaching program for new administrators. *Mentoring & Tutoring, 17*(3), 215–232.

Schön, D. (1983). *The reflective practitioner: How professionals think in action.* New York, NY: Basic Books.

Slater, C. L. (2011). Understanding principal leadership: An international perspective and a narrative approach. *Educational Management Administration & Leadership, 39*(2), 219–227.

Smith, A. (2007). Mentoring for experienced school principals: Professional learning in a safe place. *Mentoring & Tutoring, 15*(3), 277–291.

Viernes, R., & Gunzman, A. (2005). Filipino teachers' experiences of supportive relationships with colleagues: A narrative-biological inquiry. *Asia Pacific Education Review, 9*(2), 137–142.

Villani, S. (2006). *Mentoring and induction programs that support new principals.* Thousand Oaks, CA: Corwin.

Walker, J. (2008, July 30). *Super heroes or SAMS? A change in practice for a new kind of educational leader.* Paper presented at National Council of Professors of Educational Administration, San Diego, CA.

Walker, A., & Qian, H. (2006). Beginning principals: balancing at the top of the greasy pole. *Journal of Educational Administration, 44*(4), 297–309.

Wallace Foundation. (2007). *Getting principal mentoring right: Lessons from the field.* Retrieved October, 2010, from http://www.wallacefoundation.org

Weindling, D., & Dimmock, C. (2006). Sitting in the "hot seat" new head teachers in the UK. *Journal of Educational Administration, 44*(4), 325–340.

Wildy, H., & Clarke, S. (2008). Charting an arid landscape: The preparation of novice primary principals in Western Australia. *School Leadership and Management, 28*(5), 469–487.

Wohlstetter, P., Datnow, A., & Park, V. (2008). Creating a system for data-driven decision-making: Applying the principal-agent framework. *School Effectiveness and School Improvement, 19*(3), 239–259.

CHAPTER 12

LEADERS HELPING LEADERS

Mentoring After Mentoring Ends

John Daresh

The job of being a leader of schools is rapidly becoming a job that is increasingly complex, frustrating, and far less appealing to teachers who are seeking future leadership opportunities. In the past, school principals were busy people, with typical time commitments to the job approaching 65 to 70 hours of work each week. The position often included responsibilities associated with evaluating teachers and staff, maintaining the physical plant of their schools, disciplining students, planning and overseeing budgets, reporting school activities to central offices, the state departments of education, and above all, keeping in contact with parents and local community groups (Jacobson & Reavis, 1941). Time left each day would be open to focus on assisting teachers in finding ways to actually teach students more effectively and improving learning opportunities (Andrews & Soder, 1987). Today, these aspects of principals' duties also include maintaining relations with the media and overseeing the complexities associated with demonstrating compliance with laws and policies designed to track school accountability in terms of student learning. In most cases, this translates as the oversight of school and student performance on standardized testing

Best Practices in Mentoring for Teacher and Leader Development, pp. 219–240

measures (Leithwood & Jantzi, 2005). In short, those who are now entering the world of school administration as principals and assistant principals are entering a profession with traditional responsibilities such as those listed above, and with more stress associated with addressing mandates comprised of often confusing practices established by local school systems, state governments, and the U.S. Department of Education (Kruse, Louis, & Byrk, 1994). A difficult job has been made even more demanding. Concern about these known stressors faced by principals is resulting in fewer individuals considering career advancement as school-based administrators.

This chapter describes a study conducted in one urban megadistrict which implemented a mentoring program to assist new school administrators in surviving the demands of their new jobs. The Chicago Public Schools (CPS) is the third largest public school system in the United States, serving nearly one half million students who attend over 600 elementary and secondary schools each day. Throughout the 1990s and the earliest days of this century, studies of staffing needs for Chicago Public Schools projected that massive changes in school leadership were coming throughout the school district. One of the most worrisome facts concerned the need to find ways to strengthen the talent pool of potential candidates to be groomed for future placement as school principals across the city. By 2005, it was clear that within five years, the district would be facing a scenario in which more than one-third of the principals in the district would be leaving their posts because of retirements, nonrenewal because of poor performance, illness (or death), positions in less complex school districts (and better pay), or job-related stress. As it turned out, the projection of one-third of district administrators leaving was an underestimate. Nearly one-half of district principals would need to be replaced over a three-year period, from 2006 to 2009.

CHICAGO PUBLIC SCHOOL DISTRICT FACES A CHALLENGE

The Chicago Public School (CPS) district began a comprehensive approach in 2004 to address the challenge of preparing needed new principals. First, a new office—the Office of Principal Preparation and Development (OPPD) —was created to begin planning support to current campus administrators and also to search for new talent to be prepared to serve as *instructional leaders* (not just managers) for the future. Secondly, an aggressive campaign was launched to recruit and train people to step into principalships. The district already had several years of experience with "in-house" principal preparation programs for those who were already certified to serve as principals. By and large, these programs were designed and delivered by staff who worked primarily with internal candidates identified by the Chicago

Principals and Administrators Association (CPAA), an agency which had long served Chicago principals as a union. Because of the large number of new principals required, however, other strategies were identified. Agreements were reached with the University of Illinois at Chicago to work with select doctoral students engaged in the university's Urban Leadership program as a preface to service in CPS schools. Another source for future principals was tapped with an agreement wherein the city would serve as a center for the New Leaders for New Schools program, a national effort to prepare nontraditional candidates, often without classroom experience, to become ready to step into principalships. In addition, the eligibility process for those seeking careers as Chicago principals was revamped significantly, with the highest priority being placed on finding principals with more experience and insights regarding teaching and learning.

The final piece of the puzzle for seeking strong, qualified principal candidates involved securing funding from a number of sources to provide focused professional development for aspiring principals. Chicago received support from a U.S. Department of Education grant for developing urban school leadership, the Wallace Foundation, the City of Chicago, and additional grants from local industries. The bulk of the money was used to support the creation of a network of support to assist those who would be selected to serve as principals in the immediate future in CPS. A large portion of funding (approximately four million dollars in each of four consecutive years) was allocated to create and maintain a network of mentoring support for aspiring and beginning principals under programs titled Educational Leadership Improving Schools (ELIS) and the Chicago New Principals' Academy. The money was used for mentor training such as workshops related to Blended Coaching provided by the New Teachers' Center at Santa Clara, California, enrollment for some mentors at the Northwestern University Kellogg School of Management, and stipends paid to retired principals who were designated as mentors for the ELIS project. Monthly meetings for mentors and mentees were also paid for with the budget resources.

The last of the external financial support for the Academy was provided for activities carried out during the 2010–2011 school year. At that time, the formal mentoring support for newly hired school administrators concluded. Researchers wondered whether or not the mentoring support had made any difference long term and if the supportive mentoring relationships had continued. Thus, a study was launched in 2012 to determine the following:

- What aspects of mentoring initiated during a two-year commitment by experienced mentor principals to serve new school principals were maintained after the conclusion of support provided by the ELIS Project?

- What has been the nature of relationships established between beginning principals and their mentors after the conclusion of formal coaching provided during the ELIS Project?
- To what extent has the mentoring process initiated between new principals and experienced mentor principals led to increased focus on student learning and achievement?

The mentor program of ELIS was initially funded to achieve the following outcomes:

1. Mentors provide direct and purposeful support to help aspiring or new principals to perform at a high level and make observable progress toward becoming transformational instructional leaders.
2. Mentors and mentees connect leadership development efforts to improvement needs in the school, resulting in positive impact on the quality of teaching and learning as evidenced by measurable gains in student achievement.
3. The mentoring relationship is an integrated component of meeting professional needs of the mentee, as the mentor uses blended coaching strategies to improve targeted, appropriate, and timely learning and development opportunities to aspiring and new school leaders.

In addition to the identification of these three outcomes, another important event assisted in the development of more effective leaders. Before the initiation of the ELIS program, a year-long process had begun, whereby a Blue Ribbon Committee comprised of educational and community leaders came together to identify the critical skills that needed to be mastered by effective CPS principals (Cunat & Daresh, 2007). The result was the creation of five CPS Principal Competencies which outlined that effective Chicago principals would:

1. *Develop and articulate a belief system through voice and action* (e.g., lead by example, involve all members of the school community in providing support for instruction and strive to achieve a common vision).
2. *Engage and develop faculty* (e.g., develop leadership among teachers, support staff development, align staff development with school goals, and recruit and retain quality teachers).

3. *Assess the quality of classroom instruction* (e.g., use knowledge of learning theories and practices, lead standards-based instruction, and use data to improve instruction and student achievement).
4. *Facilitate and motivate change* (e.g., understand the change process for individuals and organizations, be committed to children and have high expectations for learning, and facilitate shared responsibility regarding change efforts).
5. *Balance management* (e.g., delegate effectively when needed, align resources to instructional needs).

These five competencies were deliberately crafted as behaviors and actions deemed necessary for school leaders to be successful in achieving CPS goals. These competencies were in contrast to the traditional framework for defining effective leadership which described the knowledge, skills, attitudes and values needed by principals, as promoted by the Interstate School Leaders Licensure Consortium (commonly referred to as the ISLLC Standards) (Hessel & Holloway, 2002). The Chicago Principal Competencies were well received by a wide variety of organizations and school districts which noted that the reform of educational leadership preparation should be focused on the outcomes expected of leaders, not the people themselves who served as leaders.

The CPS Competencies served many different purposes during the ELIS Project. First and foremost, they represented statements of outcomes that reflected school improvement goals for all campuses in the city. In this way, they were statements of a broader and much more complex organization beyond just a few schools. The second function of the Competencies was that they collectively represented a vision of what "good leaders" do as principals: they work effectively with faculty, they work with teachers to create a vision of school effectiveness, they know good instructional practices, and above all, they are able to walk the tightrope between leadership and management. The Competencies were stated in broad enough terms that they could be used as a template for effectiveness of leaders in all schools. These were important characteristics of leadership that were needed for a district with a diversity of cultures, languages, economic status, and many other factors found in a huge metropolitan area.

Perhaps the most valuable aspects of the CPS Principal Competencies were that they could serve as a guiding vision for the development of principals as instructional leaders, not simply building managers, and that they could be used as a guide that might be followed by those who were entering the principalship for the first time. By no means were the Competencies meant to serve as absolute measures of effectiveness by principals; they were not measurements of individuals' work, but instead, they could be used as benchmarks of progress as newcomers were "becoming leaders."

QUALITY ASSURANCE AND THE MENTORING PROCESS

ELIS grant resources were utilized to enhance the quality of mentoring programs for principals and future principals that already existed in CPS. Previously, the Chicago Principals and Administrators Association and the Chicago Academy for School Leadership offered programs that made use of experienced principals as mentors. One effort was named "LAUNCH," and it supported the efforts of aspiring principals who worked with experienced principals to learn about skills needed to manage efficient schools. Mentors also worked with another program, LIFT, to help beginning principals learn critical management skills. Both programs were viewed positively, but they were limited to assisting individuals in acquiring technical skills, rather than instructional leadership acumen. The promise of ELIS was that it would be a way for mentoring to be utilized to reach a new level of professional development for beginning principals. By and large, mentoring programs for new principals had focused primarily on helping them "survive" as leaders for the first year or two. The goals of ELIS were directed toward not only principal survival, but on long-term issues such developing instructional leadership capacity in the principals. To ensure that the efforts went beyond simply enlisting experienced principals to help solve problems faced by rookies, a Quality Assurance process (Cunat & Daresh, 2007) was created to keep tabs on the mentoring process and to monitor the effectiveness of interactions between mentors and new principals. Specifically, Quality Assurance was designed to:

1. Determine the impact of mentoring activity on new principals' abilities to grow professionally in the CPS Principal Competencies.
2. Ascertain the impact of mentoring on new principals' capacity to address the improvement needs in their schools.
3. Ensure the quality of mentoring interactions taking place to promote new principals' reflections about improving overall professional practice.

After the first year of ELIS, the Office of Principal Preparation and Development (OPPD) staff reviewed input from mentors and mentees, noting limitations of the quality of data received. On the one hand, mentees expressed satisfaction with the mentoring, indicating they appreciated the investments made in their professional development. Mentors also mentioned that they had the opportunity to contribute to colleagues' growth. These were positive statements, but they did little to confirm that the mentoring experience for the first year promoted instructional leadership. Thus, the OPPD staff identified the following questions for the second year of new principal mentoring:

1. Are new principals learning how to implement the CPS Principal Competencies as part of their behaviors as leaders?
2. Are new principals approaching their work more thoughtfully because of their interactions with mentors?
3. Are new principals' preconceived notions about the principalship being confirmed or challenged?
4. Are new principals demonstrating behaviors more consistent with instructional leaders, as contrasted with building managers? If so, what interventions by mentors appeared to be effective in bringing about such behavior?

SHIFTING FROM QUALITY ASSURANCE TO PRINCIPAL COMPETENCY DEVELOPMENT

Changes were made in the second year. First, the title of "Quality Assurance" was changed to "Mentoring Impact" to better describe the most important issue to be considered, namely whether or not changes in behaviors by new principals occurred because of interactions between experienced principals trained to serve as mentors for beginning principals. The term "Quality Assurance" made it sound as if data were being gathered to assess the quality of the mentoring activity. A second change concerned the ways in which data were collected throughout the year. In the first year, Quality Assurance forms were collected in a sporadic fashion. Several mentors did not even complete their forms in a timely manner, and there was no clear focus on collecting data related to the Principal Competencies. Finally, the single most significant change in data collection in Year 2 was related to the intentional gathering of information regarding the impact of mentoring on Competency development. The first data collection concerned Competency 1 (Articulating a Belief System through Voice and Action) and Competency 5 (Balance Management). The two remaining data collections took place with a focus on the other three Competencies: (Engaging and Developing Faculty, Assessing the Quality of Classroom Instruction, and Facilitating and Motivating Change).

The changes made between the first and second years of data collection on mentor—mentee interaction provided a great deal more useful data for the project. Mentors and mentees were beginning to develop relationships which gave rise to more intentional discussions related to the ways in which novice principals could become engaged in activity related to faculty development, instructional improvement and all of the other Competencies.

The third and final year of formal data collection from mentors and mentees resulted in suggestions for structural changes in the ways the school district might more effectively provide useful feedback to Project staff. Examples of program modifications resulting from recommendations based on three years of data collection included the following:

- Implemented more rigorous recruitment and selection of coaches/ mentors in future selection processes (the job of mentor is much more than listening to problems and sharing "war stories").
- Required summer Leadership Coach (Mentor) Training.
- Engaged in advanced training on the implementation of Blended Coaching strategies (Bloom, Castagna, Moir, & Warren, 2005) which could be seen as a continuing form of professional develop- ment for all CPS principals.
- Engaged in ongoing conversations between mentors or coaches and all district administrators to maintain professional develop- ment focus concerning how instructional leaders can be supported.
- Created ongoing support and opportunities for networking among the coaches/mentors of the ELIS Project

External support for ELIS ended in 2011, but it was not necessarily the end of the mentoring and coaching activity. Some mentors and mentees continued their working relationships for two, three, four or more years. Data gathering for this chapter ended in 2013, and a few mentees reported maintaining contact with mentors even at that time.

DESCRIPTIONS OF PARTICIPANTS

The ELIS Project resulted in 352 new principals serving as leaders of schools in Chicago. Not all of these individuals were true "rookies." Ninety of those classified as first year Chicago principals were not involved in this study because they had previous experience in other public school districts in Illinois or in other states, two had previous experiences as headteach- ers of schools in the United Kingdom, and many had been administrators in private or parochial schools. Those contacted to discern interest in being interviewed after their first three years of service in CPS served as a pool from which a random sample of new principals could be selected. Several interesting facts were discovered during this process. Out of the 262 remaining principals without previous experience, seventeen had already left their new jobs before completing three full years of service. In some cases, people relocated to new sites around the city's suburbs, but ten noted that they made the decision not to continue in the role of principal. Most had returned to their classroom assignments. Two additional principals died before they completed four years of service, and another twelve were asked to resign due to a variety of reasons not disclosed by district personnel. By the year 2011, only 231 principals who were products of the ELIS Mentoring Project remained on the job. Forty-two individuals who were invited to participate as possible research subjects chose not to do so. As a result, 189 principals agreed to be in a pool from which a sample could be asked to engage in periodic interviews with the researcher over a two-year period. From the available pool, participants were selected to reflect different age groups, gender, years of experience as teachers, grade levels served, geographic areas of the city, and other characteristics to show diversity among the principals and mentors selected for the follow-up study.

DATA COLLECTION AND ANALYSIS

On site and telephone interviews were used to collect data. Two or three interviews were conducted with each of the mentees selected for this study. Interview questions asked by the researcher included the following:

- Looking at the past (number of years) since you became a principal, how do you believe you were helped (or not) by the mentoring process provided through the ELIS Project?
- Was the process of being mentored in the first year or two of your service as a school principal helpful to you as you became more experienced as a principal? In terms of general management of the school? As a part of your duties as an instructional leader?
- Have you maintained contact with the person who served as your mentor?
- In what specific areas did you most appreciate the guidance of a mentor as part of your career?
- The ELIS Project was created largely to help future Chicago principals to become instructional leaders rather than serve as the traditional role of school building manager. To what extent do you now believe this to have been a reasonable and attainable goal for you and others with whom you still work as a principal?
- Do you sense any difference between you and colleagues who did not have mentoring support during their first two years on the job approach the job of instructional leader in your school?

As is the case of all interviews, additional questions emerged as respondents engaged in the interviews. Numerous additional probes resulted in rich data which shed light on the principals' perceptions on the value of the mentoring they received. Interview data was analyzed for thematic comments that could be reported in this chapter. Only selected findings are reported here due to space contraints.

FINDINGS

The findings reported here focus on the responses of the participating principals who maintained mentor-mentee relationships after the formal ELIS Mentoring Program ended. In general, there was great appreciation shown by principals who were still learning how to fit in as members of the administrative team in a large city school system. Following is an example of comments made by beginning principals:

> I continue to have coffee at least once each month with Dr. Johnson who served as my mentor in the Project for two years. She has asked specifically how I was adjusting as a busy urban school principal. I admit that, on several occasions, I wasn't too happy with my career choice of becoming a principal. I missed the kids and classroom and predictability of what my life was going to be like every day. And I still had Dr. Johnson to listen to my woes every once in a while. I guess I really didn't need her as much now as I did in the past. In fact, I am now mentoring a young woman who is actively pursuing a job as an assistant principal. I often hear myself saying things I remember from conversations I had with my mentor. Just having a connection to a source of wisdom about how to survive Chicago politics was most important.

Virtually every one of the new principals commented on how they appreciated knowing that "someone who cared was out there." But there was also a sense that, in a few cases, mentors were becoming more and more disconnected with the issues that principals face each day. The theme of mentors visiting schools as a personal form of therapy was common. No new principals said specifically that they wished mentors would quit stopping by the school. But it was clear that mentors often had agendas that were no longer solely focused on helping new principals succeed. This is illustrated by the following comment:

> I know that Mr. D was appointed to serve as my mentor for the Project, and he did a lot to help me understand the system I served for fifteen years before going into administration, but I think I'm sort of his mentor now. He was in his first year of retirement when he was appointed as a mentor to me, and as I recall, three other rookie principals in the city. I think he still keeps up with another person who worked with him. But I think his basic reason for continuing to drop in so often was that he misses being a principal … or at least working in a school. He told me he started working for CPS as a teacher at an Elementary School on the West Side, and then he traveled

to land jobs in a couple of other places just before retiring. I think he said he had ten or maybe eleven years in the principal's job. Needless to say, he doesn't stop in here to get paid. The money for that ran out a long time ago. I think he just wants to "talk shop" with someone ... and I'm happy that he will always feel that way.

With one exception in the sample group, principals had maintained professional relationships with their mentors. These were not continued as formal "mentoring sessions," but rather periodic and typically unannounced "drop in visits" where the mentor simply wanted to say "Hi" and offer advice, if requested. Although these were not official visits, the principals spoke at great length about the value of having someone who was not coming to the school to "check" on them. But not surprisingly, these visits generally involved some discussions about progress being made on goals for the year. One of the principals, now in her sixth year as a principal, noted that one thing she looked forward to at least once each month was a visit from the person who served as her "official" mentor during the ELIS Project. Almost every principal interviewed had a similar experience with a former mentor who just wanted to see "What's going on these days now that Arne Duncan is gone...or now that there is a new mayor in charge of the city," or a seemingly endless list of items that could tie them back to a job that they clearly loved.

In one case, a mentor went on to become an associate in a regional office (now referred to as a "network" office) and in some ways could be classified as his former mentee's "boss." But the principal noted that, although he admitted to being apprehensive at first since the mentor had seen his problem areas over the years, there had never been a sense that visits by the former mentor were "business trips" to evaluate his performance. They were more social in nature and that was a welcome experience for the teacher-turned-principal who knew he could confide in his former mentor. It was clear that, even though mentors no longer received stipends for their work, they continued to assist and support their ELIS mentees.

Some unusual situations have appeared in the years since the formal mentoring arrangements were concluded. Some of these situations appeared at first to be negative. When asked if having contact with a mentor who became a central office administrator in the school district was a positive or negative factor in one's career, one mentee replied:

When I first met Jim (my mentor for the ELIS Project), I was very unhappy. The guy really didn't seem to care about me ... he missed meetings, came late for other gatherings. He didn't return phone calls ... and so forth. But as I got to know him, I began to feel much better about some of the suggestions he made to me in terms of my reading the "politics" of the principal's job. Then I felt really foolish about many of the things I had said when I learned that my former mentor was now in a position to do a lot of damage to my career, so I stayed away from any contact when he first came in as a network administrator. But little by little, we seemed to be able to reconnect in a way that really helped me to see how much I had progressed from my first meeting with him. He was never judgmental, though I could tell when he disagreed with some decisions I had made. But he never used that disagreement in a punitive way, to knock me down on evaluations. The thing that is different now is that I think we really respect each other as people serving in administrative roles for the school district. And a lot of times, there are no "correct" or "incorrect" answers to questions.

Thus, we found that new principals did still value the mentoring they had received and were continuing to receive from their mentors. Even though mentors were no longer being paid, many of them continued to support the principals with whom they had been paired. As the data were analyzed from the interviews, three main themes emerged: New Principals Recognized the Benefits of Mentoring, New Principals Focused More on Teaching and Learning, and New Principals Experienced Increased Competence and Confidence. Each of those will now be discussed.

New Principals Recognized the Benefits of Mentoring

To a person, principals praised the work of their former mentors. A common reaction to questions about the nature of continuing mentoring relationships was that, at first, mentors were often perceived as "senior" administrators who were involved with inexperienced principals to "make certain that they knew they were the newest principals and needed to know district policy." After a few years, however, each of the principals noted that they were now viewing the former mentors as fully equal to them, and they realized the benefits they had gleaned.

Induction to the Principalship Came With Support

One principal noted that it was most enjoyable to work with and learn from people who had achieved success as principals. The greatest issue seemed to be that they were no longer "rookies" as principals, but it took them more than just one or two years of having access to experienced colleagues to answer questions that would come up throughout the school year. It was encouraging to hear that one aspect of becoming a new principal was changing. In the past, it was not unusual for new principals to realize that, coming in new in any size school district was, as one of the principals observed in his interview for this study, "sort of like becoming a member of a fraternity." The induction process was almost like a "hazing" to see if the "new people" could handle the stress of the principalship. In fact, a few years ago, it was still common to hear that beginning principals held a value that suggested that they had to "tough it out" for the first few years of the job. As one person said, "If I could survive as a new principal in this city, I knew I would succeed eventually. I didn't need a mentor to "baby sit" me." Fortunately, that type of "welcome to the principalship" seemed to be changing. The demands of being a principal were much too important to simply make people "earn their spurs" by finding their own way to survive the job. As one principal noted, "Being a principal in Chicago is not easy. And unfortunately, there aren't many sources of support every day. Thank God I had made contact with an experienced colleague that I can still call for information and help. Call him a mentor, guardian angel, or just a good, reliable colleague ... I owe a lot to Stephen."

Having Support From a Mentor Is Not a Sign of Weakness

Another principal, now experiencing a great deal of success in terms of increased student achievement scores in all areas and grade levels, noted that not all colleagues had the same working environment. The culture of the school was very different in places where there seemed to be a recognition among administrators, teachers, staff, parents, and to some extent, students, of the importance of teamwork. In the opinion of this principal, the change in his school began when teachers and others saw a principal who was willing to admit that he needed help at that times; the mentor of this principal did not interfere with the work with the teachers. And he only stopped by the school if requested by the principal. But it was clear that the principal profited from the wisdom and expertise of a trusted colleague. A spin-off of this observation was that teachers knew that there was no fault to be found when the principal still needed help on occasion, even though he was in his sixth year of serving as a principal. In this school, there was a sense that everyone needs help from time to time. Teachers knew that and so the school reflected the value of continuous learning.

New Principals Focused More on Teaching, Learning, and Student Achievement

With regard to the focus on instructional leadership rather than building management, principals noted that, when meeting with other principals in their region/network, the conversations of "ELIS Alumni" were chiefly focused on issues regarding instruction, curriculum, and learning progress made by students. This was attributed to mentor models who were perceived by the mentees as principals who did not want to complain about the central office, the state of the politics in the district, or other areas that did not deal with teaching and learning.

It was not simply a "happy coincidence" that the administrators who were selected to serve as mentors (at least in the second two years of the ELIS Project) were specifically chosen because they had reputations as strong instructional leaders. They were never principals who only talked about instructional improvement if "they could find the time." They were truly leaders who were "teachers first, and administrators if they had to be that." As one mentee noted,

> My mentor would say, and still says when we get together, to never forget the reason why I have a job. And in his eyes, that reasons was to ensure that kids are learning, that their needs in that regard were what we were doing in our jobs. My mentor spent two years with me after I got my first position. He would stop in unexpectedly to make sure I wasn't doing anything but disciplining kids, or spending a whole day fixing something that my secretary probably knew how to fix in 10 minutes. [My mentor] drove me crazy at times by pushing me to make the right decisions about where I would spend my time.

As many researchers who have studied the issue of leadership impact on students have learned, the principal's influence on student achievement has been a difficult thing to pin down (Brophy, 1986; Camburn, Rowan, & Raylor, 2003; Heck & Hallinger, 2009). And in the research reported here, the difficulty of linking what went on in the administrator's office and the learning processes for students was even more obscure, in the sense that it was very difficult to clearly see the results of actions taken three steps away from the end of the action. There is little doubt that having a mentor impacted the quality of life of new principals. That issue seems well-grounded in both theory and practice in recent years (Halverson, Grigg, Pritchett, & Thomas, 2007). In the cases in this study where student achievement scores improved, a relationship was discovered between principals who created more open climates and inviting cultures in their schools and an increased quality of teaching on a regular basis in that school. So, the question of whether the rather costly program of principal professional development in the form of early career mentoring can result in increased student learning was answered for the ELIS Program in some cases. In those cases, we discovered that the behavior of new principals did change, and principals became more tuned in to the instructional program improvement in their schools. The way that mentors fostered that change in perspective with the mentees was often very subtle. Consider the following reflection of an elementary school principal who had regular contact with an experienced mentor who started with her during the ELIS Project several years earlier:

I was skeptical about the value of mentoring when I first received word that I would be assigned to work with somebody I had never met and knew only through the fact that he was described by others as a caring principal who really liked to help new teachers and principals. But he was from a very different part of Chicago and had rarely even ventured to the northwest side where my school was located. I figured that all I would learn might be things I already knew. I had been an assistant principal for nine years before stepping in as a principal at another school. I was under the impression that having a mentor meant that I would get little more out of the experience than some tips derived from war stories that had little to do with being a principal in 2008 when I started.

At first, my mentor simply listened and walked around the building to see what was going on. He told no war stories. He didn't hint that he could have done things better had he worked here. I found myself looking forward to weekly chats with him. In most cases, he didn't advise or preach. He listened and if he was asked, answered my questions. Geez, I thought what a waste. Hope he gets reimbursed for mileage. About two months into our work together, I suddenly realized that he didn't tell me to do anything. He simply let me talk about things that I thought about doing. He asked questions here and there, but he never played the game of "When I was still a principal...." Since he didn't do that, I was sort of forced into a situation where I was answering my own questions. And as he saw that change, he smiled a lot. It was like he was saying to me, "Now you're doing your job...." No pressure, no games. From Day 1, I realized that we were equals in so many ways. My mentor has become one of the people who is truly a close friend and colleague. We have been known to talk about mutually shared ideas for hours at a time. But it was a carefully orchestrated process of allowing me to learn on my own.

The most important thing that this principal related was how she really learned a lot from her mentor about how educational change needs to come about slowly and that you cannot force another person to learn. This became a strategy that the principal had gleaned from her mentor in a very subtle learning cycle that could be best illustrated by the model of adult learning identified by Kolb (1984) in his writings about experiential learning in adults. People learn when (or if) they are ready to learn. This one example of the nuanced practices of mentoring that aids the overall climate of learning in a school was one of several things acquired by mentees without any "preaching" by mentors.

New Principals Experienced Increased Competence and Confidence

The words "feeling competent" came out more and more during the time when interviews were taking place (on the phone as well as in person). In the years following the conclusion of the program, former ELIS mentors spent very little time in the schools of their former mentees. But the confidence factor that was developed early on in the relationships between mentors and new principals provided an ongoing sense of well-being and confidence in the mentees, as indicated by this comment:

> [The mentor] does not stop by school as often now, after I have been in the "hot seat" for seven years now I'm not calling on him for as much advice as I did a few years back. But he's a great safety net. But now we're friends and colleagues. He needs no invitation to stop in here to talk. And he often asks me my opinions about how I would handle this problem or that. I feel really confident now.

In another case, a principal in her fourth year of service who had maintained contact with her ELIS mentor spoke about a lesson she learned about the importance of maintaining a leadership style that invited others to participate in decision making in the school. As the mentor and beginning principal began their working relationship, the mentor encouraged her to look at how she could involve others in decisions formulated by the school's Local Site Council. The motto of the principal became: "You are always welcome to participate in every decision that you have an interest it." In one case, the mentor helped her think through how she could involve more teachers in a discussion of the professional development budget for the school. Soon, teachers realized that their new principal was serious about giving everyone their "two cents' worth" when it came to spending "our" money. The mentor in this case was keen to provide numerous examples to his mentee which demonstrated a rather important aspect of effective leadership—distributing one's leadership. Simply stated, sharing in the decision-making process of a school creates a sense of communal responsibility related to practices in the school (Chrispeels, Castillo, & Brown, 2000). And when teachers are heard and respected for their thoughts, there is a powerful sense of commitment demonstrated by teachers who might elsewhere be shut out from the decisions made in a school. So the importance of treating people as if they are important and deserve a voice is something that was transferred from experienced mentor to a rookie.

Another area of competence that became a part of principal behavior because the mentor provided a role model for her was in the area of developing and sustaining a climate of trust among all members of the school community. This is an important ingredient in any school (Bryk & Schneider, 2002). And, virtually all of the mentoring dyads that were a part of this study articulated that the trusting dimension had to be evident in all matters in the school. This is illustrated by a statement made by a beginning principal about what she learned from her mentor: "Trust is a "cornerstone" of everything that happens in a school. If you get it started, it has to be maintained at all costs. And student learning will go with that action."

Clarity of vision is another thing that several of the new principals said that they learned through contact with their formal mentors. Each of the mentors shared the fact that when working with their new principals, they had a similar message: As principal, you must be committed to a vision and that vision must be clearly and consistently shared with everyone in the organization.

At this point, there is no absolute proof that learning or achievement will soar because mentors for principals instilled the values of trust, constancy and clarity of vision, openness to share decisions, and patience in the learning process. Mentors were paid to assist people with survival skills. But in many cases shown throughout the findings of this study, their assistance helped a new principal gain confidence and competence in instructional leadership, building a positive school culture, and developing strategies for shared decision making.

DISCUSSION

Since the end of the external financial support for the project, there has been much upheaval in the district and in the city. Several changes have occurred in the school district's top administrative personnel. At least four new Chief Executive Officers have been named by two different mayors to lead the Chicago Public Schools. Even as this chapter is being written, controversy in the central office continues to be a regular part of life in CPS. Recently, the CEO was placed on an unpaid administrative leave due to her alleged involvement in a scheme to divert several million dollars to support the work of a corporation hired by the CEO to carry out professional development activities for administrators in the district.

Ambiguity is part of daily life in the district as debates continue over the most reliable methods of measuring student performance through testing measures. It has not been clear as to the role of the Common Core Standards in the district, as they have not been fully adopted in Illinois or Chicago as the benchmarks for student progress.

Less than two years ago, the mayor, with School Board approval, closed more than 50 elementary schools in the district because of declining enrollments of population shifts from one area to another. A large number of schools which have traditionally served communities comprised chiefly of African American or Hispanic families have been closed as a way to reduce the negative effects the schools had on the state funding for public education in Chicago. Violent street crime, including several murders, have been directed at school-aged children. Although overall crime statistics for the city have been trending downward for several years, the number of murders of young people in the city has been a nationally recognized problem.

This sad lament could continue for several more pages. Funding shortfalls, low test scores, crime, corruption of elected or appointed community leaders, teacher morale problems (the city recently experienced its first teacher strike in more than 25 years by 28,000 educators), and numerous other problems of "life in the big city" are reported daily in the city's newspapers.

The massive problems stated above describe the environment in which Chicago principals have to work. Leadership at the school site level is daunting. There is nothing that suggests that these problems in Chicago City Schools can be easily cured. But the comments of the principals interviewed for this study seemed more positive than one might expect at this point. The fact that a few principals have found a way to keep relationships with mentor-colleagues who can continue to assist them through showing care and concern gives a strong indication that hope is, in fact, a part of the world of education in this megadistrict.

The research reported here documents best practice because principals were getting additional support to do their jobs in challenging times and places. Even after the funding support for the ELIS program ceased, many of the mentoring relationships established during the program continued on. The findings of this study indicate that one ingredient that may be worthy of continuing support for new principals is ongoing mentoring. It was so encouraging to find that mentoring after mentoring *was* happening, albeit informal in nature. Because supportive relationships were established, they had sticking power. A phrase that might describe what was created through the activity of mentoring in this study is "collegial trust," based on the belief that having one or more experienced principals to rely when facing the challenges of being a new principal can be a life-saver. Whether a new principal is in a huge system like Chicago or in a one-school district in some rural area, the position can often be lonely and frustrating. Many researchers have noted the power of mentorship (Crow & Matthews, 1993; Hobson, 2003; Holcomb, 1989; Riggins-Newby & Zarlengo, 2003; Walker & Stott, 1993; Weingartner, 2009). Therefore, because of the evidence found in current research that mentoring is a powerful tool to assist leaders of many different organizations, establishing and maintaining mentoring programs for newly hired principals should remain a priority. We know that they work (Villani, 2006; Weingartner, 2009).

The participants in this study affirmed the premise that mentoring programs for new principals work. Study principals expressed their gratitude for the support that came with their induction into the role, and the way that support continued over time. Participants came to understand that having a mentor was not a sign of having a deficiency or weakness, but that it was a sign that the district wanted them to be successful and persevere in the position. We found that principals were focusing on instructional leadership more as a result of the encouragement of their mentors. Teaching and learning began to be the centerpiece of their work. Every principal reported developing more competence in leadership and more confidence personally and professionally.

A surprise benefit was the fact that so many of the new principals came to view their mentors as peers and professional colleagues over time. As we noted previously, the perception that a new principal has to earn his/her stripes by figuring out how to survive alone seems to be dismantling as we note the benefits of mentoring for new administrators.

Perhaps the "best practice" that is more implicit than explicit could be stated like this: Mentees and mentors should share the responsibility for continuing a mentoring relationship after a formal mentoring program concludes. We noted in our interviews that sometimes the mentor initiated the continuing contact ("typically unannounced "drop in visits" where the mentor simply wanted to say "Hi"; "he would drop in unexpectedly"; " I think he just wants to talk shop") and sometimes the mentee initiated the contact ("I can still call for information and help"; "he stopped by if I requested it"). There has to be a mutual understanding that the mentoring relationship is continuing and that either party can initiate contact at any time. Zachary (2012) suggests that this assumption should be made explicit and should be verbalized as a formal mentoring relationship is coming to an end.

An implication from this study is for those who are designers of "good principal preparation programs" (a current project of the University Council for Educational Administration). There is a need to refer to the power of long-term mentoring or support relationships in all principal preparation programs, whether they be "in-house" programs of large school districts, nontraditional programs such as New Leaders for New Schools, or university degree and certification programs. It is unfortunate that the work of many who established the National Principals' Center Network (Barth, 1990) is largely forgotten in discussions of immediate reform of how principals are prepared, as it is likely timeless in nature. Our earlier work (Daresh, 1986) determined that there are three types of skills needed by new principals:

1. Technical skills (the "beans, busses, and budgets" diet so often used to "train" future principals through courses seen in abundance at the hundreds of universities in the United States and Canada claiming to prepare future leaders by knowing school law, budgeting, personnel selection, etc.).

2. Self-awareness skills (the development of skills to enable individual "sense making" by new [and continuing] principals; much of what has been written in the area of emotional intelligence).
3. Socialization skills (learning how to fit into the realities of the circumstances one finds him or herself in as a principal facing the "laundry list" of challenges).

The best programs to prepare new school leaders take into account the needs of new principals in all three of these domains. Each area is critical for future success, and this current study affirmed that our identification of the three most important skills principals needed in 1986 are still what they need to master in 2015. What most of the principals interviewed for this study suggested was that mentoring was particularly important in the area of developing socialization skills, as well as the other two areas of technical skills and self-awareness skills. These areas are important and deserve attention by the designers of "good principal preparation programs." However, the areas of developing socialization and self-awareness are not addressed in the current Interstate School Leaders Licensure Consortium (ISLCC) standards which guide preparation programs. Thus, faculty teaching in school leadership preparation programs will have to be intentional about including these important topics in the curriculum.

The academic community that now pleads for the creation of new ways to prepare school leaders needs support from private foundations such as Wallace and Danforth, and through the resources provided by the National Urban School Leadership grants from the federal government (USDOE). While funded research, development, and training is certainly important, the reality is that improving school leadership cannot be accomplished through creating task forces, focus groups, and commissions alone. The truth found in this research is that establishing and maintaining supportive relationships in the early stages of a principal's career is highly effective. Schools are above all places dedicated to developing people, and development of the principals is part of that. One of the ways we can improve the quality of principal preparation programs so that aspiring principals are truly made ready for the demands of the future is to encourage and teach them to find mentors for themselves when they enter the position, and embrace the support that experienced colleagues are willing to offer. If a formal mentoring program is offered in a district, that is great. But when the formal program concludes, the mentor and mentee should articulate a plan to continue the mentoring after mentoring, for the ongoing relationship can truly be mutually edifying to both.

REFERENCES

Andrews, R., & Soder, R. (1987). Principal leadership and student achievement. *Educational Leadership, 44*(6), 9–11.

Barth, R. S. (1990). *Improving schools from within.* San Francisco, CA: Jossey-Bass.

Bloom, G., Castagna, C., Moir, E., & Warren, B. (2005). *Blended coaching: Skills and strategies to principal development.* Thousand Oaks, CA: Corwin Press.

Brophy, J. (1986). Teacher influences on student achievement. *American Psychologist, 41,* 1069–1077.

Bryk, A., & Schneider, B. (2002). *Trust in schools: A core resource for improvement.* New York, NY: Russell Sage Foundation.

Camburn, E., Rowan, B., & Taylor, J. (2003). Distributed leadership in schools: The case of elementary schools adopting comprehensive school reform models. *Educational Evaluation and Policy Analysis, 25,* 347–373.

Chrispeels, J., Castillo, S., & Brown, J. (2000). School leadership teams: A process model of team development. *School Effectiveness and School Improvement, 11,* 20–56.

Crow, G., & Matthews, J. (1993). *Finding one's way: How mentoring can lead to dynamic leadership.* Thousand Oaks, CA: Corwin Press.

Cunat, M. B., & Daresh, J. (2007, April). *Mentoring for beginning urban school principals: A quality assurance process.* Paper presented at the annual meeting of the American Educational Research Association, Chicago, IL.

Daresh, J. (1986). Support for beginning principals: First hurdles are the highest. *Theory Into Practice, 25*(3), 148–161.

Halverson, R., Grigg, J., Pritchett, R., & Thomas, C. (2007). The new instructional leadership: Creating data-driven instructional systems in school. *Journal of School Leadership, 79,* 157–191.

Heck, R. H., & Hallinger, P. (2009, November). *Examining the effects of collaborative leadership and capacity building on school academic improvement: A reciprocal-effects perspective.* Paper presented at the meeting of the University Council of Educational Administration, Anaheim, CA.

Hessel, K., & Holloway, J. (2002). *A framework for school leaders: Linking the ISLLC standards to practice.* Princeton, NJ: Educational Testing Service.

Hobson, A. (2003). *Mentoring and coaching for new leaders.* Nottingham, England: National College for School Leadership.

Holcomb, E. (1989). Beginning principals' perceptions of support provided during the first year of service. *ERS Spectrum, 7,* 10–16.

Jacobson, P., & Reavis, W. (1941). *Duties of school principals.* New York, NY: Prentice-Hall.

Kolb, D. (1984). *Experiential learning as the science of learning and development.* Englewood Cliffs, NJ: Prentice-Hall.

Kruse, S., Louis, K. S., & Bryk, A. (1994). Building professional communities in schools. In *Issues in restructuring schools,* Report No. 6. Madison, WI: University of Wisconsin Center on Organization and Restructuring of Schools.

Leithwood, K., & Jantzi, D. (2005). A review of transformtational school leadership research, 1996-2005. *Leadership and Policy in Schools, 4*(3), 177–199.

Riggins-Newby, C., & Zarlengo, P. (2003). *Making the case for principal mentoring.* Providence, RI: The Educational Alliance at Brown University and the National Association of Elementary School Principals.

Villani, S. (2006). *Mentoring and induction programs that support new principals.* Thousand Oaks, CA: Corwin Press

Walker, K., & Stott, E. (1993). *Preparing for leadership in schools: The mentoring contribution.* In B. J. Campbell & E. Cater (Eds.), *The return of the mentor: Strategies for workplace learning* (pp. 77–90). London, England: Falmer Press.

Weingartner, C. (2009). *Principal mentoring: A safe, simple, and supportive approach.* Thousand Oaks, CA: Corwin Press.

Zachary, L. (2005). *Creating a mentoring climate.* San Francisco, CA: Jossey-Bass.

CHAPTER 13

BEST PRACTICES FOR SUPPORTING BEGINNING PRINCIPALS AS INSTRUCTIONAL LEADERS

The Consultant Coaching Model

Mary Bearden Martin and Linda J. Searby

The principal in a school is the leader who is responsible for ensuring that effective teaching is occurring in every classroom (Seashore-Louis, Leithwood, Wahlstrom, & Anderson, 2010). These researchers have concluded that "to date we have not found a single case of a school improving its student achievement record in the absence of talented leadership" (Seashore-Louis et al., 2010, p. 11). However, hiring and retaining the leaders needed for our schools in this age of high accountability is a challenge. Under the demands of the overwhelming responsibility for improving test scores, many principals do not survive their first few years. Troubling statistics on principal retention indicate that approximately 50% of newly hired principals will stay at a school only three to four years, and less than 30% stay for five years, with even greater turnover in high-

Best Practices in Mentoring for Teacher and Leader Development, pp. 241–278

need schools (Bettielle, Kalogrides, & Loeb, 2011; Young & Fuller, 2009; Seashore-Louis et al., 2010). New principals are also more likely to leave when test scores decline (Miller, 2009; Young & Fuller, 2009). As one principal lamented:

> The principalship is not that attractive any more. People see it as a career ender. Think about it: you go into a failing school, you're given maybe two years to turn it around, and if you don't you're gone and no longer have a job. (The Wallace Foundation, 2007, p. 8)

The revolving door in the principal's office creates a major obstacle to school improvement, as researchers have indicated that principals must remain at a school for five years to implement significant change (Fullan, 1991).

New principals have to be prepared to handle the demands of the position from the outset. Every school deserves and expects a principal to be competent and collaborative from the first day on the job (Gray, Fry, Bottoms, & O'Neil, 2007). Principal preparation programs have been criticized for failing to provide a strong foundation for beginning principals, thus, many programs are reforming and redesigning curriculum (Levine, 2005). However, no matter how strong internships and coursework have been, when school leaders are placed in their first principalship, everything seems new. Sitting in the chair of the principal is both frightening and exciting at the same time.

When new principals are appointed to a school, they do not need scrutiny by an evaluator during the first year. Neither do they need an experienced leader telling them "this is how I did it." Beginning principals need others to encourage and have confidence in them. What they need is a safe place to have professional dialogue with other colleagues. They need a guide who accepts all questions as important ones. Social interaction with others in like circumstances is helpful as well (Hansen & Matthews, 2002).

Beginning principals need high-quality mentoring and professional development tailored to their individual needs (Mitgang, 2012). This support could be achieved through a professional network of their own choosing, but that may not be sustainable over time without a more structured approach. This chapter will describe the model for new principal coaching and mentoring, known as the Consultant Coaching model that has been implemented in the Charlotte-Mecklenburg (North Carolina, United States) school district. We begin with a brief literature review on the demands on the principal as an instructional leader and the need for new principal mentoring, followed by background information on the Consultant Coaching program, and a description of the empirical methods and analysis of the data gathered in the first years of the program. We conclude with a discussion of the success of this program and the identification of promising practices that can be duplicated in other district principal induction programs.

LITERATURE REVIEW

A wealth of research exists about the important role that a school principal plays in the life and health of a school community. There has been a shift in emphasis from inputs to outcomes in the standards-based world of schools. Teachers, tests, and textbooks cannot produce results without a highly effective principal to lead a school (McEwan, 2003). We now know that sustainable school reform is led by principals and assistant principals who are committed to: sharing beliefs and understanding of what constitutes student achievement growth; striving to align the beliefs among the principal, assistant principal, literacy coach, special education resource teacher, and teacher leadership team; and staying the course toward student improvement and not letting distracters divert their energies and focus (Sharratt & Fullan, 2012). The era of the school principal who mainly focuses on school management is a bygone era. There is now a new title given to the role of the school principal: instructional leader.

The Importance of the Principal as Instructional Leader

What we know from the long line of research on school effectiveness is that instruction and classroom environments have the greatest impact on student learning, and those highly effective instructional strategies have been identified (Marzano, Pickering, & Pollock, 2001; Newmann, 1996; Wahlstrom & Louis, 2008). But effective leadership has the next greatest impact on student achievement (Seashore-Louis et al., 2010). Large scale studies have been conducted pertaining to the impact of leadership on a school (Bryk, Sebring, Allensworth, Luppescu, & Easton, 2010; Seashore-Louis et al., 2010) but others have joined in with further identification of specific characteristics of effective school leadership (Day, Sammons, Hopkins, Harris, Leithwood, Gu, & Kington, 2009; Leithwood, Harris, & Hopkins, 2008). Most of these studies identify a list of leadership behaviors and assume that leadership affects student achievement because, indirectly, it influences changes in teacher behavior.

In recent research by Leithwood and Seashore-Lewis (2012), the four core leadership practices which impact student learning have been identified, which are: (a) setting directions, (b) developing people, (c) redesigning the organization, and (d) improving the instructional program. At the school building level, the formal school leader is expected to set the direction and build a shared vision for continuous improvement, as well as provide professional development that connects to the learning needs of the instructional staff. In addition, the leader must organize the school facilities and processes to maximize a learning environment, and understand, recognize, and promote quality instruction. This means that the principal must have enough knowledge of the curriculum to ascertain whether or not appropriate content is being taught in all classrooms (Marzano, Waters, & McNulty, 2005). The effective principal is capable of giving constructive feedback to teachers on how they can improve instruction and can design a system to provide this support as well, such as creating professional learning communities. One of the most significant factors influencing whether or not professional learning communities exist in a school is strong principal leadership (Bryk, Camburn, & Louis, 1999; Louis & Marks, 1998; Wiley, 2001; Youngs, 2001; Youngs & King, 2002). "The presence of a professional community appears to foster collective learning of new practices—when there is principal leadership" (Louis, Dretzky, & Wahlstrom, 2010, p. 320).

In addition to understanding how to create professional learning communities, the principal must also understand how to interpret and use student achievement data. Sharratt and Fullan (2012) asked over 500 educators in four countries what leadership qualities would be necessary to lead schools to improve student outcomes through the use of achievement data. When they asked participants what top three leadership skills were needed to put faces on the data, the respondents readily identified three skills, as noted below:

> Leaders must first model knowledge of classroom practice—assessment and instruction—what we call *know-ability* (45%). Further, 33% said that the ability to inspire and mobilize others through clear communication of commitment was essential—what we call *mobilize-ability*. Finally, 21% said that knowing how to establish a culture of shared responsibility and accountability was crucial—what we call *sustain-ability*. These are the three factors that represent a specific focus by leaders to get results. (pp. 157–158)

To summarize, the research on the link of effective leadership to improved student achievement is strong. Almost every study of school improvement points to "the need for strong, academically-focused principal leadership" (Calman, 2010, p. 17). The principal as instructional leader must be modeling continuous learning and encouraging coleadership, and also be highly knowledgeable and participatory in both assessment and instructional practices (Sharratt, Ostinelli, & Cattaneo, 2010).

Mentoring for new principals. In one report, the claim was made that new principals are traditionally "thrown into their jobs without a lifejacket" (National Association of Elementary School Principals, 2003,

p. 8), unprepared for the demands of the position. Novice school leaders experience high stress as they try to translate their textbook understanding of school leadership into real-world practice (Lashway, 2003). In addition to adjusting to the role of the senior leader, major sources of stress for new administrators include the need to master technical skills, address demands from an array of constituents, overcome feelings of inadequacy, adapt to the fast pace of schools, and most of all, deal with the isolation inherent in the principalship (Villani, 2006). Accountability pressures center on the demand that principals must know how to supervise the instructional program that results in continuous improvement in student outcomes. There is also a growing national movement to tie principals' compensation to student test score gains in individual schools (Billger, 2007; Mitchell, Lewin, & Lawler, 1990). Researchers have established that new principals will need mentoring and 32 states are requiring this mentoring through legislation (Alsbury & Hackmann, 2006; Villani, 2006).

Most successful new principals have had intentional coaching and mentoring in their first critical years (Browne-Ferrigno & Muth, 2004; National Association of Elementary School Principals, 2003; Villani, 2006). Mentoring provides significant support to new principals by providing them with the opportunity to share their experiences and receive feedback. Sherman and Crum (2008) stated, "Protégés gain leadership knowledge and skill through dialogue with mentors and opportunities to enact best practice" (p. 110). Additional benefits of mentoring for new principals include reduction in isolation, getting outside support and an objective perspective, opportunities for deliberate reflection, and increased competence and confidence (Daresh, 2004; Hansford & Ehrich, 2006; Villani, 2006).

BACKGROUND AND SETTING OF
THE CONSULTANT COACHING MODEL

The Charlotte-Mecklenburg School district (CMS) has a stated vision: "to provide all students the best educational available anywhere, preparing every child to lead a rich and productive life" (Charlotte-Mecklenburg Schools, 2013a). Serving a system of 143,866 students in the 2012–13 school year, the district operated from a $1.3 billion budget, resulting in an $8,473 per pupil expenditure. The total number of schools is 159, and the total number of 2012 graduates was 8,130. CMS is one of the largest employers in the county with 18,143 employees. There are 9,180 certified teachers in the district, and 3,547 have advanced degrees. The district is extremely diverse with 15,505 students of limited English proficiency. These students come from 168 countries and represent 165 native languages. The percentage of students who are economically disadvantaged is 53.4%. The breakdown of students in the district by ethnicity is as follows:

American Indian/Multiracial	3%
Asian	5%
African American	42%
Hispanic	18%
White	32%

CMS operates under the direction of a nine-member school board. The superintendent has a management team of 19 executive staff members. The district operates in five regional zones, each with a zone superintendent, an executive director and a small support staff. Nine schools are currently operating in Project L.I.F.T., a program focused on improving low performing schools. This organizational structure is intended to efficiently manage and deliver instructional, human, and financial resources strategically to the schools, while also responding effectively to parents and the public.

District projections indicated that between 2010 and 2014, 37 of the 174 principals serving the district in 2008 would be eligible to retire. This number represented 21% of all principals in the district, or about one in five. According to the district leaders, principal turnover could approach 25%each year, as a result of retirements, relocations, dismissals and other factors. In addition, CMS continued to grow, opening many new schools that increased the number of school leaders that were needed (Charlotte-Mecklenburg Schools, 2013b). As a result of this growth, many new principals have been appointed each year. The district recognized this and took a proactive stance to support and retain novice principals entering the system. The Deputy Superintendent was the leading force behind this model of support for novice principals.

Creating and Refining the Consultant Coaching Model

In 2007, the Deputy Superintendent brought a team of retired principals back into the district on part-time salaries to support principal leadership efforts. In 2009, two members of this team were directed to create a plan for supporting first and second year principals. Working together, these veteran principals created the Consultant Coaching (CC) model. The model was first implemented during the 2010–2011 school year and was supported by district funds. Over time, improvements have been made to the model, based on feedback from beginning principals and Consultant Coaches. The result was a collaborative, yet structured model where new principals work within small cluster groups with an experienced consultant principal. The process is overseen by the Consultant Coach Facilitators who created the model.

A Connection to the Principal Pipeline Initiative

In 2011, the Charlotte-Mecklenburg School (CMS) District was chosen, along with five other large urban districts, to receive a Wallace Foundation grant to develop a pipeline of school leaders and to measure the pipeline's effect on student achievement (Turnbull, Riley, Arcaira, Anderson, & MacFarlane, 2013). This grant of $7.5 million was intended to help develop a larger pool of qualified, prospective principals for CMS. Key components of the initiative were collaboration with university preservice educational leadership programs, improvement of the selection process for new administrators, and a strong induction process for those hired.

Once the Wallace Foundation work began, a comprehensive five year new principal induction program was created by the school district. The CC model became the support for new principals in Year 1 and 2. During Year 2, the district initiated an additional component to the Consultant Coaching model. The new principals were trained in the School Administrator Management (SAM) project. SAM is a professional development process that helps the principal transform from manager to instructional leader. Because the CC cohort teams of principals met during the school year, the beginning principals could discuss their initial implementation of the SAM process once training was complete.

The second level of the induction program occurred in Year 3 for most new principals. During this year, Queens University offered a Leadership Institute for these principals. The focus of the training was on leadership and change. The institute introduced a collaborative framework for principals to examine their own personal leadership style. In the fall session, principals planned a change initiative for their school. When they returned for a spring session, they reported on their progress and/or struggles with the change effort. Also during this year, principals were given the opportunity to take the Vanderbilt Assessment for Leadership in Education (Val-Ed) as a research-based assessment of their own effectiveness as a school leader. The instrument, a 360° assessment in which stakeholders, peers, and supervisors evaluate the principal, focuses on learning-centered leadership behaviors that influence everyone in the school.

At the third level, generally in the fourth year of the principals' tenure with the district, they attended an Innovation Institute at the McColl Business Center, also at Queens University. This series of sessions focused on developing an awareness of the creative process and environments that can help generate innovation. During this Institute, principals learned to create school environments for producing creativity. They developed ideas and design innovations that resulted in plans for turning their new ideas into real and operable concepts.

The fourth level, generally completed in Year 5, gave the new principals an opportunity to "give back" to the system. They completed capstone projects that included, but were not limited to, serving on district decision-making committees, providing workshops for other principals, or leading an extended Professional Learning Community for principals with a common issue that could be studied. One goal for this level was to have principals prepared to be Consultant Coaches for other new principals in the future. At this point, the induction process was complete. The entire process is depicted in Figure 3.1.

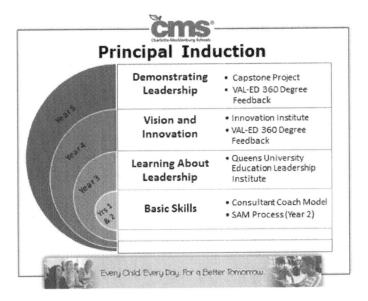

Figure 13.1. CMS Principal Induction Process.

New principals were evaluated by the Zone Superintendents each year based on the North Carolina Executive Standards. At the end of each of the induction years, they were expected to show growth as school leaders. If adequate growth was not achieved, as noted on the evaluation, principals would receive targeted support, articulated and facilitated by the Zone Superintendent. In these instances, principals continued in the induction process, but also received one-on-one coaching by a veteran principal to target an identified need of the principal.

THE CONSULTANT COACHING MODEL

The Consultant Coaching model was designed with three desired outcomes. The first outcome of the program was to ensure the success of beginning principals by providing collaborative support. Second, the principals would be equipped with the skills and competencies necessary for leading a school. The third outcome of the model was to create support for new principals to establish relationships with peers and be able to network with successful, highly skilled principals (Consultant Coaches). The "products" of the program were expected to be successful, organized, instructional leaders who are able to handle the demands of the job and who want to remain in the position. Positive results were expected through the collaboration of three groups of administrators: Consultant Coaches, new principals, and Consultant Coach Facilitators. After four years, the process has become institutionalized and a benefit to the district overall.

Selection of Consultant Coaches

In the summer, when most principals have been appointed to a school, the Deputy Superintendent of the district, with support from the Zone Superintendents, selects and then invites experienced practicing principals to serve as Consultant Coaches (CC). Coaches are chosen for specific grade levels: elementary, middle or high school. Their selection is based on the principals' summative evaluations from the Zone Superintendents, ensuring that the CC are all accomplished professionals and have the designation as a "distinguished" principal as outlined in the Charlotte-Mecklenburg principal performance evaluation.

The CCs make a two-year commitment to serve in this role. The number of CC teams and Coaches is determined by the number of first and second year principals to be served.

Role of the Consultant Coaches

Most of the CCs have volunteered to serve in a leadership capacity for the district. Meeting with the new principal teams is the primary responsibility for the CCs. They schedule the meetings and set the locations (see Appendix A). They strictly follow a set protocol for the meetings, which include focus lessons. As needed, they extend the focus lessons with their own information. They keep all dialogue in the meetings open and positive. Building trust within their group is essential for the sharing to be of highest quality. CCs provide a safe place for professional dialogue where confidentiality is secure.

CCs are encouraged, but not required, to go through the School Administrator Management (SAM) training. This process ensures that principals make time for instructional leadership. Three major components of SAM are the use of a calendar that tracks how the principal's time is spent, a daily meeting with a support team to set and reconcile the calendar, and a First Responder list to involve people other than the principal in management duties. When their second year principals go through the process, the Coaches are familiar with the expectations, understand the complexities of the process, and are able to facilitate meaningful dialogue.

CCs are expected to attend meetings scheduled with the CC Facilitators to participate in discussions, share successes, and plan for upcoming meetings with their new principal team. In these meetings, problem-solving is collaborative and reflection is encouraged.

Assignment of New Principals

The Deputy Superintendent is responsible for assigning new principals to their CC. Each of the CC teams consists of three to seven new principals and the CC. The teams are divided by school grade levels. In some cases, the Deputy Superintendent considers the drive time between schools for the participants placed together. In other circumstances, similar demographics within their schools may be considered. However, the priority is keeping the groups balanced and small in numbers.

Role of the New Principals

New principals are expected to bring something to the table at each of the CC meetings. These principals need to be open to new learning, realizing that even though they have been appointed to the principal position in a school, they do not have all the answers. New principals need to operate under a belief that it is a sign of leadership to accept and ask for help when needed. They are expected be enthusiastic, optimistic, and eager to share in the CC meetings.

Attendance of the new principals at CC meetings is required. These meetings are only interrupted by called meetings of the superintendents. Everyone is to come prepared to the meetings, having completed a homework task to share with others. They are expected to follow the norms set by their cohort team. Examples of the team agreements are: refraining from using cell phones and IPads during meetings, keeping all things shared as confidential, and that all ideas and questions have merit within the group.

The Consulting Coach Facilitators and Their Role

The Facilitators of Consultant Coaching are two retired principals from the district who are on contract with the district to provide leadership training. Their role with the CC program includes implementing and monitoring the model that has been established.

Once CCs have been appointed to the cohorts, the Facilitators begin to work with them. At the first meeting, the model and its procedures are introduced or reviewed. CCs are directed to follow the procedures and implement the model according to the adopted protocol. At each of the following meetings, one of the set agenda items is sharing instruction on research-based effective mentoring practices expected of the CCs. However, the most meaningful learning tends to result from the Coaches' own sharing of experiences in their small cohort teams. In their meetings with the Facilitators, they also discuss what is working or not working in their sessions with the new principals.

CC Facilitators organize meetings four times each calendar year with the CCs to support them and to ensure that they are maintaining the fidelity of the program. Facilitators are responsible for training the CCs on best mentoring practices, and encouraging them to operate as their own learning team of Coaches. The CC Facilitators write focus lessons on topics that are determined by the Coaches as needed and timely.

To further assess the program, the Facilitators conduct surveys at the end of each year, and share the results with the Coaches. Discussion of the results leads to revisions or changes in the model, with the goal of continuous improvement. The Facilitators must also report the results to the Deputy Superintendent.

COMMON PROTOCOLS FOR ALL MEETINGS

Established Guidelines and Procedures

Procedures for the CC model are specific and clear. Each team must follow a consistent structure for each of the small group meetings. Norms are established for the meetings and roles (minute keeper, time keeper, etc.) are assigned to facilitate an efficient session. Meetings are held once a month for three hours. In September, the dates for these meetings are scheduled for the entire year. The location of each meeting rotates between the schools of the new principal team members. Confidentiality is a nonnegotiable within the team. CCs understand that their roles are nonevaluative. Superintendents are not provided any information on the struggles or successes of the new principals from the CCs.

Agenda for Each Meeting

The common agenda for all of the meetings consists of six items and proceeds in a prescribed order. First, celebrations and accomplishments are shared to set a positive tone for the meeting. Next, homework assigned at the previous meeting is reviewed and discussed. The homework is always job-embedded and usually requires the principal to try a strategy shared at a previous meeting. The homework always stems from the last focus lesson. Then, a new focus lesson is presented by the CC. These interactive lessons, provided by the Facilitators to the CCs, are based on needs the Coaches have identified. After the focus lesson, the team conducts instructional walkthroughs in classrooms. The host principal requests that the observers pay close attention to one component of instruction that the school is working to improve. Once the walk-throughs have been completed, the CC leads a debriefing session. This professional dialogue is always encouraging and positive, yet the new principals share strategies and ideas that might help the resident principal achieve more success. The next item on the agenda is "burning issues." These topics are usually identified by the new principals and they directly relate to current situations in schools. The final activity on the agenda is the assignment of the homework to be completed before coming to the next month's session.

Time allotments for the three hour session are flexible. However, a target, projected timeline would be 15 minutes for celebrations, 15 minutes for homework review, 45 minutes for the focus lesson, 45 minutes for the walkthrough and debriefing, 30 minutes for the burning issues, and 15 minutes for closure. A 15 minute break is also included in the timeframe (see Appendix B).

Focus Lessons

The focus lessons are a key component of these meetings. The proposed topics for these lessons are provided by the CCs. In their quarterly meeting with the Facilitators, the experienced principals share the needs their new principals are facing at that particular time of the year. After brainstorming all the possible topics that the principals might benefit from, the list is prioritized by the CCs. Within the next week the Facilitators develop these focus lessons, send them out to CCs, and are available to answer any questions that might arise. These lessons are consistent across all CC groups, and they serve as a springboard for the group discussion. The focus lesson contains the basic, minimum information that is to be shared with all new principals. However, each CC is encouraged to extend or supplement the focus lesson. Examples of the focus lessons for the fall meetings would include opening of school, analyzing instructional data from the previous year, understanding the evaluation instrument, strategies for motivating teachers, and working with a new administrative team. CCs are forward thinkers, identifying topics that will be needed "just in time" for the new principals. For example, the CCs requested one focus lesson on documenting and supporting marginal teachers, to be held in December prior to the midyear conferences that were coming up in January (see Appendix C).

Homework

The new principals are expected to complete homework assignments between each session. The review of homework at each session provides the opportunity to assess the learning from the previous meeting. For example, after a focus lesson on student engagement, the homework assignment might be to hold a discussion in their school with a team of teachers on ways to increase student attentiveness, the worthiness of student work, and/or the classroom environment. Another example might be for new principals to attend a grade level or department meeting to observe the effectiveness of teacher planning time. This assignment would follow a focus lesson where teacher collaboration was the topic of discussion.

Instructional Walkthroughs

During the walk-throughs, the host principal identifies one or two areas for focus, typically aligning with instructional strategies identified for improvement in their building. They invite feedback on the observations from the rest of the cohort. Some examples of these have been student engagement, relevance of the instructional activities, appropriate uses of technology, increasing levels of rigor in the classroom, informal assessments, and so forth. The host principals benefit from the different perspectives of their colleagues. Those who walkthrough pick up many instructional ideas and can apply the discussion to their own schools.

"Burning Issues"

Each session includes an hour for discussing "burning issues" that principals need to discuss in a timely manner. Though the "burning issues" tend to be management or organizational topics, the "just in time" nature of each issue still provides valuable and necessary learning for the new principals. For example, a novice principal may ask to discuss how to conduct a beginner's day for kindergarteners and their parents or how to improve security at the high school football games. Other burning issues might include school-wide discipline, safety issues, budget issues, or district reports that are to be submitted in the next few weeks. All ideas are accepted and appreciated, including those of the CC. This item always comes after the focus lesson and the walk-through, as the primary purpose of these meetings is to strengthen instructional leadership skills. Once principals begin to discuss intense issues that they share, the remainder of the time together is often consumed with these concerns. The ending section of the meeting is an opportunity for principals to share their upcoming calendars and discuss events, committees, or other items that will require detailed planning.

COSTS INVOLVED

The CC model has not been costly for the Charlotte-Mecklenburg School district. The Coaching Facilitators are on contract to coordinate and deliver principal leadership training. The CC program is one of their assigned duties. The CCs and principals meet during the school day. Costs that have been incurred are reimbursement for travel for the coaching Facilitators and some additional materials for book studies. CCs meet a whole day per month with each other, and the new principal cohorts and CCs meet for three hours once a month. The district pays each CC a small stipend for their work. Thus, the district supports the program with "in kind" contributions (employees' time) and dedicated financial resources, as well.

IMPLEMENTATION OF THE MODEL IN
CHARLOTTE-MECKLENBURG SCHOOLS

In the first year, the CC model was a pilot to test the structure, focus lessons, and cohorts. Protocols, focus lessons, and walk-through sessions were under development. At the end of the year, CCs worked with the Facilitators to make a few modifications to the model based on informal reflections. A decision was made to have new principals stay in their same cohort with the same CC for a two year period. A second adjustment dealt with the timing and sequence of the focus lessons.

At the end of Year 2 (2010–11), the model was considered established and in full operation; thus, it was determined that a more formal assessment of the program would start with this cohort. A survey was developed by the CC Facilitators and administered to the participating principals at the end of May. Survey results were extremely positive. The new principals commented on their satisfaction with the model and noted that trust had been built in the cohorts as a result of the confidentiality, the sharing of struggles, and the bonding that occurred with principals within the group. At the end of the third year (2011–12), the assessment survey was modified to gather additional data. This feedback, while it continued to be strongly positive, also provided evidence that some of the CCs were not following the model with the fidelity that was expected. Based on these comments, the Deputy Superintendent made the decision to release some Coaches, and bring on several new ones. Additional accountability measures were put in place. The new guidelines now require that all CCs' agendas, handouts, and the attendance records for each meeting be submitted to the Facilitators. The Facilitators were asked to report the attendance and progress of the CC process to the Deputy Superintendent at least twice a year. The intent of these changes was to monitor any issues that need to be addressed earlier in the year.

The data collected in the first three years was formative as the program was in the early stages of development. Therefore, program Facilitators and the Deputy Superintendent made a decision to use survey data from Year 4 to assess program effectiveness in a formal way. The methods used to gather empirical data on the program and the results realized will now be discussed in order to highlight the best practices that were identified by the participants in the program.

EVIDENCE OF BEST PRACTICES IN
THE CONSULTANT COACHING MODEL

The CC Facilitators gathered data from all the new principal participants in the CC program to determine its impact and to establish the success of the model. Three questions were examined:

1. Were new principals who have been part of CC continuing in the principalship?
2. Was involvement in Consultant Coaching a successful approach for supporting and nurturing new leaders during their first two years of service?

   - What were its strengths?
   - How beneficial were the sessions?
   - Were new principals able to gain further skills and competencies to ensure success in their role as school leader?

- Does the model result in a close network of professionals who will support and nurture each other?

Information gathered will benefit the Charlotte-Mecklenburg school district leaders as they continue to institutionalize their induction program, but many components of the model created there can also serve as a blueprint for any school district to copy.

METHODOLOGY

To determine the success of the program and to gain information in order to refine the program in the future, two methods were employed. The first method was a review of the principals who have participated in the CC program since its inception and their retention rate in the principal role, resulting in a descriptive analysis. This step was conducted by the lead Facilitator and author of this chapter. The second method was survey methodology, employing the online service of Survey Monkey. Open-ended questions on the survey were designed to determine the strengths and weaknesses in the program. These questions are provided in Appendix D.

RESULTS

At the time of this writing, the CC program for new principals in the Charlotte–Mecklenburg school district had been in place for two years. We gathered data through open-ended surveys sent to the participants as well as statistically, in order to answer our two central research questions:

Question 1) Were the new principals who have been part of CC continuing in the principalship?

Question 2) Was involvement in CC a successful approach for supporting and nurturing new leaders during their first two years of service?

We now move to summarizing the results and reporting the impact that this program had on the participants and the district.

Question 1: Cohort Numbers and Retention Rates

In the initial years (2010–2013), the CC program served 93 new principals. Of this total number served, 77 of the principals were continuing in the role of school principal as of May, 2013. This number represented an 83% (77/93) retention rate of principals serving in the same role. Among the 77 principals, 2 were strategically moved to schools of high poverty to turn the schools around. One was promoted from a middle school to a high school, and one was reassigned from a high school to an elementary school. One was moved from an elementary to a middle school.

Fifteen (16%) are no longer in a principalship within the district. The reasons are accounted for in this list:

Retired	1
Nonrenewal of Contract	4
Moved into Central Office/Zone positions	4
Moved back into teacher/counselor position	2
Left the district	3
Other	1

The fact that 83% of the principals were retained in the position was satisfying to district officials, although that percentage could always be better. The 16% who did not remain in the position appeared to have left for logical reasons.

Question 2: Impact of Involvement in the Consultant Coaching Model

Surveys were sent to 36 principals who were participating in the CC model during the 2012–2013 school year. Twenty-eight surveys were returned, for a return rate of 78% (28/36). Eighteen of these principals were completing year one of CC. Eighteen principals were finishing their second year in the program.

When we analyzed the demographics of the principals completing the survey, we noted that the ethnicity of the group was evenly distributed, and the group was predominantly females serving at the elementary level (see Table 13.1).

Themes that Emerged from the Survey Data

We first aggregated the data from the survey, listing all of the responses to the open ended questions under each question. Then, we analyzed the responses and initially coded them (Merriam, 2007). Further coding was conducted to identify themes that emerged from the responses. We gathered information and summarized it to assess the impact of the CC model on beginning principals, and to identify the lessons learned through the process for all parties involved, and make recommendations for future refinements to the program.

Table 13.1.   Table Title

Variables	
Ethnicity	
Black	13
White	20
Other	3
Gender	
Male	10
Female	26
School Level	
Elementary	23
Middle School	9
High School	4

Four major themes emerged from the data which were used to describe the successful outcomes of the program: *constructs, competence, confidence,* and *community*. These themes are not in rank order, but result from the categories identified from the principals' comments. First, participants found the *constructs* in place for the process of CC to be very helpful. These structures required them to meet regularly and study effective instruction through focus lessons and walkthroughs. The established agenda, with a common protocol for all meetings, ensured that the busy principals' time was used wisely. Second, participants were aware that this model was an avenue for building *competence* around the principal standards set forth by the state of North Carolina, specifically those skills that integrate instructional leadership. Third, new principals completed the program with much *confidence* and security. Finally, the participants gained support and advice from multiple sources through planned opportunities for *collaboration* with colleagues who were facing similar challenges. Each theme is now described utilizing illustrative comments from the participants.

Theme 1: Constructs

The creators of the CC program of mentoring for new principals believed that a structured plan for the program would ensure that each cohort would operate under the same framework. Both participants and Consultant Coaches became comfortable with the established agenda and the norms enforced at each meeting. Therefore, collaboration time was maximized.

Monthly meetings expected. One of the nonnegotiable constructs of the Consultant Coaching model was that the cohorts would meet monthly. Monthly meetings were well-received by the participants, as illustrated by one principal who stated, "I was able to get access to valuable information in a timely fashion." Scheduling these meetings at regular intervals provided an established "guarded time" to talk. One principal claimed that "having the time set aside to stop and take a breath, to talk and connect with colleagues" helped him get through tough weeks. One principal even commented that meetings conducted more frequently would be even better.

Location of meetings rotated. New principals appreciated the opportunity to hold meetings in different locations to broaden their perspective, commenting "I learned so much through my visits. We saw diverse populations within various environments. We went across zones. It offered us a chance to see the organization and instructional focus of others schools." Rotating schools was described as a positive practice within the model where principals could see "new places for new ideas." "Getting the opportunity to see other schools made a great impact on how I view my school and the work we do at my school." As beginning principals, time to review best practices and see strategies that were working in other buildings was of great value.

One concern expressed by the new principals was the time traveling to different schools and being out of their own buildings. This monthly event is only one of several required district meetings, and when new principals are working to build relationships in their school, they are hesitant to be away. Still, new principals concurred that "there is value in visiting other schools." One principal verified the impact of these meetings by stating that the "opportunity to step away from your building and connect with others facing the exact same challenges made a difference." Overall these visits were appreciated. "It was great to see other principals in their buildings as we were getting to know each other." Another benefit noted by a principal is that "it is always beneficial to get outside of your building to push your thinking and see other ways of doing things."

The meeting protocol ensured efficiency. One of the important protocols of the CC program was that each cohort had to follow the same prescribed agenda for their meetings to ensure consistency and fidelity to the program. This structure was established in order to keep the focus on "instruction first." One principal shared that the agenda "allowed us to focus on a single relevant instructional issue at each meeting." Another commented that the meetings "flew by, but accomplished a lot." While the agenda was intended to provide structure, some flexibility was necessary to meet the needs of particular principal teams.

One comment that was made by three of the participants was that "scripted lessons should not be a mandate" in the meetings. One person suggested that the "monthly focus lessons need to align to the needs of the group." While the intent was not that these lessons be used verbatim, some Coaches took more liberty than others in modifying them. Comments from one participant indicated frustration when the consultant Coach "had his own agenda and did not regard the process with highest regard."

The amount of time participants reported focusing on instruction, however, was not consistent with expectations. According to the common agenda, 90 minutes of each session was to focus on instructional leadership. When asked how much time their team spent on instruction, 38.5% said that 90 minutes of each session concentrated on the focus lessons and walkthroughs. An equal number stated that they spent only an hour on the instructional aspects of being a principal. This area is one that CC Coaches must monitor to ensure the model is followed with fidelity.

New principals appreciated time to talk through "burning issues," or the daily tasks and responsibilities of the principal. In order to be proactive, the CCs often looked ahead to tasks that new principals would soon face. One principal appreciated that his Coach "predicts some of the concerns we may not even realize are upcoming." Having time to collaborate about strategies for handling daily work, due dates and plans of action seemed to help new principals feel prepared. Burning issues always followed the instructional aspect of the agenda and ideally, was to consume an hour of each meeting. However, only 34.6% of the respondents reported that 60 minutes was focused on burning (management) issues. Another 38.5% stated their team only spent about 30 minutes on management issues. And 26.9% stated that more than an hour was spent on this topic. Again, CCs must be aware of the time allotment for each agenda item to ensure that all needs are addressed in each meeting.

When the Consultant Facilitators requested suggestions for improvements to the structure of the model, there were few made, and most were of a general nature. One idea was not to schedule CC meetings on Fridays because of the number of events that happen at the end of the week in schools. Another thought was that a meeting should be held "maybe twice a year where all first years could get together." Participants asked for groups to remain small. Because of the cohesiveness and relationships established within the teams, one suggestion from a principal was that "once a group begins the year, do not add additional individuals midyear because it changes the relationships and the dynamics in the team." Finally, the request was made that assignments to CCs be made shortly after someone was appointed to the position of new principal.

Theme 2: Competence

New principals stated that they built their competencies and skills for leadership by participating in the CC program. While many new principals are at a level where they "don't know what they don't know," professional dialogue in a nonthreatening environment can lead to individual growth. In the survey, there was 100% agreement to the statement: Consultant Coaching helped me build my knowledge/skills to become a more successful leader. Likewise, the same feedback was given on the question: The content was relevant to the role and responsibilities of my current position. One of the new principals claimed that "Everything was applicable and I was able use new ideas and information immediately when I returned to my building."

Focus lessons emphasize instructional leadership. Each meeting of the cohort included a focus lesson on an instructional leadership topic. Participants stated that they benefitted from all of the topics. "The focus lessons gave us a jumping off point for rich discussion." Six principals said they benefitted most from the lesson on time management. One of these principals stated that processing time management strategies together helped him prioritize tasks in order to find more time to be in classrooms. Other principals mentioned the lessons on student engagement, effective use of planning time, creating action plans for teachers, and the role of the administrative team in improving achievement as the topics most beneficial for them. One principal said she always took something useful away from the discussions: "We share information and documents with each other often." When the focus lesson was on coaching skills, one principal felt that he gained a better understanding of how to make his feedback to teachers more specific. Keeping the focus of the model on instructional leadership helped new principals remember their primary responsibility in the school. These comments indicate that CC is having a positive impact on new principals, resulting in the acquisition of new skills as instructional leaders.

When specific situations were shared, the principals felt they were able to problem-solve collaboratively. "There was time, support and transparency in the sharing of ideas and concerns with other principals to work toward a resolution." When ideas or suggestions were made, feedback from others on possible ways to approach an issue was appreciated. "All of the scenarios we discussed were real," commented one principal. Through dialogue, principals were exposed to many different problems and situations. According to two responses, "While our schools vary in a number of aspects, there is a great need to hear other perspectives;" and "We were able to see challenges and successes at different schools and to discuss potential solutions."

Walkthroughs support reliability when examining good teaching. Time for walkthroughs at each school was always built into the agenda for

CC meetings. The walkthroughs were seen as a major learning experience, completely focused on instruction and the needs of students and teachers. One principal pointed out that she "learned to prioritize the needs for Coaching teachers" through the debriefing conversations that followed visits to classrooms. By using a common walkthrough format provided by the district, new principals became comfortable using a framework for analyzing instruction. Principals felt some security and affirmation knowing that they were seeing some of the same highlights or concerns they encountered in their own schools during a walkthrough. "When we visited classes, we were typically on the same page as to the quality of instruction," noted one principal. The district had recently implemented a new teacher evaluation instrument, and the walkthroughs provided an opportunity for principals to calibrate their observations: "I was validated in my assessment of my own staff. I have questioned whether my standards were too high and the principals in my group agreed I was on the right page." Another principal said that the walkthroughs helped her with norming and discussing what would be rated as "Standard," "Above Standard," and "Below Standard" performance. Stating that the walkthroughs were learning experiences, one person said they were "helpful because I learned to look for rigor."

Host principals requested that their cohort look for specific aspects of instruction during their visits and walkthroughs. Usually the principal wanted others to focus on a particular initiative of the school, in order to gain other viewpoints. Participants noted that "It was great to get an outside perspective on your building." One principal shared that "There was more positive feedback than I expected. As the building principal, you are always focusing on what needs to be improved. It felt great to hear what was going right." But one principal also noted that because of the solid trust within the group, "we were able to discuss weak areas and discrepancies in schools." One principal stated that, "We were able to give each other constructive criticism or apply our new knowledge to our own schools." Again she also realized they were not alone in needing to build capacity in their schools. As one principal summed up: "CMS still has a way to go in ensuring an effective teacher in every classroom."

Instructional walkthroughs provide opportunities for discussion of best practices. A large urban district often initiates several research-based instructional models at once. One principal wrote that it helped her to see the programs in action in other schools. In conversations following walkthroughs, questions were raised about appropriate staff professional development to support curriculum changes, scheduling techniques to maximize time to implement new strategies, and other aspects of the principal's role in promoting quality teaching. New principals were reassured of their own practice through the dialogue.

All principals felt that they took away ideas and teaching strategies for their own school from the walkthroughs in other buildings. "Debriefing allowed me to think of how to use what I saw in my building." One principal said she has gained a new perspective on the need for monitoring instructional practices after comparing her teacher performance with what she saw in other schools. "I need to be more visible and address inadequate teaching practices in a timely manner." Additionally, one of the school leaders realized that "each walkthrough provided ideas for improving school-wide culture and our behavior management system, even when we were looking at classroom instruction."

During the debriefing conversations after the walkthroughs, principals shared their observations and explored possible next steps for the teacher or school. "Observing strong teachers in disciplines where I have weak teachers in my building gave me ideas of where to help them focus their improvement efforts." One principal came away from her experience understanding that "We have a lot of great teachers in our schools. Our teachers struggle with similar issues and we should work together to provide each other support to provide the staff members meaningful learning experiences."

New principals were appreciative of the feedback they received from colleagues who participated in the walkthrough in their school. One principal was pleased to be able to share the good things going on in the building. "It was great as the hosting principal to be able to share the work my staff has been doing this year." After these meetings, the hosting principal often "shared feedback I received from other principals with my administrative team. We discussed the visitor's comments in-depth." In summary, one principal wrote that the benefits of the walkthroughs and debriefing sessions were "too many to list."

Homework puts new ideas into practice. After each focus lesson, homework was assigned to the new principals to complete before the next meeting. All of the assignments were action-oriented. Three examples of the homework were: having a specific discussion with a team in the school, looking for designated evidence of instructional strategies during walkthroughs in their own schools, or trying one new idea that was discussed during the meeting. The next month's meeting would then begin with a discussion of learning from the homework. Nineteen of the 27 (70%) responses included the exact word "reflection" in the comment. They viewed the application of prior learning from the discussion as a rich opportunity for reflection. One principal said the homework provided her an avenue to reflect on her own professional needs. Another said the reflection helped him "look at our current processes in my school and consider the need to adjust them." The primary purpose of the reflective homework, according to one participating principal, was to "give me a chance to reflect on what we talked about and how I could implement certain best practices at my school." Principals appreciated that the CC model required them to step away from the day to day routines to compare instruction in their school to other schools in the district. As one principal stated, "The opportunity to assess what was working with my leadership and overall within the school was a great benefit."

"Burning issues" need discussion to reduce new principal anxiety. An important part of each meeting agenda was the time to discuss current "hot topics" or "burning issues" that were relevant or appropriate to the principals at the meeting time. For example, when the Education Value Added Assessment System (EVAAS) roster information came out from the district, one Consultant Coach team shared strategies for how they might help teachers to ensure consistency in reporting student data. Another timely topic was focused on the implementation of the Common Core standards in schools, where different schools were approaching the roll-out differently depending on teacher needs. One principal appreciated the responses to questions about "how to spend, what to spend, and the do's and don'ts of spending money." PowerSchool was a new initiative in the school district, and one principal was glad she "had someone to learn with me so I wouldn't waste time looking for data that I needed." Finally, a principal summed up his new learning by admitting that new principals don't always know how the district operates and "it helps to hear about the ebbs and flows of the district."

In order to build the skills and competencies of beginning principals, the CC sessions needed to provide for new learning that connected to their previous experiences. New principals understand the expectation for them to be instructional leaders and they have gained strategies from each other to improve the teaching and learning in their own schools.

Theme 3: Confidence

As the new administrators realized they were skilled and competent, they felt less fear in the position of school principal. When new principals became overwhelmed with instruction and management tasks in the school, others on the team could help them prioritize the work and handle the pressures more aptly. This confidence was developed in several ways, as described here.

A safe environment where confidentiality is honored is a "must." Confidentiality was a vital team norm in the Coaching meetings. Because confidentiality in the meetings was understood by all, the CCs were able to make conversations safe. Principals were confident that what was shared between the team members would not be detrimental or come back to "bite" them. The CC groups bonded in specific ways, some sharing resources, some sharing struggles, and some telling their stories. One principal stated that we "even heard stories from our CC that were reassuring and helped us not feel so alone in this job as a school leader." One of the benefits of this model was the supportive relationships that developed among the group and with the Coach. As one principal shared, "she allowed us to talk freely and share concerns without fear of it being shared with others."

Principals felt that when the Coaches shared their own reflections and exposed their own questions or dilemmas, the result was a true dialogue where mutual trust grew. Individual confidence grew as other principals respected and valued their feedback. Teams appreciated their CCs frequently reviewing the team norms. As one principal commented, "Each time before we started the meeting, our Coach reminded us about our most important norm—confidentiality. We never had a problem because everyone respected the norms." In fact, another person noted that: "We all took the oath of confidentiality."

Beginning principals felt comfortable discussing their struggles, new experiences, and difficult concerns in the small cohorts. "It has been a way to feel less alone in the role and to be able to discuss challenges and learn new strategies in a safe environment." New principals stated the importance of being able to get answers to questions that they might not be comfortable asking others in the district. One principal stated it this way: "We were really able to talk about school issues without worry on where the information might end up." Another principal stressed the safety in the cohort: "The meeting times were extremely valuable because we were able to ask questions that we were either afraid to ask anyone else or those we did not know who else to ask." Comments were made that indicated they felt more self-assured in their leadership.

A network strengthens confidence. New principals found their own security by working with peers who were in the same position. "Getting to know other new principals made me not feel so alone." When faced with many new responsibilities, principals appreciate support from others who are in the same situations. "It has been a way to feel less alone in the role and to be able to discuss challenges and learn new strategies in a safe environment." As new principals hear the questions of others and could offer support or further information, a new found confidence surfaced. "I've learned that some of my challenges are also the challenges other new principals are facing."

Early on, novice principals began to call or e-mail each other between sessions. One principal commented: "I found myself calling one of the other new principals on my way home from work each day to share stories and check in." The team served as a sounding board for new principals before they launched any changes in their school. The new principals felt that the setting of the CC model helped principals gain confidence in themselves and the plans they were implementing in their school. At the end of the meetings, new principals felt better prepared to handle issues at school; thereby their confidence grew. "I often felt that I was ready to return to school and make a real difference." Similarly, when principals sensed that their support and ideas had been helpful to someone else, they also felt more secure in their own decision-making. "It feels good when I have something to offer," said one principal. This confidence helped new principals feel more confident in their new role.

Theme 4: Community

New principals in a large school district need to make connections with other principals. This model does not allow any new principal to struggle with these relationships. One principal commented that her cohort "found each other in the large principal meetings and sat together to feel connected."

A professional community supporting each other. Having a network of peers where principals know each other well and can really talk is critical. "I loved discussing our role with others who really know what I'm talking about." "The best part of our dialogue is that we have formed a bond. This bond has allowed us to ask for and be given support to one another." And the support did not end at the schoolhouse door. "My team was also interested in my personal life. They reminded me to stay focused not just on my job, but on family too;" and "My Coach was very supportive in May when my brother passed away."

A common thread through the discussion of the model's structure was the importance of having a strong Coach. Many principals valued the information provided by the Coach. "I also learned from the experience of the Coach as a leader." One person also provided clear feedback on the role the consultant Coach plays during the discussion. "My Coach was extremely helpful in keeping us focused on the important issues instead of getting caught up with the minor details." The participants in the team appreciated that "the Coach made herself vulnerable at times."

Participants particularly noticed the trust fostered in the groups by the CCs. Words used to describe the Coaches were open, honest, respectful, approachable, willing to listen, and nonthreatening. One person commented that her Coach was able to build trust because "she did not pass judgment at all." Being part of the team was important to some participants, as noted by the comment: "Our Coach was very down to earth and did not present a presence of hierarchy." Another principal felt the Coach was open to new ideas when she "encouraged us to share our ideas and to be candid with each other." Another principal appreciated his Coach for just being "there for us." New principals felt that their Coaches were "genuinely interested in making sure all of us are successful." Between the meetings, new principals knew that Coaches were always available, "reaching out with a helping hand," and "being ready to help no matter the day or the time that I called."

The CC teams become very close-knit colleagues, and extended their networking beyond the monthly meetings. Some CCs organized their team to attend a national conference together. Another CC held several social events for her team. Still another team, in year two, added a book study to the CC agenda, at the request of the participants. As within all strong professional learning teams, the goal was for participants to determine their own learning opportunities for professional growth.

The themes and the descriptions of the elements that comprised the best practices of the CC model are depicted in Figure 13.2.

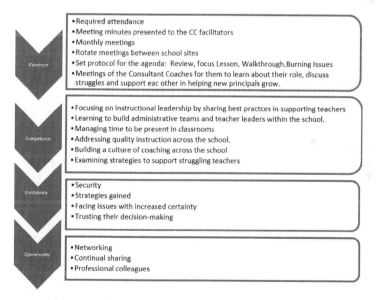

Figure 13.2.   Best Practices of the Consultant Coaching Model.

Building on Lessons Learned

The Consultant Coaching program for new principals in the Charlotte-Mecklenburg school district has been deemed a success, and is continuing as an institutional support for all new administrators. Additional focus lessons have been written to allow teams a greater range of topics to discuss. The new lessons came from suggestions provided by the new principals who completed two years in the program. Another element that has been added is requiring CCs to arrange cohort visits to schools not represented by cohort principals, as there are instructional exemplars throughout the district, led by experienced principals. In addition, a program similar to CC has been designed for Assistant Principals and is in the implementation phase.

DISCUSSION

The CC model is working successfully for the Charlotte-Mecklenburg School district at the time of this writing. Following a structured approach, the model was built on the required competencies of new principals and ensured that they were never left alone to survive on their own. Relationships and support were vital. According to the Deputy Superintendent of Charlotte-Mecklenburg Schools, "The collaborative nature of this program, and the opportunity for our administrators to serve as mentors, has helped all of us think about the challenges of leadership in a more analytical way." The success of the model is the result of much effort and planning. The CCs have also added a great deal of expertise to refine the process. The model can be easily replicated into other districts with little funding. Therefore, important lessons learned from the development and implementation of the program need to be shared.

Lesson One. Create a Solid *Construct* for Conducting a Model of Learning for New Principals That Is Safe and Focused on Instruction

Strong principals understand that collaboration is a valuable endeavor because this structure of professional learning ultimately builds trust, collective responsibility, and a school-wide focus on improved student learning (Prestine & Nelson, 2003). While principals have been considered the 'learning leader" in schools (Fullan, 2014, p. 9), the question arises: "Can we expect principals to create a collaborative culture for their teachers without firsthand experience working in such a setting with their own peers?" (David, 2009, p. 89). By participating in such a close-knit group of fellow leaders, principals will be more likely to replicate the collaborative structure in their own schools.

Within this safe place to learn, principals need to consistently address their primary goal: raising student achievement. According to Elmore (2004, para. 1), principals must "focus their efforts on instruction if they are to thrive and survive in current conditions." Therefore, maximum time on the agenda at cohort meetings should focus on instruction, and instruction should always precede any discussion of "burning issues."

Clear expectations must be set for CCs and for the novice principals. CCs need to be held accountable for submitting meeting agendas, minutes, additional information shared, and for attending meetings with the CC Facilitators. Norms must be established and enforced as new principals tend to be overwhelmed and often conversations can be dominated by one principal who is facing a problem, or time is taken up in a "whining" session. Because meetings must include walkthroughs and discussion within a set time frame, all three hours must be spent in a school. CC meetings need to be scheduled for the entire year before school opens so that new principals know when they will be leaving their buildings on a monthly basis. Likewise, the team needs to know the schools that will be visited over the course of the year. Observing in a wide range of schools helps prepare principals for any situation. The clear construct ensures fidelity with the model.

CCs need support as well, as this model is new. These experienced principals benefit from a confidential time to discuss their successes and challenges as Coaches to new principals. Coaches need time to discuss each focus lesson and become prepared to personalize the lesson to meet the needs of their group members. During these meetings they can share current research on coaching strategies and can motivate each other to be the best Coaches that they can possibly be. As a team, they need to know they are making a positive difference in the school district.

Flexibility is a key to success with this model. At times, there may be principals with several years of experience entering the district who might also benefit from spending time with new principals; others may not need this support. District initiatives may need to be added to agendas. Schedules may need to be adjusted for various reasons. In any case, decisions must be based on the needs of the first-year principals.

The CCs have considered additional projects to conduct. One example of a project was the compilation of a "master calendar" of all the important things principals need to do each month. Rather than just talking from their own "to do" lists, a more complete list of tasks was made from the collective knowledge of the Coaches that will benefit all cohorts of novice principals.

Lesson Two: Maintain a Clear Focus on *Competency* Building

Authentic leadership learning takes place when a new principal accepts the position and moves into a new setting. Principal preparation programs can only do so much (Lashway, 2003). Continued, personalized professional development after entering the principal position is of utmost importance so that new principals are never "thrown into their jobs without a life jacket" (National Association of Elementary School Principals, 2003, p. 8). Every CC session should result in participants leaving with new ideas or strategies that can be implemented immediately. Selection of the right individuals to be Coaches is imperative. Coaches must have the following qualifications: commitment to the process of CC, and willingness to follow the structure. CCs must also be successful leaders in their own school and have evidence to show they are instructionally focused. The Coaches also must be competent to lead instructional walkthroughs. Walkthroughs are a key element in the model for new learning and should not be condensed in any way. Looking for specific effective practices and debriefing on them afterwards is a key component in building competence as an instructional leader.

CCs, although veterans, also learn through their experience of assisting new principals. Often when consultant Coaches gather, they share with each other the lessons they have learned from their own experiences. Similarly, they share ideas they have gleaned from the new principals they are coaching. In this manner, everyone gains additional professional competence.

Lesson Three: Focus on *Confidence* Building

It is very common for a new principal to feel insecure and unconfident. Most principals can benefit from professional conversations that let them address problems together. One beginning principal who participated in the CC program summarized the experience this way:

> It greatly helps to see others in your seat experiencing the same fears or inadequacies. It is comforting to know in a weird sense, that the feeling of inadequacy never truly gets better, as the realm of our impact is so far reaching. However, slowly, it becomes normal to feel somewhat unsettled; the more you discuss and reflect with each other, the easier it is to move forward.

Innovative ideas need to be valued and meeting time should never be wasted on the negative aspects of the job. Instead, the CC must be able to keep conversations in a problem-solving mode and encouraging words need to be frequent.

When participants report back to their cohort on their homework from the previous session, they receive positive responses from the group. While some learning will result from things that "go wrong," the colleagues are able to turn these into lessons for the future. In either case, the reflective practice shared with others is great learning and reassures principals that they are on-track with their leadership. Our "lessons learned" include what researchers have documented: that the benefits of mentoring for new principals include reduction in isolation, getting outside support and an objective perspective, opportunities for deliberate reflection, and increased competence and confidence (Daresh, 2004; Hansford & Ehrich, 2006; Villani, 2006).

Lesson Four: Focus on *Community*

New principals learn very quickly that the principalship can be a lonely place (National Association of Elementary School Principals, 2003). They find that they need their colleagues for support. Principals do not need to stay isolated in their own buildings. Just as teachers benefit from collaborative planning, principals can gain new insights from working with others as well. Additionally, administrators thrive when they benefit from connections with their peers in learning teams (David, 2009).

The value of networking cannot be underestimated. Keeping smaller groups, maintaining the same team each of the two years, and being intentional in the selection of mentors and school leaders impacted the success of the model. One new principal, completing her second year in the district, reflected on the experiences in CC:

> The journey of the principalship is an amazing and fulfilling experience. As I have traveled through the first two years, I have realized that the support you receive as a principal in the first years of your career are critical. The support that I received from the Consultant Coach team that I was a part of during my first two years provided an enormous amount of support. It was very helpful having a mentor who was an experienced principal who was able to give relevant and timely advice and feedback when needed. Networking with the other principals in my team was an experience that I looked forward to monthly. Visiting different schools each month and conducting instructional walkthroughs in different buildings helped me grow as an instructional leader due to being exposed to best practices and strategies on other campuses. I will miss our meetings next year, but at least I have several people that I can call anytime about anything!

Several of the beginning principals wanted to continue with their Consultant Coaching team meetings into the future, although the formal program was only slated for two years. One principal stated that "It was extremely beneficial to have permission to schedule this time together each month. I would like to have this opportunity ongoing as an administrator." Even though the "formal" community of the new principal cohorts came to an end, the relationships that were established continued to be an ongoing mode of support.

CONCLUSION

Beginning principals are eager to learn and become effective leaders, yet, they need supportive constructs in order to feel competent and confident in their ability to lead. A community focused on continuous learning for new administrators connects them in an environment that is safe, supportive, and encouraging.

Participants in the CC program in the Charlotte–Mecklenburg school district have offered great insight into the benefits of this model of new principal mentoring. By listening carefully to their comments, and being open to making adjustments based on their needs, decision-makers in the district have chosen to make the Consulting Coaching model an important part of their ongoing strategy for retaining highly qualified and competent new principals. As authors, we believe this model can be replicated in other large school districts, and similar results can be achieved. Every new principal deserves this level of support for becoming a competent and confident instructional leader.

Appendix A
Example of a Cohort Schedule All
Meetings on Friday From 9:30 A.M.–12:30 P.M.

Meeting	Date	Location	Topic
1	September 14, 2012	Elon Park	Overview of Year 2 Program & Model Building School Staff Relationships Setting our Norms
2	October 12, 2012	River Gate	Creating a Culture of Coaching
3	November 9, 2012	Cotswold	Development of Appropriate and Effective Action Plans
4	December 14, 2012	Oaklawn	The Importance of Listening in the Coaching Process
5	January 25, 2013	Davidson	Components of Effective Postconferences
6	February 15, 2013	Greenway Park	A Coaching Plan in Action
7	March 15, 2013	Lebanon Road	Delegation
8	April 26, 2013	Elon Park	End of Year Processes and Procedures/Start-Up
9	May 31, 2013	Mint Hill	Celebration

Appendix B
Agenda Structure for the 3-hour Meetings

1.	What celebrations have we had? Homework review	15 minutes
2.	Focus Lesson & Discussion	45 minutes
3.	Walkthrough the building—focused instructional walkthrough	45 minutes
	a. Address specific questions that principal requests	
	b. Debriefing, feedback, and professional dialogue	
4.	Burning Issue (identified at last meeting)	30 minutes
5.	Identify Burning Issue for Next Month	15 minutes
6.	Current events: Month by Month/Sharing Calendars	15 minutes
7.	Homework Assignment and the Q and A: Discussion	15 minutes

Appendix C
Example of a Focus Lesson Provided to Consultant Coaches
Writing Teacher Action Plans

Anticipatory Set:

We have completed the first round of teacher evaluation conferences: observations, walk-throughs, review of data sources, and formative evaluation. The second round is due 1/20/12, which is right around the corner. While most teachers are continuously growing professionally, a directed growth plan may still be needed for those who are not. Our understanding of these action plans is crucial if the teacher is going to be "turned toward success."

Objective: To summarize key points of writing strong action plans

To critique a strong plan

Input:

1) Review the performance counseling letter and the state PDP form.

2) Share tips for writing strong plans (see below).

3) Critique a copy of one plan that has many/most of the elements to make it a strong example of an action growth plan. (Use plan provided or one from you school.)

Debrief the activity:

1. What are your takeaways?

2. Why is it so important that the action plans you create are in-depth and closely monitored?

(Appendix C continues on next page)

Appendix C (Continued)

Tips for Writing Directed Teacher Growth Plans

1. *Understand the brevity of the teaching situation.*

   Teachers must understand the seriousness of the need for professional growth. Teachers are placed on a Directed Plan whenever he or she 1) is rated "not demonstrated" on any standard on the Teacher Summary Rating Form, or is "developing on one or more standards on the teacher summary rating form for two sequential years, and 2) is not recommended for dismissal, demotion, or nonrenewal. Growth plans should include a specific area of teaching or learning that the teacher needs to further explore.

2. *Understand the necessity for teaching to change and for student achievement to improve.*

   Developing a directed growth plan involves a serious conversation, where the administrator impresses the need for immediate professional growth. Data is used to demonstrate the need for this growth. While teacher input is needed in order for the teacher to be invested in the learning, the principal must be certain that the goals and strategies, if addressed thoroughly, will result in improved teacher performance. The plan should be restricted to two or three goals that will directly impact student achievement. The goals may need to have a short term timeline so that additional improvements can be made within the school year.

3. *Create a support team to provide ongoing assistance.*

   Teachers on a directed development plan benefit from a support team. School leaders need to emphasize multiple forms or situations of job-embedded learning. The increased collaboration and stronger staff relationships will provide a setting where there are increased chances of successful implementation and growth. Support team members may be needed as models of good teaching, mentors to provide specific, ongoing feedback, and specific direction with lesson planning and data analysis.

4. *Begin with goal setting.*

   Once the need for improvement has been established, goal-setting should follow. The principal and teacher must determine specific improvements to be made and why they are necessary. The goals must be clearly defined so that the teacher knows exactly what is expected. Administrators must provide support writing a proper and beneficial SMART goal (specific, measurable, attainable, realistic, and timely).

5. *The action plan should be the road map towards growth and success for the teacher.*

   Student achievement must be foremost in establishing the plan. Elements of the plans should include thorough strategies or tasks, resources, and roles that will be needed for the process to be successful. A timeline must be set that is reasonable, yet reveal the urgency for change. Specific times for monitoring and sharing data should be included in the overall timeline. Support team members may be written into the plan for specific help.

(Appendix C continues on next page)

Appendix C (Continued)

Tips for Writing Directed Teacher Growth Plans

6. *Administrators provide ongoing monitoring and support for teacher growth plans.*

Although teachers are responsible for implementing the plans, the administrator needs to provide guidance and feedback on an individual basis. The timeline should include checkpoints where the principal monitors teacher progress. When the plan needs adjustments or revisions, the principal must take the initiative to modify the goals or activities. Face-to-face, frequent conversations should be held between the administrator and teacher in a more formal way when the growth plan is being monitored for evaluation purposes.

7. *Data collection is a vital part of the teacher growth plan.*

Data sources and documents that need to be collected throughout the plan should be established up-front. Evidence of improvements in teacher performance is best noted through specific charts, plans, student work, outcomes, etc. This data often indicates follow-up steps for instructional improvement. Likewise, data can be an objective source of information to verify teacher growth.

Appendix D

List of the Survey Questions

Effectiveness of Consultant Coaching 2012

1. In what way have you benefited from each month's dialogue with other new principals and your principal Coach?

2. What benefit and/or value did each month's homework provide?

3. How did the monthly focus lessons address your needs as a new principal, and/or a principal new to CMS?

   Which had the greatest value to you as a new principal?

   Which had the least?

4. What were your "take-aways" from the walkthroughs and their de-briefings?

5. How did your principal/Coach establish a relationship of trust and support with you?

6. What was the least useful aspect of the monthly meeting?

7. In what way did the monthly meetings facilitate the focus on the principal as an instructional leader?

8. Was rotating each monthly meeting to another new principal's school of benefit? If so, how? If not, why not?

9. What suggestions do you have for improving the consultant Coach model?

10. If you are completing year one, you will continue with a consultant Coach for another year. What topics would you like to have discussed in the upcoming year

REFERENCES

Alsbury, T. L., & Hackmann, D. G. (2006). Learning from experience: Initial findings of a mentoring/induction program for novice principals and superintendents. *Planning and Changing, 37*(3/4), 45–58

Beteille, T., Kalogrides, D. and Loeb, S. (2011). Stepping Stones: Principal career paths and school outcomes. *National Center for Analysis of Longitudinal Data in Education Research.* Retrieved on September 15, 2015 from http://www.caldercenter.org/upload/CALDERWorkPaper_58.pdf

Billger, S.M. (2007). Principals as Agents? Investigating Accountability in the Compensation and Performance of School Principals. Discussion Paper No. 2662, IZA.

Browne-Ferrigno, T., & Muth, R. (2004). Leadership mentoring in clinical practice: Role socialization, professional development, and capacity building. *Educational Administration Quarterly, 40*(4). 468–494.

Bryk, A., Camburn, E., & Louis, K. S. (1999). Professional community in Chicago elementary schools: Facilitating factors and organizational consequences. *Educational Administration Quarterly, 35*, 751–781.

Bryk, A. S., Sebring, P. B., Allensworth, E., Luppescu, S., & Easton, J. Q. (2010). *Organizing schools for improvement: Lessons from Chicago.* Chicago, IL: University of Chicago Press.

Calman, R. C., for the EQAO. (2010). *Exploring the underlying traits of high-performing schools.* Toronto, Canada: Queen's Printer.

Charlotte-Mecklenburg Schools. (2013a). *About us: Background, facts and history.* Retrieved November 15, 2013 from http://www.cms.k12.nc.us/mediaroom/aboutus/Pages/default.aspx.

Charlotte-Mecklenburg Schools. (2013b). *Succession planning: Find and keep the very best principals.* Retrieved November 15, 2014, from http://www.cms.k12.nc.us/mediaroom/Documents/Succession%20Planning.pdf

David, J. L. (2009). What research says about learning communities for administrators. *Educational Leadership, 67*(2), 88–89.

Daresh, J. C. (2004). Mentoring school leaders: Professional promise or predictable problems? *Educational Administration Quarterly, 40*(4), 495–517.

Day, C., Sammons, P., Hopkins, D., Harris, A., Leithwood, K., Gu, Q., & Kington, A. (2009). *The impact of school leadership on pupil outcomes.* Nottingham, UK: National College for School Leadership.

Elmore, R. (2004). *Building a new structure for school leaders in school reform from the inside out.* Boston, MA: Harvard Educational Press. Retrieved October 29, 2014, from http://www.uknow.gse.harvard.edu/leadership/leadership001b.html.

Fullan, M. (1991). *Leading in a culture of change.* San Francisco, CA: Jossey-Bass

Fullan, M. (2014). *The principal: Three keys to maximizing impact.* San Francisco, CA: Jossey-Bass.

Gray, C., Fry, B., Bottoms, G., & O'Neill, K. (2007). *Principals aren't born—they're mentored: Are we investing enough to get the school leaders we need?* Atlanta, GA: Southern Regional Education Board.

Hansen, J. M., & Matthews, J. (2002). The power of more than one. *Principal Leadership*, *3*(2), 30–33.

Hansford, B., & Ehrich, L. C. (2006). The principalship: How significant is mentoring? *Journal of Educational Administration*, *44*(1), 36–52.

Lashway, L. (2003). *Improving principal evaluation*. Eugene, OR: ERIC Clearinghouse on Education Management. 172. Retrieved October 17, 2014, from http://www.eric.ed.gov/ERICWebPortal/search/detailmini.jsp?_nfpb=true&_&ERICExtSearch_SearchValue_0=ED482347&ERICExtSearch_SearchType_0=no&accno=ED482347

Leithwood, K., Harris, A., Hopkins, D. (2008) Seven strong claims about successful school Leadership. *School Leadership and Management*, *28*(1), 27–42

Leithwood, K., & Seashore- Louis, K. (2012). *Linking leadership to student learning*. Thousand Oaks, CA: Jossey-Bass.

Levine, A. (2005). *Educating school leaders*. New York, NY: The Education Schools Project.

Louis, K. S., Dretzke, B., & Wahlstrom, K. (2010). How does leadership affect student achievement? Results from a national U.S. survey. *School Effectiveness and School Improvement*, *21*(3), 315–336.

Louis, K. S., & Marks, H. (1998). Does professional community affect the classroom? Teachers' work and student experiences in restructuring schools. *American Journal of Education*, *106*, 532–575.

Marzano, R. J., Pickering, D. J., & Pollock, J. E. (2001). *Classroom instruction that works*. Alexandria, VA: Association for Supervision and Curriculum Development.

Marzano, R., Waters, T., & McNulty, B. (2005). *School leadership that works*. Alexandria, VA: Association for Supervision and Curriculum Development.

McEwan, E. K. (2003). *Ten traits of highly effective principals: From good to great performance*. Thousand Oaks, CA: Sage.

Merriam, S. (2007). *Qualitative research: A guide to design and implementation*. San Francisco, CA: Jossey-Bass.

Miller, A. (2009). *Principal turnover, student achievement and teacher retention*. Princeton, NJ: Princeton University.

Mitchell, D. J. B., Lewin, D., & Lawler, E. E. (1990). Alternative pay systems, firm performance, and productivity. In A. Blinder (Ed.), *Paying for productivity: A look at the evidence*. Washington, DC: Brookings Institution Press.

Mitgang, L. (2012). *The making of a principal: Five lessons in leadership training*. Retrieved September 15, 2015, from http://www.wallacefoundation.org/knowledge-center/school-leadership/effective-principal-leadership/Documents/The-Making-of-the-Principal-Five-Lessons-in-Leadership-Training.pdf

National Association of Elementary School Principals. (2003). *Making the case for principal mentoring*. Providence, RI: Brown University.

Newmann, F. M. (1996). *Authentic achievement: Restructuring schools for intellectual quality*. San Francisco, CA: Jossey-Bass.

Prestine, N. A., & Nelson, B. S. (2003, April). *How can educational leaders support and promote teaching and learning? New conceptions of learning and leading in schools.* Paper presented at the annual meeting of the American Educational Research Association, Chicago, IL.

Seashore-Louis, K., Leithwood, K., Wahlstrom, K., & Anderson, S. (2010). *Learning from leadership: Investigating the links to improved student learning.* Minneapolis, MN: University of Minnesota Center for Applied Research and Educational Improvement.

Sharratt, L., & Fullan, M. (2012). *Putting faces on the data: What great leaders do.* Thousand Oaks, CA: Corwin Press.

Sharratt, L., Ostinelli, G., & Cattaneo, A. (2010, January). *The role of the "knowledgeable other" in improving student achievement, school culture, and teacher efficacy: Two case studies from Canadian and Swiss perspectives and experiences.* Paper presented at the International Congress for School Effectiveness and Improvement, Kuala Lumpur, Malaysia.

Sherman, W. H., & Crum, K. S. (2008). Navigating the waters of school administration: Women leaders in conversation about mentoring and support. In D. Beaty, W. H. Sherman, A. Munoz, & A. Pankake (Eds.), *Women as school executives: Celebrating diversity.* Austin, TX: Texas Council of Women School Executives: Tarleton State University Press.

Southern Regional Education Board (2010). *School leadership change emerging in Alabama: Results of the Governor's Congress on School Leadership.*

Turnbull, B. J., Riley, D. L., Arcaira, E. R., Anderson, L. M., MacFarlane, J. R. (2013). *Six districts begin the principal pipeline initiative.* Retrieved November 1, 2014, from http://www.wallacefoundation.org/knowledge-center/school-leadership/principal-training/Documents/Six-Districts-Begin-the-Principal-Pipeline-Initiative.pdf.

Villani, S. (2006). *Mentoring and induction programs that support new principals.* Thousand Oaks, CA: Corwin Press

Wahlstrom, K., & Louis, K. S. (2008). How teachers perceive principal leadership. *Educational Administration Quarterly, 44,* 498–445.

Wallace Foundation (2007). *Getting principal mentoring right: Lessons from the field.* Retrieved September 15, 2015, from http://www.wallacefoundation.org/knowledge-center/school-leadership/principal-training/Pages/Getting-Principal-Mentoring-Right.aspx

Wiley, S. D. (2001). Contextual effects on student achievement: School leadership and professional community. *Journal of School Change, 2*(1), 1–33.

Young, M., & Fuller, E. (2009, April). *Tenure and retention of newly hired principals in Texas.* Paper presented at the American Educational Research Association (AERA) conference, San Diego, CA.

Youngs, P. (2001). District and state policy influences on professional development and school capacity. *Educational Policy, 15,* 278–301.

Youngs, P., & King, M.B. (2002). Principal leadership for professional development to build school capacity. *Educational Administration Quarterly, 38,* 643–670.

CHAPTER 14

MENTORING MIDCAREER PRINCIPALS TO BUILD CAPACITY FOR CHANGE IN SCHOOLS

Kenyae L. Reese, Jane Clark Lindle, Matthew R. Della Sala, Robert C. Knoeppel, and Hans W. Klar

Mentoring has been identified as an important aspect of new principal development (Barnett, Copland & Shoho, 2009; Grogan & Crow, 2004; Hansford & Erich, 2006; Searby, 2010). Investigations about principals' needs for ongoing professional development suggest that mentoring should be available to experienced principals as well as newly seated ones (Duncan, 2013; Louis, Leithwood, Wahlstrom, & Anderson, 2010; Martin, 2013; Notman, 2012; Parylo, Zapeda, & Bengston, 2013). Other than these recommendations, few reports explain the complex practice of preparing and supporting mentors to assist *midcareer* principals (Louis et al., 2010). Even less information is available on *cross-district mentoring*; that is, using coaches/mentors from nearby school districts to support practicing principals (Clayton, Sanzo, & Myran, 2013).

Midcareer professionals are typically those described as having 10 or more years of professional work experience (Auster, 2001; Schneer &

Best Practices in Mentoring for Teacher and Leader Development, pp. 279–312
Copyright © 2016 by Information Age Publishing

Reitman, 1995). The midcareer stage can be challenging for these professionals as it is a time when the complexities of work and personal lives can be most severe (Auster, 2001; Schneer & Reitman, 1995). The role of principals has also become more complex (Carpenter & Brewer, 2012; von Frank, 2012). Thus, providing support and advocacy for principals at midcareer through a coach/mentoring program is one mechanism for meeting their ongoing professional learning needs.

In this chapter, we describe Leadership 3.0, a program for the development of coach/mentors to support experienced principals in school improvement. A partnership among nine school districts and a research-intensive public land-grant university was formed to implement Leadership 3.0 as one of two pilot programs that were initiated simultaneously. Leadership 3.0, the focus of this report, provided sessions designed to increase coaching and mentoring skills among district-level school leaders who were supporting midcareer principals, not employed in the same school districts. These sessions promoted the following two goals: (a) to support principals in their schools' rural contexts, and (b) to build regional leadership capacity for improved student learning through cross-district mentoring. This process involved the systematic and purposeful selection of coach/mentors (Hansford & Ehrich, 2006) from nine regional districts rather than the more traditional grow-your-own leadership development models which pair a less-experienced professional with a more knowledgeable one in the same district (Barnett et al., 2009; Daresh, 2004; Hansford & Ehrich, 2006).

As a regional leadership capacity-building initiative, the partnering districts and university coupled Leadership 3.0 with a companion pilot program, Leadership 2.0, which included nine school principals from the nine districts leading four elementary schools, three middle schools, and two high schools. Leadership 2.0 combined with Leadership 3.0 addressed repeated calls for research related to the ongoing learning needs of midcareer principals as opposed to the conventional model focused on aspiring or entry-level leaders (Hall, 2008; Harris, Ballenger & Leonard, 2004; Turnbull, Riley, & MacFarlane, 2013; Wasonga & Murphy, 2006).

The district superintendents and the university team members intended that both programs would build capacity for principals' data use related to meaningful student learning and enhanced teacher performance. The need for this was reported in the 10-year Wallace Foundation study (Louis et al., 2010):

> Leaders in high data-use schools have *clear purposes* for analyzing data. They *engage their staff collectively* in data analysis, *build internal capacity* for this work, and use data to *solve problems,* not simply to identify them.... Yet, few principals systematically collect data, and barely 50% involve staff in analyzing it. (p. 179, emphasis added)

As one superintendent stated in the planning phase, "I've got principals who get data and can analyze it. They are all over the data, but they can't figure out that next step" (Field Notes, February 15, 2012). This statement not only reflected Louis et al.'s (2010) findings, it received a collective nod of agreement from the other superintendents.

Given the importance of pushing school leaders beyond the acknowledgement of data and into plans and actions, the sessions for Leadership 2.0 focused on developing the capacities of nine midcareer principals for effectively using data. Leadership 3.0 emerged as a simultaneous pilot as the participating superintendents considered how to support their practicing principals' capacity development. They recognized the limited number of personnel in their small, rural districts who could serve as coaches/mentors to these principals in Leadership 2.0. Even though there were a few accomplished district-level leaders who had the potential to be good coaches and mentors, the superintendents agreed that those individuals would need support to work across district lines to figure out how to get principals "who might be stuck with their data, unstuck" (Field Notes, February 15, 2012). At that point, the superintendents decided to collaborate with each other to find complementary matches of mentors to protégés among their rural districts with the ultimate goal of building regional capacity for improved student performance through professional learning.

CONCEPTUAL FRAMEWORK

A partnership between a university and a group of nine school districts established Leadership 3.0 as a developmental program for coaches/mentors to support midcareer principals who participated in Leadership 2.0 to improve student and teacher performance. The processes for both programs included professional growth and learning. Therefore, we selected a model of adult professional learning and Guskey's model of evaluating professional development as the two-fold conceptual framework for the study (Brookfield, 1991; Darling-Hammond, Wei, Andree, Richardson, & Orphanos, 2009; Duncan-Howell, 2010; Guskey, 2003; Guskey & Yoon, 2009; Knowles, 1973; Zepeda, Bengston, & Parylo, 2014). The delivery framework was structured around six well-known and well-researched principles of adult professional learning (Brookfield, 1991; Knowles, 1973; Kochan, Bredeson, & Riehl, 2002), as indicated in Table 14.1. Guskey's (2000) five levels of impact for professional development provided the evaluation logic: (a) participants' reactions, (b) participants' learning, (c) organizational support and change, (d) participants' use of new knowledge and skills, and (e) student learning outcomes.

Table 14.1.   Six Principles of Adult Learning for Leadership 2.0 and Leadership 3.0 Pilot Program

Types of Knowledge	Principle #1: ... experienced professionals with experiential knowledge and tacit knowledge as background germane to research-based knowledge.	... to facilitate participants making cognitive and practical connections between background knowledge and new research-based knowledge.
Cognitive Demand	Principle #2: ... mature learners whose ability to take abstract knowledge and apply it concretely varies individually.	... to monitor individual's developmental needs and offer multiple opportunities to move from the abstract to the practical.
Pacing	Principle #3: ... busy adults with multiple responsibilities and obligations that may interrupt or intervene in learning sessions.	... to provide opportunities for learning that intentionally (with ample planning) accommodate adults' professional and personal obligations, and to monitor and adjust schedules as professional events and episodes demand.
Context	Principle #4: ... shaped by the nature of their professional roles which research has demonstrated includes high-pacing, multi-tasking, and few opportunities for sustained attention to a single issue.	... to emphasize well-planned sessions that include hands-on and active learning with brief interludes (10 to 20 minutes) of sustained direct instruction.
Feedback	Principle #5: ... highly visible and subject to spontaneous judgments as well as formative and summative evaluations of their every action.	... to offer formative and summative opportunities for feedback from all participants about the content and strategies for learning during this program.
Technology	Principle #6 ... immersed in an information-based job, with high-levels of information demand, and constantly emerging information technologies, each with an individual learning curve.	... to offer appropriate application, practice, and introduction to emerging technologies, and to demonstrate the learning environments that effectively enhance achievement and productivity with technology.

Sources: Adapted from Darling-Hammond, Wei, Andree, Richardson, & Orphanos, 2009; Duncan-Howell, 2010; Fink & Markholt, 2011; Guskey, 2003; Guskey & Yoon, 2009; Kochan, Bredeson & Riehl, 2002; Marzano, 2007.

The university team gleaned the six principles of adult learning from various literature sources (e.g., Darling-Hammond et al., 2009; Duncan-Howell, 2010; Fink & Markholt, 2011; Guskey, 2003; Guskey & Yoon, 2009; Kochan et al., 2002; Marzano, 2007). Thus, the delivery method framework included the following principles:

1. **Types of Knowledge**—Principle #1: School leaders are experienced professionals with experiential knowledge and tacit knowledge as background germane to research-based knowledge (Brookfield, 1991; Fink & Markholt, 2011; Knowles, 1973; Kochan et al., 2002).
2. **Cognitive Demand**—Principle #2: School leaders are mature learners whose ability to take abstract knowledge and apply it concretely varies individually (Darling-Hammond et al., 2009; Leithwood & Steinbach, 1995; Marzano, 2007; Spillane, White, & Stephan, 2009).
3. **Pacing**—Principle #3: School leaders are busy adults with multiple responsibilities and obligations that may interrupt or intervene in learning sessions (Brookfield, 1991; Darling-Hammond et al., 2009; Knowles, 1973; Kochan et al., 2002).
4. **Context**—Principle #4: School leaders are shaped by the nature of their professional roles which research has demonstrated includes high pacing, multitasking, and few opportunities for sustained attention to a single issue (Knowles, 1973; Smith, 2000; Spillane, Camburn, & Stitziel Pareja, 2007; Spillane, Halverson, & Diamond, 2001).
5. **Feedback**—Principle #5: School leaders are highly visible and subject to spontaneous judgments as well as formative and summative evaluations of their every action (Guskey, 2003; Guskey & Yoon, 2009; Hargreaves, 1998; Leithwood & Beatty, 2008; Notman, 2012; Wright, 2009).
6. **Technology**—Principle #6: School leaders are immersed in an information-based job, with high-levels of information demand, and constantly emerging information technologies, each with an individual learning curve (Duncan Howell, 2010; Schrum, Galizio, & Ledesma, 2011).

Specifically, the team attended to recommendations to use adult learning principles in working with leader development (Kochan et al., 2002) in designing both pilot programs (see Lindle, Reese, Della Sala, Klar, & Knoeppel, 2013).

We introduced these principles to the participants and their superintendents at the commencing event. The team distributed the university's faculty commitment to applying these principles to the new programs as a handout to model reflection on the first steps in the program, as indicated in Table 14.2. Then, we gave each group (superintendents, Leadership 2.0 and Leadership 3.0 participants) a worksheet with an empty third column. Each group discussed the principles and outlined in the third column how they planned to approach the six principles during the pilot activities, sessions, and in the nine schools.

Table 14.2. Participating District and School Demographics

District	District Enrollment	School	School Student Enrollment	School Instructional Staff Size
1	3150	Blue Elementary School	376	27
2	3926	Cyan Elementary School	341	35
3	9094	Green Middle School	674	54
4	1007	Navy High School	466	35
5	1712	Red Middle School	406	29
6	5941	Yellow Elementary School	509	34
7	3050	Orange Middle School	703	49
8	5804	Teal High School	752	51
9	2152	Purple Elementary School	309	25

In addition to the six principles for designing learning, we utilized Guskey's (2000) five-level evaluation model to gather evidence of professional learning. Guskey's levels for evaluating professional learning include the following: Level One, participants' reactions; Level Two, participants' learning; Level Three, organizational and administrative support; Level 4, participants' applications of learning; and Level Five, effects on student achievement (Guskey, 2000). Guskey argued that professional development programs rarely use more than one level of evaluation. Furthermore, Guskey noted that longitudinal pacing from awareness of new knowledge to application often takes more than one school year. Given that pacing, evaluation at Level Five could be difficult to achieve. Others interested in evidence-based models of professional learning effectiveness have supported and critiqued Guskey's approach (Coldwell & Simkins, 2011; Ringler, O'Neal, Rawls, & Cumiskey, 2013).

Guskey's (2000) observations about the difficulty of influenceing student scores with professional learning, reflects aspects of Louis et al.'s (2010) findings that most principals find it difficult to move from data awareness to capacity building that improves teaching and learning. After all, "analyzing data and taking action based on data are two different tasks. Taking action is often more challenging and requires more creativity than does analysis. Yet to date, taking action generally receives less attention" (Marsh, McCombs, & Martorell, 2010, p. 900).

Herein we report on the results of Leadership 3.0's evaluation based on Levels One and Two of Guskey's evaluation model: (1) participants' immediate impressions and feelings about their professional learning, and (2) participants' cognitive engagement and memory of their learning within weeks after a session.

BACKGROUND

In the first year of the two-year initiative, 11 sessions were held between May 2012 and June 2013 (see Appendix A: Year 1 Session Topics for Leadership 2.0 and Leadership 3.0). The three sessions held in June, 2012, occured concurrently with the state's annual meeting of school administrators. At each session, the following essential questions were posted and read aloud: (1) What are the models for data-informed decision making that the state's schools use to improve? What models could they use? and (2) What data about you and your skill sets are available for helping achieve the steps necessary for school improvement? Throughout the year, professional learning sessions included a combination of the university team's direct input on topics related to instructional leadership along with analysis and reflection about participants' individual assessments. These assessments provided both groups with feedback on their skill sets related to their capacity to create change in their schools. Participants were also provided with a set of eleven books on school improvement, turnaround schools, and best practices for instructional leadership. The participants chose three books for book studies during the year. Between breaks in the monthly sessions, the university team visited each school three times the first year. The first visit occurred during the end of the summer, just as the principals prepared to begin the new school year. The second visit occurred during the winter. The final visit involved university team members, superintendents, coaches/mentors and principals and occurred during the spring of 2013. This year-long involvement provided the basis for the report here.

During the second year, the coaches/mentors will continue supporting the practicing principals. Therefore, this study is limited to participants' perceptions at a midpoint in the capacity building process.

LITERATURE REVIEW

Educational leadership literature describes the notion of principals as both individual and organizational capacity builders for increased student achievement (Mulford & Silins, 2003; Leithwood, Louis, Anderson, & Wahlstrom, 2004; Louis et al., 2010). To accomplish these objectives, principals require ongoing professional learning that encourages continual reflection on their own practices while simultaneously building their ability to enhance the capacities of others (Day, 2000).

Capacity Building for School Leaders

Leadership 3.0 is intended to foster the capacities of midcareer principals in Leadership 2.0 to, in turn, build capacity for change in their schools. In general terms, capacity is often thought of as the ability to accomplish something. Scholars have identified various types of capacity. According to Newmann, King, and Youngs (2000), capacity can be described as "the potential of a material, a product, person, or group to fulfill a function if it is used in a particular way" (p. 261). Bredeson (2005) defined an organization's capacity as its "ability to use its collective resources in ways that help it achieve its primary mission effectively while sustaining the organization over time" (p. 2). Newmann et al. (2000) succinctly described a school's capacity as "the collective power of the full staff to improve student achievement schoolwide" (p. 261). In their study of nine successful school leaders in Australia, Gurr and Drysdale (2007) identified four types of capacity: personal, professional, organizational, and community. O'Day, Goertz, and Floden (1995) suggested that the capacity for educational reform consists of both individual and organizational capacities and that they are interdependent. Given this interdependence, O'Day et al. recommended that capacity building efforts focus on promoting the professional development of individual teachers as well as attempting to build organizational capacity. Notwithstanding the utility of the aforementioned definitions of capacity, Stoll and Bolam's (2005) definition of capacity as the "motivation, skill, resources, resilience, and conditions to more readily engage in and sustain the continuous learning necessary for improvement" (p. 51) provides clearer guidance for focusing capacity building efforts related to the schools in this study.

Scholars across the globe agree that principals are well positioned to serve as both individual and organizational capacity builders. Harris (2003) argued that effective leadership for school improvement should be primarily focused on "developing capacity and the conditions to generate and sustain improvement" (p. 3). Stoll, Bolam, and Collarbone (2002), suggested that the role of the leader as a capacity builder is "fundamental to developing learning in a complex, changing world" (p. 41). Louis et al. (2010) identified developing people as one of the four core leadership practices of effective educational leaders in most contexts. Following their two-year study of nine elementary schools, Newmann et al. (2000), identified principal leadership; technical resources; teachers' knowledge, skills, and dispositions; professional community; and program coherence as key elements of school capacity. King and Bouchard (2011), however, noted that effective principal leadership is key in that principals have the ability to affect each of these aspects in "positive or negative ways and to varying degrees, depending on the quality of their leadership" (p. 656).

Given the imperative for principals to adopt the role of individual and organizational capacity builders, the questions become: How can this be achieved? and What are the characteristics of principals who build capacities? Stoll and Bolam (2005) answered the first question in part by suggesting that capacity building involves the following processes:

- Creating and maintaining the necessary conditions, culture and structures;
- Facilitating learning and skill-oriented experiences and opportunities; and
- Ensuring interrelationships and synergy among all the component parts (p. 52).

Dimmock (2012) noted that, at its heart, leadership is capacity building with requirements for understanding people and the "knowledge and skill about how to change the school by making better use of its intellectual and social capital to produce high-leverage strategies of teaching and learning" (p. 19). Principals' potential to build capacity themselves, Dimmock suggested, is influenced by three levels of factors. The first level of factors is the personal traits, dispositions and attributes which relate to school leadership: "practical wisdom, judgment, resilience, and confidence" (p. 194). The second level includes interpersonal skills such as the ability to "communicate with, trust and motivate teams and the wider community" (p.194). The third level relates to the leaders' efficacy in regards to interacting with the school's context and culture. These three levels of leaders' capacities enable the development of their schools' capacities for which Leadership 3.0 was designed to enhance.

Building capacity in rural areas. Context and culture present additional challenges to capacity building for practicing administrators. In this case, Leadership 2.0 and 3.0 participants work with challenges embedded within their schools and the rural environments of the districts. Reviews of rural school leaders' needs regarding capacity describe conditions in primarily English-speaking countries (Duncan & Stock, 2010; Preston, Jakubiec, & Kooymans, 2013; Starr & White, 2008). The results are remarkably consistent. These reports resonate a dominating concern for rural schooling about attracting and retaining competent educators in every position (Clayton et al., 2013; Duncan & Stock, 2010; Martin, 2013; Preston et al., 2013; Ringler et al., 2013; Starr & White, 2008). These reviews also report that school leaders at both the building and district levels experience even more diffusion of duties and tasks than do their urban counterparts (Duncan & Stock, 2010; Preston et al. 2013). Clearly, rural schools and districts face capacity issues in staffing positions, as well as in building the skill sets among that staff for addressing student needs and school improvement.

These conditions illustrate the need for rural principals' capacity building in light of the juxtaposition of scarce human capital and diffusion of responsibilities in a fragmented role. If small and rural school leaders require the same abilities as urban and suburban schools in forging beyond merely unpacking student data to creative thinking about next steps (Louis et al., 2010; Duncan & Stock, 2010; Marsh et al., 2010), then their experiences should include a more distributed approach to building their capacities (Browne-Ferrigno & Allen, 2006; Browne-Ferrigno & Knoeppel, 2005; Myran, Sanzo, & Clayton, 2011; Spillane et al., 2007; Wallin, 2008). This strategy implicates the need for a network of cross-district support, which is hard to implement in rural areas (Browne-Ferrigno & Allen, 2006; Grissom & Harrington, 2010; Myran et al., 2011; Preston et al., 2013).

Building capacity through principals' ongoing professional development. Over decades, Guskey and associates (2000, 2003; Guskey & Yoon, 2009) have delineated and reviewed efforts at continuous learning for all school personnel. These researchers consistently report a gap between the use of student data to determine what school leaders need for their professional learning as well as another similar gap in the use of student data to assess the impact of professional development programs (Guskey, 2000, 2003; Guskey & Yoon, 2009).

Some literature also demonstrates concerns about ongoing development for rural principals (Clayton et al., 2013; Duncan & Stock, 2010; Martin, 2013; Preston et al., 2013; Ringler et al., 2013; Starr & White, 2008). Namely, experienced principals need professional development that enables them to use of data to improve teachers' practice and that issue is associated with the degree to which those experienced principals have backgrounds in instructional leadership (Duncan & Stock, 2010; Starr & White, 2008). Furthermore, some researchers claim that principals need to develop their soft skills in dealing with the demands of data work on teachers and students in the accountability policy era (Duncan, 2013; Leithwood & Beatty, 2008).

Professional development through coach/mentoring programs. As educational leaders strive to grow as instructional leaders and capacity builders in the age of accountability, Brondyk and Searby (2013) suggested mentoring as a strategy for meeting the professional development needs of principals. The authors stated that mentoring can take place in many contexts and different levels and it can serve multiple needs. Specific to the role of the administrator, mentoring may be offered to new assistant principals or seasoned principals with the goals of induction, time management, delegation and supervision, implementation of new processes and procedures, changing culture, and learning more about evaluation and assessment (Bloom, Castagna, & Warren, 2003; Brondyk & Searby, 2013). Further, Burch and Spillane (2003) found that principals at the elementary level are required to have a deep understanding of curriculum and that their roles are characterized by the need to interact with and support teachers.

Conversely, principals at the secondary level cannot be expected to have expertise within all content areas taught in middle and high schools. Educational leaders at the secondary level are, therefore, charged with creating productive learning environments and encouraging teachers to be innovative (Halverson, Grigg, Pritchett, & Thomas, 2007; Mulford & Silins, 2003). Clearly, principals at different points in their respective careers and those who work in elementary and secondary schools have different needs. Bloom et al. (2003) suggested that novice principals would benefit most from receiving coaching centered on district matters while all principals could be aided by the assignment of a coach whose primary focus would be problem resolution.

Mentoring Versus Coaching to Build Instructional Leadership Capacity

A variety of terms can be used to describe mentoring in education. The chosen term reflects mentors' role definition and tasks (Brondyk & Searby, 2013). Terms may also provide insights into the type of professional development necessary for the professional's career stage. For example, the term novice connotes beginner. When working with a novice, the mentor works to help the mentee develop his or her practice (Feiman-Nemser, 2001). Conversely, the term protégé is also used in the literature. This term is characterized by a more hierarchical relationship in which the mentor holds a superior rank, possesses specialized knowledge, or is seen as an accomplished professional (Brondyk & Searby, 2013). In this type of mentoring, the role of the mentor is to "transmit knowledge and skills to someone with less experience and expertise" (Brondyk & Searby, 2013,

p. 193). Crow (2012) noted that the use of many definitions when describing mentoring has limited the development of theories of mentoring and made research in the field difficult. Hansford and Ehrich (2006) articulated a definition that fits the initiative described in this chapter: Mentoring is a process whereby a more experienced practitioner works with, guides, and provides professional development to a less experienced practitioner.

Coaching, on the other hand, is a term that has been used interchangeably with the term mentor in the field of education (Fletcher & Mullen, 2012). Nevertheless, Bloom et al. (2003) noted that coaching is focused on goal accomplishment and that it addresses the needs of the individual. The authors state that "effective coaches move between instructional coaching strategies, in which the coach serves as expert consultant, collaborator and teacher; and facilitative strategies, in which the coach adopts a mediational stance, with a primary focus on building the coachee's capacity through metacognition and reflection" (Bloom et al., 2003 p. 22). For the purposes of the program described in this chapter, we argue that *coaching* requires the protégé to extend beyond meeting his or her own personal goals to address the needs of the organization. We further contend that coaching includes building capacity for a larger goal than self-advancement. However, coaching to support principals' instructional leadership also falls in the empirical research gap surrounding the term mentor (Grogan & Crow, 2004; Gross, 2009; Psencik, 2011; von Frank, 2012).

RESEARCH DESIGN

A mixed methods design was used to examine Leadership 2.0 and 3.0 participants' perceptions about the coach/mentor component of the program, as well as participants' expectations about their coach-protégé relationships during the first year of the program. We used the following research questions to guide our analysis of the participants' perceptions of the program.

1. What are the participants' perceptions as to whether their expectations were met for the Leadership 2.0 and 3.0 programs and the coaching process?
2. What are the participant's perceptions about their relationships and matches as coach and protégé pairs?
3. What are the instructional leadership challenges faced by the participants as the program moves into its second year?

Participants

Participants for the study were eight coaches who were experienced principals or district leaders participating in the Leadership 3.0 pilot program, and nine practicing principals (protégés) in Leadership 2.0 representing four elementary schools, three middle schools, and two high schools. Table 1 displays the demographics of the districts and the schools. The average school district size was less than 4,000 students with roughly 500 enrolled in each school. The schools averaged about 38 instructional personnel.

Table 14.3 shows the distribution of experience among the school principals and their pairing with the coaches/mentors. Overall, the coaches/mentors were more experienced than the Leadership 2.0 principals. Most of the principals had between 10 and 20 years of experience, while their coaches/mentors had over 20 years of experience, except in two cases.

Table 14.3.   Participant Demographics

School	Principal Tenure	Principal Professional Experience [years]	Coach/ Mentor	Coach/Mentor Professional Experience [years]
Blue Elementary School [1]	1	<10	4	>20
Cyan Elementary School [2]	5	10 to 20	9	>20
Green Middle School [3]	3	10 to 20	8[a]	>20
Navy High School [4]	3	>20	8[a]	[a]
Red Middle School [5]	2	10 to 20	7	10 to 20
Yellow Elementary School [6]	4	>20	3	>20
Orange Middle School [7]	3	10 to 20	6	>20
Teal High School [8]	1	10 to 20	3	>20
Purple Elementary School [9]	3	>20	8	10 to 20

Note [a]: This Coach/Mentor works with two schools, Green Middle School and Navy High School.

Data Sources

Data was collected from four sources: (a) an online survey of participant's expectations and satisfaction with the coach/mentoring program, (b) logs of coach/mentor and protégé meetings, (c) quotes from meetings with district superintendents, and (d) attendance records from the monthly Leadership 2.0 and 3.0 professional learning sessions. These data sources provided for the triangulation of participants' perceptions to address the research questions. More details regarding the data sources is presented below.

Online coach/mentoring perceptions survey. An online survey was developed to gauge Leadership 2.0 and 3.0 participants' perceptions about the coach/mentoring relationship, the degree to which they found the program to be effective, and challenges they faced in their current professional role. The survey also collected demographics of the participants, including years of experience in education at the district level and as a school leader. Sixteen of the 17 participants completed the survey. We eliminated three surveys from the analysis because they were incomplete. The remaining 13 survey respondents could be identified as seven Leadership 2.0 participants, five Leadership 3.0 participants, and one unidentified respondent. The survey employed a 5-point Likert scale (*strongly agree, agree, agree/disagree, disagree, strongly disagree*) where five reflected that participants strongly agreed with the statements in the survey. Descriptive statistics were conducted to analyze the data.

Coach/mentoring session logs. As a pilot program, we asked the coach/ mentors and their principal protégés to keep logs of their interactions beyond the professional learning sessions. The university team, in keeping its commitments to the six principles (knowledge, cognitive demand, context, pacing, feedback, technology) for the program, made no specific demands for meeting any certain number of hours. When asked about expectations for number of contact hours, the university team suggested that perhaps two hours a week could be expected, but made clear that this was flexible. We collected the log data in December of 2012 after a five-month period.

Superintendent visits. To garner feedback about next steps for the coach/mentoring program, we conducted one-on-one interviews with six of the nine superintendents. Due to scheduling conflicts, the other three superintendents were not available. Interviews between members of the university research team and the superintendents occurred during the summer of 2013. Follow-up interviews, or what the research team called four-way meetings, happened during the fall of 2013 and included the district superintendent, the participating principal protégé, the coach-mentor, and a member of the university research team. The research team used a field notes form to capture data from the superintendents about their impressions of Leadership 2.0 and 3.0 and their ideas regarding next steps for the program.

Attendance records. Attendance records at the Leadership 2.0. and 3.0 face-to-face sessions coordinated by the research team provide some insight into the participants' self-reports of commitments and time spent during the first year of the programs. From May 2012 to June 2013, there were 13 sessions held at a satellite campus classroom that was in a location central to all participants in the program. In keeping with the six principles that recognized the busy schedules of practicing school leaders, the university team did not pressure the participants to attend all sessions.

FINDINGS

Through this research, we intended to offer insights into participants' perceptions about the coach/mentoring program, and the relationships between coach/mentor and protégé pairs that fall within Levels 1 and 2 of Guskey's model (2000), our conceptual framework. We present findings from this study below by each research question.

Research Question One: *What are the participants' perceptions as to whether their expectations were met for the Leadership 2.0 and 3.0 programs and the coaching/mentoring process?*

We used results from the online survey to examine participants' perceptions as to whether they perceived the programs as effective and the degree to which their expectations for the coaching/mentoring process were met. In order to gauge participants' perceptions of the effectiveness of Leadership 2.0 and 3.0, we created three survey questions to ask participants whether they perceived the program as effective, whether they felt supported by the program, and whether they grew as a leader. Both coach/mentors and protégés perceived program effectiveness as low, as indicated in Table 14.4.

Table 14.4.   Perceptions of Program Effectiveness

		Please Indicate Your Level of Agreement With the Following Statements:		
Please Indicate the Program to Which You Belong		*Leadership 3.0 is Effective*	*Leadership 3.0 Provides Support for Practicing Administrators*	*The Protégé Grew as a Leader During The Mentoring Process*
Leadership 2.0 (Protégé)	Mean	2.14	1.71	2.00
	N	7	7	7
Leadership 3.0 (Coach/ Mentor)	Mean	2.60	2.20	2.60
	N	5	5	5
Total	Mean	2.37	1.96	2.30
	N	12	12	12

Nevertheless, we found that coach/mentors were more positive about the overall effectiveness of the program than their protégés. Coach/mentors also noted that they supported their protégés to a higher degree than the protégés perceived the coach/mentor support. Table 14.5 shows a further

Table 14.5.   Mentoring Experience and Perceptions of Effectiveness

Have You Officially Mentored Someone Else Before?		Please Indicate Your Level of Agreement With the Following Statements:		
		Leadership 3.0 Is Effective	Leadership 3.0 Provides Support for Practicing Administrators	The Protégé Grew as a Leader During the Mentoring Process
yes	Mean	2.33	1.89	2.22
	N	9	9	9
no	Mean	2.50	2.25	2.50
	N	4	4	4
Total	Mean	2.38	2.00	2.31
	N	13	13	13

exploration of the data by using responses where both groups indicated whether they had served as a mentor previously. The state in which these districts reside intermittently provided support for new principals, and thus, the opportunity for formal mentoring experiences was sporadic. The responses shown in Table 14.5 reflect differences in perceptions of effectiveness based on self-reported prior mentoring experiences. Those with no prior mentoring experiences saw the program as slightly more effective than those with prior experiences. In particular, those with prior experience faulted Leadership 2.0 and 3.0, stating it was not particularly effective for supporting practicing administrators.

Despite participants' low impressions of the effectiveness of the entire program, coach/mentors and protégés agreed that the coach/mentor and protégé component of the pilot programs met their expectations (Leadership 2.0 Mean = 4.01; Leadership 3.0 Mean = 4.18).

Research Question Two: *What are the participant's perceptions about their relationships and matches as coach/mentor and protégé pairs?*

In addition to participants' perceptions about the effectiveness of the programs and the expectations for the coach/mentoring relationship, through the second research question, we investigated their perceptions about their relationships and matches as coach/mentor and protégé pairs. Coach/mentors and protégés indicated on the online survey that they perceived each other's contributions to the relationship differently (see Table 14.6). Both groups were committed to the mentoring relationship, yet protégés indicated that they did not have enough time to devote to the mentoring. Nevertheless, despite time constraints, both coach/mentors and protégé participants indicated that the development of the mentoring relationship was a priority.

Table 14.6. Contrasting Perceptions of the Relationship

		Please Indicate Your Level of Agreement With Each of the Following Statements:		
Please Indicate the Program to Which You Belong		*I Am Committed to Developing an Effective and Productive Mentoring Relationship*	*I Feel That I Do Not Have Enough Time to Devote to The Mentoring Relationship*	*I Made the Development of Our Mentorship Relationship a Priority*
Leadership 2.0 (Protégé)	Mean	4.43	3.57	3.71
	N	7	7	7
Leadership 3.0 (Mentor/ Coach)	Mean	4.80	2.60	4.00
	N	5	5	5
Total	Mean	4.62	3.01	3.86
	N	12	12	12

Furthermore, information provided in the mentoring logs was analyzed to discern participants' commitment to the program. Given the rural settings and large distances between schools, the surprising aspect of these reports is the number of face-to-face sessions that were held between the mentors and protégés. Figure 14.1 shows the aggregated reports of the modalities coach/mentor and protégé pairs used to meet. Over three-fourths of these sessions were face-to-face including the professional learning sessions that the research team scheduled. The participants used e-mail to some degree, but the least utilized mode for coaching/mentoring was the telephone. The frequency of face-to-face meetings, as described in the logs, supported participants' responses to the survey that the mentoring relationship was a priority despite time constraints.

The attendance records also provide evidence of their commitment to developing the mentoring relationship, given that attendance was high at the professional learning sessions. The overall average for attendance was 82%. Leadership 2.0 participants averaged a 92% attendance rate, while the Leadership 3.0 participants averaged 73% attendance.

Research Question Three: *What are the instructional leadership challenges faced by the participants as the program moves into its second year?*

Through the third research question, we investigated the instructional leadership challenges faced by the participants as the programs moved into the second year. These responses also provided some insight into several items that showed differing perceptions about the challenges that practicing principals face. Table 14.7 displays these differences by years of experience.

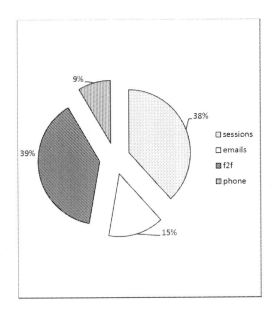

Figure 14.1.   Reported modalities of individual Principal and Coach/Mentor sessions.

Table 14.7 shows that all participants were most challenged by implementing Common Core State Standards. Educators with less than 10 years of experience reported that three of the eight components related to instructional leadership and school improvement efforts were the most challenging. Seasoned educators (30 years or above) expressed more challenges with two items: engaging teachers and other stakeholders in improvement, and the use of technology in instruction. This group also reported that four of the eight components were moderately challenging.

The group that indicated the most challenges was the midcareer group (those with 20–29 years of experience in education). Out of the eight questions within the challenges category, midcareer individuals were moderately to very challenged by six of the components: (a) implementing Common Core State Standards, (b) evaluating teacher effectiveness, (c) maintaining a rigorous learning environment, (d) engaging teachers and other stakeholders in improving educational outcomes, (e) using data, and (f) using technology to improve instruction.

Superintendent Visits

Visits with the superintendents of the Leadership 2.0 and 3.0 participants provided insights into expectations about coach/mentoring across

Table 14.7. Years of Experience and Perceived Challenges

Please Indicate Your Years of Experience in Education		How Challenging Is It For You to Do Each of the Following							
		Implement the Common Core State Standards	Evaluate Teacher Effectiveness	Maintain an Academically Rigorous Learning Environment	Engage Teachers and Other Stakeholders in Improving the Education of Students	Use Data About Student Performance to Improve Instruction	Have Strong Operational Skills, Such as Managing Facilities, Schedules, Budgets, Etc.	Use Technology to Improve Instruction	Ask For Feedback About Your Ability to Implement School Improvement Efforts
Under 10	Mean	4.00	2.50	3.50	3.17	2.83	2.67	2.83	2.50
	N	6	6	6	6	6	6	6	6
20–29	Mean	4.20	3.20	3.60	3.80	3.80	2.80	3.40	2.80
	N	5	5	5	5	5	5	5	5
30–39	Mean	3.00	2.00	3.00	3.50	2.00	2.00	3.50	2.00
	N	2	2	2	2	2	2	2	2
Total	Mean	3.92	2.69	3.46	3.46	3.08	2.62	3.15	2.54
	N	13	13	13	13	13	13	13	13

districts in these two pilot programs. Field notes from the visits indicated that superintendents desired for their participants in both programs to build capacities for instructional leadership throughout the district, rather than solely within their schools. Superintendents also desired for their principals to be more independent and risk-taking in their decision making. A comment from a superintendent captured this sentiment:

> I expect that [the person] in my district will come back and bring more to the district. Some of the principals in my district want everything to be definite and they want to be told what to do…. They should want room to make their own professional judgment and lead…. They need to get beyond the beginning years of just doing what the district office wants, and be confident in thinking about what is good for kids and then make that happen.

Superintendents also indicated that they wanted to do more four-way meetings among the coach/mentor, protégé, research team member, and themselves. Others thought the additional four-way meetings would be beneficial, but in order to increase capacity, protégés should start including teachers and other administrators in the meetings. For example, a superintendent mentioned including the curriculum coordinator for the district in the four-way meeting to harness information about effective data use practices. Other superintendents communicated this sentiment as well, stating that they continued to believe the purposes of both programs was for building capacity among school and district leaders. They also indicated that the capacity building program was designed intentionally to help all the districts, not merely the schools. To that end, a superintendent made the following comment:

> And this district needs different perspectives than the ones that are already here. With the turnover, the schools have pretty much looked inward, and with the scarcer resources, then the teachers have not had opportunities to look for other ideas. Now we need that additional help from outside.

Another superintendent expressed different reasons for wanting to focus on building capacity. His reasons surfaced issues of sustainability due to frequent superintendent turnover in some participating districts. The following quote captures the superintendents' remarks:

> I also think [the university research team] needs to think about sustainability as superintendents change. We need to keep the opportunity for people who have a different perspective than the one inside the district to help us think differently and solve problems better. I want to surround myself with people who don't know my patterns, who are different and think different[ly]. Within

a district, we can get too accustomed to our own patterns and we really cannot think differently. That's why the cross-district part is critical.

Information from the superintendents was critical to understanding lessons about the coach/mentoring components of Leadership 3.0. The superintendents lead rural districts, and their concerns are consistent with those that have been well-documented in literature about rural districts, in general (Clayton et al., 2013; Duncan & Stock, 2010; Martin, 2013; Preston et al., 2013; Ringler et al., 2013; Starr & White, 2008). Moreover, the superintendents of these rural districts voiced their expectation that synergy would be developed among the participating districts, and that they would tap into cross-district expertise. This was seen as necessary due to the reality that rural districts have limited central office personnel and those individuals play multiple roles, a fact that is supported by literature on rural schools (Duncan & Stock, 2010; Preston et al., 2013). The super-intendents' insights validated the purpose of the two pilot programs, which was to address rural, midcareer principals' need for professional develop-ment to enhance their instructional leadership.

DISCUSSION

We gleaned several lessons about the program design and implementation of Leadership 2.0 and 3.0 after collecting the feedback throughout the year. The lessons learned center around the following themes: (a) man-aging expectations about the coach's and protégé's roles, (b) addressing time and commitment constraints, (c) delving into reactive and reflective practices, and (d) understanding the challenges of midcareer principals. Examining these themes led us to making recommendations for others who may be considering implementing mentoring programs for midcareer principals. We now explore these issues and recommendations.

Managing Relationship Expectations

The results of this study revealed that the coach/mentors expressed more satisfaction about their ability to provide support and advocacy than the principal protégés perceived such help. This difference in percep-tions suggests an imbalance in the coach-protégé relationships. Literature on mentoring stresses the importance of ensuring a mutually enhancing relationship for both parties (Daresh, 2004; Mertz, 2004). Protégéship, as it is labeled in the literature, focuses on the responsibility of the protégé in the dyad, and supports the idea of protégé as equal partner (Tripses & Searby, 2008). However, protégés often need training on how to be effective mentees in order to enhance mutual satisfaction (Searby, 2008; Tripses & Searby, 2008). Our pilot programs divided the mentors and protégés on occasions to place the mentors in learning sessions about their roles in the relationship, but concurrently, the principals' sessions focused on instructional leadership issues, not their contribution or responsibilities in the coaching/mentoring relationship. Thus, the first lesson learned after the initial year of this project is that the coordinators of a leadership mentoring program should intentionally lead participants in a discussion of roles and expectations for both mentors and protégés. Then, mentors and protégés need to have what Zachary (2012) calls the "assumption hunt"—a conversation in which each party states what is assumed in the relationship. This activity serves to prevent misunderstandings and allows each party to voice expectations and concerns about what this mentoring relationship will entail.

Another aspect of this lesson learned is that time needs to be spent in additional trust-building activities between the coach/mentors and the midcareer principal protégés. Anecdotal comments from the mentor/coaches and the midcareer principal protégés led us to speculate that the protégés may have been somewhat confused about why they were selected to be mentored. Their superintendents had chosen the midcareer principals, and had framed the invitation to participate as an honor, but some seemed be unclear about the real reason they were identified for mentoring. From the university standpoint, the purpose of the mentoring program was made explicit in each of the eleven joint training sessions, as we always posted and addressed two essential questions: (1) What are the models for data-informed decision making that the state's schools use to improve? and (2) What data about you and your skill sets are available for helping achieve the steps necessary for school improvement?

Based on our gathered data and anecdotal feedback from participants, we offer the following recommendations to others who may be planning a similar mentoring program: (a) Follow our pattern of being repeatedly explicit about the purpose of the mentoring program for the midcareer principals; (b) insure that the midcareer principals perceive the mentoring as a form of professional development support for enhancing instructional leadership behaviors that are the expected norms of all current principals, not a punitive action; (c) commit time on the front end of the program for joint mentor/protégé trust building and assumption hunting activities, and if possible, include them in the structured participant meetings throughout the year. Implementing these recommendations should assist in enhancing the mentor/protégé relationships.

Addressing Time and Commitment

Both coach/mentors and protégés indicated their commitment to the mentoring relationship by taking time to meet individually, but we found from the data that the principal protégés felt that the time constraints of their busy administrative lives took precedence in the moments of choosing whether to leave their buildings to attend the three-hour sessions. Scholars have long documented the strains on principals' time (Camburn et al., 2010; Horng, Klasik, & Loeb, 2010; Wolcott, 1973), reporting a host of school improvement initiatives and accountability structures that consume their work life (Camburn et al., 2010; von Frank, 2012; Wright, 2009). The primary issue of time in this study was tied to Principle #3 from the literature on adult learning and development underlying the program design about pacing learning around busy practicing professionals' work (Brookfield, 1991; Darling-Hammond et al., 2009; Knowles, 1973; Kochan et al., 2002). For these pilot programs, participants determined the pacing, and session attendance only averaged 82%. This less-than-exemplary attendance rate may have made it harder to recover learning between sessions, provided insufficient time for reflection, or given fewer opportunities to build important trusting relationships across district lines (Bloom et al., 2003; Dimmock, 2012, Myran et al., 2011). These results reveal steep challenges in supporting midcareer individuals since finding time for the reflection that is necessary to build capacity remains an obstacle (Thompson, Brown, Henry, & Fortner, 2011). Yet, these principals and their coach/mentors perceived that opportunity as important. We felt that the participants gave us a mixed message with this data, causing us to pose the question: If the participants perceived the mentoring relationship and activities as important, why was the attendance at the structured meetings not better? We concluded that a different and deeper investigation is necessary into the time and commitment conundrum. So for this issue that emerged from our study, we do not have a recommendation for best practice, but rather a recommendation for continuing to explore ways to leverage job-embedded time for professional development for principals.

Delving Into Reactive and Reflective Practices

Another issue that we discovered, likely connected to the time constraints issue, is that the midcareer principals in our study showed a preference for reacting to problems rather than being proactive or reflective. That is, rather than engaging in an approach that made use of reflection, risk-taking, and skill acquisition for sustained change and improved schooling outcomes, these principals were driven to handle problems in the moment.

Their mentors and superintendents noted that these reflexive, rather than reflective practices hindered the principals' instructional leadership behaviors. Researchers have consistently reported that leaders in many contexts prefer a crisis-command approach over deliberative problem solving (Grint, 2010; Nguyen, Scribner, & Crow, 2012; Spillane et al., 2009), and that engaging in systematic reflection and risk-taking is challenging for many principals (Peck & Reitzug, 2012; Starr, 2012). Furthermore, such challenges often require leaders to deal with emotions, their own as well as their staff's (Leithwood & Beatty, 2008; Lindle, 2004). A principal coach/mentor needs to understand how to coach school leaders through the dynamics of school improvement efforts, acknowledging that emotions will come into play. Unfortunately, attention to the emotional aspects of school leadership is underrepresented in educational leadership literature due to its perceived lack of value (Bridges, 2012; Day, 2000; Leithwood & Beatty, 2008).

Leadership 3.0 provided practicing principals an ongoing opportunity to reflect on their practices as an alternative to resorting to reactive approaches that they might be tempted to use in their school environments. This was accomplished through an examination of case studies of the leadership practices of principals of turnaround schools in our state when we met monthly as a whole group. The coach/mentors were then expected to help the midcareer principals apply those effective leadership behaviors in their own schools. This is where the coach/mentors noted that their roles were difficult, as in the first year at least, the majority of midcareer principals did not seem to be able to make the needed changes like those that were modeled in the case studies. The coach/mentors noted that their protégés persisted in reacting to the immediate concerns rather than reflecting on ways to become better instructional leaders.

Our recommendations to those who are considering a mentoring program for midcareer principals in regards to the issue of protégés' reactive versus reflective leadership behaviors are twofold. First, we refer back to our earlier recommendation about making sure that clear expectations are explicitly shared at the beginning of the mentoring program. We took great care to outline clearly the objective that the midcareer principals were going to study best practices of turnaround principals and effective instructional leaders in order to learn how to emulate their behaviors in their own schools. We recommend this intentional and continual emphasis on the objectives as a best practice for any mentoring program. Second, we recommend that all participants understand that this program is about change, and change starts with reflection but takes time. To support the change efforts with research literature, we provided our participants with eleven recently published books on leading school improvement, and the participants chose three for book studies over the course of the first year.

As we reflected on our role as coordinators of this program, we concluded that these were best practices that strengthened the Leadership 2.0/3.0 support for midcareer principals.

Understanding the Challenges Facing Midcareer Principals

The last lesson from this multimethod look at the two pilot programs involves our need to understand the challenges of increasing midcareer principals' instructional leadership capacity. As with many principals nationwide, the principals in this study felt the intense pressures of implementing Common Core Standards. Their learning at midcareer needs to be ongoing as some of the instructional initiatives found in Common Core Standards have been created recently. In this group of principals, a few had very little classroom experience, and some had not been in the classroom for years since attaining principal positions. This reality was what caused the rural superintendents to approach us, as university partners, about helping the midcareer principals retool their skills of instructional leadership. The superintendents recognized that the midcareer principals could not encourage teachers to innovate without their own knowledge of the required innovations (Halverson et al., 2007; Mulford & Silins, 2003).

In leadership literature, we receive confirmation that the experiences of midcareer principals are different than the start-up experiences of a novice's first few years (Duncan, 2013; Louis et al., 2010; Martin, 2013; Notman, 2012; Parylo, Zapeda, & Bengston, 2013). Thus, the mentoring needs of midcareer principals are different than those of new principals. We still firmly believe that coaching/mentoring programs are an important support mechanism for midcareer principals who are faced with demands for innovative teaching and sustained improvements in student outcomes. However, the goal of the coaching/mentoring for principals in midcareer is about retooling leadership skills to bring more focus to instructional issues. As one superintendent stated, "Our veteran principals are all good people, and are really good managers and administrators, but they don't know what the "next steps" are to becoming instructional leaders."

It was very revealing to us to see that the midcareer principals (with 20–29 years of experience) admitted to struggling with six of the eight challenges that contemporary principals face. Even though the midcareer principals acknowledged their challenges, our coach/mentors found this group of principals to be somewhat confused about their superintendents' recommendation that they receive mentoring for instructional leadership, when they had been recognized as successful principals over the years. Thus, for this final issue of understanding the challenges of midcareer principals, we make the following recommendation: Do not expect behavioral change to happen quickly or comprehensively. We still hold to the tenet that there should be stated expectations and outcomes for a midcareer principal mentoring program that align with the research-based criteria for instructional leadership. However, we should take into consideration that change cannot be forced, and that intrinsic motivation has to exist for an individual to make a change. We recommend that mentors acknowledge our evaluation framework Principle #2: School leaders are mature learners whose ability to take abstract knowledge and apply it concretely varies individually (Darling-Hammond et al., 2009; Leithwood & Steinbach, 1995; Marzano, 2007; Spillane, White, & Stephan, 2009). Thus, each midcareer principal will have his/her own capacity for change. Some will grasp the new concepts immediately and intentionally work on changing multiple behaviors simultaneously. Others may only have the capacity to work on one small behavioral change. Some will not be motivated to make any changes. As coordinators of this midcareer principal mentoring program, we need to go forth into the second year of the program with these realizations in mind.

CONCLUSION

While coach/mentors and their practicing principal protégés expressed ongoing commitment to their experiences in the two pilot programs, they also shared challenges that caused us to learn lessons about the difficulty of helping midcareer principals retool their behaviors for instructional leadership. The lessons from these pilot programs serve as reminders of the time it takes to create relationships, and to make the cognitive shifts that are a critical part of the change process for adult learners, but especially for midcareer principals. We acknowledge a need to explicitly address the tensions among the time demands of school leadership roles, emotions associated with pressures and school problems, and midcareer principals' needs for changing their professional practices to align with current instructional leadership expectations. Perhaps, given the issues that rural schools face, sustained development of midcareer principals may be the most important step in ensuring capacity for innovative teaching and ongoing improvement in student achievement.

Appendix A
Year 1 Session Topics for Leadership 2.0 and Leadership 3.0

Year 1 Session #	Leadership 2.0	Leadership 3.0
	Commencing Event	
1	Principals as Learners Commitments to the 6 Learning Principles	District-level Coaches as Learners and Cross-District Commitments to the 6 Learning Principles
	What do successful SC principals do to improve and sustain high quality teaching and learning?	
2	What are the models that SC schools use to improve? What models could they use?	
3	• What data and planning strategies are available to improve schools? • What did the books you chose to read suggest about ideas for school improvement? • What data about you and your skill sets are available for helping make the steps necessary for school improvement?	
4	What does PADEPP [Note1] tell us about school leader knowledge and skills to help you take the steps necessary for school improvement?	
5	• How can you use video data to enhance your skills in taking the next steps for school improvement? • In which university degree programs might you participate to take those next steps for school improvement?	
6	Goal: Leaders in high data-use schools have clear purposes for analyzing data. They engage their staff collectively in data analysis, build internal capacity for this work, and use data to solve problems, not simply to identify them (Louis, Leithwood, Wahlstrom & Anderson, 2010, p. 179). • What are the data tools available for schools? (Halverson, 2010; Marsh, McCombs & Martorell, 2010) • What are the commitment conflicts that might hinder analysis, reflection and problem solving in schools? (Kegan & Lahey, 2001)	
7	Study Groups' discussions and planning • Learning Targets • Lexile & Quartiles • Databases	Coaching experienced leaders • Cognitive Coaching • Emotional Aspects of Policy • Asking Socratic Questions
	Video Analysis of Instruction - 5D (Fink, 2011)	
8	What did I see and how would I advise teacher of next instructional steps?	• How would I coach a principal in addressing teacher strengths and improvement? • How can I frame my coaching in Socratic questions?

(Appendix continues on next page)

Appendix A (continued)
Year 1 Session Topics for Leadership 2.0 and Leadership 3.0

Year 1 Session#	*Leadership 2.0*	*Leadership 3.0*
9	**The Next Level** • What do you see as the next level for your school? • What would you like to use Leadership 2.0/3.0 to help you accomplish by May 2014? **Reaching the Next Level** • What will it take for your school to reach the next level? • Who and what do you need to get to that level? • How can your work in your study group help you reach this level? **The Next Steps** • What, specifically, do you want to accomplish by the end of the program? • What specific steps will the mentee take to accomplish this? • What specific steps will the mentor/coach take to accomplish this? • What assistance is needed from others?	Discuss the activities we have completed so far. • What was the main "take away" for you? • How can you coach the take-aways for your protégé principal and his/her school?

10	• What aspects of your professional expertise for instructional leadership can be enhanced in the next 12 months?	
	• What focus (limited to one or two outcomes) for school improvement can you lead over the next 12 months?	
	• What are the models for data-informed decision making that SC schools use to improve? What models could they use? • What data about you and your skill sets are available for helping achieve the steps necessary for school improvement? • How can you use video data to enhance your skills in taking the next steps for school improvement?	• What are the models for coaching data-informed decision making to lead schools improvement? • What data about you and your skill sets are available for helping achieve the steps necessary for coaching leadership of school improvement? • How can you use video data to enhance your skills in taking the next steps for coaching leaders of school improvement?

Individual Reflection Time & Protégé/Mentor Discussion
How might 5D be used to inform ways in which Leadership 2.0 professional expertise is enhanced?

11	Allocating Resources for Academic Improvement from CALL (Kelley & Halverson, 2012)	

Note 1: PADEPP is the South Carolina Program for Assessing, Developing, and Evaluating Principal Performance.

REFERENCES

Auster, E. R. (2001). Professional women's midcareer satisfaction: Toward an explanatory framework. *Sex Roles, 44*(11/12), 719–750.

Barnett, B. G., Copland, M. A., & Shoho, A. R. (2009). The use of internships in preparing school leaders. In M. D. Young, G. M. Crow, J. Murphy, & R. T. Ogawa (Eds.), *Handbook of research on the education of school leaders* (pp. 371–394). New York, NY: Routledge Taylor & Francis.

Bloom, G., Castagna, C., & Warren, B. (2003). More than mentors: Principal coaching. *Leadership,* (May/June), 20–23.

Bredeson, P. V. (2005). Building capacity in schools: Some ethical considerations for authentic leadership and learning. *Values and Ethics in Educational Administration, 4*(1), 1–8.

Bridges, E. (2012). Administrator preparation: Looking backwards and forwards. *Journal of Educational Administration, 50*(4), 402–419.

Brookfield, S. D. (1991). *The skillful teacher.* San Francisco, CA: Jossey-Bass.

Browne-Ferrigno, T., & Allen, L. W. (2006, February 10). Preparing principal for high-need rural schools: A central office perspective about collaborative efforts to transform school leadership. *Journal of Research in Rural Education, 21*(1), 1–16. Retrieved from http://jrre.psu.edu/articles/21-1.pdf

Browne-Ferrigno, T., & Knoeppel, R. (2005). Training principals to ensure access to equitable learning opportunities in a high-need rural school district. *Educational Considerations, 33*(1), 8–14.

Camburn, E. M., Spillane, J. P., & Sebastian, J. (2010). Assessing the utility of a daily log for measuring principal leadership practice. *Educational Administration Quarterly, 46*(5), 707–737.

Carpenter, B. W., & Brewer, C. (2012). The implicated advocate: The discursive construction of the democratic practices of school principals in the USA. *Discourse: Studies in the Cultural Politics of Education.*

Clayton, J. K., Sanzo, K. L., & Myran, S. (2013). Understanding mentoring in leadership development: Perspectives of district administrators and aspiring leaders. *Journal of Research in Leadership Education, 8*(1), 77–96. doi:10.1177/1942775112464959

Coldwell, M., & Simkins, T. (2011). Level models of continuing professional development evaluation: A grounded review and critique. *Professional Development in Education, 37*(1), 143–157.

Crow, G. M. (2012). A critical-constructivist perspective on mentoring and coaching for leadership. *Sage handbook of mentoring and coaching in education.* Los Angeles, CA: Sage.

Daresh, J. (2004). Mentoring school leaders: Professional promise or predictable problems? *Educational Administration Quarterly, 40*(4), 495–517.

Darling-Hammond, L., Wei, R. C., Andree, A. Richardson, N., & Orphanos, S. (2009). *Learning in the learning profession: A status report on teacher development in the United States and abroad.* Dallas, TX: National Staff Development Council. Retrieved from https://www.nsdc.org/news/nsdcstudy2009.pdf

Day, C. (2000). Effective leadership and reflective practice. *Reflective Practice, 1*(1), 113–127.

Dimmock, C. (2012). *Leadership, capacity building and school improvement: Concepts, themes and impact.* New York, NY: Routledge.

Duncan, H. E. (2013). Exploring gender differences in US school principals' professional development needs at different career stages. *Professional Development in Education, 39*(3), 293–311. doi:10.1080/19415257.2012.722561

Duncan, H. E., & Stock, M. E. (2010). Mentoring and coaching rural school leaders: What do they need? *Mentoring & Tutoring: Partnership in Learning, 18*(3), 293–311.

Duncan-Howell, J. (2010). Teachers making connections: Online communities as a source of professional learning. *British Journal of Educational Technology, 41*(2).

Feiman-Nemser, S. (2001). From preparation to practice: Designing a continuum to strengthen and sustain teaching. *Teachers College Record, 103*(6), 1013–1055.

Fink, S. (2011). *School and district leaders as instructional experts: what we are learning* [online]. Seattle, WA: University of Washington. Retrieved May 19, 2015, from http://depts.washington.edu/uwcel/e_newsletter/2011.06.news/levels_of_expertise_article_4.12.11.pdf

Fink, S., & Markholt, A. (2011). *Leading for instructional improvement: How successful leaders develop teaching and learning expertise.* San Francisco, CA: Jossey-Bass.

Fletcher, S., & Mullen, C. A. (Eds.). (2012). *Sage handbook of mentoring and coaching in education.* Los Angeles, CA: Sage.

Grint, K. (2010). The cuckoo clock syndrome: Addicted to command, allergic to leadership. *European Management Journal, 28*, 306–313. doi:10.1016/j.emj.2010.05.002

Grissom, J. A., & Harrington, J. R. (2010). Investing in administrator efficacy: An examination of professional development as a tool for enhancing principal effectiveness. *American Journal of Education, 116*(4), 583–612. doi:10.1086/653631

Grogan, M., & Crow, G. M. (Eds.). (2004). Mentoring in the context of educational leadership preparation and development—Old wine in new bottles? [Special issue]. *Educational Administration Quarterly, 40*(4). doi:10.1177/0013161x04267107

Gross, S. J. (2009). Establishing meaningful leadership mentoring in school settings: Transcending simplistic rhetoric, self-congratulation, and claims of panacea. In M. D. Young, G. M. Crow, J. Murphy, & R. T. Ogawa (Eds.). *Handbook of research on the education of school leaders* (pp. 515–534). New York, NY: Routledge Taylor & Francis.

Gurr, D., & Drysdale, L. (2007). Models of successful principal leadership: Victorian case studies. In C. Day & K. Leithwood (Eds.), *Successful principal leadership in times of change* (pp. 39–58). Dordrecht, The Netherlands: Springer.

Guskey, T. R. (2000). *Evaluating professional development.* Thousand Oaks, CA: Corwin.

Guskey, T. R. (2003). What makes professional development effective? *Phi Delta Kappan, 84*(10), 748–750.

Guskey, T. R., & Yoon, K.S. (2009). What works in professional development? *Phi Delta Kappan, 90*(7), 495–500.

Hall, P. (2008). Building bridges: Strengthening the principal induction process through intentional mentoring. *Phi Delta Kappan, 89*(6), 449–452.

Halverson, R., Grigg, J., Prichett, R., & Thomas, C. (2007). The new instructional leadership: Creating data-driven instructional systems in schools. *Journal of*

Hansford, B. C., & Ehrich, L. C. (2006). The principalship: How significant is mentoring? *Journal of Educational Administration, 44*(1), 36–52.

Hargreaves, A. (1998). The emotional politics of teaching and teacher development: With implications for educational leadership. *International Journal of Leadership in Education: Theory and Practice, 1*(4), 315–336.

Harris, A. (2003). Introduction. In A. Harris et al. (Eds.), *Effective leadership for school improvement* (pp. 1-6). London, England: RoutledgeFalmer.

Harris, S., Ballenger, J., & Leonard, J. (2004). Aspiring principal perceptions: Are mentor principals modeling standards-based leadership? *Mentoring & Tutoring: Partnership in Learning, 12*(2), 155–172.

Horng, E. L., Klasik, D., & Loeb, S. (2010). Principal's time use and school effectiveness. *American Journal of Education, 116*(4), 491–523.

Kegan, R., & Lahey, L. L. (2001). *How the way we talk can change the way we work: Seven languages for transformation.* San Francisco, CA: Jossey-Bass/Wiley.

Kelly, C., & Halverson, R. (2012). The comprehensive assessment of leadership for learning: A next generation formative evaluation and feedback system. *Journal of Applied Research on Children: Informing Policy for Children at Risk, 3*(2), Article #4. Retrieved November 4, 2015, from http://digitalcommons.library. tmc.edu/childrenatrisk/vol3/iss2/4

King, M. B., & Bouchard, K. (2011). The capacity to build organizational capacity in schools. *Journal of Educational Administration, 6*(49), 653–669.

Knowles, M. (1973). *The adult learner: A neglected species.* Houston, TX: Gulf. Retrieved from ERIC database (ED084368): http://files.eric.ed.gov/fulltext/ ED084368.pdf

Kochan, F. K., Bredeson, P., & Riehl, C. (2002). Rethinking the professional development of school leaders. *Yearbook of the National Society for the Study of Education, 101*(1), 289–306. doi: 10.1111/j.1744-7984.2002.tb00013.x

Leithwood, K., & Beatty, B. (2008). *Leading with teacher emotions in mind.* Thousand Oaks, CA: Corwin Press.

Leithwood, K., Louis, K., Anderson, S., & Wahlstrom, K. (2004). *How leadership influences student learning.* New York, NY: Wallace Foundation.

Leithwood, K., & Steinbach, R. (1995). *Expert problem solving: Evidence from school and district leaders.* Albany, NY: State University of New York Press.

Lindle, J. C. (2004). Trauma and stress in the principal's office: Systematic inquiry as coping. *Journal of School Leadership, 14*(4), 378–410.

Lindle, J. C., Reese, K. L., Della Sala, M. R., Klar, H. W., & Knoeppel, R. C. (2013, April). *Building capacity for coaching leaders in practice: Addressing an impoverished knowledge base.* A paper presented at the annual meeting of the American Educational Research Association (AERA), San Francisco, CA.

Louis, K. S., Leithwood, K., Wahlstrom, K. L., & Anderson, S. E. (2010). *Learning from leadership: Investigating the links to improved student learning.* Center for Applied Research and Educational Improvement, University of Minnesota. Retrieved from: http://www.wallacefoundation.org/knowledgecenter/ school-leadership/key-research/Pages/Investigating-the-Links-to-Improved-Student-Learning.aspx

Martin, K. (2013). Principal concerns in Wisconsin: Focus on future Leaders for rural schools. Data Brief. Seattle, WA: Center on Reinventing Public Education. Retrieved from ERIC database (ED541602): http://files.eric.ed.gov/fulltext/ED541602.pdf

Marsh, J., McCombs, J. S., & Martorell, F. (2010). How instructional coaches support data- driven decision-making. *Educational Policy*, *24*(6), 872–907.

Myran, S., Sanzo, K. L., & Clayton, J. (2011). Tracing the development of a rural university-district partnership: Encouraging district voice and challenging assumptions leadership. *Journal of School Leadership*, *21*(5), 684–703.

Marzano, R. J. (2007). *The art and science of teaching: A comprehensive framework for effective instruction*. Alexandria, VA: Association for Supervision and Curriculum Development (ASCD).

Mertz, N. (2004). What's a mentor, anyway? *Educational Administration Quarterly*, *40*(4), 541–560.

Mulford, B., & Silins, H. (2003). Leadership for organisational learning and improved student outcomes—What do we know? *Cambridge Journal of Education*, *33*(2), 175–195.

Newmann, F., King, M. B., & Youngs, P. (2000). Professional development that addresses school capacity: Lessons from urban elementary schools. *American Journal of Education*, *4*(108), 259–299.

Notman, R. (2012). Intrapersonal factors in New Zealand school leadership success. *International Journal of Educational Management*, *26*(5), 470–479. doi:10.1108/09513541211240264

Nguyen, T. S. T., Scribner, S. M. P., & Crow, G. M. (2012). Tangled narratives and wicked problems: A complex case of positioning and politics in a diverse school community. *Journal of Cases in Educational Leadership*, *15*(4), 49–64.

O'Day, J., Goertz, M. E., & Floden, R. E. (1995). *Building capacity for educational reform*. CPRE Policy Briefs. Retrieved from http://www.ed.gov/pubs/CPRE/rb18/rb18b.html

Parylo, O., Zepeda, S. J., & Bengston, E. (2012). The different faces of principal mentorship. *International Journal of Mentoring and Coaching in Education*, *1*(2), 120–135.

Peck, C., & Reitzug, U. C. (2012). How existing business management concepts become school leadership fashions. *Educational Administration Quarterly*, *48*(2), 347–381. doi:10.1177/001316X11432924

Preston, J. P., Jakubiec, B. E., & Kooymans, R. (2013). Common challenges faced by rural principals: A review of the literature. *Rural Educator*, *35*(1), 1–12

Psencik, K. (2011). *The coach's craft: Powerful practices to support school leaders*. Oxford, OH: Learning Forward.

Ringler, M. C., O'Neal, D., Rawls, J., & Cumiskey, S. (2013). The role of school leaders in teacher leadership development. *Rural Educator*, *35*(1), 34–43.

Schrum, L., Galizio, L. M., & Ledesma, P. (2011). Educational leadership and technology integration: an investigation into preparation, experiences, and roles. *Journal of School Leadership*, *21*(2), 241–261.

Searby, L. (2008). A mentoring mindset: Preparing future principals to be effective protégés (NCPEA Connexions module #16930). Retrieved from http://cnx.org/contents/f7121a27-b9ca-4dec-8c27-8c3b3521f411@2

Searby, L. J. (2010). Preparing future principals: Facilitating the development of a mentoring mindset through graduate coursework. *Mentoring & Tutoring: Partnership in Learning, 18*(1), 5–22. doi:10.1080/13611260903448292

Schneer, J. A., & Reitman, F. (1995). The impact of gender as managerial careers unfold. *Journal of Vocational Behavior, 47*, 290–315.

Smith, B. (2000). Quantity matters: Annual instructional time in an urban school system. *Educational Administration Quarterly, 36*(5), 652–682.

Spillane, J. P., Camburn, E. M., & Stitziel Pareja, A. (2007). Taking a distributed perspective to the school principal's workday. *Leadership and Policy in Schools, 6*(1), 103–125.

Spillane, J. P., Halverson, R., & Diamond, J. B. (2001). Investigating school leadership practice: A distributed perspective. *Educational Researcher, 30*(3), 23–29.

Spillane, J. P., White, K. W., & Stephan, J. L. (2009). School principal expertise: Putting expert-aspiring principal differences in problem solving processes to the test. *Leadership and Policy in Schools, 8*(2), 128–151.

Starr, K. (2012). Problematizing "risk" and the principalship: The risky business of managing risk in schools. *Educational Management Administration & Leadership, 40*(4), 464–479. doi:10.1177/1741143212348221

Starr, K., & White, S. (2008). The small rural school principalship: Key challenges and cross-school responses. *Journal of Research in Rural Education, 23* (5), 1–12.

Stoll, L., & Bolam, R. (2005). Developing leadership for learning communities. In M. Coles & G. Southworth (Eds.), *Developing leadership: Creating the schools of tomorrow*. Maidenhead, England: Open University Press.

Stoll, L., Bolam, R., & Collarbone, P. (2002). Leading change: Building capacity for learning. In K. Leithwood, & P. Hallinger (Eds.), *Second international handbook of educational leadership and administration* (pp. 41–73). Dordrecht, The Netherlands: Kluwer Academic.

Thompson, C. L., Brown, K. M., Henry, G. T., & Fortner, C. K. (2011). *Turning around North Carolina's lowest achieving schools (2006–2010)*. (No. 1). Chapel Hill, North Carolina: Consortium for Educational Research and Evaluation–North Carolina. Retrieved from http://publicpolicy.unc.edu/research/TurnaroundSchoolReport_Dec5_Final.pdf

Tripses, J. S., & Searby, L. (2008). Developing a case for intentional protégé preparation in educational leadership programs. *Educational Leadership Review, 9*(2), 175–184.

Turnbull, B. J., Riley, D. L., & MacFarlane, J. L. (2013). *Cultivating talent through a principal pipeline* (Vol. 2). New York, NY: Wallace foundation. Retrieved from: http://www.wallacefoundation.org/knowledge-center/school-leadership/principal-training/Documents/Building-a-Stronger-Principalship-Vol-2-Cultivating-Talent-in-a-Principal-Pipeline.pdf

von Frank, V. (2012, Summer). Move beyond management: Coaching for school leaders translates into student improvement. *The Learning Principal, 7*(4), 1, 4–5.

Wallin, D. (2008). A comparative analysis of the educational priorities and capacity of rural school districts. *Educational Management Administration & Leadership, 36*(4), 566–587.

Wasonga, T. A., & Murphy, J. F. (2006). Learning from tacit knowledge: The impact of the internship. *International Journal of Educational Management, 20*(2), 153–163. doi:10.1108/09513540610646136

Wolcott, H. (1973). *The man in the principal's office.* New York, NY: Holt, Rinehart & Winston.

Wright, L. L. (2009). Leadership in the swamp: Seeking the potentiality of school improvement through principal reflection. *Reflective Practice, 10*(2), 259–272. doi:10.1080/14623940902786388

Zachary, L. (2012). *The mentor's guide* (2nd ed.). San Francisco:, CA Jossey-Bass.

Zepeda, S. J., Bengston, E., & Parylo, O. (2012). Examining the planning and management of principal succession. *Journal of Educational Administration, 50*(2), 136–158. doi: 10.1108/0957823121121051

CHAPTER 15

A SUMMARY OF BEST PRACTICES IN MENTORING FOR TEACHER AND LEADER DEVELOPMENT

Linda J. Searby and Susan K. Brondyk

The intent of the authors of this book was to compile a collection of recent research that would illustrate best practices in mentoring in P–12 settings that are contributing to the growth and learning of new teachers and principals. The chapters chosen for this book illustrate best practices in mentoring that meet one or more of the criteria we set forth in Chapter One, in which we stated that in order for a mentoring practice to be considered a *best* practice, it would have to:

- be effective
- be empirically proven
- achieve the stated purpose

We also noted that the practice should be rooted in recognized theory, and that the research conducted and reported in the chapters should be methodologically sound. The majority of the studies reported in this book

Best Practices in Mentoring for Teacher and Leader Development, pp. 313–324
Copyright © 2016 by Information Age Publishing
All rights of reproduction in any form reserved.

analyzed formal mentoring programs for teachers or principals that were unique in some way. From our review of them, it became apparent that there were some foundational tenets of mentoring being described that, indeed, met our criteria for best practices. There were also some new emerging trends that posed interesting possibilities for mentoring practice. The landscape of mentoring in schools is changing, and mentoring program directors are adapting their approaches to meet the needs of educators in various contexts, as well as to address constraints and barriers associated with traditional mentoring models. However, in the midst of the changes, the essential foundational tenets of mentoring relationships and programs are being preserved and should be noted. What follows is a summary of both the enduring constructs of mentoring demonstrated by the research studies in these chapters, which we deem as best practices, as well as the emerging trends in P–12 mentoring.

MENTORING IS STILL ABOUT DIALOGUE (AND NOW NEW TOOLS ARE AVAILABLE)

Discussions are a natural component of mentoring, as mentors and mentees regularly engage in both formal and informal conversations in the course of their work together. Many of the authors in this book (i.e., Cheng, Hanuscin and Volkman; Magee and Slater) supported the notion that talk promotes learning in mentees, while others provided protocols for discussions (i.e., Martin and Searby). Kralovec and Lunsford described a new teacher mentoring program in which mentors and mentees took several different self-understanding inventories, which were used as a basis for discussions when getting to know each other in the initial stages of mentoring.

Hebert and Wilkins suggested using the iterative process of inquiry as a model to promote learning. Fundamental to this process was the presence of a culture of openness, where teachers shared their practice with others in the school. Together, mentoring pairs "defined a key question, developed and acted on a plan to address that question, and collected evidence along the way to inform the question. The outcome was typically a new question, and the cycle continued" (Hebert & Wilkins). Nunez et al. described a paradigm shift in which the mentoring pair actually built knowledge through their dialogue as they "connected and exchanged beliefs, opinions, and experiences from a bidirectional process that sought to instill in the novice teacher reflective practices that were both critical and purposeful." Key to this relationship was the assumption that mentor and mentee are full and equal participants, unlike the traditional expert/novice approach that is so common in mentoring. Using a more discussion-based approach allowed the novice to contribute to the conversation, rather than all of the ideas coming only from the mentor. This not only improved the mentee's teaching, but also contributed to the formation of the mentee's professional identity.

Dialogue is at the heart of mentoring. The more mentoring partners are able to access and use new and helpful tools for having productive mentoring conversations, the greater the likelihood that mutual learning between mentors and mentees will occur.

MENTORING IN P–12 IS STILL FOCUSED ON IMPROVING TEACHING & LEADERSHIP, (AND NOW STUDENT ACHIEVEMENT IS THE PRIMARY DESIRED OUTCOME)

The goal of every mentoring program is to enhance the personal and professional development of the participants. For new teachers, support is needed for entering a new profession where the roles and responsibilities for the neophytes are the same as for the veterans with years of experience. Mentoring is needed for new teachers so they can improve their teaching . For new principals, mentoring is needed for socialization into a career, with global responsibilities and demands that call for leadership that goes from theory to practice. The authors of the chapters in this book affirm the fact that these traditional purposes of mentoring in P–12 are still viable in the 21st century. However, in this age of standards and accountability, there has been a shift from inputs to outcomes: mentoring must now result in teachers and leaders who know how to get results in student achievement.

Improved teaching. The authors of at least three chapters in this book discussed the benefits of mentoring for both the mentor and mentee. Not only did the beginning teachers' practices improve, but authors described mentors who improved their own teaching as a result of their conversations with mentees (i.e., Doone et al., Bozack, Daresh). One mentor described her experience this way:

> The decision to expose my shortfalls to both my mentee and eventually the university faculty proved, much to my surprise, to be beneficial. As a result, I have dramatically improved my ability to reflect on my teaching and best practices, help other mentees, and better bridge the theory to practice gap. I am able to critically review and constantly revamp my teaching, and teach mentees how to continually improve their own practice. I feel vibrant and passionate as a teacher, not ready to burn out despite all the demands placed on today's teachers, because I am still growing, due to my role as a mentor. (Doone et al., this volume)

Bozack also described mentors who found that "participation in the program helped them be more purposeful decision makers with a greater understanding of how those decisions impact students," which coincided with the program's mission to "promote excellence, equity and high achievement for Connecticut students by engaging teachers in purposeful exploration of professional practice through guided support and personal reflection" (ctteam.org).

Improved leadership. In every chapter on principal mentoring in this book, authors pointed out that the primary goal of their mentoring programs centered on the development of leadership competencies in the participants. It did not matter whether the context for the principal mentoring was urban, suburban, or rural, the focus was on instilling in the new or mid-career principals that they were now expected to be *instructional* leaders who had the knowledge and skills to influence school improvement and student achievement. Statements such as these were noted:

- one of the goals of the program was "to build regional leadership capacity for improved student learning through cross-district mentoring" (Reese et al., this volume);
- Charlotte-Mecklenburg School District received a Wallace Foundation grant "to develop a pipeline of school leaders and to measure the pipeline's effect on student achievement" (Martin & Searby, this volume);
- "The superintendent had become concerned about a developing pattern of assistant principals interviewing for principal openings in the district, but falling short of district expectations for their knowledge base and experience in instructional leadership." (Gurley and Anast-May).
- Chicago Public Schools developed "five competencies deliberately crafted as behaviors and actions deemed necessary for school leaders to be successful in achieving CPS goals (Daresh, this volume).

Thus, we see that one of the ways the mentoring landscape has changed in the P–12 context is that the stakes seem to be higher for participants, and results (in the form of teachers and leaders who can impact student achievement) are expected outcomes from mentoring programs.

MENTORING STILL INVOLVES REFLECTION ON PRACTICE (AND THE LESSONS LEARNED ARE HAVING A BROADER IMPACT ON MENTORING)

Reflection has always been a key component of mentoring, for both the mentor and the mentee. For both new teachers and new principals, reflection is still the primary vehicle for thinking about their practice and how to improve it, and a skilled mentor will facilitate that reflection. However, what we found from several studies reported in this book is that reflection is focused increasingly on analyzing the effectiveness of mentoring endeavors, so that the programs can be improved to better serve the needs of the participants.

Analyzing Mentoring Protocols. In the Charlotte-Mecklenburg School District, facilitators of the Consultant Coaching program for new principals realized that the quality of the program varied among the coaching cadres, as the coaches who conducted the mentoring groups were not delivering the mentoring curriculum in a uniform manner. After identifying this as a key problem, they instituted a mandatory meeting protocol with specific times outlined for the focus lessons, walkthroughs, and "burning issues" segments of the monthly sessions. When the coaches began complying with the mandated protocol, program effectiveness and mentee satisfaction increased. In Magee and Slater's analysis of three new principal mentoring cases, the authors reflected that "one size does not fit all" and that support should be individualized according to the needs of each novice. Browne-Ferrigno et al. reflected on the importance of school principals and teachers working together in a trusting relationship as coinstructional leaders, where the mentoring for those who may be aspiring to formal leadership positions takes place alongside the mentoring of teachers who will continue to lead from the classroom. Kralovec and Lunsford utilized reflective protocols based on multidisciplinary mentoring standards from the fields of teacher education, psychology, and organizational leadership. This meant that "the mentoring process began with an exploration of self-knowledge, not typical of mentoring literature in teacher education. This early focus on self set new parameters for mentor/mentee discussions." Each of these examples shows how using reflection to analyze mentoring programs can lead to improvement of processes and protocols.

Analyzing Unexpected Consequences. Interestingly, several chapter authors were honest about how analyzing the data from their programs led to new learning. Reese et al., in describing a program for mentoring mid-career principals in their increased use of student data, were candid about the varied challenges that contributed to a less-than-exemplary outcome of the program. They found from the surveys they administered to participants that a difference in perceptions of the coaches and protégés about the purpose of the program, as well as a lack of time devoted to trust-building activities hindered the success of the program. The protégés exhibited resistance to the mentoring program, and resented having to leave their respective buildings during the day to participate. The researchers learned that there were aspects of the program that they could have controlled in a better way at the beginning, but that there were also factors, such as principal-participant dispositions, that were outside of their control.

On a more positive note, Gurley and Anast-May reported an unexpected consequence of an Assistant Principal Academy that turned out to be a pleasant surprise. The Academy was designed for assistant principals in the same district to come together for professional development to increase their capacity as instructional leaders, in order to grow a cadre of prepared candidates who could move into senior principal positions quickly. Monthly sessions were structured with presentations on instructional leadership topics that would enhance the knowledge base of the assistant principals. What evolved as a by-product was a powerful peer mentoring network. Assistant principals began interacting with one another on a regular basis, connecting through e-mail, social media, or face to face at the Academy sessions. They also unofficially chose university faculty mentors and district administrators whom they could call on for needed information and resources. The result was group and peer mentoring that was informal in nature, but powerful in diversity and practicality, totally unplanned and spontaneous.

In their initial analysis of the data, Nunez et al. discovered that the mentors in their program were approaching the role very differently. Some were taking a very top-down approach and "handing out recipes" to solve situations, while others were jointly reading articles or discussing lessons. They responded to these findings by developing Reflective Rounds in order to provide mentors the opportunity to talk about their work and as way to ultimately improve their program.

PROGRAM SUCCESS STILL REQUIRES A CULTURE THAT VALUES MENTORING (AND MENTORING IS NOW MORE JOB-EMBEDDED IN THE WORKDAY)

The last enduring characteristic of effective mentoring programs that we would like to point out is that programs which are most successful are part of organizations that embody a culture of mentoring. When leaders of an organization value mentoring, they are creative in finding ways for it to take place and are able to make it part of the daily life of the school, not merely as an extra educational activity.

Cultures that support mentoring. Many of the chapters in this book described the cultural elements that supported (or hindered) effective mentoring. Bozack, Cheng et al., Reese et al., and Magee and Slater all discussed the challenges associated with finding time for mentoring. In cultures where mentoring is valued, teacher mentors are provided with the necessary time to get into classrooms to plan, observe and debrief with their mentees. In the case of mentoring new principals, districts that value mentoring make it mandatory for all new principals to leave their buildings for a half day per month to attend to their own learning (Martin and Searby). In this way, mentoring is not another responsibility or program added onto an already full school day (Bozack), but is job-embedded and given the necessary supports needed for success.

Looking across three studies, Hebert and Wilkins draw our attention to the need for broad-based collaboration and systems thinking. Using a framework for capacity building, they discuss relationship and organizational structures that have the potential to create strong and sustainable learning environments that support both new mentors and beginning teachers. Kralovec and Lunsford pointed out that mentoring programs exist within a larger context that may or may not represent a culture supportive of mentoring. They state,

> Individuals are influenced indirectly by the exosystem, which includes people with whom they do not have direct interactions but who make decisions that influence them. A school board's decision to fund a mentoring program would be an example of an exosystem's influence on mentoring. The macrosystem includes the cultural values and norms that influence all of the systems.

To summarize, we have noted some of the enduring components of mentoring programs in P–12 settings for both new teachers and administrators highlighted in these chapters. Yet, despite these consistencies, the mentoring landscape seems to be changing, largely due to the current context of high stakes assessments and demand for greater accountability for results in student achievement. Mentoring is still about dialogue, and the focus is still on teacher and leader development, reflection is still a focal habit that mentors and mentees need to utilize in order to mine the rich learning from mentoring relationships, and a culture of mentoring in schools and districts is still vital to the success of a mentoring program. These are elements of best practice in P–12 mentoring programs. We turn now, however, to some of the mentoring adaptations noted in the chapters in this book. What follows is a description of the emerging trends in mentoring in P–12 contexts.

EMERGING TRENDS IN MENTORING

The chapter authors in this book point to some important new trends in the field of mentoring, by describing how programs were created to respond to common problems associated with mentoring, such as cost, distance, limited human resources, and isolation. This body of literature helped us see how mentoring professionals in the field are beginning to "think outside the box" and move beyond the traditional mentoring models (Kralovec and Lunsford; Dennis and Parker; Cheng, Nunez et al.). We believe they have outlined some practices that help us think about new ways of working together.

Mentor Development. As some of the authors pointed out (i.e. Cheng et al., Doone et al.) learning to mentor is a developmental process which needs to be practiced and nurtured with ongoing support. In addition to learning practical elements, like observation skills (Bozack), mentors also need to be able to articulate a philosophy of mentoring (Dennis and Parker). This requires helping mentors understand the various stances and purposes behind certain philosophies of mentoring. Nunez et al. described how mentors analyzed different styles of mentoring during Reflection Rounds and found it "helpful to talk with other new mentors as they developed their new practice of mentoring and to analyze the different methods and purposes behind mentoring."

Mentors need to be able to recognize and articulate their normative view of mentoring so that they can successfully navigate the tensions that arise during the course of their mentoring. For example, Nunez et al. and Bozack both described the tension between novice's desire for practical, immediate assistance and the mentors' focus on practices, like reflection, that would form habits of mind and lead to long-term growth. Being able to articulate a mentoring philosophy, like educative mentoring (Dennis and Parker), would allow the mentor to meet both of those needs.

Reese et al. described a mentoring program for mid-career principals in a rural area in which certain superintendents realized that they did not have the mentoring expertise in their own districts to mentor veteran principals in how to use data to improve student achievement. Thus, they reached out to each other in the region to identify principals competent in data usage, and also asked for assistance from the regional university educational leadership faculty to help structure the program. Thus, going beyond the usual "grow your own" mentality of many mentoring programs, the capacity for expanded competency-building was created.

Partnerships. One of the most prevalent themes in this book is the call for stronger connections between teacher and leader preparation programs and P–12 schools. As Hebert and Wilkins so poignantly stated: "More than anything else, we need to begin building bridges between the many silos that exist in education." Several chapters in the book describe exemplary partnerships between universities and school districts for the purpose of enacting good mentoring programs.

In order for partnerships to be successful, there needs to be a shared vision of the work by all participants and stakeholders. This vision needs to be clearly articulated and understood in order to avoid situations in which members work at cross-purposes. Hebert and Wilkins expanded on this:

As Fullan (2009) describes, alignment of purpose has little impact on change if decision-making about resource allocation does not reflect a commitment to these shared purposes. This also includes communicating the vision with program leaders who have the ability to support or constrain mentoring practices. This alignment must extend to broader contexts: The new rules placed obligations on these programs that they could not effectively meet. The one-size-fits-all requirements for induction left some programs unable to participate, and inequitably impacted the new teachers being served in these contexts. The policy context plays a strong role in systemic supports that impact the effectiveness of induction implementation. Fullan (2009) lists "tri-level development" as one of eight key forces behind effective change, and this includes programmatic decisions related to the development of teachers as they transition into the classroom. This means alignment of goals and decisions across three tiers of the organizations simultaneously: the school, the district, and the state. (Hebert & Wilkins, this volume)

Aspiring administrators are also benefitting from these partnerships. Chapters on new principal mentoring illustrated how university and school district personnel cocreated mentoring programs (Reese at al., Martin and Searby, Browne-Ferrigno et al., Gurley and Anast-May, this volume), facilitated job-embedded mentoring as a form of professional development (Martin & Searby, this volume), and empowered teachers as leaders (Browne-Ferrigno et al., this volume). These chapter authors acknowledged how the national instructional leadership standards are driving mentoring practices. Daresh reported on a massive mentoring project in Chicago Public Schools funded by a multimillion dollar grant from a nonprofit foundation that invests heavily in national principal preparation, responding to a call for better quality school leadership. Dennis and Parker and Browne-Ferrigno et al. remind us that school administrators have to understand the power of mentoring and play an active role in creating space for mentoring relationships that are formed as a result of school-university partnerships.

A few of the chapters help us envision different structures for these partnerships. Doone et al. suggested, for example, using a Professional Practice Partner (PPP) to act as both P–12 cooperating teacher and university supervisor, as a way to connect teacher preparation programs and schools. One important feature of this partnership was that the PPP's supervised students both early in their program and then again during student teaching. This arrangement provided ongoing support for preservice teachers and the mentors felt more invested and connected to the teacher preparation program. One mentor felt that she was "molding a colleague" (Doone et al., this volume).

Gurley and Anast-May described how a superintendent approached the regional university Educational Leadership department faculty and asked them to establish an Assistant Principal Academy to prepare the pipeline of individuals who could step into senior principal positions knowing how to lead instructional improvement. Martin and Searby also noted the involvement of two different universities who partnered with the large, urban Charlotte-Mecklenburg district to augment the local new principal mentoring program. In addition, the Wallace Foundation was a partner in the funding and subsequent research data gathering on this program. However, the partnership concept is not universally embraced by school districts. As Kralovec and Lunsford noted from their research:

> Few school leaders have embraced the idea that preparing new teachers is *part* of the work of schools and until this idea becomes part of the preparation for school leaders, building the kind of robust partnerships that embedded, clinically-based teacher education requires will be a long way off.

Thus, we see that the formation of partnerships is enhancing mentoring programs, but also adding challenges as historically separate entities are now being required to collaborate and work together in new ways. Creating meaningful partnerships takes work and maintaining them is even harder work.

Networks. Another common theme in this book is the need to establish networks where mentoring partners can meet (virtually or in person) for the sake of supporting one another as they develop their new practice. With regard to mentors, Hebert and Wilkins explained the value of networks this way:

> Mentors need to continue to learn about mentoring as they engage in the practice, because they see new things and can apply theories and ideas to real situations. One mentor described how her experiences of putting mentoring into practice brought a new lens to what she was learning, and she was able to simultaneously be a voice of experience for those who were taking the training for the first time. (Hebert & Wilkins, this volume)

They also discussed the importance of networks for beginning teachers, explaining that novices want time to talk about their practice openly in a safe environment where they can seek advice and not feel alone. Martin and Searby pointed out that the mentors in the Consultant Coaching program met with each other and the program facilitators as their own professional learning community for the purpose of enhancing their mentoring skills with new principals. Gurley and Anast-May spoke of the powerful peer mentoring network of assistant principals that evolved out of a district program that really was not about mentoring at the outset. Daresh reported that Chicago Public Schools paid retired principals to be mentors for new principals. Thus, we see that mentoring required different types of supports for both mentors (who are learning to mentor) and new teachers and principals (who learn from interactions with other novices). In this way, both formal and informal mentoring networks are proving to be highly effective, for both mentors and mentees as they provide a community in which all can learn and improve.

Virtual Mentoring. Many of the chapters described how school districts are responding creatively to realities, such as the expense of funding mentoring programs and the distance and isolation that leave many schools with a limited number of qualified mentors. Many districts have been exploring e-mentoring as an alternative to face-to-face mentoring (Nunez et al., Kralovec & Lunsford, this volume). Hebert and Wilkins described the importance of being intentional in placing beginning teachers with mentors in their content area, which is not always possible in small districts. Instead, they suggested partnering mentors in the same content area from different districts, using technology like Skype to bridge the distance. Cheng et al. also shared how some districts were responding to the high cost of mentoring by considering virtual alternatives. They found, however, that total online mentoring had limitations. For examples, mentors reported challenges associated with developing relationships online. Instead, the Cheng chapter authors proposed a hybrid model that included both online and face-to-face mentoring. This model allowed mentor-mentee pairs to be together in person for things like classroom observations. Not only did this provide the mentors with a better sense of the mentees' teaching, but allowed them to establish relationships. Online contact was then used to debrief and for ongoing support through professional learning communities (PLC). "Having the ability to meet either face-to-face or online for PLC meetings increased the meeting frequency and resulted in an increase in the strength of the relationship and teaching practice" (Cheng et al., this volume).

To summarize, we note that four trends are emerging in P–12 mentoring programs: mentor development, partnerships, mentoring networks, and virtual mentoring alternatives. These trends have emerged in response to the changing nature of schools and the continued demands to include mentoring as a construct to improve P–12 teaching and leadership. We see each of them as having merit and the potential to further inform the efforts of educators who believe that mentoring is important as a professional development tool. It is our hope that by highlighting these thirteen research studies on mentoring for teacher and leader development, our readers will gain insight into the enduring best practices of effective mentoring programs, as well as new ideas for how to address the continuing challenges of planning and implementing quality mentoring programs in the ever-changing landscape of education.

We would welcome your responses to this volume. We can be contacted at the addresses below.

Linda J. Searby   ljs0007@auburn.edu

Susan K. Brondyk   brondyk@hope.edu

ABOUT THE AUTHORS

ABOUT THE EDITORS

Linda Searby, PhD, is a mentoring researcher and Associate Professor in the Educational Leadership program at Auburn University, Auburn, Alabama, USA. She is the co-editor of the *International Journal of Mentoring and Coaching in Education*, an editorial board member of *Mentoring & Tutoring: Partnerships in Learning* and serves on the Executive Board of the International Mentoring Association. In addition, she is a co-editor of the Blackwell Handbook of Mentoring (2018). Dr. Searby has published over 20 articles in her areas of research, which focus on mentoring from the protege's perspective, specifically on the development of a mentoring mindset in protégés, and on assistant principals and their mentoring needs as instructional leaders.

Susan Brondyk, PhD, is an Assistant Professor at Hope College, Holland, Michigan (United States) where she teaches undergraduate preservice teachers. As the Associate Director of *Launch into Teaching* at Michigan State University, East Lansing, Michigan (United States) she works with mentors and instructional coaches to support beginning teachers in struggling urban districts. In this capacity, she leads sustained, job-embedded professional development, conducts school visits to work with leadership teams, and provides one-on-one support for mentors. Dr. Brondyk's research examines mentor preparation at the pre-service and induction level. Most recently she has been studying teacher leaders as change agents.

ABOUT THE AUTHORS

Linda Anast-May is an associate professor of educational leadership at Coastal Carolina University. Dr. Anast-May's research interests include the instructional behaviors enacted by assistant principals and principals. She has recently published articles in *Planning and Changing* and *Education and Urban Society*. Dr. Anast-May has been at the university level for eight years. Before that, she served at the building and district level administration and served as School Superintendent in Indiana and Illinois.

Amanda R. Bozack, PhD, is an Associate Professor of Education and department chair at the University of New Haven, Connecticut. Her interests include the development and support of new teachers through high-quality induction programs. She is currently working with beginning science teachers, their mentors, and administrators through Project SING, an induction focused project supported by a Teacher Quality Partnership Grant through Connecticut's Office of Higher Education. She has been published in *Journal of Teacher Education, Teachers College Record,* and *The High School Journal*.

Tricia Browne-Ferrigno, PhD, is a professor in the Department of Educational Leadership Studies at the University of Kentucky. Her long-term research agenda centers on leadership preparation and development (i.e., experiences of program participants, program features and their impact on participant learning, program evaluation). She is editor of a special issue on teacher leadership for the *Journal of Research on Leadership Educator* and was project director for two grant-supported, leadership-development projects for rural Appalachian school districts. Prior to entering higher education, Professor Browne-Ferrigno worked 15 years as a teacher leader in secondary mathematics and for 2 years as the National Consultant Secondary Mathematics for ScottForesman.

Ya-Wen Cheng, PhD, is an educational program coordinator for the University of Missouri School of Medicine. Her research interests focus on designing and integrating hybrid (technology and face-to-face) learning environments for learners. She is interested in the ability of hybrid learning environment in assisting content experts to provide supports to novice learners. Now working in medical education, she is also interested in the assessment and evaluation of medical curriculum.

John C. Daresh, PhD, is professor of Educational Leadership and Policy Studies at the University of Texas at El Paso. Dr. Daresh has authored more than 20 books on supervision, instructional leadership, and principal development, and more than 100 articles and papers in scholarly journals in the United States and elsewhere. Soon to be published work include the 4th edition of *Beginning the Principalship* for Corwin Press and *Foundations for Proactive Instructional Leadership* (5th edition, due out in early 2016) for Waveland Press. Daresh also served as a Fulbright Scholar in the Republic of Kyrgyzstan and as the Senior Leadership Consultant for the Office of Principal Preparation and Development in the Chicago Public Schools.

Matthew Della Sala, PhD, is Assistant Professor in Educational Leadership and Cultural Foundations at Purdue University. His research interests include a focus on how educational policies align with broader philosophical concepts such as equity, adequacy, and equality of educational opportunity. He has published in *Journal of Educational Administration, Leadership and Policy in Schools,* and with co-author Knoeppel was awarded the 2013 *Educational Considerations* Outstanding Article of the Year.

Danielle Dennis. PhD, is an Associate Professor of Literacy Studies. Dr. Dennis serves as the Director of the Urban Teacher Residency Partnership Program and the Cambridge (U.K.) Schools Experience at the University of South Florida. Her research focuses on literacy assessment, policy, and building teacher capacity. Most recently, her research explored the ways in which content-specific coaching with pre-service teachers in the field accelerates their development as literacy educators.

Elizabeth Doon, PhD, & Karen Colucci, PhD, are faculty members in the Department of Teaching and Learning at the University of South Florida. The PDS without Wall, Professional Practice Partner (PPP) Mentoring Program was the brainchild of Dr. Betty Epanchin while Drs. Colucci and Doone worked closely with the two school district to create the curriculum and nurture the development and maintain the integrity of the PPP Mentoring Program for the past 15 years. The PPP Program is a unique mentoring model that meets the varied needs of an Exceptional Student Education Teacher Education Program.

Amanda Perry Ellis, EdD, is the Associate Commissioner of the Office of Next Generation Learners for the Kentucky Department of Education. She served eight years as principal of an elementary school, two years as a curriculum resource teacher, and six years as a middle school science teacher. She has conducted research on teacher leadership and has expertise in the area of professional growth and development of teachers and principals. Dr. Ellis is a clinical faculty member in the Department of Educational Leadership Studies at the University of Kentucky.

Bryan González, PhD, is a Psychologist and Researcher in Territorial Systems line in Horticulture Innovation Centre of Valparaíso–CERES. He is an assistant Professor in the Psychology School of Pontifical Catholic University of Valparaíso, Chile.

D. Keith Gurley, PhD, is an Assistant Professor of Educational Leadership at the University of Alabama at Birmingham. Dr. Gurley's research interests include the exploration of the roles enacted by Assistant Principals. He has recently published articles in the *Journal of Educational Change,* and *Planning & Changing.* Before moving into higher education, Dr. Gurley served as building principal and in central office administration in school districts in Kansas and Missouri.

Deborah Hanuscin, PhD, is an associate professor of science education and physics. Her research focuses on structures, strategies and supports for science teacher learning, including the focus on teacher leadership development as a focus of professional development programs. Dr. Hanuscin currently serves as Director of the Quality Elementary Science Teaching (QuEST) program, funded by the National Science Foundation, and serves on the Board of Directors of the National Association for Research on Science Teaching.

Lara Hebert is a former elementary and middle level educator, having taught math, science, and language arts to tweens and teens for 13 years. She earned her PhD from the University of Illinois in curriculum and instruction with expertise in professional learning models that combine face-to-face and virtual components. She is currently a professional learning specialist at the National Council of Teachers of English and coordinates the National Center for Literacy Education's virtual hub, the Literacy in Learning Exchange. This work is grounded in practices that strengthen collective capacity for meaningful and sustainable change within and across educator teams and organizations.

Cristina Julio, PhD, is a Professor of Special Education and has a Master's in Social Sciences and Ethics and a Doctorate in Education. In her 30 years of practice she has developed a diverse interest in these areas. In the 80s and in the political context in Chile, she worked in non-formal education settings. After earning a Master's degree and having specialized in public policy with an ethical perspective, she continued working with and implementing youth and drop out programs and policies throughout the end of the 90s. Since that time, she has worked as an academic faculty member in the field of teacher preparation and teacher training.

Hans W. Klar, PhD, is an Assistant Professor in Educational and Organizational Leadership Development at Clemson University. He has held a wide variety of teaching and educational leadership positions in Japan, Australia, Indonesia, and China. Dr. Klar's publications have centered on professional development, leadership development, and context-responsive leadership. With his co-author, his article, "Successful Leadership in a Rural, High-Poverty School: The Case of County Line Middle School," received the *Journal of Educational Administration*'s 2015 Highly Commended Award.

Robert C. Knoeppel, PhD, is Professor and Department Chair of Educational and Organizational Leadership Development at Clemson University. Prior to transitioning to academia, he worked for 12 years in public education as a teacher, school counselor, and building level administrator. His work has been regularly published in the *Journal of Education Finance* and *Educational Considerations,* the two top-tiered journals in the field of education finance. Dr. Knoeppel serves as the Associate Chair of the National Education Finance Academy and is a member of the Editorial Board for the *Journal of Education Finance.*

Etta Kralovec, PhD, is Associate Professor and Director of the Graduate Teacher Education programs at the University of Arizona, South. She was named the University of Arizona Distinguished Outreach professor in 2015. The program reported in "Crossing the Border at the Border," a teacher preparation program designed to prepare teachers for border schools in Arizona was awarded the University of Arizona Peter Likins Award for Inclusive Excellence in 2015. She is the co-author of the groundbreaking book, *The End of Homework.*

Jane Clark Lindle, PhD, Eugene T. Moore Distinguished Professor of Educational Leadership at Clemson University, has more than four decades' experience as special education teacher, principal, professor, and advisor to educational professionals in elementary, secondary and post-secondary leadership. Her more than 80 publications include research about shared governance, education policy implementation and developmentally appropriate practices in advising and mentoring non-traditional graduate students appearing in journals such as *Education Policy* and *Educational Administration Quarterly.*

Verónica López, PhD, is a Psychologist at Universidad Autónoma de Madrid. She is Associate Professor at the School of Psychology at Pontificia Universidad Católica de Valparaíso (PUCV), Chile. She is head of the Doctoral Program of Psychology at PUCV, Head of the School Climate Support

Program, and editor of the peer-reviewed scholarly journal *Psicoperspectivas*. Her research interests are school climate, school inclusion, and school improvement efforts from a democratic and inclusive perspective. She is author of more than 25 articles, 10 book chapters, and 2 books.

Laura G. Lunsford, PhD, is an associate professor in psychology at the University of Arizona South. She studies mentoring and leader development and has published and presented on mentoring teachers, mentorship dysfunction, optimizing mentoring relationships, and evaluating mentoring. She is a co-editor of the *SAGE Handbook of Mentoring* and author of *Mentoring Handbook for Program Managers*. In 2009 she was recognized by the International Mentoring Association with their Dissertation Award.

Constance Magee, EdD, is a middle school principal in Long Beach Unified School District and a Future Faculty Fellow at California State University Long Beach. She is in her 11th year as a turnaround principal and teaches Educational Administration courses in the masters and doctoral programs at Long Beach State. Her dissertation on experiences and support for new principals was published in chapter form in *Understanding the Principalship: An International Guide to Principal Preparation,* Emerald Books, 2013.

Mary Bearden Martin, PhD, is currently an Associate Professor at Winthrop University in Rock Hill, S.C. in the Educational Leadership program. She previously served as an elementary principal and curriculum director in the Charlotte-Mecklenburg Schools. Dr. Martin is a state and national presenter in the areas of teacher evaluation, mentoring new principals, coaching for continuous improvement, and collaborative instructional planning. Her publications have been in NAESP *Principal*, NASSP *Principal Leadership*, and the SCASA *Palmetto Administrator*. Her educational degrees are from Lenoir Rhyne College, Appalachian State, and the University of North Carolina-Chapel Hill, all in North Carolina

Evalyn Mujica is a teacher in the Pedagogic School at Pontifical Catholic University of Valparaiso, Chile. She works in the CostaDigital department developing projects and consultancy for the use of Computer Science in Education. She has a Master's degree in Education with a specialty in Curriculum Studies, and is in the process of earning her PhD in Educational Culture in Latin America.

Carmen Gloria Núñez earned her PhD in Psychology of Education at Pontifical Catholic University of Chile and Bordeaux. At present, she is professor and researcher of Psychology at the Pontifical Catholic University of

Valparaíso, Chile. Her research focuses on educational policies and their impact on school communities.

Audra Parker, PhD, is an Associate Professor and Academic Program Coordinator in the Elementary Education program at George Mason University. Her areas of expertise include elementary curriculum and instruction, classroom management, clinical practice, and teacher education. In addition, Dr. Parker works collaboratively with teacher candidates and K–6 teachers as a university supervisor at her Professional Development School partner site. Her areas of research serve to connect these teaching and field-based experiences and center on pre-service beliefs and practices, children's school experiences, and innovations in teacher preparation.

Kenyae L. Reese, PhD, is the Academy Principal of the Academy of the International Baccalaureate Diploma Programme at Hillsboro High School in the Metropolitan Nashville Public Schools. She has a background in business, school counseling, and leadership. Her scholarship and practice focuses on student and professional learning and development through mentoring. Her collaborative works have appeared in the *Professional Development in Education*, the *Georgia School Counselor Association Journal*, and *Political Contexts of Educational Leadership: ISLLC Standard 6*. Dr. Reese is a former Barbara L. Jackson and David L. Clark Scholar through the University Council for Educational Administration and the American Educational Research Association.

Evelyn Palma is a Kindergarten educator at Pontificia Universidad Católica de Valparaíso, Chile. She has a Masters degree in Management and Leadership in School Organizations. She is also a certificated mentor for the Ministry of Education of Chile, and a Professional Excellence Teacher certified by the same ministry. Her professional work includes teaching in technical training centers, professional development of teachers, and supporting the education of mentors.

Amy Nicole Salvaggio, PhD, is an Associate Professor of psychology at the University of New Haven, CT. She studies workplace romance and sexual behavior in the workplace, and collaborates with other researchers on a number of topics, including reading motivation, organizational climate, and gender bias. Her work has been published in *The Journal of Applied Psychology, Sex Roles,* and *The Journal of Managerial Psychology.*

Charles L. Slater, PhD, is Professor of Educational Administration at California State University Long Beach. Previously, he was Director of the Ph.D. program at Texas State University and superintendent of schools in

Alamo Heights, Texas and Brookline Massachusetts. He is a member of the International Study of Leadership Development Network, and he has published widely in educational leadership in Costa Rica, Mexico, Spain, and the United States.

Dominique Thompson is now in her 5th year as a middle school, self-contained EBD teacher. She has successfully taught in the self-contained, resource and infusion models. She serves as the chairperson for the MTSS/RtI committee at her school, is an active member of her school's SAC committee, and was instrumental in establishing a Check and Connect program at her school, for which she serves as the mentor coordinator. Ms. Thompson has conducted action research on utilizing reflection and mentoring to improve teaching. She obtained both her BS in sociology and her Masters of Arts in Teaching from the University of South Florida.

Matthew D. Thompson, EdD, serves as superintendent of Montgomery County, KY, Public Schools. For four years he served as the assistant superintendent of student learning in Scott County Public Schools and prior to that as the director of elementary schools, a principal of elementary school, and a teacher in elementary school. He has expertise in instructional leadership, leadership development, organizational change, and instructional design. He serves as clinical faculty in the Department of Educational Leadership Studies at the University of Kentucky.

Mark J. Volkmann, PhD, is an Associate Professor Emeritus of science education at the University of Missouri. His research interests focus on the development of knowledge for teaching science, as well as instructional strategies and curriculum in science. A central component of this knowledge is to understand how students learn to teach science through inquiry.

Laura Von Staden, PhD, is currently the Lead ESE teacher at a Title I, all boys, middle school. She has served as a mentor for new teachers for nearly a decade and works closely with the University in this endeavor. She currently serves on a steering committee for literacy for her school district and reviews dozens of professional books annually. Prior to going into K–12 public education, Dr. Von Staden was a cancer researcher and adjunct professor and had won several awards for her research.

Elizabeth Wilkins, PhD, is a Professor in the Department of Leadership, Educational Psychology, and Foundations at Northern Illinois University. Her active research agenda focuses on induction practices, pre-service education, student teachers, and supervision. She has published over 30 articles, co-authored two books, and several books chapters.

59484386R10192

Made in the USA
Lexington, KY
07 January 2017